The Ju/'hoan San of Nyae Nyae and Namibian Independence

The Ju/'hoan San of Nyae Nyae and Namibian Independence

Development, Democracy, and Indigenous Voices in Southern Africa

Megan Biesele and Robert K. Hitchcock

berghahn

NEW YORK · OXFORD

www.berghahnbooks.com

Published in 2011 by
Berghahn Books

www.berghahnbooks.com

© 2011, 2013 Megan Biesele and Robert K. Hitchcock
First paperback edition published in 2013

Library of Congress Cataloging-in-Publication Data

The Ju/'hoan San of Nyae Nyae and Namibian independence : development,
democracy, and indigenous voices in Southern Africa / Megan Biesele and
Robert K. Hitchcock.
    p. cm.
Includes bibliographical references and index.
    ISBN 978-1-84545-754-9 (hardback) — ISBN: 978-1-78238-059-7 (paperback) —
ISBN 978-1-78238-060-3 (retail ebook)
    1. !Kung (African people)—Namibia—Nyae Nyae—Politics and government.
2. !Kung (African people)—Namibia—Nyae Nyae—Government relations.
3. Nyae Nyae (Namibia)—History. 4. Namibia—History—Autonomy and
independence movements. 5. Namibia—Politics and government—1946–1990.
I. Hitchcock, Robert K. II. Title.

DT1558.K85B44 2010
305.896'1—dc22

                                                                        2010023850

British Library Cataloguing in Publication Data

A catalogue record for this book is available from
the British Library.

Printed in the United States on acid-free paper

ISBN: 978-1-78238-059-7 paperback   ISBN: 978-1-78238-060-3 retail ebook

Contents

﹡

List of Illustrations   vi
Preface to the Paperback Edition   vii
Preface   xii
Acknowledgments   xix
List of Abbreviations   xxi
Note on Orthography   xxiv
Chronology of the Nyae Nyae Region   xxvii

       Introduction: A Community History   1

One   Namibia and the Nyae Nyae Region   31

Two   Traditional Ju/'hoan Leadership and Governance   50

Three The Ju/'hoan People's Organization and Its Foundation   65

Four   Ju/'hoan Empowerment from Dialogue on Wildlife Issues   91

Five   The Lead-Up to Namibian Independence in Nyae Nyae   113

Six   Independence: The Years of Hope   130

Seven The Nyae Nyae Development Foundation of Namibia   153

Eight The Nyae Nyae Farmers Cooperative after Independence   168

Nine   Community-Based Natural Resource Management and
       Other Development Models   198

Ten   Nyae Nyae Conservancy Programs and the Future   227

References   245
Index   259

Photographs follow page 129

Illustrations

꧁

Maps

1. Namibia, Botswana, and adjacent nations   2
2. Namibia and its river systems   3
3. The Nyae Nyae and /Kae/kae areas in northeastern Namibia and northwestern Botswana   7
4. Namibian homelands under the Odendaal Plan   35
5. The 13 regions of Namibia   38
6. Tsumkwe District in Otjozondjupa region, showing the Kaudum National Park and the Namibia-Botswana border   41
7. Southern Africa, showing the major San language groups   52
8. The n!oresi (traditional communal lands) of Nyae Nyae   55

Figures

1. Ju/'hoan land use system   56
2. Representative Council, as outlined in the NNFC governing constitution   81
3. Organizational structure of the NNFC council, 1988–1989   81
4. Nyae Nyae Conservancy, showing organizational structure, programs, and staff   219

Tables

1. Number of San in southern Africa   4
2. Populations of San in Namibia   6
3. Land tenure situation in Namibia   34
4. Seasons of the year, according to the Ju/'hoan San of Nyae Nyae   43
5. Conservancies in Namibia's communal areas   207

Preface to the Paperback Edition

※

Recent Challenges

Since the first hardcover edition of this book was published at the beginning of 2011, challenges old and new have continued to face the Ju/'hoansi. Like San peoples all over southern Africa, the Ju/'hoansi of Nyae Nyae are responding to increased threats to their land and resource bases from pastoral and industrial interests. While they continue traditional hunting and gathering in their nationally recognized conservancy, their cultural resilience is expressed in an array of strategies ranging from gardening projects to ecotourism and maintaining a disease-free herd of buffalo (*Syncerus caffer*) for potential sale at auction in southern Africa.

Ju/'hoansi continue to negotiate to enhance their human and cultural rights at local, national, and international conferences and legal forums, as they did in May 2012 at the United Nations Permanent Forum on Indigenous Issues 11th annual meeting, which was attended by Leon Tsamkxao and Kxao Ghauz, two members of the Nyae Nyae Conservancy. Together with San from Botswana, they helped form the San Caucus, which made a statement on "The Doctrine of Discovery" that received widespread international attention.

Ju/'hoansi also work to preserve and develop the Ju/'hoan language and heritage through educational, oral history, and recording/translation projects, while at the same time strengthening group identity and developing a strong political voice. They seek to draw on their traditional knowledge system as well as to arrange community training in relevant non-traditional areas, in order to promote a healthy approach to local and regional environmental and economic sustainability.

One of the greatest current obstacles faced by the Nyae Nyae people is the continued illegal presence of more than three hundred pastoralist Herero settlers and their cattle in Tsumkwe, which is on conservancy land. The settlers have located themselves in a municipality area within the conservancy that is not controlled by the Ju/'hoan people, but their cattle cause damage to nearby conservancy land. The first wave of settlers, described in this book, occurred in April 2009 when five Herero families totaling thirty-two people from /Gam, south of Nyae Nyae, cut the Red Line, the veterinary cordon fence, and brought thirteen hundred cattle into Nyae Nyae. Although most of these animals were confiscated by the Namibian police, the Herero in Tsumkwe have since brought in new cattle. They also have large numbers of horses, donkeys, and small stock in Tsumkwe, where keeping livestock is illegal. The settlers are not paying any fees for water, sanitation, or electricity to the Tsumkwe municipality, whereas other residents of Tsumkwe are doing so. What this means is that the local Tsumkwe residents are, in effect, subsidizing their presence and their land and resource use.

At this writing, in January 2013, the issue has not been resolved despite almost four years of continuous negotiation and legal efforts. Meanwhile, the resource base of the Nyae Nyae Conservancy has suffered from pressure due to increased numbers of livestock, firewood gathering, illegal hunting, and the establishment of illegal fences. Furthermore, a large increase in the number of bush fires, some purposefully set, have injured local people and damaged their grazing and wild food resource areas.

In mid-March 2012, the regional governor of the Otjozondjupa region went to the Ju/'hoan Traditional Authority, Tsamkxao =Oma, and asked him to have the Ju/'hoansi give up a quarter of what the governor described as the "unutilized land" of the conservancy to the Herero from /Gam now living in Tsumkwe. At present, the Nyae Nyae area that has been officially set aside by the government for the Ju/'hoansi is 8,992 km² in size. Taking a quarter of this area, which is utilized intensively for agriculture, livestock production, and wild resource collection purposes, would have substantial impacts, many of them negative, on the Nyae Nyae region. It would also set a complicated precedent for all communities attempting to establish themselves in both communal and commercial freehold land in Namibia.

As of January 2013, the /Gam farmers are still living in Tsumkwe and are being supported by government assistance. Debate is raging nationally in Namibia about their continued presence. On the one hand there are those who say that the Nyae Nyae Ju/'hoansi have the law on their side, since they oversee a government-recognized conservancy that gives them some legal rights. They also now have a Nyae Nyae Community Forest, proclaimed under the Forest Act in July 2012, which gives the Nyae Nyae Conservancy more secure rights over grazing and timber resources. The nearby N≠a Jaqna Conservancy has the M'Kata Community Forest, which in 2004 was the first community forest granted such a status. Furthermore, the Ju/'hoansi were assured by the office of the president, the office of the deputy prime minister's San Development Office,[1] and the Ministry of Lands and Resettlement[2] that the resources in Tsumkwe belong to them.

On the other hand, there are those who say that the Herero and the Ju/'hoansi are both marginalized peoples and should be treated in the same way. The local council has a bylaw that makes it unlawful to have any animals in the Tsumkwe town area. The Tsumkwe council needs government support to enforce this bylaw, but has yet to receive it.

Efforts have been made to determine the applicability of the United Nations Declaration on the Rights of Indigenous Peoples (UNDRIP) and the African Commission on Human and Peoples' Rights principles and practices to this case. Namibia voted in support of the UNDRIP when it came up for a vote on 13 September 2007. Namibia is also a signatory to the African Charter. In January 2011, Namibia participated in the Universal Periodic Review (UPR) of the Human Rights Council, the main human rights review system of the United Nations. Thus far, Namibia has demonstrated strong commitment to the rights of indigenous and minority peoples and historically disadvantaged populations in the country.

In the past, the government of Namibia has provided both tacit and overt support to the Ju/'hoan claims to the land and resources of the Nyae Nyae region. The people of Tsumkwe and Nyae Nyae are hopeful that understandings and agreements with the Namibian government regarding their rights will be upheld. However, the government is dealing with demands from all sectors of the population as well as with a greatly increased interest from multinationals in Namibian mineral resources, and it is hard to say how much priority will continue to be given to the benevolent agreements of over twenty years ago. Also, a certain amount of media fatigue on the issue of illegal settlement, coupled with the numerical and political strength of the Herero pastoralists as opposed to the small population of Ju/'hoan former foragers, makes the resolution of this situation seem uncertain at best. Tsamkxao =Oma is thus left standing by his oft-reiterated statement: "The constitutions of Namibia and of the Nyae Nyae Conservancy must be our guide."

1. Since the first edition of this book was published, the San Development Program has had its name changed to San Development Office.

2. Since the first edition of this book was published, the Ministry of Lands, Resettlement, and Rehabilitation has changed its function and its name to Ministry of Lands and Resettlement.

Updates on Nyae Nyae Conservancy Programs

Some of the recent activities in Nyae Nyae include poultry and livestock projects, grazing management, community forestry activities, the collection and sale of high-value wild plant resources, and the upgrading of water facilities. The distribution of solar-powered pumps and batteries used to charge cell phones and to power lights and radios in people's homes is ongoing. Children can now prepare their lessons for school at night, something that was not possible previously. A popular project involving the raising of sweet potatoes and other crops in irrigated gardens by local garden groups with the support of the Tradition and Transition Fund is showing signs of success in southern Nyae Nyae.

On 21 August 2012, Kxao Moses =Oma, the brother of Tsamkxao =Oma, who was the member of Parliament from the Otjozondjupa region and the party whip for SWAPO, died suddenly. His funeral was attended by hundreds of people, including many senior government officials. His death came on the heels of the loss of !Kung Traditional Authority John Arnold, who passed away after a car accident in July 2012, creating uncertainty regarding future leadership.

In the face of these challenges, the Nyae Nyae Conservancy has continued to quietly build on many social and educational programs it began more than twenty years ago. One of these programs, the Ju/'hoan Transcription Group Project (JTG) described in chapter 10 of this book, has made important recent strides toward sustainability. Local takeover of the JTG project, beginning in 2010, has meant major steps toward both empowerment and sustainability for the Ju/'hoan community. The tiny library in Tsumkwe (Community Learning and Development Centre, CLDC) where transcribers and youth work and learn has become a focal point for community pride. The transcribers are in constant demand by local leaders of the Nyae Nyae Conservancy, who are mostly non literate. There are also frequent calls on the recordings archives, housed at the CLDC, to prove historical points for political meetings, such as those involving land negotiations.

The JTG book *Ju/'hoan Folktales: Transcriptions and English Translations* is being used by the Namibian National Institute for Educational Development as an enrichment material for the national school system. Thus, the transcribers are creating archives that can be used by scholars and linguists as well as by their own community for heritage and curriculum materials.

The JTG project's documentation of ancient lifeways and the contemporary creativity of young San people are both advancing well. The transcribers, the trainees, and their community increasingly feel moral ownership of the project. In 2010 the JTG was asked by the Namibian government to register as a community-based organization with the Ministry of Trade and

Industry. This move was intended to help the project toward twin goals of further employment and eventual sustainability. In August 2012, however, a much more promising approach, establishing the JTG as a community trust, was set in motion. Also, the original transcribers have added a youth component, offering pen-and-paper Ju/'hoan and English literacy lessons as well as computer literacy. Best of all, the JTG has been asked by Namibian educators to give Ju/'hoan literacy lessons to teachers of the Village Schools Project, all of whom speak Ju/'hoansi but some of whom have never had tutelage in reading and writing it. The achievements of the JTG have been described by a Namibian educator as "empowerment and development work in the truest senses."

Based on interviews of people in the Nyae Nyae region in July–August 2012, it is clear that there is ongoing support for the efforts of the Nyae Nyae Conservancy, the Nyae Nyae Development Foundation of Namibia, and the various community projects. There is broad understanding of the need for careful planning, budgetary requirements, accountability, and transparency in the dealings of the NNC Board and Management Committee. Thus, despite the challenges and some failures to meet them, Nyae Nyae can still be seen as one of the most successful San community development efforts in southern Africa.

Preface

The Ju/'hoan San, or Ju/'hoansi, of Namibia and Botswana are perhaps the most fully described indigenous people in all of anthropology. Coverage of them in writing and in film has included extensive information on their traditional ways of life and has brought their current situation substantially up to date. However, there is a critical chapter in the recent history of the Namibian Ju/'hoansi of the Nyae Nyae area around Tsumkwe, in the northeastern part of Namibia across the border from Botswana, that has yet to be effectively told. That chapter is very complex, taking place over 25 years with a few key years around the time of independence in Namibia in 1990. It is based in part on hundreds of hours of deliberation by the Ju/'hoan people about how to transform their society in the face of almost inconceivable pressure. It is the story of the formation of the people's grassroots movement that allowed this tiny group of former hunter-gatherers, speaking an exotic click language, to become a dynamic part of the new nation that grew from the ashes of apartheid in South West Africa.

The Ju/'hoan San grassroots movement went on to establish control over its own land and resources as the very first internationally recognized conservancy in the new Namibia. As of this writing, it is still defending that land and its resources against a host of threats and problems, using the social tools and new political muscle it developed around the time of independence. The major obstacles and pressures that the Nyae Nyae Conservancy faces today include the basically agricultural, land-hungry outlook of the Namibian government and the Ju/'hoansi's pastoral neighbors; the difficulty of feeding themselves in the face of reduced land and non-existent jobs; drug-resistant tuberculosis, malaria, and HIV/AIDS; and social and educational marginalization. These and other issues threaten the Ju/'hoansi at an extremely critical level: their future is very far from certain. In the estimation of some outsiders who have spent recent years working with them in the Nyae Nyae area, had the Ju/'hoansi not begun to exercise the grassroots organization and resistance that they developed in the peri-independence years, they would not be in as good a position as they are today to cope with the various challenges facing them. This does not mean, however, that they are totally in control of their own destiny.

Yet what casual observer has the chance to see the real grassroots activism of local projects or to attend the days-long conservancy meetings that still occur when transportation can be arranged by the far-flung delegates? It is not easy to interpret the torrent of meaningful, consensus-oriented talk in their own language by which the Ju/'hoansi, for the most part, still seek to include the interests of all members of their community.

In authoring this book, we hope to draw attention to the history and ongoing nature of dynamic activism in Ju/'hoan society. We marvel at the Ju/'hoansi's stamina and resilience and ability to maintain their customs and identity while adapting to the outside world and to pressures from within their own society. We see the lack of understanding of Ju/'hoan grassroots governing processes on the part of the Namibian government, neighbors, and relevant non-governmental organizations as one of the main causes of present-day Ju/'hoan suffering. Certainly, it is an enormous barrier to the Ju/'hoansi's ability to build a secure future at a time when isolation is no longer an option. This book is thus written specifically to achieve wider awareness of the heroic events that led to the establishment of the Nyae Nyae Conservancy. It focuses on the way that the Ju/'hoan people, in a complex interplay with outside forces, organically transformed their own culture of communication to serve themselves better in their transformed world.

Namibian independence having been celebrated in March 1990, this book is undeniably long overdue. But the intervening years have made progressively clearer how important and far-reaching the Ju/'hoan social transformation was to become. This time has also allowed us to accumulate a wealth of further experiences in Nyae Nyae, along with project information and written and visual materials from numerous colleagues. We have drawn upon as many of these sources as possible in the hope that our complex topic may benefit from the inclusion of differing points of view. As neither we nor any of our non-Ju/'hoan colleagues has been able to be present in Nyae Nyae during the entire span of years since 1990, writing the history of this period has had to be a collaborative project. The various contributions are acknowledged not only in the preface but also in the text and at the end of the book in the reference section. We are thankful to all those who have shared both materials and ideas.

This volume is our perspective on the history of the Ju/'hoan community in Nyae Nyae following the major international event of Namibian independence.

It is intended to provide students, colleagues, and the general public a much-requested update on the people whom they have come to know through the accounts of Richard Lee, Polly Wiessner, and other anthropologists; the films of John Marshall; and the articles and books of Lorna Marshall and her daughter Elizabeth Marshall Thomas. It focuses on the environmental and political developments that have affected and continue to have an effect on the Ju/'hoan and other San communities of Namibia and, to some extent, neighboring Botswana. Oral and written communications of Ju/'hoan individuals, particularly those who founded the Nyae Nyae Conservancy, are an important feature of the book.

Megan Biesele learned the Ju/'hoan language during her initial fieldwork with the Botswana Ju/'hoansi and has assembled a large collection of Ju/'hoan verbal materials, ranging from folklore and oral history to meetings of the grassroots organizations that have now become the Nyae Nyae Conservancy. As well as a thoroughly researched history, we have tried to provide a lively landscape peopled by the contemporary human beings who made that history through their actions and words. The book also gives newly literate Ju/'hoan people the chance to speak to the world about contemporary issues in their own voices. It thus goes a long way toward rectifying the facelessness that people such as the Ju/'hoansi have suffered in world dialogues.

We have used the actual names of individuals in order to give credit to them and, in part, because we were asked to do so. Another reason is that many of the individuals who are quoted here have been seen and heard from in numerous films, on television programs, and in the print media, and their writings and oral records are available in government documents, newspapers, reports, films, and books.

In the course of preparing this volume, we provided sample chapters and the entire manuscript to the Ju/'hoansi and to the various organizations working with them, including the Nyae Nyae Development Foundation of Namibia, the Nyae Nyae Conservancy, and the Working Group of Indigenous Minorities in Southern Africa. Our goal was to ensure transparency and to allow individuals and organizations the opportunity to comment on or take issue with what we had to say. We have attempted to correct facts, interpretations, and conclusions in light of the comments and suggestions that we received. We take full responsibility for any misinterpretations or errors that remain in this book.

No community speaks with a unitary voice, certainly not the community of anthropological colleagues and perhaps least of all the Ju/'hoan San. While delivering a basic chronology of facts and events, the book explores some of the divisive issues of the last two decades in Nyae Nyae from various viewpoints. When we offer interpretation, we clearly label it as such. In general, each chapter contains both a detailed chronicle of events and themes and a set of interpretations made by Ju/'hoansi, ourselves, and others.

A key focus is on recent development issues in Nyae Nyae and the application of anthropological research to them. Environmental and cultural rights have become very important realities for indigenous peoples and the anthropologists who work with them. The emphasis on what the Ju/'hoan people of Nyae Nyae are doing to protect their own resources and rights helps to demythologize previous images of them as noble savages or helpless victims. In sum, this book demonstrates the responsiveness of current anthropological advocacy to the aspirations of a well-known indigenous society of former foragers. It does so partly by enabling the complex story of the founding of what became the Nyae Nyae Conservancy to be told by a chorus of lively (and often argumentative) local voices.

The Structure of the Book

After a few necessary dips into the past to provide background, this book traces the complex history of Nyae Nyae from about 1986–1987—when, prior to independence, the Ju/wa Farmers Union, the first precursor of the Nyae Nyae Conservancy, was formed—to roughly 2010, with its current challenges to the Ju/'hoansi on both the local and national levels. From the beginning of this two-decade period to the present, both anthropological advocacy and the close participation of non-governmental organizations have been salient adjuncts to the Ju/'hoan people's efforts to re-establish themselves sustainably on their land after moving away from it in a futile search for an alternative livelihood. Anthropologists and development organizations have been important partners in many of the advances—and in some cases the mistakes—that the Nyae Nyae Ju/'hoansi have made.

We have striven to tell the interwoven story of these partnerships in the hope that stakeholders in similar situations in other parts of the world may find some of it useful to their efforts. Readers may find this chronicle quite complex, and for comprehension's sake we have tried to simplify where possible. However, in the last analysis the truth of this particular history lies squarely within its complexities. We present the book as a first contribution to a dialogue with colleagues and the Nyae Nyae Ju/'hoan people in which additional information and alternative perspectives will be put forward.

Several other considerations have been significant in structuring the book. First, many anthropology instructors may want updates on nomenclature and linguistic issues in reference to the San peoples, and we have covered these topics briefly but authoritatively. Second, we have provided maps at several scales to illuminate the text wherever useful. Third, throughout the volume we have sought to demythologize the Ju/'hoansi and other San. We regard it as very important that students and the general public alike be enabled to move beyond the stereotypes in the great bulk of media coverage of the San, epitomized by films such as *The Gods Must Be Crazy*. We believe that this can be done effectively through foregrounding the experiences and lively ideas of the Ju/'hoan individuals whom we came to know during these decades. Fourth, we have focused on anthropological advocacy in order to inform undergraduate students and the world's citizenry about what they can do to actualize their concerns. Lastly, in keeping with the spirit of transparency and out of respect for the Ju/'hoansi as partners in our attempt to understand their transforming society, the book project has been reviewed by the Ju/'hoan people's organization, the Nyae Nyae Conservancy, and by individual Ju/'hoansi. We regard this kind of collaboration as an appropriate continuation of the applied anthropological work we have undertaken with Ju/'hoan and other indigenous peoples.

We present our approximately 20-year history in the form of an introduction, which provides background on the Ju/'hoansi of the Nyae Nyae; two chapters on their pre-colonial way of life; three chapters on the colonial period; and five roughly chronological chapters detailing the events leading up to independence and its aftermath. The introduction focuses on the Ju/'hoan San, or Ju/'hoansi, as a group defining itself as an indigenous minority and as a people who have basic human rights as citizens of Namibia.

The story must be told thematically as well as chronologically, so each of the chronological chapters contains both an outline of important historical events for the years it covers and a discussion of the theme that is the chapter's focus. Chapter 4, for example, reaches back before its time period and then extends beyond it in order to align salient events in a comprehensible chronicle of Ju/'hoan empowerment over wildlife resources in Nyae Nyae. Many chapters also explore development and anthropology themes and problems that illustrate the politics and self-determination of indigenous peoples.

As authors and anthropologists, we keenly feel a responsibility to share our knowledge of the Ju/'hoan community's activities that we were privileged to have experienced over the years. Starting in 1970, Biesele did research in Ju/'hoan language and culture, working with Botswana Ju/'hoansi in the areas of land rights and cultural and economic development. During the 1980s, she became project director and then director of what is now the Nyae Nyae Development Foundation of Namibia (NNDFN), a foundation originally begun by John Marshall and Claire Ritchie. After an initial visit to Nyae Nyae in 1987, she was based there full-time from 1988 to the end of 1991, the years spanning the establishment of Namibian independence. She returned for the southern winters of 1992, 1993, 1995, and 1996 as an educational consultant to the Nyae Nyae Village Schools Project, which she had helped to found. Between 1996 and 2010, she made 11 more trips to Nyae Nyae, working in the areas of linguistic empowerment, mother tongue curriculum development, and cultural heritage conservation. She continues to be involved in these spheres through her work with a group of Ju/'hoan men and women trainees in an ongoing heritage text transcription project supported partly by the Kalahari Peoples Fund. Biesele additionally serves as a board member of NNDFN.

Robert Hitchcock first visited Nyae Nyae in 1987 to learn about the Ju/'hoan development projects taking place there. In 1992, he was hired by the Ford Foundation to make a comprehensive evaluation of the activities of the NNDFN and the Nyae Nyae Farmers Cooperative (the immediate precursor of the Nyae Nyae Conservancy). For that report (Hitchcock 1992), he spent several months researching, interviewing, and observing in Nyae Nyae and Windhoek. He was one of the individuals involved in the conceptualization of the community-based natural resource management program, which included the LIFE Project in the 1990s that continued into the new millennium. Hitchcock returned to Namibia in 1994 and 1995 to work on assessments of these projects. In 2001, he carried out further evaluation for the government of Namibia and the United Nations High Commissioner for Refugees (UNHCR) on the feasibility of settling Angolan refugees within the neighboring N=a Jaqna Conservancy in Tsumkwe District West, a development that, had it taken place, would have had profound effects both there and on the Nyae Nyae Conservancy. Since then, he has kept in extremely close touch with events in Nyae Nyae and in Namibia in general and has published on them widely. His work in Namibia builds upon a solid foundation of research that began in 1975 with San and neighboring communities in Botswana, Zimbabwe, and Zambia.

Hitchcock brings to the writing of this book a comprehensive background in southern African development issues and history. He conducted research among San and their neighbors in eastern and northeastern Botswana beginning in 1975. He worked for the government of Botswana in the Ministry of Local Government and Lands (1977–1979) and the Ministry of Agriculture (1980–1982) and has served as a consultant to the Department of Wildlife and National Parks in Botswana. He has also worked for the governments of Somalia, Gabon, Zambia, Zimbabwe, Swaziland, and Lesotho, and has done consultancies and project assessments for the UNHCR, the US Agency for International Development, the Norwegian Agency for Development Cooperation, and the World Bank.

Royalties from the Sale of This Volume

The Kalahari Peoples Fund (KPF), a US 501(c)(3) non-profit organization based in Austin, Texas, is designated as the recipient of royalties generated by this book. Founded in 1973 by Biesele and her colleagues in the Harvard Kalahari Research Group, the KPF was one of the first anthropological advocacy agencies in the United States and today remains a well-respected activist organization. Formed on behalf of the Ju/'hoansi and the various San, Bakgal-agadi, Nama, and other peoples of the Kalahari Desert area of southern Africa, the KPF has funded and carried out a large number of community-initiated projects, ranging from irrigation farming and protecting drinking water from elephants to land rights work, education, and heritage conservation. Biesele is currently director of the KPF; Hitchcock is a member of its board. The KPF joins us in hoping that by showing the ways in which the Ju/'hoansi have consistently acted on their own behalf, this book will enrich global dialogue on consensual decision-making, on the utility of various forms of democracy, and on sustainable development.

Acknowledgments

This book could not have been conceived of and written without the assistance and encouragement of a great many people and organizations. Our primary thanks go to the Ju/'hoan people of Nyae Nyae, who generously shared their ideas and life experiences with us for more than 20 years. We would also like to acknowledge the following people and agencies for their support. Megan Biesele acknowledges Steve Barclay, Dr. John J. Biesele, Jane Hinchliffe, Diana Burnett, Lorna Marshall, the US National Endowment for the Humanities, the US National Science Foundation, the Wenner-Gren Foundation, the Nyae Nyae Development Foundation of Namibia, Diakonia (Sweden), the Bernard van Leer Foundation, the Swift Foundation, The University Centre for Studies in Namibia, and the Kalahari Peoples Fund for partially underwriting her presence in Nyae Nyae for many years. Robert Hitchcock acknowledges the Nyae Nyae Development Foundation of Namibia, the Ford Foundation, the Working Group of Indigenous Minorities in Southern Africa, the US Agency for International Development, the Bureau of Population, Refugees and Migration of the US Department of State, the United Nations High Commissioner for Refugees, and the Norwegian Agency for Development Cooperation.

We would also like to thank Adrianne M. Daggett, who read and edited the entire manuscript and acted as research assistant, Maria Sapignoli, who read the manuscript and made extensive and useful comments and recommendations, and Victoria Goodman, who provided the very comprehensive index. Additional commentary and editing of the manuscript was done by Shawn Kendrick, whose attention to detail we greatly appreciate. A number of other people read parts of the manuscript and suggested ways to improve it, and we wish to thank them. They include Wayne Babchuk, Magdalena Broermann, Kristin Broyhill, Lara Diez, Patricia Draper, Judy Miller, Claire Ritchie, George

Silberbauer, Axel Thoma, Elizabeth Marshall Thomas, Wendy Viall, and Diana Vinding. We thank Taesun Moon for updates made to field research during 2007, 2008, and 2009. We owe Jean MacGregor many thanks for introducing us to each other in 1975.

The list of other people who helped us while we were writing the book is very long, and we are most grateful to each and every one of them. They include Stacey Main Alberts, John Arnold, the late Dan Aronson, Sonia Arellano-Lopez, the late Tim Asch, Wayne Babchuk, Jim Baird, Steve Barclay, Lesley Beake, Ben Begbie-Clinch, Barbara Belding, Lasse Berg, Dhyani Berger, John Bishop, Kristyna Bishop, Dori Bixler, Michael Bollig, Maitseo Bolaane, Andy Botelle, Alison Brooks, Marieka Brouwer, Chris Brown, Kitty and Carl Brown, Alec and Judy Campbell, Beverley Carpenter, Roger Chennells, Catherine Collett, Andrew Corbett, Aron Crowell, Janette Deacon, the late Patrick Dickens, Ute Dieckmann, Jim Ebert, Silke Felton, Judy Frost, Diane Gelburd, Rob Gordon, Mathias Guenther, Wilfrid Haacke, Jennifer Hays, Melissa Heckler, Janet Hermans, Manfred Hinz, Thekla Hohmann, Nancy Howell, Dianne Hubbard, Kazunobu Ikeya, Margaret Jacobsohn, Ruud Jansen, Trefor Jenkins, Brian Jones, Gerson Kamatuka, the late Ulla Kann, Beata Botlhoko Kasale, Melinda Kelly, Leo Kenny, the late Susan Kent, John and Jill Kinahan, Ryan Klataske, Aaron Kohn, Andrew and Joan Kohn, Melvin Konner, Anke Kooke, John Ledger, Richard B. Lee, the late Braam le Roux, Willemien le Roux, Johanna Loermans, Ingrid Lofstrom-Berg, Bernt Lund, Yo-Yo Ma, Tony Manhire, the late John Marshall, Shebby Mate, Alice Mogwe, Ketsile Molokomme, Marshall Murphree, the late Mark Murray, Levi Namaseb, Elizabeth and George Nicolaou, the late Larry Northam, Alan Osborn, Garth Owen-Smith, Michael Painter, Richard Pakleppa, Rosie Pauly-Kurz, Holly Payne, the late Yvonne Pickering, Oliver Piersson, the late Andrew Quarmby, Larry Robbins, Harriet Rosenberg, Sten Rylander, Beatrice Sandelowsky, Sidsel Saugestad, Ted Scudder, the late Marjorie Shostak, Patricia Skyer, Andrew D. Smith, Jackie Solway, Irene Staehelin, Nancy Stone, Trine Strom Larsen, James Suzman, Renee Sylvain, Akira Takada, Jiro Tanaka, Elizabeth Marshall Thomas, Philip Tobias, Jane Tomlinson, Mark Tracy, Linda Troman, Steve Turner, William Ury, Chris Weaver, Paul Weinberg, Thomas and Dagmar Widlok, Polly Wiessner, Marlene Winberg, Barbara Wyckoff-Baird, John Yellen, Hosabe / Honeb, Joram /Useb, and Joshua //Hoebeb. There were many others not named here who assisted us in a variety of ways, and we wish to extend our thanks to all of them as well.

Our deepest gratitude goes to Marion Berghahn, Ann Przyzycki, Elizabeth Berg, and the editorial team at Berghahn Books. We very much appreciated the thoughtful advice we received while bringing this volume to completion.

— *Megan Biesele and Robert Hitchcock*

Abbreviations

AIDS	Acquired Immune Deficiency Syndrome
BERP	Basic Education Reform Program
CAFOD	Catholic Agency for Overseas Development
CASS	Centre for Applied Social Sciences (University of Namibia)
CBNRM	community-based natural resource management
CBPP	contagious bovine pleuropneumonia (lung plague)
CCN	Council of Churches in Namibia
CLDC	Captain Kxao Kxami Community Learning and Development Centre (Tsumkwe)
CITES	Convention on International Trade in Endangered Species of Wild Fauna and Flora
DNC	Department of Nature Conservation
DTA	Democratic Turnhalle Alliance
ELCIN	Evangelical Lutheran Church in Namibia
EPC	Environmental Planning Committee
FPK	First People of the Kalahari
GDP	gross domestic product
GRN	Government of the Republic of Namibia
HIV	Human Immunodeficiency Virus
ICCO	Interchurch Organization for Development Cooperation
IRDP	Integrated Rural Development Program
IRDNC	Integrated Rural Development and Nature Conservation
IUCN	International Union for the Conservation of Nature and Natural Resources (also known as the World Conservation Union)
IWGIA	International Work Group for Indigenous Affairs

JBDF	Ju/wa Bushman Development Foundation (formerly, the Cattle Fund)
JFU	Ju/wa Farmers Union
JTG	Ju/'hoan Transcription Group
KPF	Kalahari Peoples Fund
KPN	Kalahari Peoples Network
LAC	Legal Assistance Centre
LIFE	Living in a Finite Environment Project (Namibia)
MAWF	Ministry of Agriculture, Water, and Forestry
MET	Ministry of Environment and Tourism (formerly, the Ministry of Wildlife Conservation and Tourism)
MLGLH	Ministry of Local Government, Lands, and Housing (Botswana)
MHSS	Ministry of Health and Social Services
MLRR	Ministry of Lands, Resettlement, and Rehabilitation
MWCT	Ministry of Wildlife Conservation and Tourism (formerly, the Department of Nature Conservation)
NACSO	Namibian Association of CBNRM Support Organisations
NAMAS	Namibia Association of Norway
NDP1	National Development Plan 1
NDP2	National Development Plan 2
NDP3	National Development Plan 3
NEPRU	Namibian Economic Policy Research Unit
NGO	non-governmental organization
NNC	Nyae Nyae Conservancy (formerly, the Nyae Nyae Farmers Cooperative)
NNDFN	Nyae Nyae Development Foundation of Namibia (formerly, the Ju/wa Bushman Development Foundation)
NNFC	Nyae Nyae Farmers Cooperative (formerly, the Ju/wa Farmers Union)
NORAD	Norwegian Agency for Development Cooperation
NUNW	National Union of Namibian Workers
SADC	Southern African Development Community
SADF	South African Defence Force
SDR	Swiss Disaster Relief
SIDA	Swedish International Development Cooperation Agency
SWA	South West Africa
SWAA	South West Africa Administration
SWAPO	South West Africa People's Organization
TUCSIN	The University Centre for Studies in Namibia
UN	United Nations
UNAM	University of Namibia

UNDP	United Nations Development Programme
UNHCR	United Nations High Commissioner for Refugees
UNTAG	United Nations Transition Assistance Group
USAID	United States Agency for International Development
VSP	Village Schools Project
WCED	World Commission on Environment and Development
WIMSA	Working Group of Indigenous Minorities in Southern Africa
WWF	World Wildlife Fund (US)

Note on Orthography

The Ju/'hoan language is far from simple, and therefore the orthography used in this book was not easy to develop. It was important that the language's representation should not be simplified, as that would reduce the number of the myriad meanings it encodes, meanings on which the Ju/'hoan "Old Way" (Thomas 2006), as well as the Ju/'hoansi's vital, transforming present history, intimately depends. Thus, although the click symbols and other conventions that Western readers will encounter in this book may seem awkward, using them is our way of paying respect to the complexity and specific verbal art of the Ju/'hoan language. The failure to record and use faithfully an endangered language such as Ju/'hoansi would be to hasten its disappearance—an intellectual as well as a human rights disaster.

The sounds of Ju/'hoansi are a case in point. Among global phonological systems, the Khoesan languages (of which Ju/'hoansi is one) contain the largest inventory of consonants found in any languages that have been surveyed. Khoesan consonants use a large number of combinations of clicks and other features, making these languages uniquely phonetically complex. As David Crystal (2002: 57) writes in his book *Language Death*, "[I]f Khoisan [Khoesan] languages had all died out before linguists had described them, it is unlikely that we would ever have guessed that human beings would use such an apparently minor feature of sound production to such complex effect."

The orthography we use was developed by Patrick Dickens (1991), a linguist from the University of the Witwatersrand, Johannesburg, when he was in the employ of the Nyae Nyae Development Foundation of Namibia (NNDFN). As detailed in chapter 10 of this book, Dickens worked for three years with Ju/'hoan trainees to render Ju/'hoansi a professionally documented and taught language. Basing his orthography on a much more complex one by Jan Snyman

(1975) of the University of South Africa, Dickens produced an orthography to international linguistic standards that was elegantly streamlined and could be typed on any keyboard. With it, literate and non-literate Ju/'hoansi alike could learn to write their language in a matter of hours.

Dickens's *English-Ju/'hoan, Ju/'hoan-English Dictionary*, whose manuscript was completed by the time he died of AIDS in October 1992, was published in 1994 (Dickens 1994). The Ju/'hoan grammar he wrote was also published posthumously (Dickens 2005). These books have become indispensable tools of literacy and scholarship for the Ju/'hoan community and for linguists of the Khoesan languages. After Dickens's death, the KPF became the scholarly custodian of his linguistic work.

At the same time, the Ju/'hoan people's organization, then the Nyae Nyae Farmers Cooperative (NNFC), became the community custodian of Dickens's linguistic materials and the education program that they made possible. The NNFC advanced the Ju/'hoan agenda of effective national and international communication by formally adopting Dickens's orthography for educational and political purposes. After independence, the Namibian Ministry of Basic Education and Culture was successfully lobbied to adopt Dickens's orthography as the official one for the Nyae Nyae Village Schools Project (VSP) and other Ju/'hoan schools. Because of this language activism, the Ju/'hoan language was accepted under the Namibian Basic Education Reform Program (BERP) as the medium for a pilot project in curriculum development for the years 1991–1996. Ju/'hoansi was one of the nationally recognized languages used at the Namibian National Conference on Land Reform in 1991. Now part of the Namibian national educational system, the VSP is ongoing today. The language revitalization that was aided by Dickens's orthography has contributed a great deal to the growing confidence and political effectiveness of the Ju/'hoan voice in Namibia.

Pronunciation

For the benefit of those who do not speak click languages, we provide here a few pronunciation guidelines. The letters "oa" are pronounced like "wa" in English. The word /'hoan, meaning "real" or "harmless," in the compound word Ju/'hoan—rendered "harmless people" by Elizabeth Marshall Thomas (1958)—can be pronounced "twan." The name of the people can be reasonably pronounced "Ju-twan."

The Ju/'hoan language has four clicks (some Khoesan languages have five). For the first two Ju/'hoan clicks, / and = (with the latter sometimes written as ǂ), we suggest substituting "t." For the last two Ju/'hoan clicks, ! and //, we suggest substituting "k."

Nomenclature

In this book we follow the *Style and Typing Guide for Khoe, Ju, !Ui and Taa Languages* developed by linguist associates of the Working Group of Indigenous Minorities in Southern Africa (WIMSA 2001) for the spellings of the names of peoples and languages. We reproduce here, with permission, the relevant portion of that guide.

Ju Language Family

> !Xun (used to be !Xû): the language and the people
> Ju|'hoansi: the language and the people
> Ju|'hoan: use only as an adjective
> !Kung: the language and the people

Khoe Language Family

> Khoekhoegowab: language of the Hai||om, Nama, and Damara peoples
> Khwedam: language of the Khwe people
> Khwe: the people (used to be Kxoe)
> ||Anikhwe: part of the Khwe peoples, mostly in Botswana
> Naro: the language and the people
> G|ui or Cgui: the language and the people
> G||ana or Xgana: the language and the people

Taa Language Family

> !Xõó or !Xoon: the language and the people

!Ui Language Family

> N|u: the language of the southern Kalahari
> N||n‡e: speakers of N|u
> ‡Homani or ‡Khomani: people who used to speak N|u and |'Auo
> |'Auo: extinct language
> |'Auni: speakers of |'Auo
> |Xam: extinct language. The San Cultural Centre is called !Khwa ttu, this is
> |Xam for 'water pan'
> ||Xegwi: extinct language

Chronology of the Nyae Nyae Region

1850s	First recorded encounters of Ju/'hoansi with Europeans
1862–1870	Nama-Herero Wars, northward expansion of Hereros into areas near Nyae Nyae
1884	Establishment of Namibia as a "German Protectorate" (named Deutsch-Südwestafrika)
1890	Germany annexes territory of South West Africa (now Namibia)
1896–1897	Rinderpest epidemic affects wildlife and livestock in Namibia and Botswana
1904–1907	German-Herero Wars, the first genocide in the twentieth century, resulting in substantial lives lost and at least 6,000 Herero moving into Botswana
1911–1915	Police zone established in northern Namibia; the "Bushman Problem" or "Bushman Plague" in northern Namibia included attacks by German troops, police, and settlers on San communities and San men being forced into labor
1915	Germany surrenders territory of South West Africa to South Africa
1922	South Africa establishes "native reserves" in South West Africa
1949	Commission for the Preservation of the Bushmen appointed
1951–1958	Marshall family undertakes expeditions to Nyae Nyae
1959	Establishment of administrative center at Tsumkwe
1964	Odendaal Commission report on South West Africa
1965	Border fence erected between Namibia and Botswana

1966	Namibian War of Independence begins and lasts until 1988
1970	Bushmanland created as a magisterial district in South West Africa
1978	UN Security Council Resolution 435 on Namibia passed, outlining a cease-fire and UN-supervised elections
1981	The Cattle Fund (later, the Ju/wa Bushman Development Foundation, JBDF) is founded; survey work by John Marshall and Claire Ritchie begins in Nyae Nyae
1982–1983	First groups of Ju/'hoansi leave Tsumkwe to re-establish themselves on their *n!oresi*
1984	Plan to turn Nyae Nyae into a game reserve is announced
1986	The Ju/wa Farmers Union (JFU) (later, the Nyae Nyae Farmers Cooperative, NNFC) is formed
1988	Run-up to independence involving meetings with government and NGO officials
1989	Cease-fire declared on 1 April; UNTAG enters Namibia; SWAPO wins November elections
1990	Namibian independence declared on 21 March 1990; Ju/'hoansi take part in the celebrations
1991	Namibian National Conference on Land Reform and the Land Question held in Windhoek, 25 June–1 July 1991 with Ju/'hoan participation; an incursion of Herero into Nyae Nyae ends peacefully with the government of Namibia backing Ju/'hoan land rights
1992	Crisis in the Nyae Nyae Development Foundation of Namibia (formerly, the JBDF) and the NNFC
1995	Outbreak of lung plague among cattle across the border in Botswana, resulting in the government's destruction of 320,000 head
1995–2002	Implementation of the LIFE Project by USAID, GRN, and WWF in the Nyae Nyae area
1997	Demonstrations by Hai//om to claim ancestral land in Etosha National Park
1998	Founding of the Nyae Nyae Conservancy (NNC) (formerly, the NNFC) and the announcement of Nyae Nyae as the first conservancy on communal land in Namibia; recognition of Tsamkxao =Oma as the Ju/'hoan Traditional Authority
2001	A devil's claw project piloted by the NNC with the Ministry of Environment and Tourism is initiated; elephant damage to wells and gardens in Nyae Nyae increases

2003	Status of conservancies for protecting land tenure rights in Nyae Nyae and other communal areas is questioned by Namibian government officials
2005	Food situation in Nyae Nyae is serious; questions are raised about the effectiveness of the NNC
2008	Plans made for the establishment of a Nyae Nyae Community Forest
2009	Late April invasion of Nyae Nyae by Herero farmers from G/am, prompts the Ju/'hoansi to seek legal advice and support from NGOs and the government
2010	Tsamkxao =Oma attends the UN Permanent Forum on Indigenous Issues in April; as of September 2010, the issue of the Herero and their herds in Nyae Nyae remains unresolved
2011	Herero in Tsumkwe built up their cattle numbers and illegal fences were constructed in the conservancy in the area north of the main road to Tsumkwe. Gardening activities in southern Nyae Nyae expanded.
2012	Two Nyae Nyae Conservancy members attended the 11th annual meeting of the United Nations Permanent Forum on Indigenous Issues in New York from 7–18 May 2012. The Nyae Nyae Conservancy Forest was proclaimed in July. The United Nations special rapporteur on the human rights and fundamental freedoms of indigenous people, S. James Anaya, visited Tsumkwe in September 2012.

Introduction

A Community History

The Ju/'hoan San of Nyae Nyae are a people who today see themselves as an indigenous minority who have basic human rights as citizens of the southern African country of Namibia. This book describes the process by which they have developed that perspective. It examines the wide array of changes that have occurred in Nyae Nyae, looks at the responses that the Ju/'hoansi have had to these challenges, and describes how they have been able to become political actors on the national and international stage, seeking greater recognition of their human rights, their right to development, and their right to participate in public policy decisions.

The Ju/'hoansi today are citizens of Namibia, a relatively new nation in Africa, which achieved its independence in March 1990. Namibia is located in southern Africa, with the Atlantic Ocean to the west, Angola to the north, Botswana to the east, and South Africa to the south (see map 1). Namibia also shares a border with Zambia along the north of the Caprivi Strip. Covering an area of approximately 824,000 square kilometers, Namibia is slightly more than half the size of the American state of Alaska. As a country, Namibia is heavily dependent on the mining industry, agriculture, fishing, and tourism, as well as on receipts from the Southern African Customs Union (Republic of Namibia 2006; World Bank 1992, 2008). Today, it is a member of the Southern African Development Community (SADC). Like all of the countries of southern Africa, Namibia has a complex history, some of which is outlined in this book.[1]

---

1. For additional literature on Namibia's history, see Green, Kiljunen, and Kiljunen (1981); Leys and Brown (2005); Leys and Saul (1995); Marais (1984); Melber (2003); and Rotberg (1983).

Map 1 Namibia, Botswana, and adjacent nations

Namibia is one of the most arid countries in Sub-Saharan Africa. Rainfall varies between 25 millimeters per year in the Namib Desert in the west to 700 millimeters per year in the Caprivi region in the northeast. Water is a limiting factor in many areas, and the variability in the timing, distribution, and amounts of rainfall has to be considered carefully by planners and by local people. Namibia's only perennial rivers flow along portions of its northern and southern borders, the Cunene River in the north and the Gariep (formerly the Orange) River in the south (see map 2). The people, wildlife, and livestock of Namibia are almost entirely dependent upon ephemeral rivers, surface water after rains, small springs, and groundwater (Chenje and Johnson 1996; Jacobson, Jacobson, and Seely 1995). The water table in the country has dropped significantly in some areas over the past several decades, in part because of water extraction to supply human domestic needs, livestock, agriculture, towns, industry, and mining. According to Gleick (2006: 241, table 3), 20 percent of Namibia's population lacks access to safe drinking water. Obtaining access to sufficient land and procuring adequate water supplies to meet basic needs have been two of the major challenges facing local people in Namibia.

From an ethnographic standpoint, Namibia is a diverse country, with about 28 different languages spoken and a large number of ethnic groups, some of them, such as the Ovambo, quite sizable. Some of the groups in Namibia, including the San and the Nama (Khoekhoe), consider themselves to be indigenous to the country. While a number of these ethnic groups have been

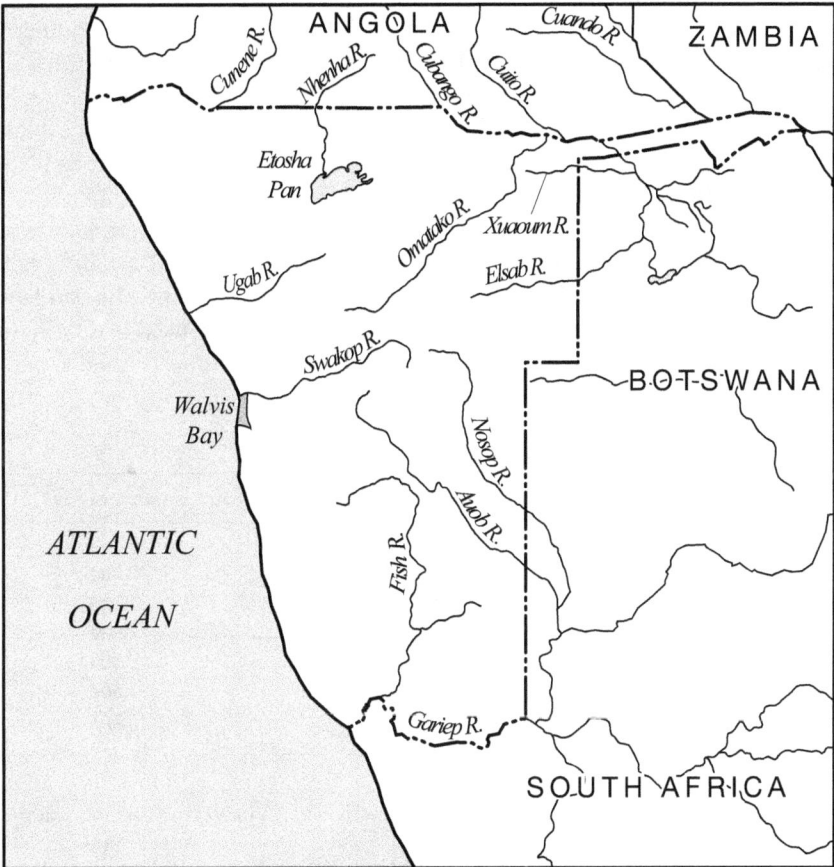

Map 2 Namibia and its river systems

investigated by social scientists (Gewald 1999; Hahn, Vedder, and Fourie 1928; Malan 1995; Schapera 1930), a significant amount of attention has been paid to the Ju/'hoan San, who in the past were sometimes labeled the !Kung.

The Ju/'hoan San have been the subject of anthropological study and interest for over 50 years (Barnard 2007: 53–58; Biesele 1986; Gordon and Douglas 2000; Hitchcock 2004; Lee and DeVore 1976; L. Marshall 1960, 1961, 1976; Thomas 2006: 48–51; Wiessner 1977, 2002). As a result, the Ju/'hoansi are some of the best-known and most thoroughly documented indigenous peoples on the planet. In some ways, they are considered southern Africa's "model people" (Jenkins 1979). James Suzman (2001b: 39) points out that the Ju/'hoansi have received a disproportionately greater amount of attention relative to their numbers than any other group in Namibia. He goes on to note: "This high profile is also reflected in the extent of non-government organization activity in the area" (ibid.).

The Ju/'hoansi are one of a number of different San groups in southern Africa.[2] There are approximately 100,000 San living in six southern African countries today (see table 1). The San population is made up of a diverse set of self-identifying groups who speak a wide variety of languages and who exhibit both similarities and differences in customs, traditions, economic practices, and histories.

There is much debate in the anthropological and linguistic literature over the most appropriate term to be used for Ju/'hoan peoples (Barnard 1992, 2007; Lee 1976, 1979a). The term "!Kung" is actually the name of a San language that is closely related to the Ju/'hoan language. It is used primarily to refer to !Xun who reside in the north of Namibia and southern Angola, with

Table 1 Number of San in southern Africa

Country	Population	Size (sq km)	Number of San
Angola	13,068,110	1,246,700	3,500
Botswana	2,029,207	600,370	48,000
Namibia	2,128,471	825,418	34,000
South Africa	49,109,107	1,221,912	7,500
Zambia	12,056,823	752,614	1,300
Zimbabwe	11,651,858	390,580	2,500
Totals	90,043,776	5,037,594	96,800

Note: Figures estimated as of July 2010.

Source: Data obtained from the Working Group of Indigenous Minorities in Southern Africa (WIMSA).

2. For some overviews of the San, see Barnard (1992, 2007); Hitchcock et al. (2006a); Hohmann (2003); Schapera (1930); Smith et al. (2000); Suzman (2001a, 2001b); and Tobias (1978).

some members living in what is now Tsumkwe District West (formerly Western Bushmanland) (Barnard 1992: 39, 45–46; Pakleppa and Kwononoka 2003; Suzman 2001b: 38–39, 42). The people with whom we deal in this book prefer to be known by the name "Ju/'hoan," which means true or ordinary people.

The Ju/'hoansi are northern San whose language contains four click consonants, a feature of great interest to linguists (Crystal 2000: 56–57). There is also considerable interest in the Ju/'hoansi and their neighbors on the part of geneticists, biological anthropologists, and demographers (Howell 2000; Nurse, Weiner, and Jenkins 1985; Tishkoff et al. 2007, 2009; Vigilant et al. 1989). The Ju/'hoansi exhibit a number of interesting features, ranging from the ways in which they adapt to their environment, share goods and services, and engage in consensus-based decision-making and conflict management (Lee and DeVore 1976; L. Marshall 1976; Thomas 1958, 1994, 2006).

Estimates of the numbers of Ju/'hoansi vary, depending on the source of the information. In 1979, Lee (1979a: 35, table 1) estimated that there were 4,000 Ju/'hoansi in Namibia and 2,000 in Botswana, for a total of 6,000. Gordon and Douglas (2000: 7) said that there were 7,000 Ju/'hoansi in Namibia, mainly in the Grootfontein, Tsumeb, and Bushmanland (now Tsumkwe) districts. The Summer Institute of Linguistics volume on world languages, *Ethnologue* (Lewis 2009), suggests that there are 28,600 Ju/'hoansi in southern Africa, which we believe is an overestimate. The Working Group of Indigenous Minorities in Southern Africa (WIMSA) recently put the number of Ju/'hoansi in Namibia at 6,000 (Axel Thoma, pers. comm., 2007; Joram /Useb, pers. comm., 2007). We estimate that the total number of Ju/'hoansi in Namibia and Botswana today is approximately 11,000 people. We have to admit, however, that this figure is a mere approximation, since getting accurate census data that take into account ethnic identity is a complex process in southern Africa. Southern African governments are reluctant to include questions relating to ethnicity in national censuses, and there are both logistical and methodological difficulties inherent in population censuses. An additional problem is that individuals sometimes shift their identities and do not always give the same answers to questions about their backgrounds.

The Ju/'hoansi represent the second largest group of San in Namibia (see table 2 for a summary of the populations of San in Namibia). The largest San population is the Hai//om, who reside in northern Namibia and whose ancestral territory included what is now Etosha National Park, the largest protected area in Namibia.[3] Another sizable population of San in Namibia is the Khwe, some of whom reside today in Tsumkwe District West close to the Ju/'hoansi, and the majority of whom reside in Kavango and Caprivi to the north. Some

---

3. For excellent overviews of the Hai//om, see Dieckmann (2007); Longden (2004); Suzman (2004); and Widlok (1999).

Table 2 Populations of San in Namibia

Group Name(s)	Location	Population Size
//Anikwe	West Caprivi	400
Khwe	West and East Caprivi, some in Tsumkwe District West, Otjozondjupa region	5,000
!Xun	Okavango, Otjozondjupa regions	6,000
Ju/'hoansi	Tsumkwe East, Otjozondjupa, Omaheke, Gobabis	7,000
Hai//om	Oshakati, Uutapi, Tsumeb, Outjo, Etosha National Park, Grootfontein	11,000
Naro	Omaheke region, Otjinene and Gobabis districts	2,000
=Au//eisi	Omaheke region, Otjinene and Gobabis districts	2,000
!Xõó	Omaheke region, Otjinene and Gobabis districts, Mariental region, Hardap district	300
|'Auni	Mariental region, Hardap district	200
N|u (/Nu-//en)	Mariental region, Hardap district	100
Total		34,000

Source: Data compiled from reports and documents on file in the WIMSA library, the Namibia National Archives, the library of the Kuru Family of Organizations, and published literature (e.g., Gordon and Douglas 2000: 7; Suzman 2001b: 3, table 1.1).

of the Khwe and the !Xun ex-soldiers and their families opted to go to South Africa with the assistance of the South African Defence Force (SADF) prior to Namibian independence in March 1990.[4]

The area where the Ju/'hoansi reside today stretches across the Botswana-Namibia border from Tsumkwe and areas to the west into Botswana as far as Gomare, Tsau, and Sehitwa near the Okavango Delta in the east (see map 3). There are Ju/'hoansi residing in areas in the southern territory of Nyae Nyae, including the Omaheke portion of the Gobabis farms region of eastern Namibia (Suzman 1999: xxii–xxvi; Sylvain 1999, 2001) and the Grootfontein farms to the west (Suzman 2001b: 12–13). Ju/'hoansi also live in some of the towns of Namibia, including Grootfontein, Otjiwarongo, and Windhoek. The majority of the Ju/'hoansi reside in the Kalahari Desert region of northeastern Namibia and northwestern Botswana. Thus, Ju/'hoansi are, like many indigenous groups around the world, transboundary peoples, having to deal with all of the social and political complexities that that status implies.

4. For discussions of the resettlement of the !Xun and Khwe soldiers and their dependents, see Robbins (2006, 2007); Robins, Madzudzo, and Brenzinger (2001); Sharp and Douglas (1996); Uys (1993); and Hitchcock (in press).

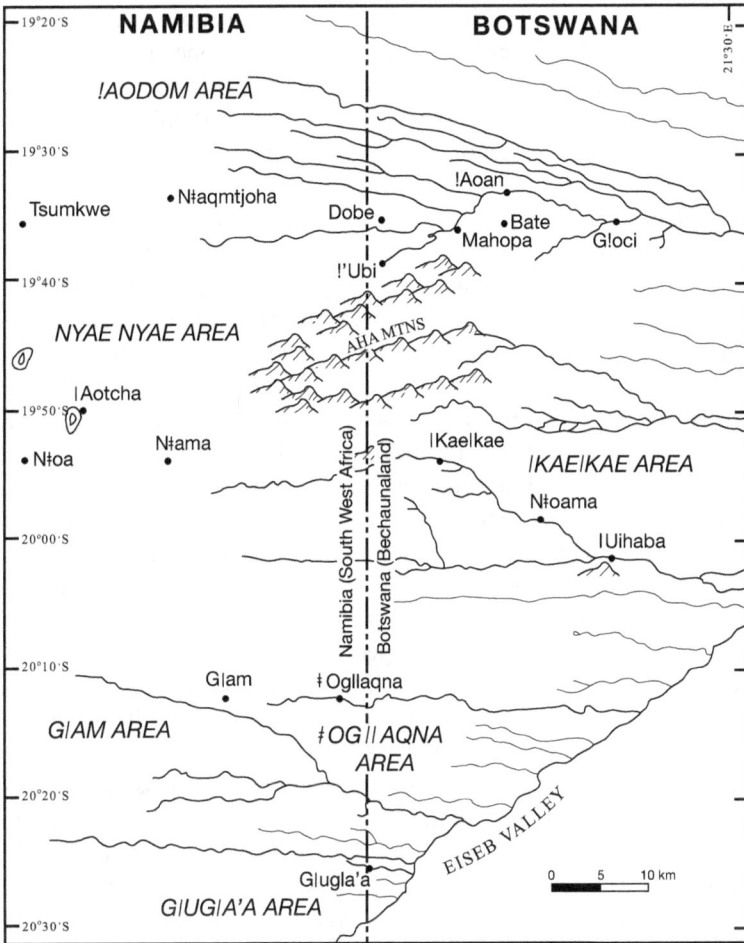

Map 3 The Nyae Nyae and /Kae/kae areas in northeastern Namibia and northwestern Botswana

Anthropological Research on the Ju/'hoansi

While anthropological observations were made about the Ju/'hoansi and their San neighbors in the nineteenth and early twentieth centuries (Gordon and Douglas 2000; Guenther 2005; Schapera 1930), it was not until the 1950s that serious, long-term, and detailed ethnographic work was carried out among Ju/'hoan populations. In 1950, Laurence Kennedy Marshall retired as president of Raytheon Corporation in the United States. As Lorna Marshall (pers. comm.,

1990) noted, retirement provided her husband with an opportunity to pursue his interests. In addition to spending time with his family, one of the things that he wanted to do was to sojourn in Africa, which he had read about extensively as a child. Stories about the "lost city of the Kalahari" had particularly intrigued him. Marshall approached the Peabody Museum at Harvard University to see if there was any interest in carrying out an expedition to the Kalahari Desert of southern Africa. J. O. Brew, the director of the Peabody, said that, if they were to go to the Kalahari, the Marshalls might spend some of their time looking for "wild Bushmen," meaning those people who lived solely by hunting and gathering.

In 1950, Laurence and his son John made their first trip to the Kalahari. They heard at /Kae/kae in Botswana that there were groups farther to the west who were living independently of other groups and who were foraging. In 1951, the Marshalls, including Laurence and his wife Lorna, son John, and daughter Elizabeth (now Elizabeth Marshall Thomas), set off for what is now Namibia. Their objectives were to visit places that had "been relatively little explored" (Thomas 2006: 46, 48), to establish contact with people living in remote areas (L. Marshall 1976: 2–3), and to learn about the hunting and gathering way of life.

Doing fieldwork in South West Africa in the 1950s was a complex undertaking. At the time that the Marshalls worked in the Nyae Nyae region (1951–1961), there were incidents of local people being captured and pressed into service in the mines or on cattle posts, ranches, or farms. In some cases, the farmers who came into the Nyae Nyae area persuaded local Ju/'hoansi to join them and took them away to their farms (L. Marshall 1976: 60). The Ju/'hoansi were also faced with the prospect of Herero and other groups moving into the Nyae Nyae region and establishing cattle posts. Some of the Ju/'hoansi were only too happy to work for the Herero because they were able to get access to milk and meat and sometimes were given gifts of food, clothing, and tobacco. In 1957, when Laurence Marshall again visited the Nyae Nyae area, he heard more details about the ways in which some of the Ju/'hoansi were being treated on the cattle posts, and he reported the matter to the South West African authorities. In response, the South West Africa Administration (SWAA) sent police patrols to the Nyae Nyae region, and the officers convinced the Herero to return to their homes in Botswana (L. Marshall 1976: 60; Lorna Marshall, pers. comm.).

The Marshall family expeditions had a profound impact on the Ju/'hoansi, providing not only much entertainment and a periodic source of food and income, but also, according to Ju/'hoansi informants, a more positive sense of themselves. The expeditions to the various pans in the Nyae Nyae region led to increased numbers of local visitors in the places where they stayed. The larger numbers of people in the camps had both costs and benefits. On the cost side, local people had to go farther to get sufficient bush food to sustain themselves, except when they were being provisioned by the Marshalls. There were also more conflicts in the camps than when the camp sizes were smaller and there were fewer people from different bands living together, according to the Ju/'hoansi. On the benefit side, the greater degree of sedentism meant that there were more opportunities for people to engage in social interactions, for marriages to be arranged, and for exchanges of goods and services to occur, not to mention the possibilities afforded by the presence of the Marshalls and their co-workers.

The Marshalls did not have an easy time carrying out their work in South West Africa. There were logistical difficulties, such as vehicle problems (e.g., broken springs and overheated radiators) and the limited availability of water. Lorna Marshall says that she reported on the arduous nature of the journeys into the Nyae Nyae region because she believed that the grueling travel conditions were "so important a protective factor for the !Kung maintaining their way of life" (L. Marshall 1976: 13).

At the time of the expeditions, the Ju/'hoansi and other San in Namibia were under the administrative oversight of the South African Department of Bantu Administration and Development (L. Marshall 1976: 13). The South West African Native Affairs Administration Act of 1954 laid out the bureaucratic structure under which the Ju/'hoansi and other Namibian "native" populations fell. Essentially, the Ju/'hoansi were at the bottom of a several-tiered bureaucratic and socio-economic system in South West Africa. They had no right to self-representation; they had no leaders who were recognized by the SWAA; and they had no say over what could be done with regard to the land that they occupied and the water sources on that land.

The pace of change in the Nyae Nyae region began to quicken during the time of the Marshall expeditions in the 1950s (L. Marshall 1976: 13–14, 60–61). The Witwatersrand Native Labor Association began recruiting Ovambo and Kavango men for mines in the area just to the north of the Nyae Nyae region, and some of the mine labor recruiters visited the Nyae Nyae area, following the tracks of the Marshall vehicles (Lorna Marshall, pers. comm., 1990).

The Settlement at Tsumkwe

The next episode in Ju/'hoan history, from 1959 to the late 1970s, was characterized by several South West African government decisions regarding land use and zoning and the establishment of administrative infrastructure and management systems. These decisions had a series of ever widening social and economic implications for the residents of the area. The administrative center for Nyae Nyae, called Tsumkwe, was established in 1959. The center was meant to be a location of permanent and sedentary resettlement for the Ju/'hoansi, a way of incorporating them into "modern" life. The South West African government promised the Ju/'hoansi jobs, agricultural training, and access to medical care. It also encouraged them to come to Tsumkwe by offering them food and water.

Infrastructure development at Tsumkwe included drilling a borehole, preparing land for agricultural fields, and setting up a police station, a store, and a housing scheme (J. Marshall 1989: 46–49; L. Marshall 1976: 73). Paid jobs were made available, but only for a few people. The high population density and low rate of employment, combined with the availability of alcohol at the store, resulted in a whole series of social, economic, and health problems. The degree to which people in Tsumkwe could depend on wild foods declined. Resources were depleted relatively quickly in the vicinity, and because the people were now sedentary, these resources were not replenished as would normally occur when a group would move elsewhere in the annual mobility pattern. The diet deteriorated as people became increasingly dependent upon maize meal rations provided by the administration and foodstuff purchased from the local store. When people refused to share the few resources that they were able to obtain, reciprocity systems were disrupted and social tensions increased. Rape, domestic abuse, and interpersonal violence were common in Tsumkwe.

According to the Ju/'hoansi, life in Tsumkwe was characterized by poverty, ill health, apathy, and social dissatisfaction. Tensions increased to the point that fights would break out fairly frequently. The mortality rates from homicide and illness were so high that Tsumkwe became known to the Ju/'hoansi as "the place of death." It should come as no surprise, therefore, that many Ju/'hoansi eventually began to look for an opportunity to leave and, if possible, return to their former homes.

The first borehole was drilled in Tsumkwe in 1961. By 1964, there were at least four gardens being maintained by Ju/'hoansi in Tsumkwe. Goats were introduced by the SWAA in 1965, and nine people obtained them on the understanding that they would give the progeny back to Claude McIntyre, the commissioner of Bushman Affairs, who would then redistribute them to other people. By 1969, there were 12 Ju/'hoan communities that had settled in and around Tsumkwe, 9 of which kept goats and 10 of which had gardens in which crops were grown. A total of nine people had formal employment in Tsumkwe. Cattle were introduced at Tsumkwe by the administration in 1972, and 49 adult Ju/'hoan males either bought or were given cows. Some of these men already had had experience managing cattle, having worked on farms in Grootfontein or Gobabis. Losses of livestock to lions and other predators were high.

From a political standpoint, the first Bushman *rada* (council) was formed in 1967. By the late 1980s, the government was providing the *radasi* (members of the *rada*) with salaries. The militarization of the Tsumkwe region occurred in the mid- to late 1970s as the war of independence heated up, and by 1980 there were eight military bases in Bushmanland. Approximately 150 Ju/'hoansi joined the SADF, and three times that number of !Xun and Khwe were in the military in Western Bushmanland. By 1981, a significant percentage of the Tsumkwe population was at least partially dependent on salaries and food supplied by the military. Only four families continued to maintain gardens, and just 4 out of 30 cattle owners were milking their cows (John Marshall, pers. comm., 1987). The majority of the residents of Tsumkwe survived on rations provided by the SWAA and, to a lesser extent, goods purchased through cash earned by Ju/'hoansi who were in the military or who had jobs.

The South African police force began to use San as trackers in the early 1970s (Lee and Hurlich 1982: 334). Subsequently, !Xun and Khwe San from Angola and the Caprivi were recruited by the SADF as soldiers. By 1975, the SADF had two major military bases, Alpha and Omega, in the Caprivi. According to Gordon and Douglas (2000: 185), Omega housed some 3,000 San and their families in 1978. The soldiers received high salaries, and their dependents were provided with rations, blankets, and other goods.

The impact of the militarization of the San has been addressed in detail by a number of researchers.[5] John Marshall (1989; pers. comm., 1996) estimated that there were as many as 12,000 San in the military during the 23-year-long civil war. He also noted that three out of every four people in Western Bushmanland were directly or indirectly part of the military. According to Marshall (1984: 13), many of the people living in the military settlements led "idle, debilitated lives."

In 1978, Bushman Battalion 36 was established at Tsumkwe, and the SADF began to recruit Ju/'hoansi (Lee and Hurlich 1982: 335; Ritchie 1986: 313). Major Pinkie Coetzee arrived in Bushmanland and began work on military training and development activities, including training in livestock keeping. The military built roads and drilled boreholes, especially in Western Bushmanland. The major's goal was to settle family groups with livestock around each borehole in order to help them become economically self-sufficient. Agriculture was attempted, but yields were low.

Approximately 1,000 Bushmen from Angola, the Caprivi Strip, and Kavango were brought to the Nyae Nyae region by the SADF in the late 1970s. They were settled at an army base at Mangetti Dune in Western Bushmanland. According to informants, tensions ran fairly high between the immigrants and the Ju/'hoansi. Jealousies caused by the flow of money and goods into the region were felt especially by people on the margins of the sharing network (Ritchie 1986: 313). One of the most significant effects of the SADF presence in northern Namibia was that local people, including many San, became more dependent upon the money, food, goods, and services provided by the military. Economic stratification was seen in the settlements where well-paid

5. See, for example, Biesele et al. (1989: 144–146); Bixler (1992: 41–43, 122–124); Gordon (1984); Gordon and Douglas (2000: 2–3, 57–58, 183–208); Kolata (1981); Lee (1979a: 428–431; 1979b: 312; 1985: 38–41); Lee and Hurlich (1982); J. Marshall (1984: 13; 1989: 26, 38–41); Marshall and Hartung (1986: 25, 34–35); Marshall and Ritchie (1984); Ritchie (1986: 313–314; 1987: 61–63); Robbins (2006, 2007); Robins, Madzudzo, and Brenzinger (2001: 9–10, 61–64); Suzman (2001b: 41–42, 55–56).

soldiers were stationed; essentially, there were a few relatively wealthy people and substantial numbers of poor ones.

Challenges Faced by the Nyae Nyae Ju/'hoansi

We present our history of Nyae Nyae in terms of a number of challenges and crises that faced the Ju/'hoan people, and the ways in which these issues were either resolved or not resolved. The principal matters that this book covers are the following:

- the mid-1980s bid of the South West African Department of Nature Conservation (DNC) (later the Ministry of Wildlife Conservation and Tourism, MWCT) to make Eastern Bushmanland into a game park and effectively exclude the Ju/'hoansi from their land;
- the late-1980s question concerning which political party the Ju/'hoansi would align with, the conservative Democratic Turnhalle Alliance (DTA) or the liberation party, the South West Africa People's Organization (SWAPO);
- the post-independence possibility that the Ju/'hoansi would lose their land through national communal land allocation and the general issue of land reform;
- internal organizational issues in the Nyae Nyae Development Foundation of Namibia (NNDFN), which John Marshall and Claire Ritchie established as a way of aiding the people of Nyae Nyae, and problems affecting Ju/'hoan society, such as generational strife, jealousy over the perceived formation of an elite, and questions of equity in the distribution of jobs and benefits;
- development-related topics that included water provision, land and natural resource management, land tenure, agriculture, and political participation at the local, regional, and national levels; and
- continued uncertainty about the status of land tenure in the Nyae Nyae region and surrounding areas, given recent Namibian government statements about the land and plans for resettlement of people from other parts of Namibia in the area (e.g., Tsumkwe District West).

The Main Challenges in Context

In recent years the Ju/'hoansi faced a number of major challenges. Their economy was eroding, and hunger was all too common. There were threats to their land base from other groups who wanted to utilize the water, grazing, wildlife, and mineral resources in the area. Namibian government planners were considering turning areas in and around Ju/'hoan ancestral land into commercial farms and establishing a large refugee camp nearby (Hitchcock 2001; Pakleppa 2001, 2002; Pakleppa and WIMSA Team 2004). The Ju/'hoansi had faced these situations before during the colonial era, when the minority white government of then South West Africa reduced the land base of the Ju/'hoansi from an estimated 91,000 square kilometers to an area less than 10 percent of that amount.

By the early 1980s, people in Tsumkwe were chafing to leave in order to get away from what they saw as inhospitable conditions. Many if not most of the Ju/'hoansi were living in virtual squalor, and the levels of violence and mortality were among the highest in the world (Marshall and Ritchie 1984). As a number of Ju/'hoansi noted in meetings and interviews, there was a relatively high level of dependency on government welfare and assistance programs. Many people said that they would prefer to be socially and economically self-sufficient. They reasoned that if they were able to have clearly defined rights to areas where they could live, forage, raise livestock and crops, and engage in social activities, they would be better off than staying in large settlements.

In the early 1980s, some of the Ju/'hoansi, assisted by anthropologists John Marshall and Claire Ritchie, began to move back to their original territories in Nyae Nyae in an effort to avoid the complexities of life in Tsumkwe. This decentralization or out-migration trend, which also can be characterized as a kind of back-to-the-land movement, is reminiscent of what happened among Aboriginal Australians in the Northern Territory of Australia in the 1970s (Berndt 1978, 1982; Young 1995). To make this possible, the Ju/'hoansi had to have access to water for domestic use and for their animals. There were boreholes at some of the places where the Ju/'hoansi had lived prior to their move to Tsumkwe, but they needed to be equipped with pumps. The Ju/'hoansi faced resistance from government officials, some of them from the MWCT over issues relating to hunting and the use of water at boreholes that had been drilled for wildlife. In a number of cases, there were confrontations between Ju/'hoansi and MWCT personnel, several of which were recorded by John Marshall (2003a) and his film crews.

The government of South West Africa had planned to turn Nyae Nyae into a game reserve where the Ju/'hoansi would be allowed to stay only if they remained "traditional," in other words, dressed as foragers in skins for tourists to observe. John Marshall (1984: 14) described this approach as one that condemned the Ju/'hoansi to "a plastic Stone Age." The Ju/'hoansi and their supporters, including the Ju/wa Bushman Development Foundation (JBDF), protested the government's plans and sought to have the Ju/'hoansi take over water points that were designated for wildlife, much to the chagrin of representatives of the MWCT. In spite of the difficulties they faced, several Ju/'hoan communities established themselves around boreholes, some of which were equipped using funds drawn from a grant provided by the Marshall family.

What became the Nyae Nyae Integrated Rural Development Program (IRDP) in northeastern Namibia began with the help of anthropologists in 1981. Initiated originally as a "cattle fund," the program was aimed at providing Ju/'hoansi with livestock, tools, and seeds so that they could re-establish themselves on their traditional lands as farmers. The rural development effort was also aimed at facilitating the process whereby Ju/'hoansi could gain a greater say in what happened to them and to the area in which they lived.

By the late 1980s, the larger political handwriting was on the wall: South Africa was not going to be able to retain its control of South West Africa. The United Nations came to South West Africa in 1989, and preparations were made for democratic elections and independence in the country that was to become Namibia. The Ju/'hoansi avidly discussed the implications of the upcoming elections and the meaning of democracy. Some of them worked for representatives of various political parties who were seeking office. On 21 March 1990, Namibia gained its independence. Several Ju/'hoansi attended the celebrations in Windhoek, the capital city, while those remaining in Nyae Nyae also paid homage to the new democratic nation-state of Namibia.

An important concern of the Ju/'hoansi in the run-up to independence and the years following was how to ensure that their voices could be heard at all levels in the new country. One way to do this, they felt, was to have representatives attend national-level meetings on issues of concern to the Ju/'hoansi, such as those relating to customary law, land administration, and development. A second way that the Ju/'hoansi could make their voices heard, they believed, was to have respected individuals in their communities recognized as traditional authorities, elected to Parliament, or selected to serve in national- or regional-level administrative institutions. A third strategy that some Ju/'hoansi wanted to pursue in order to enhance their chances of participation in public policy discussions and decision-making was to form alliances with political parties such as the DTA and SWAPO. There were also Ju/'hoansi who felt that links should be established with faith-based institutions involved in the liberation struggle, such as the Council of Churches in Namibia (CCN) and the Evangelical Lutheran Church in Namibia (ELCIN).

Some San joined what came to be known as the Bushman Alliance, part of the DTA, one of the many political parties formed during the period of the liberation struggle prior to Namibian independence. Members of a number of San groups supported the efforts of the South West African Territorial Force and the SADF in their military campaigns against SWAPO, in some cases serving in the South African military (Gordon and Douglas 2000; Kolata 1981; Lee and Hurlich 1982; Marshall and Ritchie 1984; Robbins 2006, 2007; Uys 1993). There were also San, including some Ju/'hoansi, who supported the objectives of SWAPO. Many San privately believed that the institutionalized racism of the apartheid system practiced in South West Africa was a violation of human rights, and they hoped that the liberation movements would be successful in their efforts to bring democracy to Namibia.

Much of the effort of the Ju/'hoansi following independence focused on establishing and running a representative body. One option that they investigated was to form a cooperative, a type of institution that, prior to independence, was not available to Africans—only to whites. As described in this book, there were discussions among the Ju/'hoansi in the 1980s about the formation of a farmers union and other kinds of institutions. There were also deliberations about how to form an overarching body—a kind of supra-communal organization—with representatives drawn from the various communities spread across a large area with few roads and no public transport.

The setting up and running of such a large-scale democratic organization was something that the Ju/'hoansi wanted very much to do. Many of them had no illusions about how complex this task would be. The democratic election of representatives to take part in a regional body caused many people to feel uncomfortable. In the past, the Ju/'hoansi had practiced what could be described as direct democracy, in which everyone—theoretically, at least—had a say. The notion of having someone else speak for an individual or a group was not something that came easily for them, given their fierce egalitarianism (Lee 1979a: 24, 244) and their strong sensitivity to the social problems that result from what Polly Wiessner (2005: 122) has called "big-shot behavior." In spite of their reservations, Nyae Nyae Ju/'hoansi from as many as two dozen or more communities participated in the meetings. These large gatherings were often noisy affairs in the early days of political organizing, with a wide range of individuals putting forth their views. Some of the patterns that existed then have continued to the present day.

Land Tenure

In June to July 1991, the Government of the Republic of Namibia held a conference in Windhoek on "land reform and the land question" (Republic of Namibia 1991), and Ju/'hoan representatives were in attendance. At this meeting, the Ju/'hoansi said that they should be recognized by the new Namibian government as the legitimate "owners" of the Nyae Nyae region. Not long after the conference, the Ju/'hoansi faced a major test of their land rights when Herero pastoralists from the south moved with their cattle herds into the Nyae Nyae region. Both the minister of lands, resettlement, and rehabilitation and the president of Namibia, Sam Nujoma, declared that the Ju/'hoansi had rights to their land. The Ju/'hoansi and the non-governmental organization (NGO) working with them—the NNDFN—peacefully escorted the Herero out of Nyae Nyae. Since that time, however, questions have been raised about whether or not the Ju/'hoansi have the security of land tenure in their area. The Ju/'hoansi have thus faced the possibility of dispossession, and in April–May 2009 they confronted once again an unlawful Herero invasion (Hays 2009). Since independence, the question of land tenure has never been far from their minds, and they have actively engaged in numerous activities aimed at solidifying their hold over the land and its resources, sometimes going against the advice of advisers and NGOs working with them.

As we note in this volume, the Nyae Nyae region is one of the few communal areas in Namibia where the San were able to retain a portion of their land and resources. Approximately half of all San in the country live in communal areas, meaning that they do not have *de jure* (legal) land tenure rights (Suzman 2001b: xviii, 6, 26; Odendaal 2006a, 2006b). The government of Namibia maintains that although the communal areas are occupied by local people, the land belongs to the state. The significance of this position is that, in the government's view, local communities hold a "use right" but have no private or collective "ownership rights" over the land. It also means that the San can legally be moved against their will without compensation in kind—that is, without being provided alternative land of equal or greater value than the land that they have lost. It also means that, potentially, they have less of a say about the ways in which the land and its resources are managed.

Harring and Odendaal (2006a: 52) have argued that Nyae Nyae provides one of the best opportunities for Namibian San to make a legal land claim based on aboriginal title. Their reasoning builds on the fact that the San still reside on some of the land that they have occupied for generations and have undertaken various kinds of development activities, such as well-digging and borehole establishment, giving them at least customary rights over the surrounding land. Rights to land and natural resources and fair treatment before the law have been rallying cries of the Ju/'hoansi and other Namibian San for decades (Biesele 1992a, 1992b, 1992c, 1994; Hitchcock and Vinding 2004; Le Roux and White 2004; Suzman 2002; Sylvain 2002, 2005). It is interesting to note that the Ju/'hoansi have opted thus far not to pursue legal strategies through the courts to obtain rights to their land, in contrast to some of the other San groups, such as the Khwe, =Khomani, G/ui, and G//ana, in Namibia, South Africa, and Botswana.[6] Other indigenous non-governmental organizations, such as the First People of the Kalahari (FPK) in Botswana, have vigorously pursued legal strategies in order to gain or regain access to land and resources.

---

6. For a discussion of land claims efforts by southern African San, see Barume (2010); Chennells (2002); Chennells and du Toit (2004); Hitchcock (2006); Hitchcock and Babchuk (2007); Saugestad (2005); and Taylor (2007a, 2007b, 2007c).

According to Marshall and Ritchie (1984: 6), the year 1970 marked the next turning point, following the establishment of Tsumkwe, in the history of the Ju/'hoansi. This was the year that the Odendaal Commission recommendations concerning the establishment of a homeland for Bushman peoples in Namibia were put into effect. The Odendaal Commission had recommended that West Caprivi and Bushmanland could be designated as Bushman homelands (RSA 1964: 29–40, 81, 99–101). West Caprivi was subsequently turned into a game reserve, despite the fact that sizable numbers of Khwe resided there.

Government decisions in 1970 saw 40,000 square kilometers of the Ju/'hoansi's ancestral territory ceded to other groups (the Herero to the south, the Kavango to the north). A portion of the Ju/'hoan area in the north was designated as the Kaudum Game Reserve. Eventually, the Ju/'hoansi were left with approximately 6,300 square kilometers of their ancestral land, an area less than 10 percent of what it had been originally. They also lost most of the pans that were the foci of their *n!oresi* (plural of *n!ore*)—their traditional territories.

Bushmanland was formally designated as a homeland in 1976 under Proclamation 208. This same proclamation called for the establishment of a Bushman Advisory Council, whose members would be made up of individuals elected by people then called "Bushmen" (Ritchie 1987: 67). Council members were intended to serve as liaisons between Bushmen and the administration, although this did not happen to the degree that many Bushmen had hoped. In exchange for their services, council members were supposed to receive salaries from the government; however, as time went on, the council received criticism for not consulting with local people and for making top-down decisions.

Threats to the Land Base: The Game Reserve

In addition to the concentration of people at Tsumkwe, the mid- to late 1970s saw another shift relating to land in the Nyae Nyae region. In 1976, Eastern Bushmanland was declared a nature conservation area under the Native Areas South West Africa Proclamation R188 (Ritchie 1987: 65–66). The fact that the Ju/'hoansi had largely vacated their traditional areas and settled in Tsumkwe made the Nyae Nyae region even more attractive as a potential game reserve. Another reason that it was viewed as a significant conservation area is that the region becomes a vast wetland in the summer rainy season and attracts numerous species of birds, including flamingos, pelicans, herons, and rare wattled cranes (Jones 1988a: 87). It also contains a variety of habitats, including 14 permanent and 9 semi-permanent pans, open plains, undulating fixed dune areas, thick stands of timber and shrubs, and mongongo groves (Hines 1992; Jones 1996; J. Marshall 1957; L. Marshall 1976: 62–76).

As Ritchie (1987: 66) notes, by the end of the 1970s, a formal plan had been worked out to declare the entire area from Tsumkwe east to the Botswana border—virtually all that was left of the Ju/'hoan territory—as a game reserve. Only a small portion of the area's existing population would be permitted to stay and work for the reserve. However, due in large part to a successful campaign mounted by the Ju/'hoansi against the plan, it was eventually abandoned.

One of the problems facing the Ju/'hoansi in Bushmanland was that the region was seen as having great potential by a number of different groups. The DNC had its plans, but so too did the military and the Department of Agriculture. Mineral resources were being sought by Consolidated Diamond Mines, and the Forestry Department wanted control over the timber in Western Bushmanland. In addition, there was the ever present threat of pastoral populations, who saw the region as having both water and grazing. The land issue became (and still is) the central concern of the Ju/'hoansi. They realized that if they wished to keep their land, they needed to take steps to re-establish their occupancy rights in their traditional areas. At the same time, they were aware that if they were to be successful economically, they had to diversify their subsistence economy, establishing, in effect, a mixed system of foraging, farming, and livestock production.

Three Ju/'hoan communities were successfully established in 1982, 7 more were re-formed by 1987, and over 30 fully re-formed *n!ore* groups existed by 1992 (Hitchcock 1992). Eventually, this number grew to 36, where it stands today. It should be noted, however, that there have been fluctuations over time in the numbers and distributions of local communities, depending in part upon the condition of the water points and on social factors.

According to informants who moved out of Tsumkwe and into the initial farming communities, some of the socio-economic benefits that they experienced included a reduction in social tensions, a positive change in the degree to which generalized sharing and exchange was practiced, and a greater tendency for people to feel a sense of community. There were more people involved in productive labor in the farming settlements, as well (Marshall and Ritchie 1984: 129). Women were working more than they had in Tsumkwe, and this contributed to their regaining a higher social status (Claire Ritchie, pers. comm.). Overall, the Ju/'hoansi in the new settlements were encouraged by what they had been able to achieve.

The success of the initial farming settlements served to instill a desire in other Ju/'hoansi in Tsumkwe to return to their traditional lands as well. The difficulty was that most of the people lacked the resources necessary to underwrite the costs of moving back to their *n!oresi*. There were also pressures exerted by the SWAA, which actively discouraged people from returning to their former territories. As some people in Eastern Bushmanland noted in discussions, the desire to leave Tsumkwe was there, but the means to do so were hard to come by.

The Cattle Fund: Establishing Land and Water Rights

In early 1981, a scheme was worked out by John Marshall and Claire Ritchie for a Cattle Fund, which would help Ju/'hoansi start their own herds and sustain themselves economically. The Cattle Fund purchased livestock and made the animals available to communities that agreed to undertake the work necessary to establish viable farming communities. The conditions for receipt of livestock were that people would build kraals and that they would manage their animals with care. The Cattle Fund arranged for the purchase of livestock from several sources. It also advised people on how to perform the tasks necessary for maintaining their herds.

In 1982, an administrative board was set up to oversee the Cattle Fund. The new board included representatives from the government, the private sector, and local Ju/'hoan communities. After the first board meeting was held in Windhoek, a Constitution was written up, and rules were outlined for the management and operation of the fund. The various documents and plans were discussed at length with the Ju/'hoansi in Tsumkwe and in the farming communities.

The Ju/'hoansi and the administrators of the Cattle Fund saw the utility of establishing dispersed settlements based on a mixed economic system. It was believed that development could be carried out more easily in small, widely distributed communities where pressures for sharing were lower and the number of accessible resources was higher. The problem was that the Ju/'hoansi did not have secure access to water points away from Tsumkwe. Marshall and Ritchie began to see their main assistance challenge as the provision of water so that viable *n!ore* groups could go back to the land.

During the 1980s, the South West African government expanded the facilities at Tsumkwe, constructing additional housing, offices, and a farm to be used for livestock demonstration. Some Ju/'hoansi were able to learn livestock breeding and management techniques from government agricultural officers at the livestock farm, and on occasion they were able to buy a calf or two.

However, the most vexing problem for the Ju/'hoansi remained that of land rights. The fear that the land would be taken away continued to be a subject of discussion at meetings held in Nyae Nyae. The people who had left G≠aing≠oq were prevented from returning to their area by the DNC, which claimed the place because it had installed the water pump there. The DNC continued its policy of drilling boreholes in Eastern Bushmanland, particularly in the northern part of the region. Efforts were made by what had by then become the JBDF to compile data on land claims, using a hired lawyer, Pierre Roux. The JBDF arranged for a drilling contractor to establish two additional water points, but the commissioner of Bushman Affairs, Johan Swanepoel, did not allow the rig to be brought into the area.

The Ju/wa Farmers Union

The establishment of the Ju/wa Farmers Union (JFU) in 1986 was another turning point in the history of the Ju/'hoansi of Eastern Bushmanland. The JFU was a people's organization that emphasized consultation, information dissemination, and decision-making about development strategies. The JFU was called a farmers union to emphasize the fact that its aim was to develop a mixed-subsistence economy. The organization's major goal was to establish self-sufficient communities that were capable of determining their own political, social, and economic future. The JFU also wished to develop institutional capacity for handling public policy issues. According to members of the original union, a crucial objective was to have a voice in national-level forums about matters in northeastern Namibia, such as land and local government.

The JFU was also a forum in and of itself for addressing policy issues that included gaining secure access to land, coping with outsiders wanting to move into the area, and working out ways to distribute livestock and other goods. The organization played a significant role in consciousness-raising. In many ways, its most important work was communicating new understanding and skills that were needed to re-establish the Ju/'hoansi communities at a time of great political change in southern Africa.

The JFU was founded and developed in tandem with a support organization, the JBDF, an outgrowth of Marshall and Ritchie's Cattle Fund. The JBDF assisted the JFU in fund-raising, technical assistance, and suggesting options for consideration by the JFU's members. Together, the JFU and the JBDF addressed matters such as the potential effects of the declaration of Eastern Bushmanland as a game reserve and the impact of predators on Ju/'hoan livestock herds. As one JFU member noted, "The foundation helped us by giving us the means to address our problems." Another noted that the JFU became "the voice of the people," while the JBDF worked to make sure that the people's voice was heard by the government.

According to the Constitution of the JFU, an objective of the organization was "to improve and establish farming communities in Eastern Bushmanland and neighboring unoccupied areas which were traditionally 'the land of the Ju/ wa people'" (JFU 1986: 1). It did this in part by encouraging people in Tsumkwe to move back to their *n!oresi*, and also by identifying areas in Nyae Nyae unclaimed by Nyae Nyae groups and allowing San from outside the area, such as those from the Gobabis farms to the south, to settle in them. People noted the fact that the DNC claimed rights to parts of Bushmanland, particularly in the north, and had constructed a camp at Klein Dobe without consulting the Ju/'hoansi. Meanwhile, Herero pastoralists were attempting to make inroads in the south. As one man, Debe Dam, put it, "We must help people settle in those places because we will lose them."

By mid-1986, 10 Ju/'hoan farming settlements had been established in Eastern Bushmanland (Marshall and Hartung 1986: 1). One problem that they faced was the threat of predators. For example, the people of one community, G=aing=oq, were forced to leave their *n!ore* as a result of frequent difficulties with lions: at one point, a Ju/'hoan speared and killed a lion that was hanging on to the belly of his bull. The predation rate in 1986 was high (John Marshall, pers. comm., 1987).

There were indications in 1986 of tacit government support of the efforts of the JFU. The fact that Andreas Shipanga, minister of conservation and natural resources, and other members of the interim government expressed a desire to meet with JFU representatives, combined with the assistance given to Ju/'hoan farming efforts by the Ministry of Agriculture, Water, and Forestry (MAWF), showed that the administration was changing its position on development in Eastern Bushmanland. There were still problems, however, as was seen in the decision by the government to establish a 25-kilometers-wide development-free strip along the Botswana border. The JFU immediately began to make its concerns heard.

In 1989, during the lead-up to Namibian independence, the JFU council played an important role by disseminating information and lobbying. Members of the council traveled around Eastern Bushmanland and talked with people in the communities about the implications of the United Nations Security Council Resolution 435 of 1978, which outlined a cease-fire and UN-supervised elections, and the impact of decolonization and independence. They addressed questions concerning the various political parties that would be involved in the election process (e.g., SWAPO and the DTA) and discussed what it would mean to Ju/'hoansi to be part of a multi-racial state after Namibian independence. As a result of these efforts, the Ju/'hoansi were able to take part in the elections as well-informed voters.

The UN resolution went into effect on 1 April 1989 with the declaration of a cease-fire, and in April the United Nations Transition Assistance Group (UNTAG), which was to supervise the process leading up to free elections, entered Namibia. UNTAG established offices in Tsumeb and Grootfontein, while a small satellite office was opened in Tsumkwe. Starting in June 1989, UN representatives held a series of meetings with Ju/'hoan communities. These meetings were significant in part because it was the first time that a major international body had shown direct interest in the welfare of the Ju/'hoansi. They also gave local people the opportunity to interact with officials other than those of the government and NGOs, thus enhancing their sense of self-worth.

In mid-1989, the JFU and the JBDF engaged a drilling company to drill boreholes in a number of *n!oresi* in Eastern Bushmanland. The council representatives played a very important role in this process, helping identify *n!oresi* so that the company knew the areas in which to search for water. They also went out to the potential sites with the drilling contractors and introduced them to the local people.

The latter part of 1989 was taken up with deliberations on matters such as cattle distribution to people who would be occupying the new farming communities. Substantial efforts were put into information dissemination concerning the national elections, which were to be held in November. The JFU had played a major role in establishing contacts with the various communities and by providing people with ideas about what it would mean to vote and to be citizens in a new Namibia. By the end of 1989, the Ju/'hoansi had had the opportunity to take part in a political process and to make decisions, both as individuals and as members of a representative body that was broad-based in its orientation and involved in local-level politics. There was still a great deal of uncertainty, however, about the ways in which democratic processes would work in Nyae Nyae.

The Nyae Nyae Farmers Cooperative

The 1990s brought even more substantial changes to the Ju/'hoansi. After Namibia achieved independence, the JFU was formally renamed the Nyae Nyae Farmers Cooperative (NNFC). The new president of Namibia, Sam Nujoma, paid a visit to Eastern Bushmanland, accompanied by the prime minister and other government officials. Discussions were held between the NNFC and administration officials in Tsumkwe. There were also meetings with representatives of donor agencies and with people from the Kuru Development Trust, an organization devoted to assisting Bushmen in western Botswana.[7]

By the time of independence, there were 23 farming communities in place, most of which had gardens and herds of livestock. One of the first orders of business was to work out the mechanisms by which cattle were to be distributed. A new policy of selling livestock at subsidized prices was established, replacing the previous policy of giving cattle to people. Work continued on gardening, crafts, and other projects.

After independence, a major change occurred in the relations between the Ju/'hoansi and some of the government ministries, most notably those involved in the issue of land use. What had been a problematic set of relationships evolved into a more cooperative interaction. In January 1991, the NNFC and the NNDFN worked with representatives of the Ministry of Wildlife Conservation and Tourism (MWCT, formerly the DNC) and Integrated Rural Development and Nature Conservation (IRDNC), a Namibia-based NGO, on an environmental survey and land use planning exercise in Eastern Bushmanland.

---

7. For a description of the Kuru Development Trust, now the Kuru Family of Organizations, see Bollig et al. (2000).

Several suggestions arose out of this exercise, including the recommendation that a joint committee, composed of ministry officials in Bushmanland and local representatives, be set up (Biesele and Jones 1991). It was also recommended that local people be allowed to take part in decision-making concerning natural resource use and management, and that a system be put in place in which local people would get income from trophy hunting and tourism.

The year 1991 was crucial for the NNFC and the Ju/'hoansi. The Conference on Land Reform and the Land Question was held in Windhoek from 25 June to 1 July, and the NNFC played an important role. Representatives from the NNFC who were in attendance at the meeting made a presentation on the *n!ore* system and the work done by their cooperative. Subsequently, government officials, including President Nujoma and the minister of land, resettlement, and rehabilitation, recognized the legitimacy of the NNFC as the traditional authority for Eastern Bushmanland. This recognition was to prove useful later when there were incursions of outsiders with cattle.

During 1991, several groups of pastoralists, especially Herero, came into the Nyae Nyae area and requested permission from individuals at some of the communities to move their cattle there to share water and grazing. This occurred at Djxokhoe, for example, where an elderly man responded favorably to a Herero request. The Herero brought in a herd, and, according to local people, "There were so many that soon there was no grass, and our cattle had only sand to eat." Representatives from the NNFC came to Djxokhoe to talk to people about the potential problems posed by the presence of the Herero cattle. At first, the people of Djxokhoe did not agree with the cooperative's decision that the Herero should leave, in part because they were getting some of the milk from the herd. After lengthy discussions, however, it was decided that it was for the best if the Herero departed. Eventually, the Herero and their cattle were escorted out of the area by the NNFC.

In the latter part of 1991, several Herero began building what they described as a quarantine camp for their cattle in the eastern part of the Nyae Nyae region close to the Botswana border. There were fears that this was the vanguard of a general move of what was rumored to be 26,000 cattle and 3,000 Herero from Botswana into Namibia, a fear that proved somewhat true. By 1997, there were over 500 cattle belonging to Herero in eastern Otjozondjupa. Efforts were made by the NNFC to convince the Herero to stop the construction, but to no avail. The NNFC appealed to the Namibian administration, pointing out that President Nujoma had told them during his visit to the area on 18 August 1991 that the government recognized the right of the Ju/'hoansi over their land. Protracted discussions were held between the NNFC and the Herero and between the NNFC and the Namibian administration.

In August 1991, the NNFC, in conjunction with government representatives, convened meetings with the Herero involved in the quarantine camp construction. The discussions eventually led to the decision by the Herero to leave the camp and move out of the area. Importantly, in this case the NNFC was backed up by the Namibian government. The NNFC was thus able to represent the interests of its constituency in negotiations with both the government and other groups. Its members also learned some valuable lessons from this experience, particularly in terms of ways to defuse potentially difficult land conflict situations.

The NNFC leadership also played a significant role at the Regional Conference on Development Programs for Africa's San Populations held in Windhoek in mid-June 1992. The NNFC representatives argued forcefully for the legal recognition of San land rights in southern Africa. They also pointed out the importance of local people gaining benefits from the natural resources in their areas. Protection of their land was imperative, they said, and it was vital to have a representative body speaking for them on resource management issues. In addition, they addressed topics such as education, training, and curriculum development, saying that it was crucial that the lessons taught in school be relevant to local needs and that they be presented as much as possible in local San languages. The experiences and ideas of the NNFC helped to shape many recommendations that issued from the San conference (Republic of Namibia 1992: 14–19).

Following the recommendations of the team that worked on the land use planning survey and subsequent discussions in NNFC and government meetings, an Environmental Planning Committee (EPC) was established in Bushmanland in March 1992. The NNFC was one of several organizations that were represented on the EPC. Several EPC meetings were held between March and July, including a large-scale gathering of officials and local people that took place at Klein Dobe.[8] This meeting helped crystallize a number of the conservation and development issues that faced Bushmanland, including wildlife management as a land use practice, tourism, and the need for an integrated land and resource development policy.

The NNFC participated in exchange visits with other groups in communal areas of Namibia, including Kaokoland (Cunene region), where the Himba, Herero, and Damara were engaged in community-based resource management activities. The Ju/'hoansi also met with Saami and Australian Aboriginal representatives to discuss issues relating to indigenous peoples. Representatives of the NNFC attended national and international conferences on indigenous peoples, as was the case in June 1992 in Windhoek, in October 1993 in Gaborone, Botswana, and in April 1996 and July 1997 in Cape Town, South Africa (Bank 1998; Biesele and Hitchcock 2000; Saugestad 2001). There was another regional

---

8. Details can be found in the EPC's minutes of these 1992 meetings.

San meeting held in Gaborone in September 2003. Some NNFC representatives also attended sessions of the Working Group on Indigenous Populations in Geneva and, in 2010, the United Nations Permanent Forum on Indigenous Issues. At these gatherings, members of the NNFC shared their experiences and sought to learn how others have dealt with political, economic, and social problems. When they returned to Nyae Nyae, they discussed with local communities what they had learned at the international meetings.

The Era of Community-Based Natural Resource Management

From 1992–2002, the Living in a Finite Environment (LIFE) Project, a joint effort of the United States Agency for International Development (USAID) and the Government of the Republic of Namibia, provided technical assistance and funding to the Ju/'hoan San communities to assist them in their efforts to become self-sufficient through community-based natural resource management. Emphasis was placed on social and economic development, as well as human resource development involving formal and non-formal education and training. The workers associated with the LIFE Project used a variety of participatory development strategies that stressed communication and self-determination at all levels, although this goal was not always realized in practice, according to some of the Ju/'hoansi interviewed at the time.

Benefits of the LIFE Project included increasing the number of wild animals in the region (Weaver and Skyer 2003; WWF 2000) and facilitating the process whereby the NNFC was able to establish a conservancy in the Nyae Nyae area (Berger et al. 2003). Under wildlife management policies of the Ministry of Environment and Tourism (MET 1995a) and the Nature Conservation Amendment Act of 1996 (Republic of Namibia 1996), this type of institution gave communities, in a kind of collective proprietorship system, the right to benefit from wildlife on communal land and from tourism concessions (Jones and Murphree 2001: 42–45).

The NNDFN and the LIFE Project both had important impacts in Nyae Nyae in terms of creating jobs and distributing income (Berger et al. 2003; Weaver and Skyer 2003; Wiessner 2004). Some employment opportunities were related to the NNFC, which had a number of openings in leadership positions and the everyday management of the organization. There were also jobs that arose out of work with private companies and safari operators. There has been some mineral surveying and exploration in the region by an Australian firm, Mount Burgess Mining, which at one point had 13 Ju/'hoan employees. The Ju/'hoansi are not sure if diamonds or minerals were found. A few Ju/'hoansi were hired by lodge owners and safari companies that operated in the Tsumkwe area, and, over the years, anthropologists, ecologists, and other researchers and development workers have also employed Ju/'hoansi to assist them in their work. From the perspective of the Ju/'hoansi, the number of people employed by various agencies and organizations, including the government of Namibia and the Nyae Nyae Conservancy (NNC), could and should be increased substantially.

Nyae Nyae after the LIFE Project

In the years following the closure of the LIFE Project, many unsettled issues still pervade Nyae Nyae communities. For example, transportation continues to be a problem: some people go by donkey or horse, but most go on foot. On occasion, people need to leave Nyae Nyae *n!oresi* to go to Tsumkwe to get food, pick up their pension checks, or go to the clinic. There are four churches in Tsumkwe, and some Ju/'hoansi attend them. Serious medical problems are treated at the hospital at Mangetti Dune in Tsumkwe District West or at the larger regional hospital in Grootfontein.

A major concern of Ju/'hoansi and other San in Namibia relates to the crucial need to strike a balance between conservation and development. Sustainable development can be defined as development that "meets the needs of the present without compromising the ability of future generations to meet their own needs" (WCED 1987: 43). It consists of a set of strategies whereby the social and material well-being of people is raised without sacrificing the environment or the viability of socio-economic and cultural systems. Along with individuals and NGOs around the world, many Ju/'hoansi see sustainable development as a fundamental right of all people. Many also believe that access to water and natural resources, including wildlife and wild plants, is a fundamental human right.

Another development strategy that the Ju/'hoansi have explored in collaboration with international, national, and local NGOs is eco-tourism, defined by the World Conservation Union (i.e., the International Union for the Conservation of Nature and Natural Resources, IUCN) as "environmentally responsible travel and visitation to relatively undisturbed natural areas, in order to enjoy and appreciate nature (and any accompanying cultural features—both past and present) that promotes conservation, has low visitor impact, and provides for beneficially active socio-economic involvement of local populations."[9] The problem for the Ju/'hoansi is that, in spite of the rhetoric about public participation and the benefits of tourism that are supposed to accrue to local populations, eco-tourism programs, more often than not, serve to dispossess poor local people and have only limited social and economic benefits—as well as many risks.

9. See http://cmsdata.iucn.org/downloads/parks_feb00.pdf.

Development Dilemmas and Debates

The contexts in which changes have taken place among the Ju/'hoansi in the Nyae Nyae region have led to debates about the best ways to promote development, democracy, and broad public participation. Is having a community-based organization the most effective way to reach decisions that affect a wide array of people, some 2,000 of them in as many as 36 small villages scattered across the broad, semi-arid Kalahari landscape? Should the members of the community-based organization be satisfied with the economic returns of a safari operator bringing clients to their area to engage in hunting and photo-tourism, or should greater efforts be made to seek alternative sources of income and employment? Are community-based resource management and local-level tourism the most appropriate sources of economic support for the Ju/'hoansi, or should more investments be made in livestock production and agriculture?

The Ju/'hoansi learned some lessons from their kin and friends in Botswana, who, in 1995, had to face an outbreak of a livestock disease, contagious bovine pleuropneumonia (CBPP). The Botswana government opted to destroy all of the cattle in the area, estimated at 320,000. Local people were put in a position of depending on government food and cash supports, and some opted to fall back on foraging (Hitchcock 2002a). Agricultural initiatives have had some impact in the area, but even today crop production provides only a relatively small part of the diet. Would it not be better, as some Ju/'hoansi and NGO advisers contend, to have a diversified subsistence and income-generation system that allows for flexibility and ensures that there is at least some food and cash for people to depend upon?

The Ju/'hoansi of Nyae Nyae, like many indigenous peoples around the world, are caught up in a complex globalized system where decisions are all too often made outside of local communities. At the global level, the passage in 1973 of the Convention on International Trade in Endangered Species of Wild Fauna and Flora has meant greater protection for large terrestrial mammal species such as elephants. Yet the Nyae Nyae Ju/'hoansi today are faced with a sizable number of elephants, a thousand or more, preying on their water points and gardens (Berger et al. 2003: 38–42; J. Marshall 2003a, 2003b; Thomas 2006: 203–205, 297–299; Wiessner 2004: 153). Their only recourse is to attempt to keep the elephants away with fences, rocks, and reinforced cement barriers. The Ju/'hoansi view elephants as magnificent animals—but also very dangerous ones. They sometimes comment wryly about the fact that, at the international level, elephants are on Appendix 1 of the Convention on International Trade in Endangered Species of Wild Fauna and Flora (CITES) and are considered threatened or endangered in a number of other African countries, while they themselves are having to deal with sizable numbers of elephants causing substantial destruction in their area.

A major debate erupted over the kinds of development and conservation strategies that the Ju/'hoansi of Nyae Nyae should follow, perhaps best illustrated in John Marshall's (2003a) classic documentary, *A Kalahari Family*. As described later in this volume, this film, which has generated considerable public and academic interest, has helped raise concerns about the ways in which development issues are being addressed in the Nyae Nyae region. Marshall's filmography provides a powerful record of events that took place in the Nyae Nyae region over the past five decades.[10]

In some ways, the development work in Nyae Nyae has been innovative and a model example of how development programs should be structured. At the same time, there have been serious difficulties, not least in the area of establishing a viable local economy and ensuring that the voices of people with diverse and varying interests are heard. Some of the successes can be attributed to the role that anthropologists have played in the research and development work in Nyae Nyae. However, it should be stressed that some of the problems that have occurred are also due to decisions made by anthropologists (Garland 1994, 1999; Garland and Gordon 1999; J. Marshall 2003a; Tracy 2005; Wilmsen 1999, 2004). In spite of the controversies and disagreements over development strategies, the establishment of the NNFC can be seen as a remarkable example of how social scientists, governments, civil society, and local people themselves can help promote development and human rights at the local and national levels in an African country. At the same time, it provides lessons on some of the limitations of the approaches that have been employed, particularly in the area of establishing a viable local economy.

A major focus of this book is on recent development issues in Nyae Nyae and the application of anthropological research to them. Environmental and cultural rights have become very important realities for both indigenous peoples and the anthropologists who work with them. The emphasis on what the Ju/'hoan people of Nyae Nyae are doing to protect their own resources and rights helps to demythologize previous images of them as either noble savages or helpless victims. In sum, this volume demonstrates the responsiveness of current anthropological advocacy to the aspirations of a well-known indigenous society of former foragers, partly by allowing the voices of that society to be heard.

Ju/'hoan Voices

Independence in Namibia awoke the Ju/'hoansi to the necessity of explaining themselves to a world that they were quickly coming to see as very different from

10. For additional discussions of Marshall's films, see Biesele and Hitchcock (1999); Biesele, Hitchcock et al. (1996); Ritchie (1993); Schrire (2004); Sylvain (2004); Tomaselli and Homiak (1999); Wilmsen (1999, 2004).

their own. Tsamkxao =Oma, the visionary first chairperson of the NNFC, which later became the NNC, put it this way:

> Our old people long ago worked hard talking together to decide how to share resources. Today we are still working hard to come up with good ideas for how to use our resources under the new government. We consider part of our work to be finding new ideas to help the new government keep the peace among the people. The new government is listening to us as we do our work of thinking. We don't need a new government to tell us how to get along with each other. We already know this.

In 1991, as part of the Ju/'hoan delegation to the Namibian National Conference on Land Reform and the Land Question, Tsamkxao explained that the Ju/'hoansi placed relationships among themselves at the heart of their economic lives:

> When my mother and father bore me and I was on this land, I looked at the land and they told me, "This is your father's father's father's *n!ore.*" My mother said, "This is my father's father's father's *n!ore*, and I hold rights in it, and so through me do you."

> So it is with my people. All of us are related, and we greet each other in specific ways, and we understand each other. We live together.

> We sit together and are related and greet each other as kin and understand each other. We agree together about who is going to live together in this *n!ore*, and who is going to live together in THIS *n!ore* over here.

> A *n!ore* has its responsible person, who holds the rights in it for everyone else who has rights there. Up to now, we had been holding our *n!oresi* in this way, not sharing with a government our say over the land.

> We are not a people who buy land. We ourselves do not buy land. Instead, we are BORN on land. My father taught me about his father, who taught him about the foods of our land. Your father's father teaches you. People have taught each other and taught each other and taught each other. People have died but the teaching has gone on.

Tsamkxao no longer chairs the NNC; instead, he is recognized by the Namibian government as a Traditional Authority with national responsibilities.

After a few necessary dips into past history as background, this book traces the complex history of Nyae Nyae from roughly 1986–1987, when Tsamkxao spearheaded the formation of the first precursor of the NNC prior to independence, to roughly 2010, with its current challenges to the Ju/'hoansi on both the local and national levels. From the beginning of this two-decade period to the present, both anthropological advocacy and the close participation of NGOs have been salient adjuncts to the Ju/'hoan people's efforts to re-establish themselves sustainably on their land after moving away from it in a futile search for an alternative livelihood. Anthropologists and development organizations have been key partners in many of the advances—and in some cases the mistakes—that the Nyae Nyae Ju/'hoansi have made.

This book strives to tell the interwoven story of these partnerships in the hope that stakeholders in similar situations in other parts of the world may find some of it useful to their efforts. Readers may find our telling of the story quite complex. For comprehension's sake we have tried to simplify where possible, but in the last analysis the truth of this particular history lies squarely within its complexities. We present the book as a first contribution to a dialogue with other information and perspectives—coming both from colleagues and the Nyae Nyae Ju/'hoan people.

Heritage and Critique

Despite its continuing problems, the Nyae Nyae community today is actively pursuing not only political advantage but also heritage preservation activities. Trainees are digitally recording older people's stories and folktales, along with chronicles about how some of them became healers, and accounts of the composition of medicine songs and how they were transmitted across the landscape by teaching and sharing. Via books, articles, and the Internet, literate and non-literate Ju/'hoansi alike are now able to publicize their own critiques of their situations—and of outsiders' views of them—to a global audience. Life stories about the Ju/'hoansi, both imaginary and historical; essays, both thoughtful and critical; and images, both moving and still—these must all be seen as part of the complex legacy that has resulted from the collaboration of concerned outsiders with the ongoing Nyae Nyae people's movement.

As we discuss in the pages that follow, numerous anthropologists, government officials, and development experts have worked closely with the Ju/'hoansi on local-level development, education, and land claims. These efforts have not been without controversy. Debates have ensued about the best ways in which to approach development in the Nyae Nyae area (see, e.g., Biesele, Hitchcock et al. 1996; J. Marshall 1996, 2003a, 2003b; Thomas 2006), and there have been those, including some Ju/'hoansi, who have argued that the people and habitats of the region should simply be left alone. The Ju/'hoansi themselves express a number of different opinions about what needs to be done so that they can live economically self-sufficient lives.

Chapter One

Namibia and the Nyae Nyae Region

Although the Government of the Republic of Namibia (GRN) has made significant strides toward realizing its national development objectives since independence was achieved on 21 March 1990, the country continues to face socio-economic conditions that are markedly inequitable. The wealthiest 5 percent of the population controls 75 percent of the gross domestic product (GDP), while over 50 percent of the population controls only 3 percent of the GDP. Poverty levels are high, with 34.9 percent of the population living below US$1 per day, and 68.5 percent living below US$2 per day (World Bank 2008: 335). About 70 percent of the country's population lives in rural areas and depends upon natural resources[1] and on agriculture, an important part of Namibia's economy.

During the 1990s and into the new millennium, residents of rural Namibia witnessed the dismaying spectacle of land-hungry people from other marginalized communal lands, as poor as the Namibians themselves, traveling around the country, looking for land. This was the situation that faced the Ju/'hoan San of northeastern Namibia, who were deeply concerned that people from other parts of Namibia might move into their own area. What was most disconcerting about this process was that the GRN was facilitating the movement of people into new territories, where they competed with local residents for land and resources.

From a socio-economic standpoint, the San, including the Ju/'hoansi, occupy the lowest levels of Namibian society (Suzman 2001a, 2001b, 2002). Most San in Namibia are impoverished and landless; as a result, they have to eke out an existence under difficult conditions. At the beginning of the new millennium,

1. See http://geneva.usmission.gov/2010/04/20/usaid-biodiversity/.

nearly half of the San in Namibia were farm workers, either on the cattle posts of livestock owners or on commercial ranches (Harring and Odendaal 2006a). Unemployment and underemployment among the San are common, and the majority live below the poverty datum line of US$1 per person per day. As a result, many San are dependent on other groups or the state for their survival.

Namibia's natural environment provides an important source of food, materials, and income for a sizable segment of the country's population. As noted in *Namibia's Green Plan* (MWCT 1992), the country's economy is almost totally reliant on natural resources, both renewable and non-renewable. These natural resources include fish, minerals (diamonds, uranium, copper), wildlife, and grasses for livestock grazing and roof thatching. The country has considerable mineral wealth, and mining makes up a significant proportion of the national economy.

Namibia's *National Development Plan 1* (Republic of Namibia 1995a, 1995b) argued that environmental constraints needed to be taken into account at all levels. It also stressed that shifting the pattern of development onto a more sustainable path was to be the major challenge during the ensuing years. Such a shift required substantial changes in both policy and practice. This was especially important in the communal areas of the country, where the majority of the population resides. If Namibia is to meet its environmental and development challenges, it will require substantial inputs from its own people and moderate, well-targeted, and innovative assistance from outside agencies, including donors.

At independence, the GRN set the following national development objectives: reviving and sustaining economic growth, creating employment opportunities, reducing inequalities in income distribution, and alleviating poverty. As noted in *National Development Plan 1* (NDP1), which covered the period 1995–2000, these goals committed the GRN to the pursuit of policies that were aimed at achieving growth with equity. Article 95 of the Namibian Constitution stresses the responsibility of the state to improve the welfare of its people and to protect the environment for future generations. The country's national development plan is thus aimed at promoting growth in the economy while working to eradicate societal inequalities.

The objectives outlined in the environment section of NDP1 were, first, to promote sustainable development within all sectors and across all regions in order to ensure that present and future generations of Namibians gain optimal benefit from the equitable and sustainable utilization of Namibia's renewable resources, and, second, to protect biotic diversity and maintain ecological life support systems (Republic of Namibia 1995a, 1995b). Additional goals in NDP1 included promoting the training of Namibians and institutional strengthening in the field of environmental management. They also called for integrating planning and management of land and other natural resources.

In *National Development Plan 2*, which covered the years 2001–2006, the GRN expanded on some of the aims of NDP1 and added some new objectives, including increasing both the amount of land in agricultural production and the number of people on the land and diversifying the livestock industry (Republic of Namibia 2001). As detailed in *National Development Plan 3*, covering the period 2006–2011, the GRN seeks to ensure that the economy is stable and that resource exploitation and use in the country are sustainable over the long term (Republic of Namibia 2006). It is interesting to note that Namibia was the first country in the world to incorporate environmental protection into its Constitution. It is also of interest to observe that although Namibia was one of the African countries that challenged a draft of the United Nations Declaration on the Rights of Indigenous Peoples in 2006, it eventually voted in favor of the declaration when it came before the United Nations General Assembly in September 2007 (Barume 2010; Garcia-Alix and Hitchcock 2009).

Namibia: A Brief History with Special Reference to Land

In 1884, Namibia became a German colony, and the German colonial occupancy lasted until 1915, when the country was taken over by South Africa, then under British control. When the Treaty of Versailles was signed in 1919, South Africa was granted a mandate over the territory under the League of Nations. The governor-general of the then Union of South Africa had the power to enact legislation and to oversee land allocation and other political and economic matters. The privatization of land that occurred in Namibia under Germany, and later under the South West Africa Administration (SWAA), saw the establishment of rigid land boundaries and fences (Republic of Namibia 1991; Werner 1989, 1991, 1993). People who had lived on the land that was now alienated (i.e., turned over to private use by white farmers and ranchers) were required either to become laborers on the farms of other groups or to move to the towns or the crowded communal areas (Harring 2004: 64–66). The communal sectors in Namibia, which in the past were called "native areas," today cover 218,300 square kilometers, or about 26.5 percent of the country's land (see table 3). A larger portion of the country's land was designated as commercial farms and ranches (in essence, freehold land); today it makes up roughly 469,100 square kilometers, or approximately 57 percent of the total land area. Some of the land in Namibia (21,600 square kilometers, or 2.5 percent) was taken by the state for the purposes of mineral exploration and exploitation, with a focus in part on diamonds, uranium, and other valuable sub-surface resources. Most of this state land is leased out to private companies, some of which are large transnational corporations.

Table 3 Land tenure situation in Namibia

Land Tenure Category	Size (sq km)	% of the Country
Commercial land (freehold)	469,100	57.0
Communal land	218,300	26.5
Conservation area (parks, game reserves, etc.)	114,500	13.9
Diamond area	21,600	2.5
Walvis Bay area	1,124	0.1
Total	824,624	100.0

Source: Data from Odendaal (2006a).

Forced removals of people from prime farming and ranching areas occurred throughout the period of South African occupation, from 1919 until the late 1980s (LAC 1991; Werner 1991, 1993). Local people also moved of their own volition, seeking more productive land or places where there was less competition with other groups. The result was that conflicting claims arose among the various ethnic groups and sub-groups in Namibia and among individual households. As Harring (2004: 65–66) notes, "The call for 'land reform' is meaningless without a clear understanding of 'who benefits' from the acquisition and redistribution of those lands." Given that over half of the land was in the hands of 4,500 white farmers, while well over a million Namibians were living in communal areas that were often overcrowded and not very productive agriculturally, the pressure for land reform was considerable at the local level.

Whereas the San peoples had previously lived throughout Namibia on their own lands, in the late nineteenth and early twentieth centuries they experienced dispossession, marginalization, and, in some cases, genocide (Gordon 2009; Gordon and Douglas 2000: 49 85). Substantial portions of the traditional lands of the San were either given to other groups or turned into state land. Efforts were made, however, to set aside land for them. The idea of a "Bushman reserve" was recommended by the Commission for the Preservation of the Bushmen, on which P. J. Schoeman, an Afrikaans writer, sat. This commission, which was appointed in 1949, submitted its report to SWAA in 1953 (Gordon and Douglas 2000: 160–165). The final report of what came to be known as the Schoeman Commission recommended a single reserve for the San, that of Bushmanland (Le Roux and White 2004: 110–116). Other government commissions made similar recommendations. The Game Preservation Commission, for example, recommended in its 1949 report that Game Reserve No. 1 near Etosha be either abandoned or turned into a Bushman reserve, although this recommendation was not implemented (Gordon and Douglas 2000: 161).

Following World War II, much of the discussion about the San in South West Africa focused on issues surrounding "vagrancy," livestock theft, and the desire on the part of white farmers for inexpensive labor (Gordon and Douglas 2000: 162–171). In the 1950s, the practice of "blackbirding" (abducting workers by means of deception and kidnapping) was relatively common, extending even into remote parts of Namibia such as Nyae Nyae (Gordon and Douglas 2000: 169–171; L. Marshall 1976: 60). Sizable numbers of San were part of the rural labor force, especially on settler farms and cattle posts.

In 1962, SWAA appointed the Commission of Enquiry into South West African Affairs, sometimes referred to as the Odendaal Commission. Under this commission, the "native reserves" in Namibia were consolidated into ethnic homelands organized along tribal lines, for example, Hereroland for the Hereros, Ovamboland for the Ovambo, Damaraland for the Damara (see map 4).

Map 4 Namibian homelands under the Odendaal Plan

Ultimately, however, they all were under the jurisdiction of SWAA. While the Odendaal Plan, which was formally presented in 1964, designated an area as "Bushmanland," little effort was expended to make this delineation a reality. The Odendaal Plan did result in an infusion of capital into South West Africa, but few of these funds were devoted to the development of Bushmanland, other than maintaining the administrative structure at Tsumkwe. Finally, in 1968, Bushmanland was created in the remote northeastern part of the country, located between Kavango (the land of the Kavango people) in the north and Hereroland (the land of the Herero and Mbanderu) in the south. Bushmanland was proclaimed as a "homeland" for "the Bushman nation" (Act 54 of 1968, Act 46 of 1969, Proclamation R208 of 1976, South West Africa).

Bushmanland was occupied primarily by a single San group, the Ju/'hoansi, who at the time numbered only several hundred. Bushmanland was never given self-governing status; rather, it was turned over to a regional administrator who worked for SWAA. Under apartheid, the Ju/'hoansi did not have their own tribal councils or traditional authorities, nor did they have leaders who were recognized by the state. Bushmanland essentially was a homeland for political purposes. It was not viewed by the San in Namibia as a homeland for all San, although there were SWAA officials who considered the idea of using Bushmanland as a resettlement location for people, including San, from other areas.

One of the problems that the Ju/'hoansi had to deal with in the 1960s was that they had moved from their traditional lands, their *n!oresi*, to a government-sponsored settlement at Tsumkwe. In the 1970s, SWAA, in conjunction with the South African Defence Force (SADF), established military bases at Tsumkwe and at nearby Mangetti Dune. !Xun and Khwe soldiers from Angola and northern Namibia and their families were resettled in Bushmanland, primarily in the western portion of the area, a region which at the time was largely waterless. The SADF had boreholes drilled and laid out agricultural plots from 4 to 7 hectares in size, which were then made available to the former soldiers and their families. In the 1980s, additional !Xun and Khwe from Angola and Caprivi were resettled in Western Bushmanland. The interactions between the Ju/'hoansi and the !Xun and Khwe generally were positive, although there was some resentment on the part of the Ju/'hoansi due to the fact that the !Xun and Khwe were receiving salaries and fairly significant amounts of assistance from the government and from NGOs, such as the Evangelical Lutheran Church in Namibia (ELCIN).

Post-independence Transformations in Namibia

Some of the actions that the GRN undertook, once it was established in March 1990, included the following: rehabilitation of the country's economy, demobilization of soldiers, transformation of the roles of traditional authorities, land tenure reform, and reorganization of the various districts (Hangula 1995; Hinz and Joas 1995; Hopwood 2007; Odendaal 2006a, 2006b; Republic of Namibia 1991; Thoma and Piek 1997; Werner 2001). In 1992, the GRN passed the Regional Councils Act (Act No. 22 of 1992). The idea behind this legislation, which took effect officially in 1998, was that planning and administration would be decentralized, with regional councils becoming responsible for planning development.

Regional delimitation and regional representation both had repercussions in terms of practical land rights. The GRN entered into an extended process of establishing land tenure policies, setting up two "technical committees" (one for communal lands and one for commercial lands) to consider the various options for dealing with land management and administration. One matter of continuing vagueness was the supervision of land in the communal areas, including the former Bushmanland. Improvement of livestock and crop production and provision of services in the communal regions were stated goals of the government.

Locally sensitive programs required much more responsive administrative structures that would have to be created anew out of situations that had been racially constructed in the past. In order to abolish the token homeland local government legacy of the colonial era, the GRN embarked upon its new system of local governments and regional administrations. As a result of a study by the Delimitation Commission, authorized by the new Constitution, the former tribal and ethnic homelands system was eliminated and replaced with new regions that were defined on the basis of a number of factors, including population, infrastructure, the presence of municipalities, and economic viability.

The former racially divided municipal governments have been merged into single municipal councils, and the communal administrations and former regions have been replaced with 13 new regions (see map 5). Each region has a regional commissioner, who serves as an officer of the Ministry of Regional, Local Government and Housing and Rural Development; a chief administrative officer; and an elected council. The regions have advisory and planning authorities and are able to impose taxes, in a limited capacity. The regional governments are not intended to fulfill service provisions or production functions, which remain the responsibility of the central government ministries.

Although the report of the Delimitation Commission had been submitted, the new regions had been officially proclaimed in March 1992, and regional elections had taken place early in 1993, evidence of the new administrative structure was only unevenly apparent as late as 1995. Legislation to finalize the definition of the new structures took a very long time. Many Namibians, whether at the government or "bottom rung" level, recognized that local government was in a formative state throughout the 1990s. They understood that

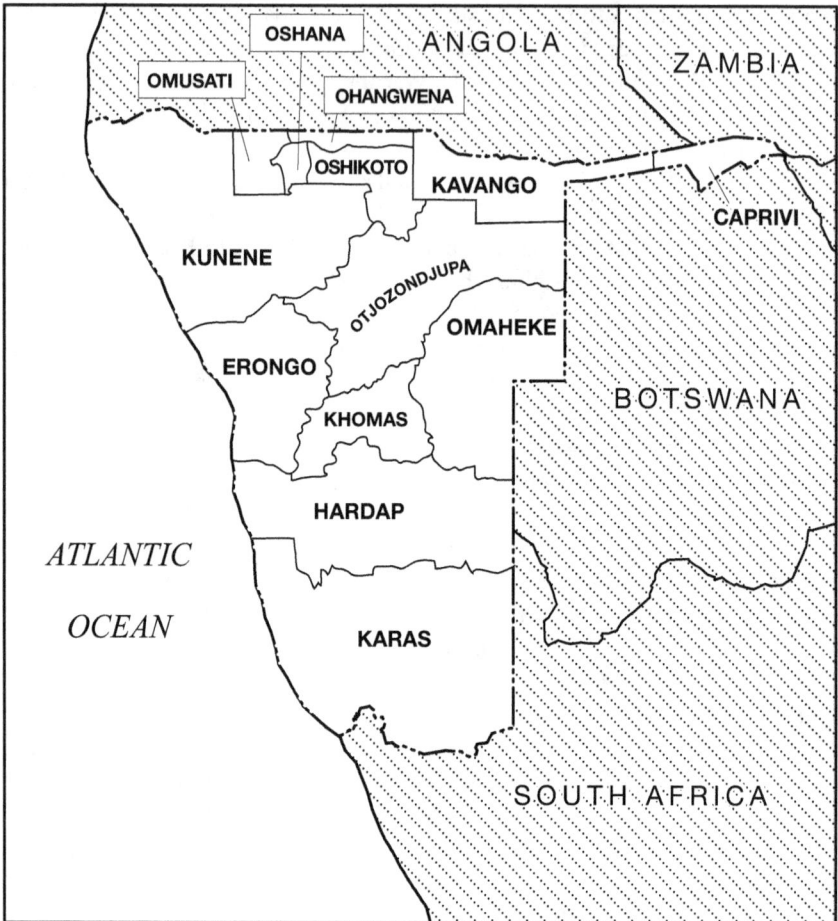

Map 5 The 13 regions of Namibia

new regional power bases would be formed, but many questions remained: How exactly would the local government structure be implemented? What kind of relationship would the regional councils have with the national government? How responsive would the regional councils be to local constituencies? What relationship would local land boards, if any were indeed to be established, have to the regional councils?

The lengthy state of indecision contributed to a sense of insecurity for local institutions, especially those in communal areas whose land tenure had not been established. As with land tenure, indecision regarding the official status of local government created disincentives for sustainable resource management. These issues needed to be resolved so that local communities such as Nyae

Nyae could embark on development and resource management programs with the full knowledge that they would receive the benefits from them.[2]

It was apparent that people in the communal areas and in land surrounding national parks and game reserves wished to have greater access to natural resources, including wildlife and veld (wild plant) products. Efforts were made by the GRN to come up with policies and programs that would increase the benefits flowing to rural communities from natural resource utilization.[3] Tourism was seen as an important strategy for increasing local employment and income. Agriculture, fishing, mining, livestock production, and the exploitation and cultivation of high-value plants (e.g., morama and Hoodia) were also seen as important. In order to ensure that natural resource management benefited local people, it was necessary to change national level legislation, to facilitate the establishment of local institutions, and to recognize traditional authorities.

One of the 13 regions established as a result of the Regional Councils Act was Otjozondjupa, which at the time of its declaration was 105,327 square kilometers in size and contained some 85,000 people. The Otjozondjupa region is considered the most under-developed in Namibia. It contains a number of districts and several municipalities, including Grootfontein, but much of it is rural, with a relatively low population density and widely dispersed inhabitants. Tsumkwe is a center for two of the region's districts that are of main concern to the Ju/'hoansi: Tsumkwe District East, roughly equivalent to what used to be known as Eastern Bushmanland (Nyae Nyae), and Tsumkwe District West, made up mostly of what formerly was Western Bushmanland, where some Ju/'hoansi reside and which they utilize for purposes of hunting, gathering, and grazing domestic animals.

In March 1998, the GRN announced that 31 traditional authorities and, as Daniels (2004: 50) put it, "hence 31 Namibian 'traditional communities' had been granted official recognition." Six San groups had applied for recognition, but none of them was awarded that status (Thoma and Piek 1997). The San groups complained formally to the government, and they were allowed to submit their claims in writing to the Investigating Committee on Tribal Disputes. Eventually, the committee recommended that the two San groups that retained a portion of their land base—the Ju/'hoansi in Tsumkwe District East and the !Xun and Khwe in Tsumkwe District West—should receive official government recognition, and the GRN accepted this recommendation (Daniels 2003: 57; 2004: 50; Manfred Hinz, pers. comm., 2001). The two leaders appointed as Traditional Authorities were Tsamkxao =Oma of the Ju/'hoansi of Tsumkwe District East and John Arnold of the !Xun of Tsumkwe District West.

2. The matter of resource management will be examined in greater detail in chapter 9.

3. For discussions of some of these policies, see Corbett and Daniels (1996); Jones (1996); Jones and Murphree (2001); Taylor (2007a); Weaver and Skyer (2003).

The Environment of the Nyae Nyae Region

The area in which this study took place falls within the Otjozondjupa region and includes a portion of eastern Otjozondjupa (Tsumkwe District East). The traditional lands of the Ju/'hoansi incorporated part of what is now Kaudum National Park, where there is a fossil river valley, the Kaudum, that stretches into Botswana (see map 6). The southern border of the Nyae Nyae area was at G/am, which today is a Herero settlement. The eastern border of the Nyae Nyae area is the north-south border fence with Botswana, beyond which is the Dobe-/Kae/kae area, where members of the Harvard Kalahari Research Group worked (Lee 1979a, 1979b; Lee and DeVore 1976). The western border in the past was defined in part by the area of waterless land dotted with *mogau* (*Dichapetalum cymosum*), a plant poisonous to cattle, which was considered Western Bushmanland, now Tsumkwe District West.

Named by Lorna Marshall (1960: 325–326; 1976) from old German maps, the Nyae Nyae area (in Ju/'hoansi, N//oaq!'ae or "area of broken rocks") corresponds to the land occupied by the Ju/'hoansi in the northeastern part of Namibia. It lies in area approximately 19 degrees 5 minutes and 20 degrees 20 minutes south latitude and 20 degrees 10 minutes and 21 degrees east longitude. The Nyae Nyae region consists of a roughly oval-shaped area that is approximately 144 kilometers (90 miles) north to south and 78 kilometers (60 miles) east to west, with a total area at the time of the Marshall family's research of approximately 25,900 square kilometers (10,000 square miles). When SWAA created Bushmanland in 1976, it aligned the area east to west. Portions of ancestral Ju/'hoan territory were granted to the Kavango in the north and to the Herero in the south as part of Hereroland East.

As we use the term in this book, Nyae Nyae corresponds today to what is defined in maps of Namibia as Tsumkwe District East. Tsumkwe District West, to the west of Nyae Nyae, was largely waterless and had relatively low numbers of people utilizing the area, except for occasional hunting and gathering trips. Small groups of !Xun, Ju/'hoansi, and some Hai//om resided in the area, which stretches from Nyae Nyae west to the Omatako Valley.

Water in the Nyae Nyae region is obtained by people from surface sources, such as springs, during the rainy season and from groundwater sources through wells and boreholes throughout the year. Lorna Marshall (1976: 64) noted that the Nyae Nyae region had waterholes "in which underground water wells up to the surface in outcroppings of the underlying rock." Permanent waterholes were crucial to the well-being of the Ju/'hoansi. As Marshall put it, "'There are vast stretches of the desert which cannot be inhabited because there are no waterholes." Elizabeth Marshall Thomas (2006: 27) says, "In the six thousand square miles known as Nyae Nyae, there were only seven waterholes that the Ju/'hoansi considered to be permanent." She went on to note that these waterholes had never failed in living memory, even during drought.

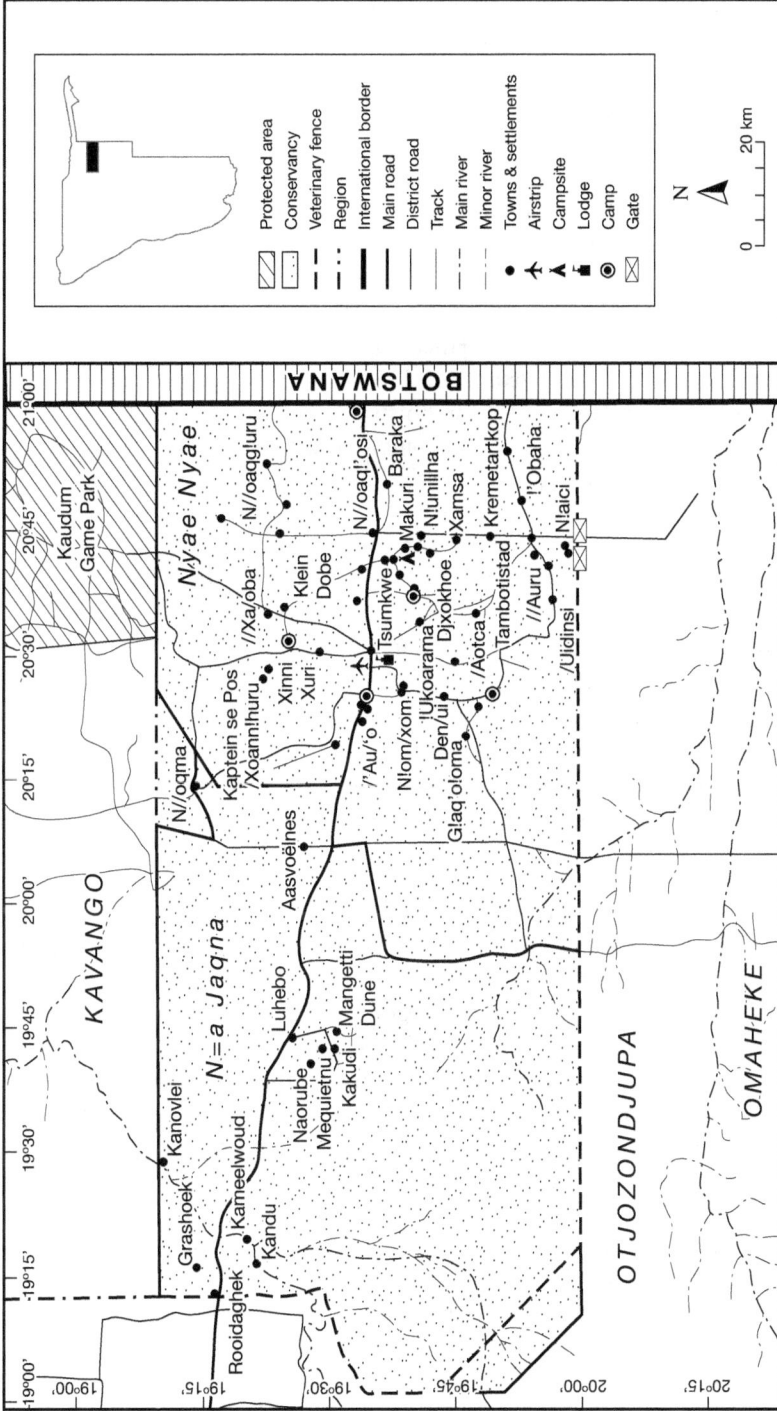

Map 6 Namibian Tsumkwe District in Otjozondjupa region, showing the Kaudum National Park and the Namibia-Botswana border

There are smaller pans that hold water after the rains and that attract birds, antelopes, and other species. People also get water out of the holes in trees after rainfall, and there is evidence of pegs that were placed in some of the trees in the area, notably baobabs (*Adansonia digitata*), so that people could climb up to get water, honey, and other resources and could look for game. In the past, melons (e.g., *Citrullus naudinianus*) and sometimes roots (e.g., *Raphionacme burkei*) served as sources of liquid and sustenance for resident populations at certain times of the year.

An important geographical feature in the Nyae Nyae-/Kae/kae region are the Aha Hills, which stretch across the Botswana-Namibia border. In Botswana, there are the /Uihaba (G/wihaba) Hills, some 35 kilometers west of /Kae/kae, and the Koanaka Hills, approximately 22.5 kilometers southwest of /Uihaba, are also on the Botswana side of the Botswana-Namibia border. /Uihaba and Koanaka contain caves of major paleontological and environmental significance. Local people use the hills for resource procurement purposes, while tourists and, on occasion, scientists visit the hills. In some places the area is dotted with pans—low-lying depressions on the landscape that contain rainwater during the rainy season and sometimes into the dry season (May–October). Another geographical feature are fossil river valleys (*omirimbi*), which in the past saw surface water flows but today are largely dry. Besides the hills, pans, and dry river beds, the main topographical feature of the region is a system of parallel longitudinal dunes (called *alab* dunes), 8 to 80 kilometers in length and 1.5 to 8 kilometers apart, which are oriented roughly west-northwest to east-southeast. These dunes are presently stabilized by vegetation, including grasses, shrubs, and trees (Grove 1969; Yellen 1977; Yellen and Lee 1976). The Nyae Nyae region is characterized as northern Kalahari semi-arid tree and bush savanna (Thomas and Shaw 1991: 98–106).

The semi-arid climate of the Nyae Nyae area features a four- to six-month rainy season in the summer and moderate to cool winters, with little to no rainfall. Figures for Tsumkwe in the period from 1966 to 1992 reveal that the rainfall averaged 474.9 millimeters per year (23 years with data), ranging from 219.8 to 627.8 millimeters (Botelle and Rohde 1995: 199). Rainfall at !Xangwa in Botswana, which is just across the border from Nyae Nyae, averaged 469.4 millimeters per year and ranged from 224.7 to 935 millimeters in the period from 1983 to 1990 (ibid.). More recent data from the Namibia Meteorological Service indicate an annual rainfall ranging from 400 to 700 millimeters at Tsumkwe.

The hottest mean temperatures in the region usually occur between October and February, when the temperature reaches 33 to 43 degrees Celsius (93 to 110 degrees Fahrenheit) in the daytime shade. The coldest months are June and July, when nighttime temperatures drop to freezing and daytime temperatures average between 24 and 27 degrees Celsius (70 to 80 degrees Fahrenheit). Table 4

Table 4 Seasons of the year, according to the Ju/'hoan San of Nyae Nyae

Season Description	Month(s)	Ju/'hoan Term
Coldest season, dry	May–August	*!gum*
Hottest season, dry	September–October	*!ga*
Hot, little rain	November	*!gabu-!gabu*
Hot, little rain	December	*!kuma*
Warm, big rain	January–March	*bara*
Warm, no rain, or occasional downpour	April	*//obe*

Source: Adapted from L. Marshall (1976: 67–71).

presents data on the various seasons recognized by the Ju/'hoansi of Nyae Nyae. It can be seen that there are significant differences between the wet season (usually November–April) and the dry season (usually May–October).

Annual and seasonal droughts are common in the Nyae Nyae region, as are periodic crop failures and reductions in the number and variety of wild plants and animals. Low crop yields due to drought or insufficient rainfall occur approximately every second or third year in the Tsumkwe District, according to officials of the Ministry of Agriculture, Water, and Forestry (MAWF). The rainfall patterns, combined with the nature of the soils, which generally are Kalahari sands with some pockets of black cotton soils, have important implications for agricultural crop production. Agriculture is a risky activity in the Kalahari. Yields are modest even in the best of times, and nutrient-deficient soils tend to limit agricultural potential even when a year-round supply of water is available. Most soils in the area are poor, lacking in humus, and are relatively high in alkalinity. Only a small portion of Namibia as a whole—less than 1 percent—is considered to be agriculturally productive.

From hydro-geological information obtained by the GRN and various private firms engaged in water exploration and development in Tsumkwe District, it appears that the water table is higher and thus more accessible in Tsumkwe District East than in Tsumkwe District West. Dozens of boreholes have been drilled in the two areas over the past several decades, some of which are used to supply the domestic and agricultural needs of local people. It is difficult to get accurate data on the number of boreholes that have been drilled in the Nyae Nyae area, but government officials and NGOs involved in water provision have estimated that at least 40 boreholes have been drilled. At any one time, only a portion of them are fully functional.

During our fieldwork, it was evident that local people in the Nyae Nyae region perceive water availability as a major problem. Efforts have been made by MAWF to provide water sources in the area, and there have been privately sponsored initiatives as well, such as those financed by the Kalahari Peoples Fund, the Redbush Tea Company of London, Dr. Polly Wiessner, and the Nyae Nyae Development Foundation of Namibia. A particular problem involving water sources relates to elephants (*Loxodonta africana*), which have been responsible for destroying pumps, troughs, and water storage facilities in recent years, as noted by John Marshall in his films and his writings (see J. Marshall 1989, 2002, 2003a, 2003b, 2003c).[4]

There are numerous trees, shrubs, and vines that provide fruits, nuts, gums, barks, and roots that are used for food, fuel, construction, medicinal and ritual purposes, household implements, and crafts.[5] Ju/'hoansi exploit over 150 species out of a total of some 500 plants in the area (Lee 1979a: 158–204; L. Marshall 1976: 82–123). Some are large trees that bear nuts, such as mongongo (*Ricinodendron rautanenii*) (also called mangetti or *g//kaa*), and others are vines that also bear nuts, such as morama (*Tylosema esculentum*) (also called gemsbok bean or *dshin*), the pods and roots of which are used for food. Also important is marula, or *kaqe* (*Sclerocarya caffra*), a tree that bears edible fruits that some people sell commercially for the production of wine (amarula). Other economically important plant species include devil's claw (*Harpagophytum procumbens*) (in Ju/'hoan, *//xamsa//oqro*), which is used for headaches, often in the form of a tea; baobab (*Adansonia digitata*) (=ʼom), the pods of which are consumed both for their taste and for medicinal purposes; Kalahari truffle (*Terfezia spp.*) (*dcoodcoo*), a subterranean fungus that is used for food; and aloe (various species) (*n//hoqʼoru*), which is used to treat burns.

In the past, the Ju/'hoansi exploited some 150 species of plants and over 40 species of mammals; thus, they could be described as being generalists in terms of their subsistence (Lee 1969, 1979a). In July 1964, the Dobe Ju/'hoansi worked an average of 12–19 hours a week in order to obtain sufficient resources to sustain themselves (Lee 1968: 37). It should be noted, however, that the labor inputs of Ju/'hoansi varied both over time and from place to place (Lee 1979a, 2003; Yellen 1977). The Ju/'hoansi of the /Du/Da region south of the Dobe-/Kae/kae area in Botswana, for example, expended considerably more hours in subsistence procurement, in part because of the absence of mongongo nuts and lower resource densities in general (Patricia Draper, pers. comm.).

Ju/'hoan women are involved in many activities that are based on their keen observation of the environment and their special skills as botanists (L. Marshall 1976: 95). These skills include their extensive knowledge of plants, animals, insects, and other resources that have significant potential as food, medicines, and

---

4. The issues surrounding the presence of elephants are dealt with in later chapters, including more detailed discussions in chapters 4 and 9.

5. For lists of economically important plant species, see Lee (1979a: 158–175, 182–204); Leffers (2003); and L. Marshall (1976: appendix 1).

tools (e.g., baskets, nets, digging sticks). In the past, Ju/'hoan women would range out from their homes, often on a daily basis, to collect wild plants. The plants they collected were either picked up by hand or obtained through excavation, using hands or a digging stick. The plants were then placed in a carrying bag or net that was worn over the shoulder. Sometimes people put the plants in buckets or plastic bags. These goods were usually consumed by individuals and their families.

Some of the plants and other items (e.g., ostrich eggshells) that people foraged in the bush were used to manufacture crafts, were exchanged with other people, or were sold to generate income. Women, men, and sometimes children are able to earn at least a little cash from the sale of items that are collected or manufactured (see Leffers 2003; Terry, Lee, and Le Roux 1994). On occasion, craft sales can generate a significant amount of income, as much as N$200–$500 (equivalent to about US $26–$66 at the time) per annum, according to people whom we interviewed in the 1990s and in the early part of the new millennium.

Fauna and Hunting

The Nyae Nyae region supports a diverse array of wild animal species, from elephants to bush squirrels. Nearly all of the major antelope species common to southern Africa are found there, as is the full range of large and small predators (Hitchcock et al. 1996; Lee 1979a: 96–102; L. Marshall 1976: 124–130; Yellen and Lee 1976). The bird populations are also of significance, in terms of science and conservation, as well as their contribution to local diets (Hines 1992, 1993; Yellen 1977). There are pans on both sides of the border, especially on the Namibian side, that provide stopover points for migrating waterfowl and other birds, a number of which are very rare.

In the past, hunting was seen by the Ju/'hoansi as an important activity, one that provided not only food but also goods and materials crucial to the local economy. Women contributed to men's hunting success through their extensive tracking knowledge and by sharing information they had obtained during the course of gathering trips (Biesele and Barclay 2001). One of the concerns expressed to us by a number of older Ju/'hoansi was the fact that members of the younger generation often did not have the desire to learn how to hunt. Some people saw this situation as being extremely problematic, noting that the younger Ju/'hoansi have few means to earn a living besides foraging, farming, or craft production, with dependency on government support as the only other option. At the same time, it should be noted, some younger people said that they did not want to hunt because it was "too dangerous" or "too difficult." Gathering, too, was not easy, as it requires knowledge of plants and the conditions under which they grow. Collecting wild foods, they said, was "hard work," and unless they were able to get significant cash returns, it was not worth the effort.

Foragers or Farmers?

A question that kept coming up in discussions with government officials, development workers, researchers, and members of the media was whether the Ju/'hoansi are primarily hunter-gatherers. In fact, the Ju/'hoansi can be described as having a mixed economy that consists of a small amount of foraging, agriculture (growing crops such as maize, beans, and melons), livestock raising, and transfers (food and other necessary goods obtained from relatives and friends) (Berger et al. 2003; J. Marshall 1989, 2003a; Wiessner 2004). The Ju/'hoansi rely on cash, food, and other goods provided by the government and NGOs, with a sizable number of people receiving most or even all of their food from the state.

Sometimes people use the term "hunter-gatherer" in an economic sense, with subsistence and other basic needs being met from the exploitation of wild plant and animal resources. Food and material consumption patterns are not always easy to assess in the field, and researchers and government game scouts sometimes simply ask people whether or not they hunt or look for evidence of wild animal remains in their homes and camps. While many rural people in northeastern Namibia consume at least some wild plant and animal foods, practically none are totally dependent on wild resources.

An assumption made about hunter-gatherers is that they are self-sufficient societies—that they do not depend on outside agencies for any inputs at all. In fact, few, if any, Ju/'hoansi households in Nyae Nyae are totally self-sufficient. Nearly all of them get at least some of their food from the state or purchase it with cash that they have earned by working for the government, NGOs, or private companies. Some people also get food (e.g., milk, maize meal) from livestock owners, in exchange for herding and other work, or from agriculturalists, whose fields they help plant, cultivate, weed, and harvest.

In the view of some Namibians and some researchers, hunter-gatherers are people who lack domestic animals (i.e., they are non-livestock holders). One has to consider, however, those people who engage in *mafisa*, a form of long-term loan in which livestock is exchanged for labor, a practice also known as agistment. Under this system, Ju/'hoansi who are employed as herders to manage the livestock of others are given a calf in exchange for their labor. The Ju/wa Bushman Development Foundation, as well as other NGOs (e.g., ELCIN), and Namibian government ministries, including MAWF and what used to be known as the Ministry of Lands, Resettlement, and Rehabilitation, have given livestock (cattle and goats) to people in the major settlements (Tsumkwe and Mangetti Dune) and some of the outlying communities in Tsumkwe District.

Yet another assumption made about hunter-gatherers in Namibia was that they did not plant domestic crops or till the soil using hoes or plows. In actuality, even so-called mobile foragers used fire to increase yields of melons and morama (*dshin* beans), went on their annual moves, and returned to harvest the crops that had survived the depredations of wildlife and cattle.

Some people in Namibia define hunter-gatherers on the basis of the kind of technology that is used. If people employ bows and arrows, digging sticks, and carrying bags made of skins, they are considered to be hunter-gatherers. Ministry of Environment and Tourism officials told Hitchcock that they use the criterion of whether or not individuals wear leather clothing (especially breech-cloths, in the case of adult males) as the basis for determining if a person is a "traditional hunter-gatherer." A person wearing modern clothing who was seen hunting outside of the Nyae Nyae area would likely be stopped by a game scout, questioned, and, in all likelihood, arrested for contravening wildlife laws.

Theoretically, hunter-gatherers are also characterized by the use of human energy, that is, energy derived from their own physical labor. From the stand-point of some of the government officials, journalists, and researchers with whom we spoke, hunter-gatherers are not supposed to use diesel fuel, electric-ity, wind energy, water power, or draft animals—sources of energy that many Ju/'hoansi do use when they have the opportunity to do so. For instance, many of the water points in the Nyae Nyae communities are equipped with diesel engines or windmills, and some of the people draw water from the boreholes for their small gardens, using pipes to direct it onto their fields. It is apparent, therefore, that most Ju/'hoansi prefer to keep their options open when it comes to economic decision-making.

Agriculture and livestock production were promoted in Tsumkwe District by the GRN and its predecessor, the government of South West Africa. When the government settlement of Tsumkwe was established in the late 1950s, one of its purposes was to provide local people with training in agriculture and livestock husbandry. While the agricultural training activities of agricul-tural extension personnel and administrators who oversaw Tsumkwe in the late 1950s and 1960s, experienced their ups and downs, a sizable number of Ju/'hoansi gained practical knowledge in planting and cultivating crops and in managing cattle and small livestock (goats and sheep).

As Elizabeth Marshall Thomas (2006: 280) notes, after McIntyre moved to Tsumkwe, he "established a clinic and introduced primitive farming along the lines of ordinary European-type farming, which was at the time the only para-digm, beginning with a herd of goats and an experimental planting of corn and millet." McIntyre chose goats, according to Thomas, not only because they would provide milk, but also because they are small enough so that they could be dispatched for food without having to be shared with other people. In fact, as Thomas (ibid.) points out, the meat of goats, just like that of cattle, would have been shared with others.

As it turned out, keeping goats was not easy, in part due to predation of hyenas, leopards, jackals, and lions. There were debates over whether or not goats were "bad for the environment," a position that many Ju/'hoansi rejected but which some government officials and members of conservation organizations supported. The Ju/'hoansi acknowledged that goats could be problematic, especially when they ate the thatching grass used in the construction of roofs and walls of some homes or consumed clothing and blankets in people's yards.

Agricultural production also posed challenges. The Ju/'hoansi and other residents of Tsumkwe planted maize, sorghum, millet, beans, and melons, among other crops. Water, which was not always easy to come by, had to be hand-carried to the fields. Later, pipes were laid to some of the larger fields, but the maintenance of the pumps and pipes was a problem. Sometimes crop yields were good, but people had difficulty keeping birds and animals, both domesticated and wild, out of the fields, and on occasion whole fields of maize or millet were devastated by pests. Attempts were made to construct fences around the fields using acacia thorn branches, but these were not always effective. The Ju/'hoansi farmers reportedly tried hard to keep animals out of the fields, something that required vigilance and enormous amounts of time and effort.

Government ministries and NGOs occasionally provided wire and fence posts to people in the area, and fence construction was undertaken by a number of Ju/'hoansi. Some of the farmers in Nyae Nyae experimented with different kinds of crops, which they hoped would be drought-resistant or pest-resistant. It was not unusual for a visitor to the area to be asked if he or she would go to Grootfontein or Windhoek to get seeds for people. Over time, faced with droughts and predation on agricultural fields and gardens by both fauna and other humans, many Ju/'hoansi got discouraged about the efficacy of crop production. As Elizabeth Marshall Thomas (2006: 281) concluded, "Nyae Nyae was no ordinary farmland, and the experiment collapsed, to everyone's disappointment."

Land Reform and Development Plans

By 2007, the GRN was focusing its attention on trying to achieve a more equitable land ownership structure through a land distribution and resettlement scheme that would give the historically disadvantaged majority (black Namibians) access to some of the commercial (freehold) land that was largely owned by whites. As a result, the prospect of being allotted arable and grazing land has attracted people from other places to some of the communal land areas. Plans were being made to turn part of Tsumkwe District West, just to the west of Nyae Nyae, into a potential area for land distribution for farming and ranching purposes (Harring and Odendaal 2006a, 2006b, 2007; Odendaal 2006a, 2006b). These plans could well affect the Ju/'hoansi in Nyae Nyae, with larger numbers of people, some of them farmers and pastoralists, coming into the area and utilizing the grazing, soil, water, plant, and wildlife resources.

In 2007–2008, the GRN was also considering the possibility of moving the veterinary cordon fence that cuts across northern Namibia to an area farther to the north along the Namibia-Angola border. This fence, the so-called Red Line, was established during the colonial period to prevent the spread of animal diseases from the communal areas in the north to other parts of the country. The advantage for those living below the Red Line is that they can market their cattle to other parts of Namibia and to places overseas. While this could have benefits for the Ju/'hoansi in terms of increased cattle prices and sales, given the fact that most people had relatively small livestock herds, it will likely have only minimal economic impacts. The real problem is that it will make the Nyae Nyae area—already of interest to outsiders because of its permanent water, relatively rich grazing, and open areas where fields could be planted—a place to which people could move with their livestock and set up what in effect would be cattle posts. Several Herero and Kavango told us that an added advantage of the Nyae Nyae area was its resident Ju/'hoan population, who could be pressed into service as herders, field hands, and domestic workers.

The government had already been thinking about how to handle things in the Nyae Nyae area. In the latter part of 2005, it announced the establishment of a San Development Program, to be overseen by the office of the deputy prime minister. This program is aimed specifically at poverty-stricken people who are part of the historically disadvantaged population of Namibia. Thus far, it has provided training in income-generating projects; draft animals, tools, and seeds; and scholarships for San children. In early 2007, a training course for San coffin makers was offered as part of this development program. At the graduation ceremony held for the participants, Deputy Prime Minister Libertina Amathila called upon regional councilors to make sure that they empowered the San people. She went on to say that the San needed a special program in order to "fast track their integration into the economic mainstream" (quoted in Bause 2007). The Namibian government went to great lengths to explain that this program was not, in fact, ethnically based, but was being implemented because "the San are a very poor community." In other words, the San Development Program was part of the government's overall efforts to alleviate poverty and raise living standards throughout the country.

The GRN's long-term plans for the Nyae Nyae area and the Otjozondjupa region as a whole are still unclear, but it is apparent that the goal is to diversify the economy and to reform, if only in a limited way, the basis of land tenure in the region. This situation poses both risks and opportunities for the Ju/'hoansi. The real question is whether the Ju/'hoansi and their neighbors will be informed directly of the government's plans or if they will be overlooked during negotiations with large international donors to fund development initiatives that could well have substantial impacts on the Nyae Nyae region and its people.

Chapter Two

Traditional Ju/'hoan Leadership and Governance

Many changes in what Elizabeth Marshall Thomas (2006) refers to as the "Old Way"—how the Ju/'hoansi of Nyae Nyae generally lived their lives in the past—were occurring long before 1986. This chapter summarizes the pressures that caused these changes and shows how they brought about a strongly felt need among the Ju/'hoansi to alter the way in which they governed themselves. Nevertheless, 1986 emerges as a watershed year because of the formation of the Ju/wa (Ju/'hoan) Farmers Union in Nyae Nyae. Thus began an era of change in Nyae Nyae Ju/'hoan community governance that has little precedent in any San society. It started a process of transition from consensus-based, small-group regulation and decision-making to a form of regional representational government—a development that is still evolving more than 20 years later.

Why such a transition was necessary, in the face of national and international changes affecting the Ju/'hoansi, and how it has been negotiated among them since Namibian independence in 1990 are the main themes of this book on recent Nyae Nyae history. To understand the Ju/'hoansi's courageous attempt at countering the challenges they faced during the unraveling of the apartheid-era South West Africa Administration (SWAA), under which they had found a fragile, ignominious, and temporary shelter, we must take a look at how they governed themselves in the past. This chapter examines traditional Ju/'hoan leadership and governance, a system that worked so well even up to recent times that we may assume it also had a long period of development, going back substantially into prehistory.

The "Old Way": Land and Leadership

Leadership and decision-making among the Ju/'hoansi have always, at least as long as has been documented ethnographically and via oral history, been inextricably linked to land and its resources. More importantly, Ju/'hoan governance has been inseparable from kinship and thus from mutually satisfactory ways of regulating access to sustenance, so that the means of life can be available to all. The Ju/'hoansi have long had clearly defined genealogical ties to resource areas, called *n!oresi*. This means that hereditary "owners" (*kxaosi*) or stewards of *n!oresi* have collective decision-making and conflict-resolution powers, and family groups have claims to specific *n!ore* areas through their relationships to the "owners." Unlike many other San in southern Africa (see map 7, in which the San are designated by language groups), most of whom have been, since the beginning of European colonization, dispossessed of land rights and scattered as serf laborers on both white and black farms and in towns, the Ju/'hoansi are fortunate to have maintained both a substantial fragment of their former foraging territory and the social rules, amounting to a social technology, by which they regulate the relationship of their population to the territory's resources.

Traditionally, and specifically prior to 1986, the *n!oresi* of the Ju/'hoansi were roughly circular land areas with undefined borders that were oriented around a water source, each providing the resource needs of a traditional hunter-gatherer group (band) of 30 to 50 people. Although rights to the wild vegetable resources of each area were known and respected by all the bands, the *n!oresi* did not have defended boundaries. Instead, their permeable edges were often crossed by Ju/'hoan hunters in pursuit of wounded game. Lorna Marshall described a hunting area as a vague region extending south and west, for instance, of a certain line of hills or a water pan. Animals within a *n!ore* belonged to no one until they were shot or wounded, and even visitors were permitted to hunt them.

John Marshall reported that a kill of 15–18 large mammals per year was usual for a single Ju/'hoan band, averaging 25 people per band (J. Marshall 1958a, 1958b; see also L. Marshall 1976: 140). When an animal was killed, its owner had the right to distribute the meat. Without fail, meat was shared with virtually all members of the local group, along rather definite lines of sharing. Even those who might never have primary access to meat with which to reciprocate at a later date—women, the disabled or elderly, and even men who could not or chose not to hunt—were given their shares. Certainly, the distribution of meat was a point of high tension in Ju/'hoan and all San societies: if anyone were to be left out, a great deal of bad feeling would result.

Vegetable foods, which were more abundant and far outweighed meat in the total diet, were not shared as strictly as meat. Wild foods were shared by the woman who gathered them, mostly within her own nuclear family, in a

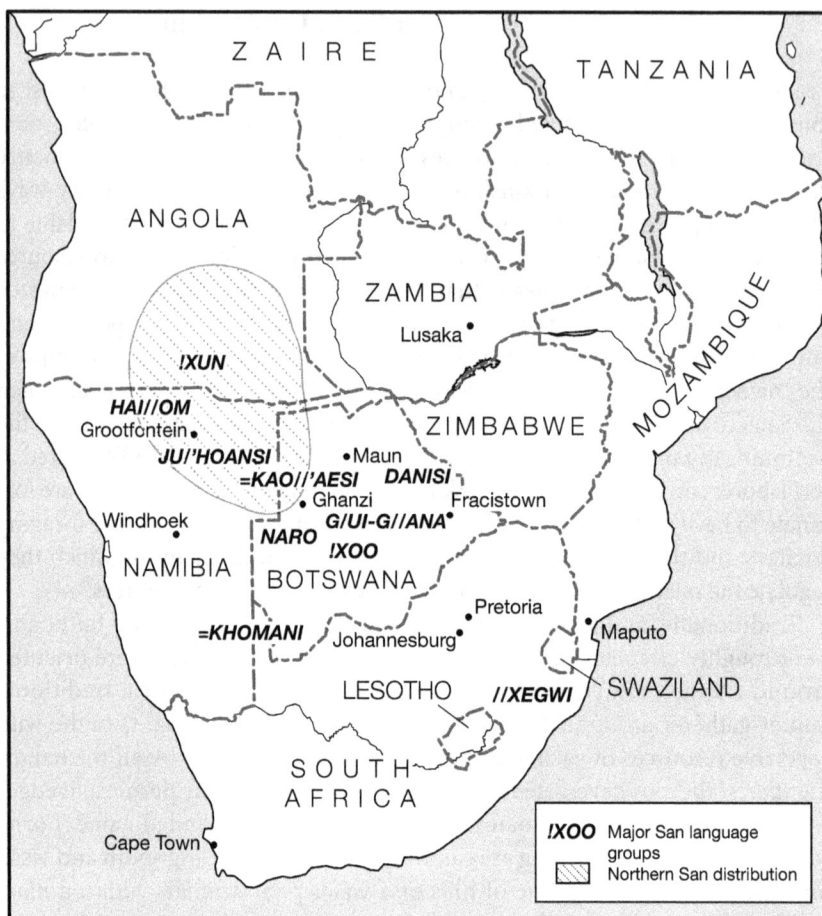

Map 7 Southern Africa, showing the major San language groups

manner that was more casual than was the case with meat. However, specific gathering places were owned by specific bands. This rigorous ownership facili- tated the adaptation of the size of the band to the quantity of vegetable foods available. Although nuclear families are the units within which gathered foods are shared, a single nuclear family could not sustain the arduous gathering full- time. Families organized into bands, though, could do that job. Bands usually provided enough men in cooperation and in rotation for hunting and enough women to guarantee companionship and mutual help for both gathering trips and stay-at-home child care.

Bands are social units made up of families and individuals linked through kinship, marriage, friendship, and economic ties. The Ju/'hoansi term for these units is *n//abesi*, which means "the people who live together" (L. Marshall 1976: 156). These groupings vary in size but often consist of several families who cooperate together for at least part of the year. Sometimes several bands use the same waterhole, but in these cases they generally occupy different areas around the waterhole. Some of these bands, especially those consisting of families that have been together a long time, have names, often drawn from the geographic features of the land where they reside.

Bands formed alliances with neighboring groups whose resources could be used in time of need. With this fluid, overlapping, and interactive use of land and resources, the Ju/'hoansi resembled other San, even those in areas with considerably less rainfall, such as the Central Kalahari Desert of Botswana. In discussing band alliances among the G/ui San there, George Silberbauer (1979, 1981a, 1981b) stressed the importance of this flexibility in alleviating local food shortages in times of drought. Because rainfall in the Kalahari may be uneven, one band may have experienced famine while another was finding plenty of food. In the case of allied bands, an extended visit to the favored region would probably occur. H. J. Heinz (1972, 1979) wrote of the "band nexus" among the !Xoo San, a low-intensity system of cooperation among up to seven bands in adjacent territories. The Naro San of the Ghanzi area of Botswana are also said to have employed such a system in earlier times (Mathias Guenther, pers. comm., 1981).

In years of severe drought, however, food scarcity was universal, so there was no point in visiting an allied band's territory. Silberbauer (1979, 1981a, 1981b) found that in the Central Kalahari this fact prevented explosive situations of conflict over scarce resources from occurring. The flexible use of territories belonging to allied bands is an example of the controlled opportunism with which San people successfully exploited the Kalahari ecosystem. Alliances with other bands were used when they were profitable; isolation within separate territories occurred when moving to another region was useless and potentially detrimental.

Ju/'hoan bands were allied by marriages and cooperated with each other because of the kinship ties formed by these unions. Thus, consanguinity was one mechanism that matched the needs of the population to the available resources. As Claire Ritchie (1988: 36) pointed out, "The conditions of their environment require[d] a flexibility of borders" (see also Marshall and Ritchie 1983). Richard Lee (pers. comm., 2009) explained that the Ju/'hoansi would "consciously strive to maintain a boundaryless universe." What we and these authors are referring to are social and cognitive habits honed over millennia, a form of ecology-driven social evolution that eventually came to fit seamlessly with the demands of what was, for most of that time, a semi-arid environment (Thomas and Shaw 1991; Tyson 1986). These long-established habits of mind are the backdrop to the immense changes that the Ju/'hoansi have been challenged to make in a very short time over the last few decades.

An important social feature of the Ju/'hoansi relates to the exchange of non-food items such as ostrich eggshell jewelry through a network that ties together consanguineous kin. This gift-giving system, known as *hxaro*, involves a balanced and delayed exchange of goods that links people together in a complex system of mutual reciprocity in the northwestern Kalahari Desert (Wiessner 1977, 2002). The reciprocal exchange system serves to reinforce social alliances and facilitates the mobility of people who are connected through kinship and *hxaro* ties. As Wiessner (2002: 421) notes, *hxaro* relations serve as a proxy for long-term mutual support among Ju/'hoansi.

Social Rules for Resource Management

The Ju/'hoansi have had a powerful, unwritten social technology of resource management that has made their economic adaptation possible in the Nyae Nyae region for a period of up to 25,000 years (Alison Brooks, pers. comm., 2008; John Yellen, pers. comm., 2008). In this social technology, leadership was traditionally tied to stewardship of the resources of each *n!ore* by a core group of siblings. Usually, the oldest man or woman within this group, known as the *n!ore kxao*, or *n!ore* owner (master), had guardianship but not exclusive authority over the resources of the *n!ore*. Leadership in these areas was and still is tied to generally agreed upon genealogical connections through parents, spouses, and/or special kin "name relationships" to the particular *n!oresi* that they inhabit.

Of 300 known, named *n!oresi* in the 6,000 square kilometers of territory known as Eastern Bushmanland (Nyae Nyae) after its delineation by SWAA's Odendaal Commission in 1970, about 200 have been mapped by Ju/'hoan people using GPS, and perhaps another 100 remain to be located in less accessible areas. Map 8 shows the distribution of *n!oresi* as documented by Ju/'hoansi in conjunction with the Nyae Nyae Development Foundation in the early 1990s. The *n!ore* system has considerable time depth in Nyae Nyae. This is known from both oral history evidence and archaeology. Except for trade goods and ceramics dating back over the past century and a half, little evidence of permanent (in the sense of long-term, rather than sedentary) occupation of the region by any people other than hunter-gatherers has been found in Nyae Nyae.[1]

N!ore Rights and the Right of the Kxa/ho

There are two key concepts of land tenure and resource use in the Ju/'hoan *n!ore* system. These are *n!ore* rights and the right of the *kxa/ho*, the larger land area of

---

1. It should be noted that although archaeological research in the larger northern Kalahari region does indicate the presence of livestock, ceramics, and trade goods going back well over

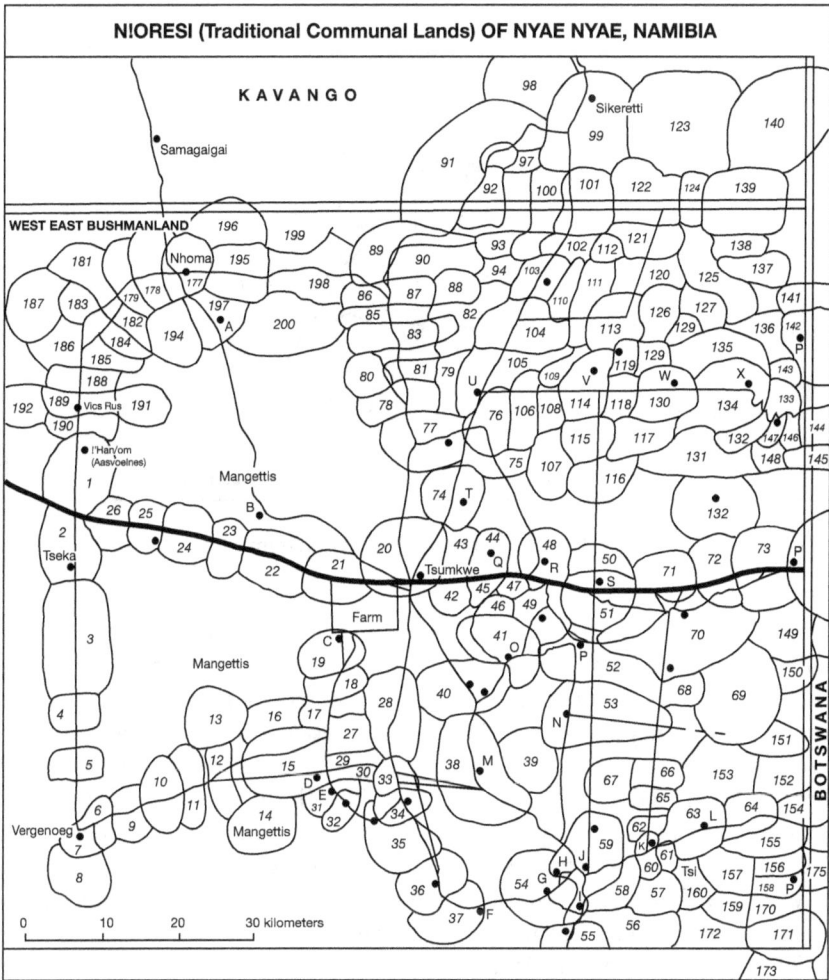

Map 8 The *n!oresi* (traditional communal lands) of Nyae Nyae

Nyae Nyae under which *n!oresi* are subsumed. The *n!ore* rights are subject to the underlying right of the *kxa/ho*. However, the *n!ore* rights are considered by the Ju/'hoansi to be stronger than the right of the *kxa/ho*.

As explained earlier, a *n!ore* is a named place that contains various natural resources. Some *n!oresi* are residential while others are used only for hunting and gathering (see fig. 1 for a diagram of the Ju/'hoan land use system). Each residential

1,000 years, the core area of Nyae Nyae where the permanent pans are (e.g., at /Aotcha) does not contain much in the way of these kinds of materials. For further information, see Lindholm (2006); Smith (1996); and Smith and Lee (1997).

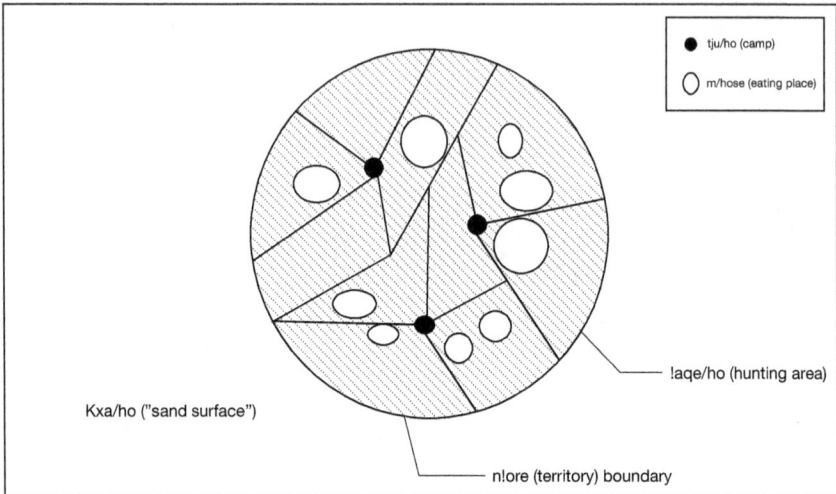

Figure 1 Ju/'hoan land use system

n!ore has one or more "eating places" (*'m/hosi*), which may or may not be shared with contiguous *n!oresi*. Each residential *n!ore* also has an associated "hunting place" (*!aqe/ho*) or direction of usual hunting (sometimes more than one), and this too may or may not be shared with nearby residential *n!oresi*. The sharing of resource areas associated with *n!oresi* is organized along lines of kinship, historical association, and specific local resource availability. The *n!ore* system and its under-standings provide a flexible and usually agreed upon method for adapting socially and numerically in order to make good use of unpredictable wild resources.[2]

Where *'m/hosi* are shared, the inhabitants of each *n!ore* have a special but ultimately non-exclusive relationship to the portion of the *'m/ho* closest to their *tju/ho* (village). This portion is called a *g/ani*, defined as "the gathering area that

2. The San territorial unit is also known as a *gu* (G/ui), *g!u* (G//ana), *no* (Kua), *n//olli* (!Xoo), or *nong* (Naro). The importance of these land units among Ju/'hoansi has been emphasized by a number of researchers (see, e.g., Albertson 1998, 2000; Hitchcock 2005; Hitchcock and Bartram 1998; Lee 1979a: 58–61, 117–119, 334; L. Marshall 1976: 71–72, 93, 103, 131–132, 184, 187–189; Marshall and Ritchie 1983; Thomas 2006: 74–86; Wilmsen 1989: 168–186; Yellen 1977: 37–41, 54–64). These units vary in size. Lee (1979a: 335) says that the *n!oresi* in the Dobe-/Kae/kae area of Botswana measure roughly 300–600 square kilometers in size. Yellen (1977: 53–56) notes that the Dobe *n!ore* was 320 square kilometers in size in the late 1960s. Albertson (1998) states that the *n!oresi* around Dobe ranged in size from 40 square kilometers at !Arin//ao to 244 square kilometers at G/hi=ahn in the late 1990s. In the latter case, the *n!oresi* were measured in the field using both geographic positioning systems (GPS) instruments and the data recorded in geographic information systems (GIS) files. This information was used as part of the evidence to make land claims before the Tawana Land Board and the North West District Council in Botswana.

is behind you," in the sense of it being "in your backyard." As one informant stated to the authors in June 1992, in response to questioning about exclusive rights to resources in his *g/ani*, "Look, even if bush food is 'in my backyard,' it doesn't belong to me alone. It belongs to all of us." He then went on to describe how a hungry person from another *n!ore* should request access to the *g/ani* of a *n!ore kxao*. He should say, "I've seen food out back of you." Then the *n!ore* owner would say, "Where is it?" and join him in eating it. Clearly, this sort of sharing has an information-spreading function, as well as a risk-reduction one, in an area of patchy rainfall. In fact, over much of the Kalahari area of both Namibia and Botswana, cooperative "nexus" systems of foraging bands, similar to that of the !Xoo identified by Heinz (1972, 1979), have been demonstrated.

The right to reside permanently in a *n!ore* is inherited by individuals from their parents, and siblings share this right equally. This right cannot be sold, given away, or willed to anyone. A person or group may travel through other people's *n!oresi*, but no one may settle in a *n!ore* without the permission of the *n!ore* owner. The rights of *n!ore* owners are understood to include the right of permanent, exclusive possession, with resource access modified, as indicated above, by flexible, environmentally modulated sharing with associated neighbors. They also include the right to gather all bush foods in the *n!ore*, to trap game there, to start poisoned-arrow game pursuits there, and to use the water sources. Lately, *n!ore* owners and their extended families have been assumed to have the right to raise livestock on their *n!oresi*, to develop any necessary infrastructure, and to cultivate crops as well.

The *kxa/ho* (literally, "sand surface" or "sand face") is all of the land traditionally inhabited by the Ju/'hoansi and its water, bush foods, game, grazing, wood, minerals, and other natural resources. In other words, the *kxa/ho* encompasses all of the individual *n!oresi*. To express the meaning of *kxa/ho*, the Ju/'hoansi say "our land and all the things *!Xu* [God] has placed in it." The right of the *kxa/ho* is a communal land right acquired by individuals through descent. It is a key part of what it means to define oneself as Ju/'hoan and is crucial to how the Ju/'hoansi view their own struggle for land tenure.

The right of the *kxa/ho* is usually exercised in the following ways: the right to the waters of the land, particularly in times of drought; the right to travel freely through the land and to drink water, hunt, and gather while on the journey; the right to shoot and follow wounded game anywhere in the land; and the right to gather key bush foods anywhere.

Today, anyone who speaks Ju/'hoansi and refers to himself or herself as Ju/'hoan is assumed to possess the right of the *kxa/ho*. According to the Nyae Nyae Farmers Cooperative Constitution of 1988, the *n!ore* rights and the right of the *kxa/ho* "have kept the peace among us and served us well." There is not a single known instance of death as the result of a dispute over territory in Nyae Nyae in over 100 years (John Marshall, pers. comm., 2004).

Territory (Occupants and Kinship)

Under the traditional system of land tenure, Ju/'hoansi inherited rights of residence in specific areas from their parents. Individuals also established subsidiary rights in other *n!oresi* through marriage, with bride service in the form of hunting for the wife's parents an important determinant of residence for at least part of the husband's life span. Richard Lee (1979a: 61) writes of the contiguous Botswana Ju/'hoansi: "A camp is built up gradually through time by the addition of in-marrying spouses of the core siblings. These spouses in turn bring in their siblings and their spouses, so that the basic genealogical structure of the camp assumes the form of a chain of spouses and siblings radiating from the core."

The name relationship (L. Marshall 1976: 238–242; Wilmsen 1989: 174–178), as an added dimension of kin-relatedness, provides subsidiary ties to further possible *n!oresi*. This complicated system of name use can be summarized as follows. A child is named by its father. By tradition, the first-born son and daughter are named for the father's father and father's mother. This occurs about 70 percent of the time (Draper and Haney 2005). The next-born son and daughter may be named for the mother's father and mother's mother, although this appears to be more variable. However, children are almost always named for a relative of the grandparental generation (a prime exception being when the father is not Ju/'hoan). As a consequence, only a limited number of names are used and reused across generations in Ju/'hoan society.

The practice of namesake, no matter from which relative the name is derived, has broad and significant social implications. The person for whom the child is named is referred to as the "big name," and the namesake child is referred to as the "small name." A special namesake relationship exists between the big and small name pairs, and people who are relatives of the big name will refer to the small name using the kinship terms that apply to the big name. For example, if a woman has a namesake relationship with a granddaughter of hers, that woman's sister would refer to the woman's granddaughter as *her* "sister," even though it is plain that, biologically speaking, this is untrue. According to Draper and Haney (2005: 256), modern informants of both Ju/'hoan and Euro-American origin report that these naming practices among the Ju/'hoansi of Botswana and Namibia have continued into the present times.

This practice has several purposes, some of which are to place a child firmly within existing social networks that allows him or her land and water access rights; to reaffirm an older generation's ties with a younger one (in contrast with the often distanced relationships between generations in American society, where the two have little in common); and also possibly to maintain in living memory older sets of genealogical ties (as suggested by L. Marshall 1976: 238–242; see also Draper and Haney 2005; Lee 1986; Takada 2008). All of these functions enhance the socio-economic survival strategies needed to live in the finite Kalahari environment. A parallel may be drawn with the flexibility of use and sharing of names, group membership, exchange relationships, and *n!ore* use, all of which have the purpose of risk reduction.[3]

All people who have a name relationship—who share a name—are considered to be related. As one Ju/'hoan woman put it to us in 1995, the name relationship "create[s] a sense of belonging." Another woman explained that the name relationship and the associations among the Ju/'hoan people through exchanges—both material and social—give them a sense of identity that is important and comforting to them. Those people who lack these connections, who are from other groups, are considered by the people of the Nyae Nyae and /Kae/kae regions to be *ju dole* (strangers).

The namesake relationship reflects the need to have several options open, since one's *n!ore* residence may be shifted in response to environmental pressures (e.g., scattered rainfall and variable local resources) or as a result of social strains (e.g., group incompatibility). This flexibility is subsumed within an overall pattern, the "Old Way," that has ensured high social agreement and low conflict for the Ju/'hoansi.

Why a "New Way" Was Needed to Meet Recent Challenges

As described previously, during the 1950s, the Ju/'hoan economy was eroding on a reduced land base, and hunger was all too common. There were also ongoing threats to their land from other groups, who wanted to utilize the water, grazing, wildlife, and mineral resources in Nyae Nyae. In the late 1950s, the Ju/'hoansi moved temporarily into Tsumkwe, an administrative center, in a futile search for an alternative livelihood. By the late 1970s, they wanted to re-establish themselves sustainably on their land. Many people had resented the short-sighted paternalism of the SWAA's plans for them in Tsumkwe and declared that they would prefer to be socially and economically self-sufficient. They reasoned that if they were able to have clearly defined rights to areas where they could live, forage, raise livestock and crops, and engage in social activities, they would be better off than if they were living in large settlements where their former risk-reduction strategies no longer worked.

Tsamkxao =Oma, the visionary first chairperson of the Nyae Nyae Farmers Cooperative (NNFC), the successor organization to the original Ju/wa Farmers

---

3. The social ties created by the reciprocal—although not always equal—material goods exchanges and the name relationship system were important because they facilitated the sharing of information about the state of the environment in various areas. They also resulted in a widespread network of people who possessed mutual rights and obligations and who could be called upon for aid in times of stress.

Union (JFU), called for a bridge from the "Old Way" to a "New Way" for new times. Tsamkxao spoke as part of the Ju/'hoan delegation to the Namibian National Conference on Land Reform and the Land Question in 1991. As quoted in the introduction to this volume, Tsamkxao explained that in the "Old Way" of governance, relationships among the Ju/'hoansi were at the heart of their economic lives.

With the mounting problems of hunger and illness in Tsumkwe and the ongoing threat to their land rights, the people at Nyae Nyae had already realized by the late 1970s that they had to go back to their *n!oresi*, if they were to hold onto them. They also saw that they must supplement hunting and gathering with alternative, and more intensive, economic means in order to survive on a reduced land area.

Change: Causes and Effects

The Ju/'hoan effort to convert to a mixed-subsistence economy has been far from easy, as was pointed out in chapter 1. The Ju/'hoansi have struggled with lions that kill their cattle, elephants that trample their gardens and pull out water pumps, and hostile SWAA officials, who believed them incapable of development. They have also struggled among themselves, in the course of adapting the cultural rules and values that underwrote the old foraging way of life to the very different ones of agriculture.

Of course, it is accepted by now that the foraging peoples of southern Africa have often gone back and forth between hunting-gathering and agriculture, and, depending on the social and environmental circumstances, have in fact often combined the two in order to sustain themselves (Vierich 1981; Vierich and Hitchcock 1996; Widlok 1999). The rules by which most Ju/'hoansi were living until recently, however, and for which generations of their children were socialized, were embedded in the demands and opportunities of a foraging relationship to their Kalahari environment. So while these learned rules and values did not constrain the Ju/'hoansi in any irrevocable way, the long-term success with which they had formerly used their environment did pose challenges when change was called for.

In very general terms, hunting-gathering involves great individualism of labor, situation-specific decision-making, relatively non-delayed rewards for effort, and egalitarian sharing rules. Agriculture, in broad contrast, implies collective labor, organized more or less hierarchically; undifferentiated, repetitious, and arduous labor patterns; greatly delayed rewards; and often stratified sharing (wealth differentials). Thus, large abysses of inexperience opened beneath the efforts of even the most motivated Ju/'hoansi as they struggled to enlist their extended families in puzzling new labor patterns with uncertain returns.

In general, the Ju/'hoan people's life experiences, until then limited mostly to foraging and to working as cattle serfs for others, had not prepared them for the disciplines and social relations of agriculture. Instead, their history and background had built up in them vast amounts of environmental information and other resilient and no-less-logical habits of mind, which had long stood them in good stead. These mental habits were enabling and flexible ones, like those that allowed foragers in other parts of southern Africa to go back and forth between foraging and agriculture in prehistory, as environmental and social conditions allowed. Where the Ju/'hoansi were concerned, the limitation in these mental habits was that of having worked, if at all, as an economic underclass to other regional agricultural groups, with no practical experience of the relevant planning processes and long-term rewards. Work as a hands-on cattle serf did not translate immediately into large-scale herd management expertise.

Establishing a Mixed Economy and Going Back to the Land

When the Ju/'hoansi began to discuss their problems in Tsumkwe, prior to moving out of it, strong leadership for the *n!ore* groups evolved from necessity. People opened their hearts and minds to individuals who they believed could lead them out of "the place of death," as Tsumkwe had come to be called. One such leader was =Oma Tsamkxao of /Aotcha, who led his people back to their *n!ore* in the early 1980s. "He stopped our feet [from wandering]," his relatives said. =Oma's son Tsamkxao, in his turn, played a significant part in the Nyae Nyae *n!ore* resettlement as the first chairperson of the people's organization, the JFU, which arose out of a grassroots movement and eventually became the Nyae Nyae Conservancy, the first internationally recognized conservancy established in Namibia after independence. Encouraged by John Marshall and members of Marshall and Ritchie's Cattle Fund (later to become the Ju/wa Bushman Development Foundation), Tsamkxao followed in his father's footsteps and energetically facilitated the relocation of three other *n!oresi* during the early 1980s. That number had risen to 12 by the end of the decade. Leaders like =Oma and Tsamkxao, and the need for organized decision-making and arbitration that they began to fill, led the way for the eventual development of formal organizations such as the JFU.

The setting up in 1986 of the Ju/wa Farmers Union (later renamed the Nyae Nyae Farmers Cooperative and still later the Nyae Nyae Conservancy) marked a decisive moment of change in both leadership and political consciousness among the Ju/'hoansi. Several leaders at the relocated *n!oresi* proposed a new form of the *n!ore* system, spearheaded by an organization to represent those communities that had gone back to the land. This organization, the JFU, was to help the Ju/'hoansi hold onto their lands and to enable dispossessed groups to settle on available land along the old *n!ore* lines of settlement and resource use. Each community was to have two representatives acting as voices for their communities on matters of *n!ore* allocation, *n!ore* group viability, cattle allocation, and the organization of farming labor. Increasingly, this body formed an important forum for the discussion of macro-environmental issues as well.

Since the JFU/NNFC was begun, the Ju/'hoansi have been subject to unprecedented external pressures. Not only did they undergo a long period of militarization during South West Africa's war against the South West Africa People's Organization, but they also experienced interim government obstruction of their development goals in the name of centralized "administration" of their population. Before independence in 1990, the wildlife of their area was purposefully depleted by the South West African Department of Nature Conservation and various sub rosa operations of the South African Defence Force. Overexploited by hunters and trophy-seeking safari companies, wildlife also died by the hundreds as a result of fences that were erected in total disregard of game migrations.

Drought, too, took its toll on the wildlife of Nyae Nyae during this period, with a very dry spell from 1981 to 1988 followed by a brief respite before another drought. Around the time of independence, tourists in unmanageable numbers flocked to Nyae Nyae, and the Ju/'hoansi became anxious about threats to their game posed by careless campers and campfires built near key waterholes and pans. At the same time, however, Namibian independence, with its breath of fresh political air and sense of opportunity for marginalized communities to develop in their own way, brought home to the Ju/'hoansi the challenge of constructing a brighter future.

Perhaps the most galvanizing aspect of both the problems and the possibilities confronting the Ju/'hoansi, however, was the threat of the loss of the land base posed by alternative economic models and incoming interests. These included both conservation efforts that excluded the presence of people and pastoral encroachment on the relatively unspoiled grazing of Nyae Nyae.

The Challenge of Creating an Egalitarian Society

To understand the challenges that the Ju/'hoan people, and other small-scale groups like them, are facing in managing their resources in new, nation-state contexts, we must look briefly at the social characteristics of their traditional society. Although there is substantial disagreement among scholars about the degree of economic isolation in which the Ju/'hoansi have lived over the last 2,000 years, the immensely detailed environmental information at their command would itself alone argue for a substantially independent foraging existence, one consonant with certain social concepts and forms that are by now well-known to anthropology. These elements include the absence of hierarchical leadership and the presence of pervasive power-sharing mechanisms; sharing and leveling as important social technologies to spread resource access; general sexual egalitarianism and complementarity of economic roles; nurturant and permissive child-rearing and a lack of ageism; ad hoc leadership characterized by facilitative rather than autocratic roles; sapiential authority in an information-intensive economy; democratic inclusion of personal opinion in consensual decision-making; stewardship, rather than ownership, of land; communication and healing skills viewed as multiplied rather than divided by social sharing; and the absence of activity specialization in favor of flexibility, which generally accompanies a hunting-gathering economy. Although much of Ju/'hoan society is in transition to a mixed-subsistence economy, the hunter-gatherer habits of the past are still very much in evidence in areas relating to economic organization, authority, and decision-making.

In confronting the recent need to develop a wider social form than the extended family group in which these characteristics were embedded, the Ju/'hoansi face a number of cultural problems. These include an ideological and practical difficulty with the concept of representation in government. In their small, face-to-face groupings, they had always followed the principle that if each person's opinion was not physically heard, there would eventually be trouble. Sometimes this concern was expressed in an idiom of health: it was said that repressed opinions could create sickness. This traditional tolerance of each person's views, including those of women, youth, and elders, has given rise to practical problems in new contexts. When the JFU/NNFC began in 1986, its general meetings at first consisted of hundreds of people, and the meetings went on for many days. In later years, this problem has been alleviated somewhat, partly through the availability of new models besides the hierarchical ones of the Ju/'hoansi's neighbors. As part of their ongoing self-analysis, the Ju/'hoansi have sought the means to deal with many new decisions in increasingly smaller amounts of time.

One of the major problems confronting the JFU/NNFC has been the "tall poppy syndrome," the propensity for traditional community members to fear standing out from the crowd due to the social censure directed at those who self-aggrandize. A correlate of this attitude, of course, is a difficulty in getting individuals to stand out in any way or to commit themselves publicly to a course of action before a general poll is taken. Yet both stands have become necessary in the course of consolidating community strength and entering national politics in Namibia.

The Ju/'hoansi eventually solved these problems—and the fear of institutions and of leaving out people's opinions—by opting for government by committee. The history of the people's organization that will unfold in later chapters in this book details the discovery process and changes in leadership since the formation of the Ju/wa Farmers Union in 1986, which became the Nyae Nyae Farmers Cooperative in 1989 and the Nyae Nyae Conservancy in 1998.

In both apartheid and black governments in southern Africa, it was often said that San people, having no traditional headmen, must therefore be incapable of governing themselves. Indeed, the forms of headmanship or chieftainship that have been made familiar by pastoral and agricultural societies do not characterize leadership in the Ju/'hoansi or other recently studied hunting-gathering groups. Instead of hereditary headmen with status and wealth exceeding those of others, as in stratified societies, San groups have leaders who lead rather by virtue of a combination of genealogical ties to resource areas and personal qualities that may arise in individuals—qualities that are not necessarily passed on to heirs. In the case of the Ju/'hoansi, both of these traditional sources of authority are being creatively extended in the development of new leadership patterns. Similarly, and in a closely related development, creative extension is being made of the traditional resource management rules. In the chapters to follow, we look at the pressures that caused social and resource management rules to change rapidly in Nyae Nyae after 1986 and the often innovative ways that the Ju/'hoansi responded to them.

Chapter Three

The Ju/'hoan People's Organization and Its Foundation

≋✿≋

In discussing changes that occurred in Nyae Nyae after the formation of the Ju/wa Farmers Union, we must remember that, compared to other completely dispossessed San people of southern Africa, the Ju/'hoansi were in a fortunate situation. Unlike thousands of other San, they had managed to hold onto at least a fragment of their former hunting and gathering territory. In this they were aided, ironically, by the apartheid system itself: separate development meant that communal land was set aside for them, to keep them in isolation. Although this system reduced their traditional territory and prevented them from developing normal economic ties to the outside world, it had the positive effect of protecting their environment from overgrazing and, to some extent, from overhunting.

Thus, as early as 1950, the approximately 1,200 Ju/'hoansi in the Nyae Nyae region of then South West Africa were some of the only San people able to support themselves solely by hunting and gathering, which they could do because their environment was largely an enclave apart from cattle herders. All other San in Namibia, including Ju/'hoansi who lived outside of Nyae Nyae, were dispossessed, and most had been so for at least three generations. Without land or rights to land on which to farm and produce subsistence, and without work in a declining and increasingly mechanized ranching economy, most San wandered from farm to farm in small groups, in search of occasional jobs or relatives with jobs and rations to share. Many of these San, including Ju/'hoansi in areas such as the white-controlled Gobabis farming district south of Nyae Nyae, were dying at a young age of hunger and malnutrition. Other San managed to support themselves in northern Namibia and Botswana with a mixed subsistence—livestock and seasonal cultivation combined with uneasy hunting and gathering on lands that were not their own (Cassidy et al. 2001; Hitchcock et al. 2006a; Robins, Madzudzo, and Brenzinger 2001; Saugestad 2001; Suzman 2001a, 2001b, 2002)—but their lives were dominated by insecurity and by prejudice from white and black neighbors alike.

As mentioned previously, Bushmanland was established by the South West Africa Administration (SWAA) in 1970, although it was not proclaimed until 1976. It was to be the only homeland for the people classified as "Bushmen," a "wastebasket" category in the country at that time into which people of mixed or uncertain parentage were regularly "dumped" for administrative convenience. The Ju/'hoansi lost most of the Nyae Nyae region and all but one of their permanent waters. Southern Nyae Nyae, including the major water at G/am, was given by SWAA to the Herero (it became Hereroland East). Northern Nyae Nyae, including the waters of Tco/'ana (Sigaretti) and Samangaigai, was incorporated into Kavango and later proclaimed the Kaudum Game Reserve. Western Bushmanland—two-thirds of the proclaimed homeland—is mantled in deep sand and waterless forest. This environment has always been relatively unfit for human habitation, although it was utilized for foraging purposes. Today, except in parts of the Omatako Valley (a dry riverbed with water deep beneath it that can be drilled in some places), people in Western Bushmanland live only at boreholes on former military bases or in communities that have water points.

In the absence of bush foods and game, San people could not support themselves by hunting and gathering while they developed subsistence farming. After 1970, the Ju/'hoansi were left with about 6,000 square kilometers of communal land in Eastern Bushmanland (which is the equivalent of Nyae Nyae), where at most about 170 people could support themselves by hunting and gathering. The "Old Way" economy, about which John Marshall's sister Elizabeth Marshall Thomas wrote in her 2006 book, *The Old Way: A Story of the First People,* permanently collapsed.

The rights of access to water and other resources, as traditionally shared among the Ju/'hoansi through the *n!ore* system, had depended upon sufficient land to provide these materials. Once the traditional area of Nyae Nyae was substantially decreased, it was no longer possible for Ju/'hoansi to support their population solely by hunting and gathering. They needed a more intensive form of economy to add to foraging, which remained their fail-safe. The story of the attempt to do this by the Ju/'hoansi, through their Ju/wa Farmers Union and its successors (supported by the Ju/wa Bushman Development Foundation and its successors) is the subject of John Marshall's extraordinary films of this period, including *N!ai: The Story of a !Kung Woman* (1979), *Pull Ourselves Up or Die Out* (1985), and *To Hold Our Ground* (1990).

The obstacles encountered by the Ju/'hoansi as they tried to provide a mixed subsistence for themselves were charted by John Marshall, Charles Hartung,

Claire Ritchie, and later Megan Biesele in position papers, grant proposals, and requests for government cooperation written in the late 1980s under the auspices of the Ju/wa Bushman Development Foundation (JBDF). These papers are priceless documents for anthropologists and historians, particularly since under the South West African regime, which still practiced apartheid, most foreign researchers either did not choose to work in the country or were denied entrance if they did. Thus, there is heavy reliance in the rest of this chapter on internal JBDF documents as the sole source of uncensored information available about Nyae Nyae prior to independence. These papers and reports outline both the problems and the options that some concerned outsiders foresaw for the Ju/'hoansi at the time.

In *Ju/wa Farming in Eastern Bushmanland: Problems and Recommendations*, Hartung and Marshall (1988) wrote about the JBDF's attempt to help the Ju/'hoansi develop subsistence farming:

> Several problems [were] encountered by the Ju/wasi, their Union and Foundation. The problems [arose] largely from opposition by the Department of Nature Conservation to Ju/wa farming in Eastern Bushmanland; from exceptional difficulties Ju/wasi experience in obtaining licenses for rifles to protect themselves and their livestock from lions and other predators; from [the] inability to benefit commercially from farming and collectively from the resources of their land. Ju/wasi cannot sell their cattle on the Namibian/South African market because of the Red Line [the quarantine fence ostensibly erected to protect commercial cattle herds from diseases like hoof-and-mouth carried by game populations, but actually built to protect white economic interests]. They cannot benefit directly for agricultural development from trophy hunting because the license fees go into the Central Fund, [since] Ju/wa communal land rights are not recognized by the Government. Ju/wasi are under constant threat of dispossession (e.g. for 10 years by the proclamation of a game reserve until Minister A. Shipanga stopped it in 1986) from lack of representation. Despite an active local government in the Ju/wa Farmers Union, Ju/wasi are neither represented in the Government nor adequately consulted about government decisions concerning their land, their resources and their future.

Hartung and Marshall continued:

> [A] mixed economy simply means that some family members farm on communal lands, producing a subsistence and engaging in limited commerce, while others work for wages or go to school. Neither subsistence farming nor wage-work alone can support the majority of Namibians today. Subsistence self-sufficiency is impossible ... The mixed economy depends on communal lands where relatively large numbers of people can produce a subsistence in contrast to commercial farming in which large areas of land support a single family and a few laborers ... Ju/wasi are committed to the mixed economy by necessity and choice. They are not pastoralists. They do not have the time or inclination to evolve the social and religious patterns

of a culture based on cattle (e.g. like Herero people). The Ju/wa farming economy will not be based on owning vast herds for social and religious purposes.

Ju/wasi regard cattle as economic assets providing milk and beef for subsistence, and as a source of money if/when they can sell some of their stock. Their farming will thrive in Eastern Bushmanland if they can participate in the commercial economy. This is important. It means that on their fragment of land a significant number of Ju/wasi can support themselves with small herds by the mixed economy without massive grazing pressure.

Hartung and Marshall's arguments rang true at the time, and they continue to do so today. There are ongoing debates about the degree to which the Ju/'hoansi should focus their energies on livestock production and agriculture and on wildlife-related activities, but there were a number of Ju/'hoansi who in the 1980s agreed with the general positions taken by Hartung and Marshall.

Establishment of the Ju/wa Bushman Development Foundation

With these careful justifications for promoting a mixed economy in Eastern Bushmanland in place, the JBDF was started by John Marshall, Claire Ritchie, several Namibians living in Windhoek, and several Ju/'hoansi, with a legacy from John's father, Laurence K. Marshall. The need was dire. In 1981, there were 920 Ju/'hoansi living in the rural slum at Tsumkwe with few jobs and no subsistence resources. There were 30 births and 31 deaths that year; the deaths included 9 out of 12 babies born in three government housing projects. The JBDF was initiated, wrote Marshall and Hartung (1986: 23), "to help Ju/'hoansi get out of [Tsumkwe], start farming on their *n!oresi* and survive."

Cattle, tools, and materials were purchased with income from the original Cattle Fund. The plan for the JBDF was formalized in May 1981, and John Marshall discussed it with members of several communities (/Aotcha, //Auru, and //Auru Ma). The information spread, and people began seeking access to cattle, donkeys, and goats. As Ritchie (1987: 65) notes, the principal goals of the foundation, whose motto was "Helping people to help themselves," were to help raise funds to assist Ju/'hoansi in developing subsistence farming communities and to work as a lobbying group to help protect Bushmanland. One of the problems that the Ju/'hoansi faced was a lack of experience in dealing with the media and with higher-level government administrators. The JBDF helped people, on the one hand, by publicizing their situation and, on the other, by serving as a kind of community liaison and advocacy body. One government administrator described the foundation as a go-between, sharing information about local people's opinions and desires with the government and helping to explain the government's plans to the Ju/'hoansi.

The most important constraint facing those Ju/'hoansi who wished to return to their *n!oresi* was access to water. In some cases, there were no boreholes in their areas. In other cases, boreholes existed but lacked pumps. Many of these boreholes had been drilled by the Department of Nature Conservation (DNC), and the administration was reluctant to allow people to establish themselves and their herds at these places. In a number of cases, the Ju/'hoansi were denied permission to install new pumps or repair existing ones.

The Cattle Fund worked hand in hand with the Ju/'hoansi in setting up the farming communities. The number of farming settlements began to grow, although there were complications, including problems such as elephants destroying pumps and officials telling people that they could not stay on government boreholes. In spite of the difficulties, people constructed kraals and gardens in a number of localities in Eastern Bushmanland. As John Marshall (1989: 53) points out, "Experience with the Cattle Fund showed that a few thousand dollars for additional cattle, basic tools, and equipment such as hand pumps and wire was enough to help Ju/'hoansi develop a viable subsistence in stable communities."

In early 1981, Ju/'hoansi made several short trips from Tsumkwe to their traditional territories. By March 1981, a kraal had been started at /Aotcha, but the project proceeded only by fits and starts. The /Aotcha people moved out to their *n!ore* several times, returning to Tsumkwe when fires burned down their kraal and affected the grazing. One of the factors that motivated people to move away from Tsumkwe, according to informants, was the opening of a liquor store with funding derived from a government loan. The expanded availability of alcohol exacerbated already existing social tensions. Returning to their *n!oresi*, therefore, was seen by Ju/'hoansi as a way to alleviate conflict while at the same time re-establishing occupancy rights in the face of the threat of the proposed game reserve. As Ritchie (1988: 36) notes, people made the decision to leave Tsumkwe "to regain their independence and self-sufficiency."

The decentralization trends among the Ju/'hoansi were enhanced in the early 1980s by a desire on the part of local people to establish a mixed economy and secure their rights to land and natural resources. Ritchie (1987: 63) stresses that the idea to move back to their *n!oresi* came from the people themselves. It was facilitated in part by lengthy discussions among the residents of Tsumkwe. Some Ju/'hoansi referred to a kind of push-pull process. Tsumkwe was an unpleasant place to be, which provided the push factor, while the pull came from their *n!oresi*, described by a Ju/'hoan man as "the places where our ancestors were buried and where we could live in contentment."

In 1982, several communities moved out of Tsumkwe to /Aotcha, N=aqmtjoha, N=anemh, Mashorro, and Xamsa, although the residents of the last two gave up and returned to Tsumkwe within three months. The process of adjusting to life in the dispersed settlements was not easy. In some cases, government officials tried to convince people to remain in Tsumkwe; in other cases, they went so far as to actually shut down boreholes. There were internal difficulties, as well. Conflicts occurred in some of the communities, especially /Aotcha, where there was a general feeling that there were too many spongers and that the set-up was top-heavy (Ritchie 1992: 8). Disagreements also arose over matters concerning access to livestock, the disposition of bulls, and which families were to go to the various *n!oresi*.

In spite of the difficulties, three Ju/'hoan communities were established in their traditional areas by 1982. One of them, /Aotcha, had 119 people and 101 cattle. A second, N=aqmtjoha, had 60 people and 9 cattle, while a third, N=anemh, had 33 people and 7 cattle (Marshall and Ritchie 1984: 149, 151, table 12). There were vast differences between these dispersed communities and Tsumkwe. First of all, the population densities of the former were much lower. Secondly, the degree to which foods that had been obtained through foraging contributed to the diet was much greater in the decentralized settlements. Ritchie (1987: 64) estimates that wild foods made up 20 percent of the diet, livestock products 15–20 percent, and gardening 30 percent, with the remainder coming from foods purchased or obtained from government or military sources. Thus, the members of the farming communities had a more balanced and nutritious diet than did the people in Tsumkwe, who depended much more heavily on maize meal as a staple part of their subsistence.

The period 1980–1986 in Nyae Nyae paralleled the "outstation movement" that took place after World War II among the Aboriginal people of Australia, who left farms and sheep stations and returned to their ancestral lands (Coombs, Dexter, and Hiatt 1982; Young 1995). These years saw the departure of the first three re-formed *n!ore* groups for their traditional areas in the hope of securing a self-sufficient future. Over the next six years, some 500 Ju/'hoansi left Tsumkwe to re-establish *n!oresi* in Nyae Nyae. By 1987 there were 10 settlements containing 342 Ju/'hoansi at places such as /Aotcha, Xamsa, and N=ama. This number increased substantially in the period 1989–1991, when the Nyae Nyae Development Foundation (the successor to the JBDF) undertook the majority of its borehole drilling efforts. By early 1992, there were more than 30 settlements in the Nyae Nyae region, each with its own water source, with a combined population of over 1,000 (with the addition of other new settlers from the Gobabis farms area). Currently, the Ju/'hoansi are inhabitants of 36 rural communities. These communities demonstrate the ability of the Ju/'hoansi to hold onto the land and show a substantial presence and willingness to retake control of local natural resources. All along, their goal has been to establish a mixed-subsistence economic pattern to counter the recent shrinkage of their land base.

The year 1984 was a turning point for the Ju/'hoansi in their efforts to assert their land and water rights. An incident occurred at //Auru in which Ju/'hoansi who had installed a hand pump refused to leave when asked by SWAA officials to do so. They insisted that //Auru was Ju/'hoan land and that the water and the pump belonged to them. They also pointed out that the JBDF was assisting them, rather than being in charge of the activities in Eastern Bushmanland. Subsequently, three Ju/'hoan communities submitted requests to the attorney general in which they stated their desire to return to their traditional areas in order to live there.

After these events, according to John Marshall (cited in Ritchie 1992: 18), a new atmosphere could be felt in the communities outside Tsumkwe, evidence that a sense of strength, place, and solidarity existed. The political consciousness of some of the Ju/'hoansi, including community leaders, was on the rise, and the seeds of what became the Ju/wa Farmers Union were sown, as the desire of the Ju/'hoansi for self-determination intensified. More groups applied for land, and more new settlements were established.

Establishment of a Ju/'hoan People's Organization

Between 1984 and 1988, the Ju/wa Bushman Development Foundation evolved into a non-profit association based in Windhoek, with a Namibian board of trustees. It received grants from Namibian, South African, European, and American donors for its salaries and direct expenses. One of its most important functions was mentoring the people's organization, the Ju/wa Farmers Union (JFU), which was established in 1986 and whose membership was composed of all the Ju/'hoansi who were involved in farming in Eastern Bushmanland. By 1988, the JFU had a council composed of two representatives from each of the then 12 farming communities. The council was unpaid and met relatively regularly.

The JFU received funding for direct development, such as boreholes, pumps, livestock, and tools. It had a Management Committee, and its first chairperson was Tsamkxao =Oma. The JFU and the JBDF had an agreement whereby the latter's staff helped the JFU raise funds and manage affairs that its members had not yet learned to undertake for themselves. All the while, it was the common objective for the JFU to operate independently as soon as possible through education, training, and experience.

From the first, the JFU operated like a local government. It set development policy and distributed development assistance. For example, it decided which groups to help with boreholes, livestock, etc. It communicated, as a body, directly with the government of South West Africa. It elected its officers and resolved disputes by discussion and consensus. This is not to say, of course, that there were no internal disagreements or that the government always consulted with the JFU about matters affecting Nyae Nyae and the Ju/'hoansi.

One of the functions of the JFU was collating information about traditional territorial claims of Ju/'hoansi. By 1986, the genealogical and land claims data showed that there were over 300 named *n!oresi* in all, over 150 of which were claimed through kin ties by living Ju/'hoansi (Ritchie 1987: 20) and some of which could not be settled with farming communities, due to the difficulty of establishing water points. This information was compiled with the assistance of the JBDF and was greatly augmented with help of the JBDF's successor, the Nyae Nyae Development Foundation of Namibia. Subsequently, it formed the basis for a map of the *n!oresi* in Eastern Bushmanland that was used at the National Conference on Land Reform and the Land Question in 1991 (Republic of Namibia 1991).

The JFU aimed to be a participatory organization that also served as a representational body for its members. In October 1986, the Constitution for the JFU was drafted and was discussed at length at a public meeting held in /Aotcha. During the course of the deliberations, a Management Committee for the JFU was elected. The process by which this occurred is best described in the words of Claire Ritchie (1992: 20), an eyewitness to the meeting: "It is clear that people are taking this seriously. [They] feel the importance of what they are doing for themselves. The concept of nominating and voting, especially in public—hands raised for all to see—is alien. Some people vote with their eyes closed, one, sometimes both hands in the air, feeling obviously awkward. Some of the older men refuse to vote. It is painful to pick out one person and repudiate another. In the beginning everyone votes for every candidate." After lengthy discussions and voting, one individual, a young man, was chosen as chairperson of the Management Committee, partly because he was literate and had done well in school. As Ritchie (ibid.) went on to point out, "Ju/'hoansi lay great store by the ability to read and write ... Pieces of paper have great symbolic importance."

According to the Constitution, the JFU membership consisted of all adults over the age of 16 residing in the farming communities in Eastern Bushmanland (JFU 1986: 1). Meetings were held in which dozens and sometimes well over 100 people participated, each putting forth his or her views. Sometimes these meetings would last for days, and according to Ju/'hoan informants, there were so many people speaking at once that at times it was somewhat difficult to follow the discussions. The lack of formal governmental structures among the Ju/'hoansi meant that the move toward representational democracy was something of a challenge. There was a certain discomfort with the idea of specific individuals having the right to speak for others. The egalitarianism inherent in the Ju/'hoan system dictated against individuals accruing power or authority. As a consequence, the leadership issue was of critical concern.

In addition to a Management Committee, the original JFU Constitution provided for a Membership Committee, which would be elected by the members of the Representative Council (JFU 1986: 1). The length of term for Management and Membership Committee members was to be a year, whereas the members of the council were to serve two-year terms. At the same time that council representatives were chosen, the JFU had to ensure that everyone had an equal say about decision-making. Given the consensus-based system of the Ju/'hoansi, it was important that all were able to make their views heard. Sometimes, however, government officials wanted to meet only with representatives of the various farming communities, as was the case with ministers from the new interim government in June 1986. In such cases, at preliminary meetings at the community level, the representatives were able to gauge local opinions, which they drew upon in later meetings.

The discussions in the JFU meetings underscored the significance that people attached to the land and resource rights. The people of Eastern Bushmanland realized full well that the settlements they were establishing represented their best hope for maintaining access to a portion of their ancestral territory. They also recognized that they needed an organization to represent them in their dealings with the government on land issues. There was much discussion about the importance of forming a representational organization to work on their behalf.

The Ju/'hoansi continued to have meetings in 1986–1987 to discuss the issues of land rights and the establishment of settlements. Tsamkxao =Oma, the JFU chairperson, pointed out that the people in Eastern Bushmanland did not want outsiders coming in and telling them how to use their land; rather, they wanted to make their own decisions about land allocation. Another member of the JFU, /Ui G/aq'o, noted in a meeting at Tsumkwe in late 1986, "This isn't just us here speaking. I know that all Ju/'hoansi around think the same way—to hurry up and help, and help us build up our *n!oresi*. That's the only way we will have any strength to build up our life, our future."

The Ju/wa Farmers Union and the South West Africa Administration

Government policies and non-recognition of San added to what was rapidly becoming bureaucratic domination of the Ju/'hoansi from every conceivable angle (Hitchcock and Holm 1993). It was obvious that the intention of the DNC was to crush Ju/'hoan farming and community life in Eastern Bushmanland, not only with the above punitive measures, but also by increasing the number of elephants. People became afraid to go out hunting and gathering, or even to fetch water, due to the unprecedented number of new elephants in the region. The DNC also promoted uncontrolled growth of the lion population.

Perhaps even more insidious was a government policy that officially classified about 32,000 highly diverse people in Namibia as Bushmen. Regardless of their actual ethnicities, they were placed in a wastebasket category, which was the only so-called ethnic group without a "second tier" or "ethnic" government of any kind. Of the various ethnic homelands, Bushmanland (proclaimed in 1976 as a homeland around the same time as the creation of the wastebasket category) was the only one held in trust by SWAA and the only land on which Bushmen were allowed to settle. Since Western Bushmanland was waterless, Eastern Bushmanland was the only habitable portion of Bushmanland.

At any time, the government could allow, encourage, or facilitate the settlement in Eastern Bushmanland of large numbers of people who had been classified by SWAA as Bushmen. Among those who could be relocated into Eastern Bushmanland were 8,000 Angolan Bushman mercenary soldiers and their families, whose geographical, economic, linguistic, and cultural backgrounds were hugely disparate from those of the Ju/'hoansi. These Angolans had been displaced while serving in two wars, first under the Portuguese colonizers of Angola, and then under the white South African-dominated South African Defence Force (SADF), which was battling forces of the South West Africa People's Organization (SWAPO) in northern Namibia and Angola. These desperate, brutalized people, who came from a more agricultural background than the Ju/'hoansi and who possessed guns, could rapidly decrease the number of lions, elephants, and other animals in the region. Under this policy, which would diminish the Ju/'hoansi's hunting-gathering resources, the Ju/'hoansi themselves could be easily overwhelmed and displaced.

Further, through the 1980s, SWAA made no effort to acknowledge Ju/'hoan traditional communal land rights in Eastern Bushmanland. Nor did it intend to recognize or establish any form of Ju/'hoan local government that would have authority over Eastern Bushmanland and control over its resources. Basically, SWAA believed that it could settle whomever it liked in the area and could dispose of the region's resources without consulting the local people, who had been its stewards for millennia.

Administrative Reorganization and Rhetorical Confusion

In the late 1980s, a new Constitution was being promoted in South West Africa that would, to all intents and purposes, eliminate homelands by including them in newly created administrative districts. Bushmanland was to fall under a district that would encompass Hereroland, part of Gobabis, and part of Grootfontein. With neither local government nor recognized tenure, the Ju/'hoansi would remain a despised minority, and their land would be easily expropriated. The new dispensation was apparently based on deliberately fostered disinformation: that "local" government is the same as "ethnic" government and that "communal lands" are the same as "homelands" (see also Ritchie and Marshall 1988: 3–5).

In fact, of course, communal tenure was the legitimate, historically established tenure of black peoples in South West Africa where they had kept part of their lands after the onslaught of white commercial and governmental expropriation. Homelands, as products of apartheid policy and enactment, recognized nobody's land rights; the land belonged to the national (white) government. Established to expropriate non-white people's land and to deny non-white people national citizenship, homelands were simply imposed on the lands where these people lived. Communal tenure had historical legitimacy; homelands had none. Government recognition or denial of traditional communal tenure had nothing whatsoever to do with either the erection or the dismantling of homelands.

By fostering confusion between communal tenure and homelands, and by promoting the rhetoric of abolishing homelands so "everybody can live wherever they want" (without providing sufficient opportunities or the means to do so), while refusing to recognize communal tenure, the government was simply acquiring the "legal" (as opposed to justifiable or ethically legitimate) means to continue to expropriate black people's lands. Communal lands were to be divided up into "commercial" units. A few rich Namibians, foreigners, and foreign investors would own Namibia. Hundreds of thousands would be dispossessed.

The disinformation was deepened by equating local and ethnic government. Local government was based on residence and meant what it said—that people who live in a place have a measure of control over their land and resources. Ethnic government, then called the "second tier," was based on spurious classifications. All the people classified as an ethnic group—whatever their background and interests, wherever they resided, and however they made their living—were ruled and represented by officials based in Windhoek who could not possibly have local constituencies' interests at heart. Where the Ju/'hoansi and Eastern Bushmanland were concerned, 32,000 totally disparate, scattered people defined as Bushmen would "vote" on the disposition of Bushmanland under an ethnic or second tier government. As Ritchie and Marshall (1988) put it, the Ju/'hoansi "would be dispossessed of Eastern Bushmanland without a sound."

However, no ethnic or national government was going to expropriate the communal land of—and thereby risk losing the backing of—600,000 Ovambo, 100,000 Herero, 100,000 Damara, 60,000 Kavango, 60,000 Nama, or any of the other 135,000 people living under communal tenure at that time. When the powers of the president of South Africa, as the trustee of native lands in South West Africa, were transferred to the SWAA administrator general in 1977, and then to the second tier or ethnic authorities in 1980, jurisdiction over Bushmanland and the people classified as Bushman remained vested in the Department of Governmental Affairs in the central government, their appointed ethnic authority. With no representation whatsoever, the Ju/'hoansi and Eastern Bushmanland were the country's only feasible targets left for expropriation.

Mentoring the JFU for Area-Wide Cooperation

Pervasive pressure and fear defined Ju/'hoan circumstances in Nyae Nyae when John Marshall and Claire Ritchie invited Megan Biesele to South West Africa in 1987 to consider the position of project director for the Ju/wa Bushman Development Foundation. Biesele had been working for some years with Botswana Ju/'hoansi for the Botswana government in a posting funded by Lorna Marshall via the Kalahari Peoples Fund (KPF).

Biesele came to work in Nyae Nyae in 1988, after the JFU was started and when the *n!ore* reorganization plan promoted by the JBDF was in full swing. She benefited from the massive background experience that Marshall, Ritchie, and their associates had gained in their many years of confrontation with agencies of the South West Africa government in the Nyae Nyae area. The degree of threat was huge and palpable. The situation seemed one of permanent crisis, and the pace of both the JBDF's challenge and the government's response to their challenge was breathless. JBDF was at once working furiously to help Ju/'hoansi establish a visible economic presence on their land and fighting the forces of ignorance, avarice, and anger that seemed to drive government policies where Ju/'hoansi were concerned.

The JBDF had been working closely with the fledgling JFU to establish the 20 farming communities that were initially planned for Eastern Bushmanland, 8 more than the 12 that were in existence by 1988. The JBDF believed that 6 to 10 more communities would add enough demographic, economic, and social strength to retain the land and establish a local government. While the main work of the JBDF at this time was practical and promotional, the main work of the Ju/'hoansi seemed to be hammering out *among themselves* the new social understandings by which they would strive to hold onto their land and its resources and their ability to make decisions about their own affairs.

The duties of the JBDF's two previous co-project directors, Charles Hartung and Adrian Strong, had been growing exponentially with the continuing state of emergency in Nyae Nyae. They had been tasked with establishing additional farming communities and protecting the gardens, livestock, and water infrastructure against elephants and lions. Now a stepped-up lobbying effort and press campaign were seen as necessary, along with fund-raising and on-the-ground management of the interlocking elements of a complex rural development project.

Biesele's first assignment on arrival for work in July 1988 was recording the ear-tagging of JFU cattle at the various *n!oresi*. This job, carried out inside dusty and dangerous kraals full of charging cattle, was practical in the extreme, and it also fully engaged the Ju/'hoan language ability for which Biesele had been hired. At the same time, Marshall made it clear that Biesele's real work was to be of a much more subtle and profound nature. He wisely saw that the Ju/'hoansi were undergoing changes in the span of a single generation that other peoples of the world had taken hundreds or thousands of years to process, and that what they needed was a kind of "talk therapy" to aid them in comprehending and bringing about the necessary transformations. Marshall told Biesele that her most important task was to listen and facilitate as the Ju/'hoansi struggled with themselves and with each other to remake their social understandings.

Nyae Nyae and the Nation

With the mentoring of the JBDF, the Ju/'hoansi had also started to expand their activities from the *n!oresi* and kin networks of Nyae Nyae to a national level in order to protect their interests. Partly in response to this perceived "community organizing," a commissioner of Bushman Affairs had been appointed by SWAA, and a Bushman Advisory Council had been formed. The JFU had managed, through negotiations with this council and by virtue of their renewed, economically active presence on the land, to diminish the threat of a game reserve in Eastern Bushmanland. During 1987, confrontation and negotiation with SWAA, over issues ranging from social services to natural resource management, began in earnest.

It was conflict over the Ju/'hoan people's control of the wildlife resources of Nyae Nyae that had, in 1987 and 1988, finally initiated their general politicization. The JFU confronted many issues with the DNC in those years, and the JBDF made earnest attempts to explain, and to advocate for, the Ju/'hoansi's involvement in decision-making about their livelihoods, land, and future. The decades-long relationship of the Marshalls with Nyae Nyae families, the careful filmmaking efforts of John Marshall, and, starting in 1987, the sound recordings and translations made by Biesele of the formal meetings that the Ju/'hoansi held among themselves and with outside entities—all of these elements worked together to help Ju/'hoan voices be heard on a national level as never before. In 1987 and 1988, three of the main topics at these meetings were cooperative principles and internal governance, relationships with SWAA, and the use of Nyae Nyae's wildlife.

The highly emotional wildlife resource issue served to focus the Ju/'hoansi's attention on the dual necessity of better community governance and improved communication with SWAA about economic planning. Tsamkxao =Oma and other Ju/'hoan leaders had already established a long-term relationship with the then minister of conservation and natural resources, Andreas Shipanga. By 1986, when the JFU was formed, Minister Shipanga had helped the Ju/'hoansi to begin to feel safe from the threat of a game reserve on their land. In early 1988, a safari hunting concession for Nyae Nyae was granted to Anvo Hunting

Safaris by SWAA. The JFU believed licensing fees from the concession would come to them for Nyae Nyae development.

Under this concession, which allowed trophy hunting in Eastern Bushmanland, R78,000 (about US$30,000 at the time) in licensing fees was paid to the central fund of the government. The fact that this comparatively huge sum remained in SWAA coffers and did not make its way to Nyae Nyae, despite what the JFU thought was an understanding with Minister Shipanga, sparked a controversy between the Ju/'hoansi and the DNC that was to go on for many years. In fact, for a time before independence it became the single most disputed and heatedly discussed area of outside interaction for the Ju/'hoan people. This controversy and the incursions on people's privacy, food resources, and drinking water by the SADF, who were massed in the area to fight SWAPO in Angola, provided flash points that led to the increasingly political rhetoric used by Ju/'hoansi in meetings during the years just prior to independence.

Central to discussions both within the Ju/'hoan communities and between Ju/'hoansi and outsiders were the linked issues of conservation and economic planning for the future of Nyae Nyae. Could people whose past and traditions were steeped in detailed hunting and gathering knowledge of their once-extensive *n!oresi* make the economic changes that would allow them—in the face of many threats—to hold onto their remaining land and reliably feed their children?

The JBDF and the Establishment of the Nyae Nyae Farmers Cooperative

In 1978, the United Nations Security Council adopted Resolution 435 in support of the transition to independence for South West Africa from its status as an illegal mandate of South Africa. The long history of South West Africa as an apartheid-era "stepchild" of the white controlled, monolithically powerful, and racially troubled South African state made this resolution seem, from the perspective of the Ju/'hoan and other San peoples, completely impossible to implement. The UN decision had taken place far away on an unimaginable international stage, and people who had spent their lives at the bottom of the apartheid ladder had few illusions that independence would ever come to pass or affect their lives for the better. Nevertheless, a decade later, as the UN resolution moved closer to being implemented, the Ju/'hoansi and their allies, along with other marginalized national groups, now began pro-actively to refer to the country in which they lived as "Namibia."

The Ju/'hoansi continued to fight locally to preserve their rights to hunt and to manage the game and veld food resources on which their lives depended. Outreach was made to Botswana Ju/'hoansi, who began to consider moving back to the *n!oresi* that they had vacated in South West Africa/Namibia when the international fence was constructed in 1965. There was considerable cross-border movement by Ju/'hoansi in the 1970s and 1980s, something allowed by both Namibia and Botswana.

A number of events and meetings in 1987 affected Nyae Nyae both nationally and internationally. When Biesele made her initial visit that year, she was joined by ethnographic filmmaker Timothy Asch and anthropologist Robert Hitchcock. Asch went on to help make John Marshall's body of work a masterpiece of ethnographic film, and Hitchcock laid the groundwork to return later to make a professional assessment for the Ford Foundation of the JBDF's relationship with the people of Nyae Nyae (Hitchcock 1992). Biesele began, during that first trip, to make the recordings of community meetings and interviews that eventually became the Nyae Nyae Tape Archive.[1]

Also that year, the late Braam le Roux, accompanied by his wife Willemien, visited from Botswana to share ideas before starting a Botswana organization similar to the JBDF. Their Kuru Development Trust, broadened later into the Kuru Family of Organizations, has been a consistent ally and partner to the JBDF and JFU, and to the KPF in the US, which has continued to support community endeavors in both countries. In May 1987, Regopstaan of the Kruiper family of =Khomani San at Welkom, South Africa, was driven to Nyae Nyae by a tour operator, and contact was begun in that way with a San group located far across another international border. During July, three meetings in Tsumkwe in the course of two days underscored the ever closer approach of national political events in Namibia to the once isolated Nyae Nyae.

On 21 July 1987, the South West Africa Agriculture Ministry convened an informational meeting that, for the first time, included Ju/'hoan people as the official spokespersons for their own environment and economy. On 22 July, coinciding with a JFU meeting held in Tsumkwe, the Democratic Turnhalle Alliance (DTA), the major conservative political party, held a meeting to recruit Ju/'hoan followers and to turn them against SWAPO, which was still in exile but beginning, after the UN Security Council ruling about transition, to make plans to return home. It was clear that the Ju/'hoansi, a small but not insignificant number of people in a sparsely populated country, were to be wooed as potential voters. The need for an official body to represent the Ju/'hoansi at political assemblies, where gifts of T-shirts and *braaivleis* (South African barbecue) were handed out, and to inform the Ju/'hoan constituency about the platforms of the various political parties became more and more clear. This need dovetailed well with the purposes of the JFU.

---

1. These recordings have all been digitized, with community permission, and are in the process of transcription by the Ju/'hoan Transcription Group, as described in chapter 10.

By 1988, the complexity of the issues facing the JFU prompted the formalization and institutionalization of its organizational structure; it needed nothing less than to remake itself as a de facto people's governing body for Nyae Nyae. The JBDF and the JFU worked in tandem to refine the idea of the JFU and brought it into a nationally recognizable form in late 1988 as the Nyae Nyae Farmers Cooperative (NNFC). The word "cooperative" was chosen because SWAPO leaders advised about the importance of the cooperative movement that was taking place in other parts of Namibia. The JBDF and JFU agreed that cooperative principles most closely defined what was needed in Nyae Nyae. Representatives from the JFU visited Paul Vleermuis, one of the founders of the cooperative movement in Windhoek and the leader of the Namibia Community Cooperatives Alliance, and learned how to apply this organization's experiences to their own situation.

After lengthy discussions involving representatives from all the Nyae Nyae *n!oresi*, the NNFC adopted a governing Constitution, written in both Ju/'hoansi and English. During this process, John Marshall had held up for the Ju/'hoansi the model of the US Constitution, and they spent many hours discussing how it might apply to their situation. Eventually, a Constitution was drawn up in the Ju/'hoan language and in English, and the JFU became the Nyae Nyae Farmers Cooperative.

Membership requirements for the NNFC were defined in its Constitution under Section 2, Articles 5 and 6, as "All persons who speak Ju/'hoansi and call themselves Ju/'hoan and who are over the age of 18." Another criterion for membership was that of residence; people who had lived in the area for 10 years could become members. It was also noted that other individuals could apply formally to the council for membership rights. Such a provision was important for those Ju/'hoansi who wanted to come into the area from the Gobabis farms in Namibia or move across the border from Botswana to establish new farming communities.

The Representative Council, outlined in Articles 16 to 23 of the Constitution (see fig. 2), was to include two persons from each community in Nyae Nyae, including "municipal areas" such as Tsumkwe. Required to meet for a three-day period at least once every six months, the council members had the right to select a chairperson and representatives for an Executive Committee, which was to be made up of individuals from "each quarter of Nyae Nyae" (Article 22). In 1988, because of the uncertainty over the status of land in the west, there were only three areas of Nyae Nyae that had representatives on the Executive Committee: the northern area, the central area, and the southern area (JBDF 1988b: 5). A diagrammatic representation of the organizational structure of the NNFC in 1988–1989 is presented in figure 3. At that time, the Executive Committee consisted of a chairperson, a secretary, and three regional representatives.

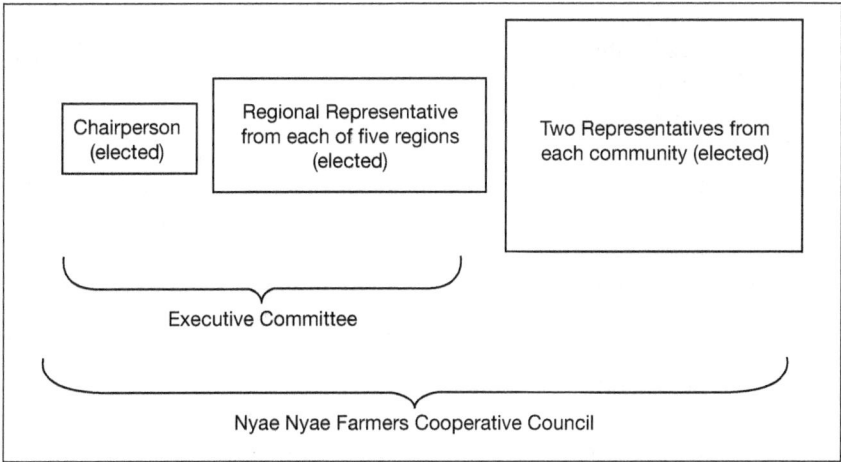

Figure 2 Representative Council, as outlined in the NNFC governing constitution

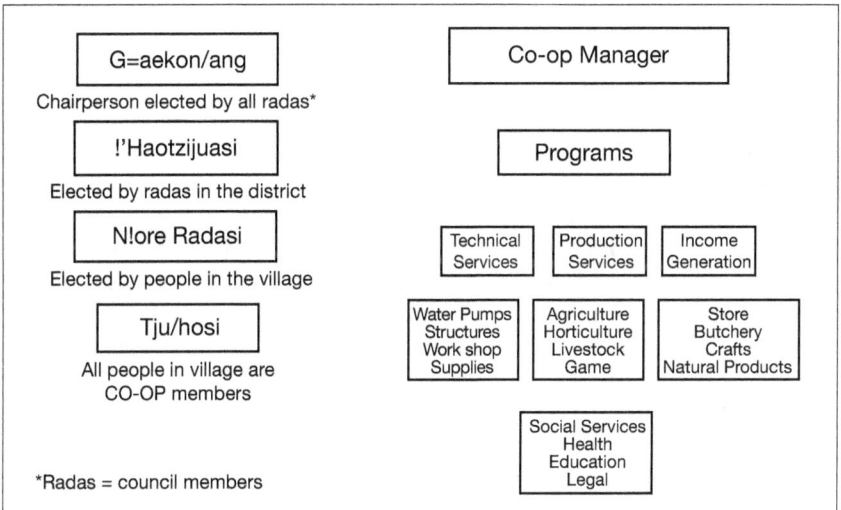

Figure 3 Organizational structure of the NNFC council, 1988–1989

The functions of the council were outlined in the Constitution (Article 20). These included allocating land for farming or other purposes, drilling boreholes, and installing water facilities. There were also provisions relating to conservation and resource management, including the authority to limit or prohibit the hunting of certain species of animals and to prevent the setting of bush fires. As a legally constituted body, the council had the authority to initiate legal action and to receive and manage funds from the government and other sources.

The key policies and priorities of the NNFC and the JBDF were the following: to help as many Ju/wa groups as possible to establish farming communities in Eastern Bushmanland;[2] to help Ju/'hoansi improve their farming and related skills; to help Ju/'hoansi participate as much as possible in the mixed economy through the sale of crafts and other items; and to help Ju/'hoansi, through practical education and training, to manage their affairs and compete realistically in the world in which they live. The goal was to assist, first, Ju/'hoansi who had *n!oresi* in Eastern Bushmanland; then Ju/'hoansi from Nyae Nyae who were dispossessed in 1970 after the Odendaal Commission; and, lastly, Ju/'hoansi who were landless, unemployed, and living in desperate circumstances in neighboring districts.[3] The problems that the Ju/'hoansi faced were identified in 1988 as the following: government opposition, wildlife, predation, trophy hunting, restrictions on farming, land security, and representation.

Government Opposition

Active opposition by the DNC to Ju/'hoan farming included the removal of reservoirs and taps for drinking water. People sometimes had to drink from game troughs, and when there was no wind to turn the windmills, both people and cattle went without water. Government hand pumps that were pulled out by elephants were not restored by the government, and the Ju/'hoansi lacked the tools, such as jackhammers, to do the work themselves. Many communities experienced a series of attempts to dislodge them from their boreholes in favor of letting the water be used by game.

Wildlife

In 1987, the DNC drilled three boreholes—two of them successful—for elephants and other game in the northeast quarter of Eastern Bushmanland. Neither the

---

2. To this end, in 1988, the JFU/NNFC had begun drilling boreholes around which viable *n!ore* groups could settle.

3. With steady, appropriate development on communal land (not a homeland) and the possibility of the Ju/'hoan people participating fully in the mixed economy if/when the Red Line was removed, it was believed that Eastern Bushmanland could support a considerable proportion of the Ju/'hoansi in Namibia. At least one group of "Bushmen" would have a chance to survive and progress.

JFU nor the involved communities were consulted. John Marshall wrote that "it was explained by Mr. Swanepoel, Mr. B. Beytel of Nature Conservation and others that the game waters were provided to draw the elephants in Eastern Bushmanland away from the farming areas in the south. When asked why the elephants couldn't use the waters to travel south as well as north, no adequate explanation was forthcoming" (Hartung and Marshall 1988: 7).

In 1988, government officials stated that Ju/'hoansi should not farm in the region around the game waters and that one community should be moved south. Marshall pointed out that this would in effect be dispossession. The JBDF position was that the boreholes drilled by the DNC were attracting many more elephants than Nyae Nyae could support. In 1986–1987 there were an estimated 600 elephants in Nyae Nyae, and in 2006 Elizabeth Marshall Thomas put the figure at 1,000—a population that was causing terrible problems for the people. To be sure, there were other reasons for the elephants' migration into the Nyae Nyae area, such as "poaching, culling, and loss of habitat resulting in an overcrowded population" (Thomas 2006: 297), but initially, at least, they were attracted by the waters provided by the DNC. The costs of trying to protect water installations and gardens from elephants were prohibitive for small organizations like the JFU, the NNFC, and the JBDF.

Predation

Despite all pressures, including predation, the Ju/'hoan herds grew by 9 percent in 1986. However, fluctuations in predator populations caused significant changes in herd sizes over time. In some years, predation by lions made cattle farming virtually impossible in Nyae Nyae, especially as the Ju/'hoan farmers, unlike other farmers in South West Africa, were prevented by government policy from killing lions in their area. For example, in October 1987, lions killed 19 Ju/'hoan cattle at /Aotcha, a total of 21 percent of the small herd (Hartung and Marshall 1988: 8). The kills were reported to the local DNC officer, who did not attempt to shoot the lions. The attitude of DNC officials was that lions were more valuable to the national economy, via trophy hunting and tourism, than the people (or at least those non-whites who did not contribute a significant percentage of marketable meat products to the national economy) whose herds were being decimated by them.

Ju/'hoansi were unable to obtain licenses to use the few guns given to them, so they resorted to using bows, arrows, and short spears. Several lions were shot using poisoned arrows, with potentially dangerous consequences. One Ju/'hoan man killed two lions with his spear. In 1987, a leopard attacked and wounded three people at one farming community; the people had to kill the leopard with their knives. The official attitude toward allowing Ju/'hoansi to have guns was explained thus: Ju/'hoansi would hunt game indiscriminately if they had guns. The people's long stewardship of their own resources and their effective social methods of sharing were never taken into account.

The Ju/'hoansi were incensed that they were being treated this way. Tsam-kxao =Oma said to Minister Shipanga, "You protect the lions here, so they are like your dogs. If your dog kills my animal, don't you have to pay me for it?"

Trophy Hunting

Trophy hunting could have benefited the Ju/'hoansi, as they would have made excellent guides and natural resource stewards, but in the late 1980s there were several problems with this idea. For one thing, trophy hunting was licensed to a private safari company. To keep making money, wrote Charles Hartung and John Marshall (1988: 9), "It will be in the interest of the company, the Department of Nature Conservation and the Government to maintain and even increase the population of lions and elephants in Eastern Bushmanland." Also, despite assurances from Minister Shipanga and others that the license fees from trophy hunting in their area would go toward the development of Ju/'hoan farming, the fees went into a central government fund and were used according to a priorities list on which agricultural development in Nyae Nyae was at the bottom. Lastly, the decision to allow trophy hunting in Nyae Nyae was made by the government and its cabinet with little or no consultation with the Ju/'hoansi.

As with the threatened proclamation of the game reserve, the people were not adequately informed, had no chance to discuss the complexities, and simply did not know what they were getting into. If Ju/'hoan farming were to be crushed by elephants and predators, Hartung and Marshall (1988: 9) continued, it would "have the same effect as if Ju/'hoansi were dispossessed by the game reserve. The people will not survive."

Restrictions on Farming

In 1986, Minister Shipanga had told members of the JFU and JBDF at Tsumkwe that Ju/'hoansi could settle and farm anywhere in Eastern Bushmanland. Later, there were statements by government officials denying Ju/'hoansi the right to farm within a strip 25 kilometers wide along the Botswana border. This restriction was explained alternatively as necessary for veterinary reasons or for non-disclosable reasons. This bureaucratic obfuscation created a further outcry among the Ju/'hoan communities.

Land Security and Representation

In 1987, the Ju/'hoansi of Nyae Nyae were represented on the national level by an advisory council that had been appointed by the Department of Governmental

Affairs. The council was to give advice to a committee composed of various government departments that claimed an interest in Nyae Nyae. The Ju/'hoansi had no assurance that their interests would take precedence. The only land security that seemed viable at the time was to occupy their land and be seen to be engaged in visible economic activities upon it—essentially, to lay claim to squatter's rights. Hunting and gathering were never visible or esteemed in this context, so settling and farming as quickly as possible became their priority.

In light of the above problems, the JBDF and the JFU had made a number of recommendations in 1987. First, they asked for recognition of land rights in Nyae Nyae. It was a historical fact that Ju/'hoansi and their predecessors had been living in Nyae Nyae for thousands of years. Citing the intention expressed by the then Transitional Government of National Unity toward recognition of communal lands, the JBDF asked for Ju/'hoan land tenure in Nyae Nyae to be recognized nationally.

The JBDF also suggested creating a clear-cut policy on agricultural and conservation matters in Nyae Nyae. JBDF spokespersons pointed out that farming seemed to occupy a lower position on the government's priority list than conservation. They asked for greater community involvement in decision-making and for recognition of the JFU, which had been disregarded by the government since its formation in 1986. The JBDF pointed out the need for development training and education in areas such as water infrastructure maintenance, cattle husbandry, gardening, and tool-making. It also called for informal training at the Agricultural Demonstration Farm near Tsumkwe and for in-service training of local game wardens, to avoid importing people from elsewhere to watch over the Nyae Nyae game populations. It recommended armed local predator control and greatly improved communication channels between Ju/'hoansi and the officials charged with their welfare.

JBDF Development Project Background

At the same time that the JBDF was lobbying SWAA, it was seeking support overseas to aid the Ju/wa Bushman Rural Development Project and its educational component, with the goal of training a cadre of Ju/'hoansi in literacy and practical skills. Specifically, it sought funds to provide for the following: a salary for a project coordinator and manager; continued prospecting and drilling for water; the establishment of communities; protection against elephants and lions; and transportation in order to tie the diverse communities together for mutual information exchange and decision-making.

Beyond the now diminishing prospect of a game reserve, identified threats to tenure and survival included the possibility of expropriation by other groups and by other means. The Ju/'hoansi particularly feared a possible Herero occupation. Also, the JBDF had been asked in June 1986 by the then minister of agriculture, Eben van Zyl, what they would think if 280 "colored" farmers from Namaland in southern Namibia were subsidized to settle in Eastern Bushmanland. Although this question turned out to be rhetorical and the Namaland farmer settlement never materialized, the possibility was devastating to contemplate.

The Herero threat was in fact much closer and had already caused problems from time to time, starting in the 1950s. Herero cattle farmers had established a cattle post at G/am, a traditional Ju/'hoan waterhole only 50 kilometers south of Eastern Bushmanland. G/am was expropriated from the Ju/'hoansi when the entire southern Nyae Nyae region was proclaimed Hereroland East in 1970. The Herero, whose large herds tend to overgraze their land when not managed properly, had sought to occupy the waters and grazing of Eastern Bushmanland. They had invaded Nyae Nyae at least three times in the 1950s and were turned back by police patrols. In 1987, Herero from G/am began visiting and pressing Ju/'hoansi to let them graze their cattle in Eastern Bushmanland. Herero people also actively pressured the government and various political parties—notably, the DTA—to "open" Eastern Bushmanland for "everyone" to graze their cattle. There were also approximately 30,000 Herero in Botswana seeking to return to their "traditional" lands in Namibia, their cattle having by then virtually destroyed the grazing in Western Ngamiland, Botswana. "Under various fictions," wrote Claire Ritchie and John Marshall (1988: 1), "these Herero claim[ed] Eastern Bushmanland. Thirty thousand Herero votes, bought with Eastern Bushmanland, could mean a lot to the DTA."

Meanwhile, the DNC, apparently with the collaboration of the Department of Agriculture, officially continued active measures to destroy Ju/'hoan farming communities and to obstruct Ju/'hoan farming development. Among these actions in 1987–1988 were the following:

- The Department of Agriculture dismantled a *mangel* (chute) and kraal at the Xamsa farming community, removing poles and wire that they had originally given to the Xamsa people.
- The DNC, intending to reserve drinking water for game only, removed the water cistern and faucet from the windpump at Djxokhoe, thus denying clean water to the local farming community and forcing them to drink from the elephant trough.
- The DNC planned to create a large waterhole for elephants virtually in the middle of the N=anemh farming community, which would be physically destroyed by the elephants.
- The DNC planned to drill three boreholes and create three new elephant waterholes in the northeastern quarter of Eastern Bushmanland. The increase in elephants would be detrimental to the economic

infrastructure of Ju/'hoan communities and ultimately fatal to the communities themselves.

- The DNC forbade the JFU to install a large cistern for drip irrigation at the G=aing=oq windpump.
- The Department of Agriculture identified only two agricultural development sites in Eastern Bushmanland: /Aotcha and N=o!au. At a meeting with members of the JFU, an official explained that the Department of Agriculture intended to develop Western Bushmanland for commercial farming. He stated that Ju/'hoan families could apply for fenced-in farms in the west if they had "a hundred cattle and the means to operate a commercial farm" (which none, or very few, of them did).
- At a meeting between members of the JBDF and local DNC officials, it was explained that Ju/'hoansi were forbidden by law to hunt with bows and arrows; were allowed to hunt only kudu, warthog, and gemsbok with rifles (which no Ju/'hoansi could afford); were forbidden to gather many bush foods (because they were "protected" species); were not allowed to cut down most trees to make kraals; and would be prosecuted if they tried to kill lions with their arrows and spears—no matter how severe the predation and even if lions were in their villages—because Eastern Bushmanland was "common" land and lions could be killed only with the permission of the DNC on fenced-in farms. These prohibitions cut off nearly every subsistence strategy available to the Ju/'hoansi besides wage labor and craft production.

The Integrated Rural Development Program of the NNFC

In 1988, the NNFC, together with the JBDF, set up the Integrated Rural Development Program (IRDP) as one of its first actions. The IRDP was based on principles of both cooperation and development that had been observed in other parts of rural southern Africa. By early 1989, the NNFC had 20 *n!ore* communities back on the land, and the IRDP aimed to foster a further 10 by 1992. As outlined in a funding proposal written by Ritchie and Biesele (1989: 1–2), the IRDP called for the following six areas of development: resettlement of Ju/'hoansi groups on traditional land; water development; mixed-subsistence economy (cattle husbandry, horticulture, and hunting-gathering); vocational training; adult literacy and numeracy; and community health education.

The program, directed jointly by NNFC chairperson Tsamkxao =Oma and Biesele, by then the project director of the JBDF, was made possible by many years of previous work undertaken by both the Nyae Nyae people of the JFU/NNFC and the founders of the JBDF, especially John Marshall, Claire Ritchie, and Charles Hartung. Over the ensuing years, the IRDP was to provide personnel inputs in the areas of cattle husbandry, dryland agriculture, vocational training, health management, and life skills education. It also planned to use consultants for environmental impact and planning, the utilization of game products, and economic diversification.

The emphasis throughout the program was on human resource development and heavy community involvement, rather than on the provision of physical infrastructure. The NNFC emerged as the single most important vehicle for participatory development. Ritchie and Biesele (1989: 5) wrote: "Political experience and organizational experience have been gained and the conscientization process has taken on a momentum of its own. The Cooperative is fashioning itself into an effective, flexible body for both internal communication and external representation." As the decision-making body for all economic issues that went beyond the level of the individual, the NNFC deliberated upon regional matters, such as the viability of new groups and their applications for water points and infrastructure. More recently, the NNFC became a forum for political discussion about the participation of the Ju/'hoansi in the future of an independent Namibia.

The Hunting-Gathering Legacy and the Future

The Ju/'hoansi had a vision of their past, with its limited but adequate resources and survival skills, and this vision was far from mere folklore. These were people who knew the details of their past and present subsistence very well; they had to, in order to endure. This fact is well documented in anthropological records, such as John Marshall's films (e.g., 1958c, 1979, 2003a) and Richard Lee's (1969) input-output analysis of their subsistence. In a society living so close to the environmental and economic margins of survival, there was—and is—no advantage to lying about food availability.

Many of the older Ju/'hoansi of Nyae Nyae remembered idyllic childhoods in an environment that was both sufficient and sustainable for hunter-gatherers. But by the 1980s, the Ju/'hoansi and other San, known collectively in southern Africa as the "people of the eland," had not seen or eaten an eland in a long time. To replace their lost protein sources, the Ju/'hoansi had to make a huge and unprecedented effort. Undertaking livestock farming in a hostile environment with artificially high numbers of predators and protecting their stock with laboriously built thorn kraals (since they were prevented from using firearms), they became a sort of latter-day pastoral pioneer. The JBDF came up with the term "Agtertrekkers" (on analogy with the Afrikaans term "Voortrekkers") as a useful trope to help explain the Ju/'hoan predicament (and Ju/'hoan heroism) to audiences in South West Africa. In particular, the JBDF needed to convey to outsiders the creativity that the Ju/'hoansi were exercising in adding farming to their more familiar social traditions of hunting and gathering. Despite the difficulties, a more intensive form of economy had to be found to replace the livelihood sources that had been lost when the Ju/'hoan land base was reduced. The JBDF's main point was that the Ju/'hoansi, many of whom had worked as pastoral serfs for others, were people for whom a mixed subsistence—primarily, low-level cattle herding in conjunction with hunting and gathering—was a logical next step, especially if agricultural training were available.

The Mixed Economy and Multi-tasking in Nyae Nyae

The Ju/'hoansi showed the JBDF that this level of cattle herding, combined with hunting-gathering, could be put into practice using the kind of political organizing that was increasingly becoming necessary. One clear, hot morning in 1988 Tsamkxao =Oma set off early with four companions to travel by truck through heavy sand to a number of communities in the far north of the area. They were taking to these people the latest political news that had arrived the previous day from Windhoek. Tsamkxao was wearing a new suit coat and pants that had been purchased to match the formality of the occasion. When a kudu ran across the track in front of the truck, he braked, flung off his coat and shoes, grabbed his bow and quiver of poisoned arrows, and went off in the direction that the kudu had disappeared. In a few minutes, he had returned to the truck, placing unused arrows back in the quiver. The arrowhead embedded in the kudu would do its work slowly, and Tsamkxao would return later to track the dying animal. He put his coat back on and resumed his business day. His knowledge of the Nyae Nyae area, combined with the reliability of the poison technology, allowed for some flexibility so that hunting could co-exist with the demands of a challenging political career. Similarly, the opportunistic, multi-tasking mental habits long favored in the hunting-gathering context seemed uniquely fitted to the model of a mixed economy based on diverse activities.

John Marshall, Claire Ritchie, Charles Hartung, Megan Biesele, and others in the JBDF, working on behalf of the Ju/'hoansi in 1987–1989, were in agreement about the necessity for economic change. They believed that the reduced land base of the Ju/'hoansi meant that the "extensive" economy of hunting-gathering had to be replaced by something more "intensive." In other words, a land base that could support only about 170 people by traditional means now somehow had to support 2,000 people. The JBDF's position was that the kin-based *n!ore* groups of Nyae Nyae would have to rely on different group members' access to different kinds of resources, pooling them to create a mixed economy. The "pillars" of this economy, as John Marshall put it, included sustainable cattle raising, gardening, and wage income from those few employed by SWAA in Tsumkwe, in addition to hunting-gathering at a reduced level.

Many NNFC members, especially those who had experience working on farms in Botswana or the commercial areas of Namibia, incorporated this vision into their exhortations to other community members, some of whom were slower to accept the possibility of change.

However, coming up with the right formula for a mixed economy was harder—for both the Ju/'hoansi and the JBDF—than generating rhetoric about it. In addition to the high levels of predators and elephants, many factors countered an easy transition to cattle keeping. For one thing, the pastoral models of the Ju/'hoansi's near neighbors, the Herero and Batswana, partook of "cattle complex" symbolism, which held that the larger the herd, the better. The social capital garnered from owning large numbers of animals was more important than the health of the environmental system that supported the cattle. For another, the sharing ethic of the Ju/'hoansi, coupled with the prevalent hunger, made it difficult for an individual to build up his herd for milking or sustainable off-take, that is, animals, used for food or sale, taken from a herd large enough to maintain growth despite this periodic reduction. Instead, pressures from relatives forced animals to be slaughtered and eaten prematurely. Isolated as they were behind the Red Line veterinary cordon fence, the Ju/'hoansi found it difficult to purchase cattle to build up their stock at the start, not to mention that they were forbidden to market animals or meat products beyond their communal area. The development of a cattle industry in Nyae Nyae, a future possibility, could hardly be expected to flourish without any marketing outlet at all.

Gardening to provide food was even more problematic. On average, rainfalls could produce crops—even those that were desert adapted—only one out of every three years in the Kalahari area. Although irrigated gardens became possible due to boreholes that the JBDF drilled at some communities, it was hard enough to get sufficient drinking water out of the ground, not to mention the technical difficulties with irrigation. Birds and other agricultural pests were a constant problem, as were elephants, which ravaged gardens as well as water installations.

Rational planning for the future in Nyae Nyae thus involved enormous social and educational challenges. Debates among the Ju/'hoansi, the NNFC, the JBDF, and the DNC engaged all of these challenges. In the next chapter, we trace a controversial exchange that began in 1988 in the pages of *African Wildlife* magazine—one that examined all of the above issues and added wildlife management and eco-tourism as options for consideration in the Ju/'hoan future.

Chapter Four

Ju/'hoan Empowerment from Dialogue on Wildlife Issues

Why do Europeans get together and talk to each other and decide everything and then tell us about it as if we were little babies still nursing? Long ago we said we didn't want Nature Conservation to have control of everything. There wasn't one person who wanted it.

— =Oma N!ani

We should have long ago written a letter to Nature Conservation about ivory. It's clear that the money which should come to us from these things is being stolen. Other people are eating our money while we just sit with nothing.

— N=aisa G/aq'o

Before Namibian independence was established in March 1990, the Ju/'hoansi were becoming increasingly critical of top-down decision-making about their resources on the part of the Department of Nature Conservation (DNC). In particular, they were bitter that revenues from wildlife products in Nyae Nyae were being drained into the central government with no advantage to Ju/'hoansi.

Debates with the DNC also focused on whether conservation planning in the Nyae Nyae area was to benefit people as well as animals. For years, the DNC had ignored any Ju/'hoan attempts to establish meaningful dialogue on this issue. After strenuous communication efforts, however, in 1988 the DNC approached the Ju/wa Bushman Development Foundation (JBDF) for the first time about a joint effort. The JBDF—but not, tellingly, the people's organization, the Nyae Nyae Farmers Cooperative (NNFC)—was invited to participate in a "full moon count" of large animals at the Nyae Nyae waterholes in order to generate baseline planning numbers.[1]

This overture, although newly positive, was considered wrongheaded by both the JBDF and the NNFC. It ignored the issue of Ju/'hoan control over land and resource rights, for which the NNFC was so earnestly working. It also failed to address the communication impasse that had long existed between the DNC and other South West Africa Administration (SWAA) entities, on the one hand, and the Ju/'hoan community, on the other. However, close observation of the communication issues showed that the white officials involved, while appearing irredeemably arrogant to the Ju/'hoansi, not only were ignorant of Ju/'hoan forms of conversational politeness, but were, in fact, socially shy. And since Ju/'hoansi have a hard time "coding" shyness or avoidance on the part of white people as anything but anger and arrogance, misunderstandings abounded on both sides. With apartheid still the de facto social mode and law of the land, no forum had yet been created in which the two cultures could have a meaningful exchange of views. For example, differing views on the social use of space commonly led to misunderstandings. To SWAA visitors, a *n!ore* appeared to be mostly an empty, "natural," and therefore socially neutral space, whereas to the Ju/'hoansi, since all of the *n!ore* is their residence, passing through it without acknowledging the people living there was equivalent to cutting across one's backyard without saying hello. Occurrences like this incensed the Ju/'hoansi. Tsamkxao =Oma said about SWAA visitors:

> It's a good thing, visiting. But just traveling across someone else's *n!ore* and then going home is a useless thing. Certain white people who come here just leave again without saying anything to us. Sometimes they don't even come to our village—just camp by the pan. Sometimes it is even people who have met me, and they don't even drop by!
>
> When you come to a place, you should go by and say hello to the people. You go by and say, "People, hello! I've been traveling this way or that way and have arrived here." And people would say, "Great! What have you been doing? What work are you here to do?" Then you'd say "My work is thus and so," and people would say, "Oh! I see! Now I know why you're here. Now we understand each other." That's how people should tell each other things and give each other an agreement.
>
> A truck could break down, and if no one told us, we wouldn't know. Sometimes one of us tells another, "Yesterday there was a truck here, but I don't know what it was doing here." How would we know if no one told us? Don't they like to tell us things? They just keep us in the dark, and it's hard for us not to think they're doing something bad out there. Really, there should be a law about this.

---

1. A "full moon count" is an expedition in which volunteers utilize the high visibility generated by a full moon to count the number of animals that visit a waterhole over the course of an entire night.

In particular, the Ju/'hoansi found it hard to convey to the DNC the deeply nuanced nature of the *n!ore* system that, for centuries, had so well regulated their relationship to the land and resources of Nyae Nyae. The *n!ore* concept was not just about space; it was also about rights to resources, with social sharing and conservation mechanisms built in. The *n!oresi* were seen as emotionally and symbolically important in a host of ways that were celebrated in oral history. They were also tied to persons via kinship. On the occasion of the death of Tsamkxao's father, =Oma Tsamkxao, in 1988, Tsamkxao's wife //Uce spoke of her feeling about /Aotcha, the *n!ore* to which she belonged through her marriage to Tsamkxao:

> My husband's father's death is something terrible, something with which I can't make peace. He's been like my own father and has held me to this *n!ore*. His *n!ore* was my mother-in-law's *n!ore*. My father-in-law has died and put me into great pain. I'm still crying and feeling pain. I'm asking myself, what will I do? He was the one who "caused me to live" here [the phrase used was *n=ai !xoana*, an emotionally loaded and highly respectful term]. And I say to myself, "Yes, even though I'm crying, I'll still stay in this *n!ore*, to which he held me. This is my *n!ore* now, and I'll just stay here where he died, and not go somewhere else. I'll just die with his *n!ore* too. What would I be looking for if I went somewhere else?" My great, great father died here, and why should I die somewhere else? It's only death that has separated us: nothing else could.

Embedded in the concept of the *n!ore* and in discussions about it, as shown in Tsamkxao's quote in the introduction of this book, is much traditional information about survival. Further embedded in the concept is the motivation to survive, using the environmental knowledge specific to the *n!ore*. For the Ju/'hoansi, it was an important course of commitment to the future and to cooperating for the health of the specific, beloved areas of land that had provided their sustenance. Thus, they were amazed that explanations of their long-operating and successful system of *n!ore* ownership fell on deaf ears when they tried to tell SWAA officials about it. Kaqece /Ukxa said in 1988:

> It's Ju/'hoansi *n!ore*, but they have the say. Swanie [J. M. Swanepoel, the commissioner of Bushman Affairs in the Department of Governmental Affairs] took [our *n!ore*] /'Aig!oan and gave it to Nature Conservation. =Aqbace went to Nature Conservation too. All those places. I don't know by what authority they've done this. All these *n!oresi* belong to Nature Conservation, and I don't know where they found the law to do this. They don't see that Ju/'hoansi have any authority over their *n!oresi*. They just walk right by us, asking "What's a *n!ore*?" and not waiting for an answer. If that's how it's going to be, it's wrong.

Later that year, Tsamkxao =Oma dictated a letter to the DNC, offering his observations about wildlife, along with traditional information about the *n!oresi* of Nyae Nyae:

We want to give you our thoughts on Nature Conservation and the sickness of wild game. We see that the game remains healthy here in our *n!oresi*, unlike in Tsintsabis and the Tsumeb area, which four years ago had many deaths among kudus from a scalp and horn disease. The reason, we think, is that the kudus were drinking water where many other animals have to drink. In our area there is only one place of sickness, G=aing=oq, where Nature Conservation put an artificial waterhole for elephants and lions. Many vultures drink there, too, and G=aing=oq is the only place where many of our cattle have died of lung disease. At the other places, where cattle numbers are few and game is at its usual level of numbers, both cattle and game stay healthy. The game has been healthy in our area for a long time, long before Nature Conservation was working here.

So far we haven't seen any help from the Department of Nature Conservation where people's lives are concerned. I am a grown man, and I haven't seen that people have been helped to have good lives by this Department; they only have help for the animals. Why are they here if they are not helping people? Sincerely yours …

After this letter, Tsamkxao was finally asked by the DNC in a pro forma way for access to his environmental knowledge through participation in a later full moon count. But he asked a further question: why should this information be given without hope of ameliorating the situation, and without visible returns? In another letter to the same official, he likened participation in the full moon count—using his knowledge of tracking, giving observations, and turning in found trophies such as elephant tusks—to "returning someone's lost wallet and receiving no reward":

Tsamkxao =Oma greets you and asks the following: if you drop your wallet and I pick it up and give it to you, isn't that better than if I steal it? So if I pick up something which belongs to the Government and return it, isn't that better than if I keep it and hide it? We have been told that elephant tusks we find in the bush belong to the Government. But won't the Government get back more of its property if we who sweat to find these things receive a percentage from them? Otherwise, why shouldn't we leave them where they lie, or even bury them?

This is only I, Tsamkxao, speaking, not the JBDF, nor Megan who is writing it down for me, nor anyone else. I know many people have been confused because we have been told if we pick up a diamond, we'll get a percentage from it. Why shouldn't it be the same with ivory? Some of us have received pieces of paper when we turned in ivory, and we thought we would be paid, but that has not happened. Finding tusks is a matter of sweat. People who just drive on roads are not going to see dead elephants, and the ivory will just be wasted.

Finally, how do I know this is really the law, and not just your idea? I'm interested in your plan to gather people together so we can all hear what is the law. When we asked you to show us a piece of paper about this, you said there wasn't one. Won't you take our thoughts together with yours when the law is made?

In Botswana, life is lived with laws. Police and other officials are there to help people learn the laws, not just to slam them into jail before they have a chance to find out what they are. Why can we not find out what laws we are living under in Bushmanland? We need to make plans about how we will live. Sincerely ...

This inability to make plans was perhaps the single greatest source of frustration for the Ju/'hoansi during the years leading up to independence. It was based on officials' misunderstanding of the rational basis of Ju/'hoan traditional subsistence, their "Old Way." The health and power of their strategies for survival were obscured for these officials by the dual myth that cast the Ju/'hoansi as "children of nature," floating somehow above the land with no real resource needs, and as "lazy, shiftless, and primitive" people. The JBDF struggled to help the Ju/'hoansi communicate the reality behind these stereotypes, yet during these years before independence, even trained expert advocates could not penetrate the fog of hazy areas in the DNC laws that had been manipulated by local officials. In general, the officials' answer was "no" to all reasonable suggestions, "no" to all applications for gun permits to protect cattle from an artificially elevated lion population, and "no" to whether specific game species, long the mainstays of the Ju/'hoan diet, might still be legally killed. In these years, the Ju/'hoansi lived with the uneasy sense that they might be violating many rules whenever they went hunting, gathering, or even collecting house-building materials in the bush. Many of the best hunters spent months in the Grootfontein jail for hunting violations that they did not know beforehand were illegal. Their incarceration caused enormous hardship for the families they had to leave behind in Nyae Nyae.

Trophy Hunting

Families deprived of meat by capricious and punitive laws did not look kindly at first on the safari hunting concession, which further strained resources on which they had relied. The concession, granted in 1988 to Volker Grellmann of Anvo Hunting Safaris, was contentious in many ways. One example was that Grellmann was invited to participate in a government economic and land-use planning exercise called "Bushmanland 2000," which took place on 1 August that year in Tsumeb—but neither the Ju/'hoansi nor the JBDF was included, except for a one-year planning document that the JBDF was allowed to submit. In fact, the JBDF felt that the invitation itself signaled a wish to control the people and the JBDF, rather than work collaboratively with them. Not only did one white man gain greater political clout than 2,000 non-white people could command, but the action further emphasized the Ju/'hoansi's painful status as "wards of the state," who were being systematically separated from their former protein sources.

Attempting to replace the game protein that they had been deprived of when they lost many of their *n!oresi* at the creation of the "homeland" of

Bushmanland, the Ju/'hoansi had been trying, with John Marshall's help, to raise cattle in a sustainable way. Yet the trophy hunting concession further increased the difficulty of raising cattle by encouraging the growth of the lion population for sport hunting. It appeared that the DNC's interest in the full moon counts was mostly to set quotas for the white hunters in order to develop game resources for government revenue, instead of for the Ju/'hoan people.

Although the hunting concession was in later years to generate substantial funds for the Nyae Nyae Conservancy (NNC), which grew out of the NNFC, at the start its proceeds went into the central government and did not benefit the Ju/'hoansi. When the Ju/'hoansi complained, they were told by Grellmann and the DNC that Anvo Safaris would be providing large amounts of meat, mostly elephant, to the communities from game shot by safari hunters. Unfortunately, Grellmann and the DNC failed to understand the Ju/'hoansi's explanation that few of them would or could eat elephant meat, as elephants were not native to their area and were thought anatomically and socially too close to human beings.[2]

Part of the discussion concerning the concession focused on the DNC's claim that the Ju/'hoan "Old Way" epitomized what they called "the cruelest treatment of game." They based this judgment on the fact that the Ju/'hoansi were supposedly making no special arrangements for game to flourish. Instead, the white hunters and the DNC favored setting out "game waters" to raise game numbers artificially, as was done in the country's Etosha National Park. Hai//om San peoples who once co-existed with game at Etosha had been moved out long before, despite a great deal of archaeological, oral, and historical evidence to support co-existence in the past (Dieckmann 2007; John Kinahan, pers. comm., 1992, 2002). Park rangers at Etosha no longer remembered a time before the Hai//om had been trucked out, or before game numbers had been hugely elevated. The JBDF and the Ju/'hoansi, for their part, were asking why a co-existence model that had worked so well in the past, as reflected amply in the oral history and folk stories still being told in Nyae Nyae in 1988, could not be included in the planning process.

The Power of the Media

As in many other circumstances surrounding the Ju/'hoansi, a media event—this time in print instead of on film—had profound effects on environmental planning in Nyae Nyae. We trace a 1988 exchange that took place in the pages of the South African journal *African Wildlife* among Brian Jones (1988a,

---

2. In later years, however, hunger in the Nyae Nyae communities has been so great that this food avoidance has been breaking down. As a result, many Ju/'hoansi now eat elephant meat, although unwillingly.

1988b, 1988c), Andrew B. Smith (1988), and John Marshall (1988). Jones's original article (1988a, vol. 42, no. 2) was titled "Bushmanland: Fate in the Balance." The final item in the exchange was John Marshall's reply (1988, vol. 42, no. 6), entitled "Bushmanland: Lives in the Balance." This dialogue involves all the issues of rational conservation planning for the future of Bushmanland outlined in chapter 3, with the addition of arguments for and against "conservation status" for Nyae Nyae. The discussion laid the groundwork in Namibia and neighboring countries for greatly increased interest in the wildlife resources of Bushmanland and how they were to be managed for the good of the region as well as for local people.

In turn, this outside interest enabled a gradual amelioration of communications and relations between the Ju/'hoansi and officials of the DNC, who were thus exposed to relatively enlightened international attitudes about indigenous peoples' participation in conservation. In this chapter we trace the growth of Ju/'hoan empowerment and increased participation in local environmental planning, using quotes taped at a series of meetings with conservation officials just before, and for a time after, independence. These quotes reveal the rhetorical skill that Ju/'hoan leaders and their young Ju/'hoan translators were honing during these years. This skill eventually brought about a high degree of unity in the messages that the Ju/'hoansi conveyed to the Namibian government about their wants and needs.

The growing rhetorical unity among the Ju/'hoan spokespersons was at first vigorously paralleled by the unity of public positions taken by JBDF personnel on Ju/'hoan issues. But the latter part of 1988 saw the start of a division in the JBDF between two main approaches to communication with the governmental entities "responsible" for Eastern Bushmanland. These approaches diverged on two main axes: first, cooperation versus confrontation with South West Africa governmental entities and those who would succeed them after independence; and, second, agriculture versus wildlife management and eco-tourism as sound options for the Ju/'hoansi's future. The divergence was increased by the fact that John Marshall returned to the US in late 1989 and was gone until 1991; thus, he did not have the opportunity to participate in the increasingly positive communications that the Ju/'hoansi were having with the DNC about planning in Nyae Nyae.

Planning for Balance in Wildlife Management

Brian Jones, a former environmental writer who became a public relations officer for the South West Africa Department of Nature Conservation and later a staff member in the Ministry of Environment and Tourism, wrote in his original 1988 article, which marked the beginning of the exchange in print over

Bushmanland use rights, that Eastern Bushmanland was "a conservationist's dream." He enumerated wildlife resources of interest to the Ju/'hoansi and outsiders alike, including a buffalo herd, a large population of wild dog, elephant, giraffe, bat-eared fox, blue wildebeest, duiker, steenbok, ant bear, leopard, honey badger, red hartebeest, reedbuck, silver jackal, eland, roan, tsessebe, and other kinds of antelope. He also wrote that it was "the only pan-veld system in SWA/Namibia" and called for its flamingoes, wattled cranes, great snipe, and other beautiful and endangered species to receive conservation status for protection. He cited the main factor preventing such protection as attempts by government and "private development programs" in Nyae Nyae to develop cattle farming, with potentially disastrous results for the wildlife and their habitat.

Anthropologists or the Ju/'hoansi themselves could have told the South West Africa officials why Bushmanland was still unspoiled. Originally, the Ju/'hoan hunter-gatherers and the animals they depended on had plenty of land area; the Ju/'hoansi pursued a very rational use of resources based on their *n!ore* system; the technology they used sufficed for the people's needs and did not destroy more than they needed; the people had their own religious conservation ethic about game; sharing was enforced among them by symbolic means; and many leveling mechanisms were in place in their society so that no person or group could self-aggrandize—say, by overhunting—at the expense of any other. In short, the *n!ore* system and its cultural ramifications regulated the number of people to the productive capacity of the land.

Jones did argue for trophy hunting to be allowed, "with proceeds being held in trust for the Bushmen." He asked for the Ju/'hoan people to be included in the conservation area but stopped short of advocating that they establish land ownership or usufruct rights to the products of the land. In the climate of that time, before South West Africa became Namibia, the most Jones could do was to ask for a kind of clientage status for the Ju/'hoansi on their own ancestral land.[3]

In response, Andrew B. Smith of the Archaeology Department at the University of Cape Town wrote to *African Wildlife* to say that Jones's article was an outrage. Imagine the reaction, he said, if white farmers were to be asked to accept such an arrangement on what they regarded as their own land. Smith said further that the Ju/'hoansi and other San needed a sense of identity that could grow, that the *n!ore* system should be *de jure* institutionalized, and that conservation should be run locally by a cooperative decision-making body. Lastly, he said that since communal lands used for foraging do not degrade on their own, but will degrade with pastoral practices and values, some of the hunting-gathering ethic should be kept as conservation insurance for the future.

_____

3. As we see later in this chapter, however, with the changes that came at independence, Brian Jones and some other DNC officers were able to espouse more radically defined notions of Ju/'hoan empowerment with regard to the land.

In reply, Jones decried Smith's letter as overemotional and said that returns from trophy hunting would be given to local people, who would be involved in the "self-determination" of their relationship to their resources. Unfortunately, he put the word in quotation marks, which neatly encapsulated the problem of rhetorical, not actual, commitment that characterized the whole exchange. John Marshall then oared in from the point of view of the "private development program" that Jones had criticized in the first place. Marshall wrote that the wide dispersal of small settlements in Nyae Nyae (the re-formed *n!ore* communities) favored co-existence with game species. He also said that it was not the "programs" but the Ju/'hoansi themselves who were re-establishing their communities on the land: "Does anyone really think that someone could compel ... desperately poor and inexperienced people to undertake the struggle of farming in Eastern Bushmanland against their wishes and without the motive of survival?" The real conflict, Marshall wrote, was between lives and money. The dispossession was happening so that tourists could enjoy an expensive "Darkest Africa." He asked that Jones's suggestion of "limited" agriculture and cattle ranching be changed to "managed," that is, "managed by Ju/'hoansi and for their benefit."

In the background of Marshall's thinking was the experience of San people some years earlier in the West Caprivi area to the north of Nyae Nyae. Contrary to popular belief, the South African Defence Force (SADF) did not depopulate West Caprivi for security reasons. Instead, Marshall said, the proclamation of a game reserve there in 1968 initiated the same slow "war of attrition" that the Ju/'hoansi had long been victims of in Nyae Nyae. The Khwe San people were forbidden to hunt, gather, fish, plant crops, possess livestock, or even cut reeds for houses. Some of these people abandoned their land to seek subsistence elsewhere, while others were moved to military bases by the SADF. A hidden purpose of this process was to remove the "inconvenient" indigenous people in order to create a sanitized experience for high-end tourists.

Marshall was adamant that the same fate should not befall the Ju/'hoansi. Later, after independence, debates such as the one in *African Wildlife* had generally positive outcomes for the various San peoples, as they made Namibian government officers aware of the new attention being paid to the empowerment of indigenous peoples in other parts of the world. But at the time, the 1988 journalistic exchanges only served to alienate from each other two potentially powerful allies of the Ju/'hoan people. Marshall felt vindicated in his belief that the Ju/'hoansi would get nowhere by negotiating with national government personnel, and he advised them in even stronger terms than before not to cooperate with government plans for the Ju/'hoan area. On the other hand, the government that Brian Jones represented was teetering on the brink of a massive democratic change that would ultimately enfranchise people like the Ju/'hoansi beyond anyone's apartheid-era dreams. Thus,

Jones and government officials were bemused by the confrontational stance that Marshall was still advocating and tended to maintain a skeptical distance from the NGO that he had founded, making it difficult for the JBDF to accomplish many of its aims.

The Eco-tourism Alternative

While John Marshall was making a series of visits to the US in 1988–1991, events began to flow much more quickly and surely in the direction of independence. Others in the JBDF were concerned that the isolation that the organization was experiencing might cause the Ju/'hoansi to miss out on the potential benefits of changes that were on the horizon. To steer the dialogue with the DNC toward positive alternatives, Megan Biesele, Charles Hartung, Adrian Strong, and others in the JBDF began at this time to cite examples of local people acting as game conservators and of human-animal co-existence in conservation areas around Africa. Conservationist Garth Owen-Smith and anthropologist Margaret Jacobsohn were letting South and South West Africans know about a fledgling system of local conservators among the Himba in Kaokoland and Damaraland, South West Africa, where local people were charging R5 per day for tours in order to teach outsiders that sacred sites should not be desecrated. In Niger, Touareg game guides were protecting the addax, a type of antelope. In Rwanda, conservation jobs were being created for local people in order to protect mountain gorillas.

Stemming from these positive examples, early eco-tourism discussions in the JBDF found Claire Ritchie, Megan Biesele, and others considering what conservation efforts could look like in Bushmanland under a true partnership with the DNC. Rather than riding around with a white hunter, visitors could be accompanied by Ju/'hoan trackers, benefiting from their high level of traditional and local environmental knowledge. A dignified tourism system run by the Ju/'hoansi, which would control access to areas and limit the number of participants, could start a return of revenues to local communities and create a chance for the Ju/'hoan people to get life skills education and jobs. The Ju/'hoansi are natural hosts. Not at all averse to visitors, they are instead hospitable, friendly people, when visitors take the time to greet and get to know them.

Around this time, recent breaches of etiquette by visitors had gravely upset the Nyae Nyae *n!ore* dwellers. A composition written in Ju/'hoansi by a 16-year-old girl in Biesele's creative writing class for Ju/'hoan trainee teachers in the Nyae Nyae Village Schools Project (see chapter 10) portrays a head-on collision of cultures on /Aotcha pan, an important part of the wetland system identified in Brian Jones's article:

The Day the Tourists Pretended We Were Flamingoes, by N!hunkxa /Kaece

One day, on the Sunday before Christmas, we went down to swim in /Aotcha pan. While we were swimming, some white people came in two cars. We went towards them. One car drove this way, and the other car drove that way, and they tried to chase us with the cars. When we wanted to get out of the pan, they blocked our way so that we had to run back into the water. When we were in the water again, they would stop. When we wanted to get out again, they would do the same thing again. So we went back and forth, back and forth, over and over again.

When they tried to drive into the pan with one of the cars, its tires slid and it got stuck. So we got out of the water and ran back to the village with nothing on but our underpants. When we told the other people what had happened, Tsamkxao (=Oma) went down to the pan with all the people from the village. Tsamkxao asked the white people, "Yau! What is this about chasing our children while they're swimming?"

The white people said, "We only wanted to chase the flamingoes." So Tsamkxao said, "Why is it that the children have always swum in that water but never chased the flamingoes, and now you are trying to kill the children but say you are just chasing the flamingoes?"

Then the white people wanted to hit Tsamkxao. They said he was like the sand under their feet. (Pfaffe 2003: 25–26)

Another infuriating incident in 1988 also involved tourists and the people's water sources. Seg//ae Kxao, the woman who represented the N=aqmtjoha *n!ore* in the NNFC and continued to represent it in the NNC until early 2010, when she went blind, said that tourists had been bathing in their water troughs, even washing their clothes, and in the process had fouled the drinking water: "I went to talk to these two whites. And I saw that they had stopped their car and entered the reservoir and were swimming. And I said, 'Yau, why have you jumped into our drinking water and put your dirt into it? If you do that, what water am I supposed to drink? This isn't swimming water.' And these school kids got their car number: we had no pencil but they wrote it down with a cinder."

Excitement erupted around this issue. Other people who were there with Seg//ae connected this lack of control over local resources with other, similar issues, such as tourists taking photographs without permission, tourists paying rip-off prices for traditional handicrafts, and SADF personnel driving through the area, insulting old people and throwing beer cans behind them. Aggrieved attitudes like these went back to 1986, when Minister of Nature Conservation Andreas Shipanga came to Tsumkwe and promised the Ju/'hoan people that they would receive the revenues from trophy hunting in their area. Up to 1989, and even into 1992, these revenues were still flowing solely into the coffers of the central government, despite Shipanga's promise.

During 1989, although not much had changed outwardly with regard to Ju/'hoan-DNC relations, a wind of change was blowing ahead of the impending governmental transition at independence, and it was to have far-reaching consequences for Ju/'hoan control of their own resources. As the public relations officer for the DNC, Brian Jones was instrumental in establishing a path toward better communication with various local Namibian communities. As we know from his writings in *African Wildlife*, Jones took a special interest in Eastern Bushmanland, also called the Nyae Nyae area. He knew that a new national mandate would be established for the DNC after independence and that community-based consultation would be the starting point for all environmental planning. Jones was instrumental in promoting dialogue in the Nyae Nyae case and eventually saw to it that Nyae Nyae became one of the first areas to participate in a community survey of resources and local opinions about how they should be used. He facilitated the series of three meetings between the NNFC and the DNC, discussed below, that illustrate the improvement of communications before and during the independence process.

The first meeting, in December 1989, took place in the slightly improved atmosphere of imminent governmental change. It was the first time that Ju/'hoan people had ever been invited to the DNC camp, Klein Dobe, which had been established without community permission and had caused a great deal of resentment. People's general attitude toward Klein Dobe was that it was a place where white officials from Windhoek met to drink beer and *braai* meat together, make plans for local people without consulting them, and then drive back to Windhoek. However, although the Ju/'hoansi were glad finally to be meeting at Klein Dobe themselves, the form of the meeting (conducted mostly in Afrikaans and a little English) was rigid and hierarchical, emphasizing the attitude of the chairperson, Hennie Theron, a DNC official from Otjiwarongo, and his propensity to dictate to the Ju/'hoansi rather than listen to them. The content of the conference—which lasted only one day, for at that time and in that place it would have been impossible to have anything like a mixed-race overnight social event—centered around the very low DNC payments for found ivory, the hindrance that artificial game waters and elevated problem animal populations were creating for the new *n!ore* communities in their farming efforts, and the need for "better communication" between local people and the DNC. The tone of the conference was relatively hopeless, and social embarrassment on both sides at being together in the same meeting room seemed to paralyze the atmosphere. But seeds had been sown.

The year of independence, 1990, was a whirlwind of political activity (see chapters 5 and 6), so it was not until January 1991 that the next meeting was held at Klein Dobe. However, it was clear that, in the meantime, the new mandate of the DNC had been ironed out in Windhoek, and a Planning Unit had been formed under the direction of Brian Jones and his colleague Chris Brown. Both were younger, forward-looking, and English-speaking (as opposed to Afrikaans-speaking) DNC employees who were dedicated to the promotion of participatory planning. Jones and Brown were pushing for a community-based surveying and planning process to be implemented in the communal lands, and in late 1990 they began with the first survey in Western Caprivi, where the Khwe San had been disempowered by the declaration of conservation status. Representatives from NNFC and the JBDF (by then called the Nyae Nyae Development Foundation of Namibia, or NNDFN) were invited to take part, in order to prepare them for a survey in their own area planned for January–February 1991.

In preparation for the eventual Klein Dobe meetings, the NNDFN had been asked, as far back as October 1989, to conduct a mini-survey of opinions in a few Nyae Nyae *n!oresi* to determine whether the local people wanted mixed subsistence (agro-pastoralism and income-generation added to hunting-gathering) and control over their natural resources. These questions were asked by Biesele, assisted by an NNFC representative, G/aq'o =Oma, who had previously worked for the Department of Wildlife in Botswana and thus had a wide perspective on the issues. Answers to the questions received at N=aqmtjoha and //Auru were revealing and clearly implied high interest in the (soon-to-be politically possible) process of collaborating with the DNC rather than working at cross-purposes with it. A lively conversation occurred over the possibility of restocking with eland and other indigenous game, as shown in this extract:

Bospiki: If Ju/'hoansi had strength, maybe they could think of catching lots of elands and maybe roans, and farming with them. But until the election, we have no strength. The white people still have all the strength in this land. Right now, if you tried to sell an animal like that, you'd go straight to jail. But maybe after the election we could do it.

These days, if you drive through our land without even seeing an eland or a roan, it's because of the fences which have been put up: that's the only reason. The animals and their calves have been taken to the west and then the fences were put between. Long ago the elands used to cross Nyae Nyae according to the season, but one season the fence was closed on them, and they haven't returned.

When I was the age of this kid [maybe 20 years ago], there were plenty of elands here—and not many lions. There were some lions, but few. They'd only come near you occasionally.

N=amce: What we have to do is get rid of the fences. Our children didn't use to die like they do now. People would split up and go off hunting different ways, and then come back with food. Today we're not eating! Nature Conservation came to help, but all we know of them is that they put us in jail.

Positive Outcomes of Pre-independence Communication with Officials

Because issues and attitudes like these were finally being addressed, the second Klein Dobe survey and meeting were altogether more participatory and interculturally dignified than the first meeting had been. Participants from many government departments, NGOs, local communities, and the NNFC camped together for 10 days in rustic bungalows and tents, gingerly learning to share food, beer, and even, eventually, the fire-heated showers. Each day, teams made up of local and government people traveled out to the *n!oresi* of Nyae Nyae and asked a set of open-ended questions about resources and their use and about attitudes to resource ownership. The meetings in Klein Dobe were report-backs, and most people there had a sense of working together as a research team. The exercise opened with a first day of ecological orientation to the area via short presentations by scientists. Attention was paid to translations for the Ju/'hoan people, and plenty of time was given to this effort.

Unfortunately, there was criticism leveled privately at the two NNFC leaders by the more conservative DNC officials, who suggested that the ideas they were expressing "must have been put into their heads by the translator [Biesele], because they couldn't have had such ideas on their own." This criticism was in fact a blessing in disguise. It so angered the NNFC officials that it made them realize that efforts at direct communication and government recognition of their ideas could no longer be delayed. As Tsamkxao =Oma said at that time, "The white road from the west brings us visitors as numerous as birds before the rains. If these visitors want to know the thoughts which are inside my head, they have only to ask."

The 1991 survey and the second Klein Dobe conference began the process of establishing mutual trust between the Ju/'hoan people and the DNC (now the Ministry of Wildlife Conservation and Tourism, MWCT), so that a collaborative consultative body could be set up. Another outcome was the joint drafting of a land use plan for the region that would ensure sustainable human development while at the same time maintaining essential ecological processes and biodiversity. The approach of the survey was based on modern participatory development principles and the policies adopted by the MWCT following independence, which held "[t]hat local people should be fully consulted at all stages of the development project, that they should participate in its design, and that they should be empowered to take decisions over the resources they are using" (Biesele and Jones 1991).

The many socio-economic issues covered during the conference and survey included the following:

- The dismantling of the feared "Meesterplan" to create Boesmanland Nasionale Park, the game reserve plan that had originally galvanized the movement of the Ju/'hoansi back to their *n!oresi* from Tsumkwe
- The problem of unemployed soldiers and the hole in the local economy left by the departure of the SADF
- Dependency and food aid, which was made necessary by the aid given to the ex-SADF population of Western Bushmanland and the government's desire to provide an equal service to Eastern Bushmanland

- The equitability of the local safari company/trophy concessionaire's purchase of crafts in the various communities
- Trophy revenues and elephant meat handouts
- Tourist fees
- Possible educational tourism
- The increasing scarcity of game in the area
- The possibility of using non-traditional hunting methods
- Problem animals such as lions and elephants, which prey on cattle and destroy water installations and gardens
- Transport problems and government service problems
- The inroads on traditional hunter-gatherer knowledge made by schooling and by incoming economic attitudes
- The threat to cattle posed by *gifblaar* (*Dichapetalum cymosum*), a poisonous plant
- The difficulty that non-literate people have in competing for scarce jobs
- Conflicting messages from government entities regarding how people should find their subsistence in the future on reduced land
- Theft caused by hunger, due to depleted bush resources in heavily populated areas like Tsumkwe
- Tourist behavior and control over their activities
- Difficulties communicating in the past with DNC officials
- Punitive measures against poaching that did not address the economic realities
- Photography by tourists and remuneration
- Hunting laws and the possibility of changing them
- Sustainable hunting and gathering levels

The second Klein Dobe conference clearly put many more Ju/'hoan cards and concerns on the table, and it was the first chance for many of the outlying *n!ore* inhabitants to see that a positive relationship with the MWCT might be possible. It was necessary for the leaders of the NNFC to act as go-betweens in this effort, however. At each *n!ore* settlement visited, people were mistrustful until the purpose of the visit was explained by the NNFC leaders and the MWCT personnel were introduced. Many of the old guard nature conservators were unable to enter into the new spirit of dialogue at all, remaining silent at all of the meetings or staying back at Klein Dobe on the pretext of cooking for those who were out working. But in general the new format espoused by the fledgling Planning Unit personified in Brown and Jones carried the day: it was clear that the new mandate of community consultation could not be denied.

Common ground arrived at between the MWCT and the Nyae Nyae people during Klein Dobe II included the following:

- That wildlife should prosper and be utilized sustainably, with appropriate controls being applied for problem animals
- That wildlife is an essential resource for local people, who should be viewed as de facto owners of game with concomitant rights and responsibilities
- That there should be shared responsibility and decision-making over wildlife utilization
- That controls are required to ensure the sustainability of resources such as game and wild foods, particularly if new methods of hunting are introduced
- That cattle numbers need to be limited to avoid overgrazing and that the local people need advice and help on this issue
- That there should be a land use and management plan, based on the accepted land use systems of the community, and that land allocation and settlement should be in terms of this plan
- That there should be a joint management and land use planning committee
- That benefits from local natural resource utilization (e.g., trophy hunting income) should accrue to local people
- That there should be control over tourism to the region and that fees and other financial benefits should accrue to the community
- That local traditional knowledge and scientific knowledge should be combined in informing management decisions and research
- That employment locally within the MWCT should as far as possible, and within the government's policy against discrimination, go to local people
- That there should be a program of training for local people in wildlife utilization and management, problem animal control, etc.
- That there should be a community game scout system
- That hunting and gathering rights should be recognized
- That amounts paid for ivory compensation should be greater

The Concept of an Environmental Planning Committee

In August 1991, there was a follow-up report made to the NNFC at one of its own meetings concerning the MWCT's response to the survey and events that took place at Klein Dobe in January 1991. By this time, the MWCT had realized what a good piece of press it had in the relatively well-organized NNFC, and they had their own film crew on hand to create a media event for television and their own journalist to do an article on public participation in environmental planning. One of the most important issues discussed at the August meeting was that of a planned auxiliary game guard system for Nyae Nyae, some of whose costs would be met by the MWCT and some by the NNFC. This plan involved issues of horse and gun use and was tied by the NNFC to its own evolving plan for splitting Nyae Nyae into five districts (*!aotzisi*) for ease of administration.

A second main issue on the agenda in August was that of proposed hunting law changes. At Klein Dobe, some of the younger men interviewed had expressed a desire to be allowed to use guns, horses, and dogs in pursuit of game, rather than being limited to traditional weapons (bows and poisoned arrows, spears, and *sansevieria* snares). This issue was taken up again in the context of wider Namibian hunting laws. Brian Jones explained to the Ju/'hoansi that the limitation to traditional weapons was in fact a protection for them—that if they were to be allowed to use guns in the future, any other Namibians, likewise using guns, could come into their area and quickly decimate their game. He underscored the value of their specialized traditional knowledge, which was not shared by any other hunters.

The older Ju/'hoan hunters were quick to realize the importance of this point. N!ani Kxao said, "I got my bow and arrows from my father. They are something I will never abandon ... Your bow and your arrows hold you fast to your *n!ore* ... Hold fast to your bow and arrows. If you drop your bow and arrows, you will just sit there with nothing, watching other people. It is our bows and our arrows which have laid down our *n!oresi* for us to live from." An older man from another *n!ore* (//Xa/oba) said, "We are Bushman people. We have the sense not to kill everything. We kill one animal and then eat it, and then go kill something else. We will keep the young men from carrying guns because they do not have enough sense to do this." The idea "not to kill everything" and a commitment to the use of traditional weapons and food-gathering methods are largely what the success of future mixed-economy strategies in Nyae Nyae rested upon. Convincing skeptical MWCT officials that the Ju/'hoansi would keep that commitment in the long term was one step in the process toward regaining control over their land.

Shortly before this August follow-up meeting, the NNFC and its NGO, the NNDFN, had been contacted by USAID/World Wildlife Fund in connection with new programs possibly to be implemented in Namibia in the area of community resource control. The single most important recommendation that came out of a site visit to Nyae Nyae by USAID/WWF staff was that a full-time environmental liaison person be employed by the MWCT to facilitate communications between the communities and all relevant government divisions (especially MWCT). All developments that took place after early 1992 benefited from the speedy creation of this position, which was filled by Holly Payne. By the time of the third Klein Dobe meeting, held in July 1992, Payne had been on the job for some months and had facilitated the convening of the first few Environmental Planning Committee (EPC) meetings, the recommendation for which had come out of Klein Dobe II.

The third Klein Dobe meeting, underwritten by SIDA and NORAD (Swedish and Norwegian aid agencies), was an event as different from the first one as could perhaps be imagined. Involving over 100 people, it was convened by the NNFC's EPC itself, along with the MWCT. Government representatives, including the minister of agriculture, attended as invited guests from as far away as Windhoek (a distance of 750 kilometers). The NNFC also invited the leaders and representatives of what was then named the Nyae Nyae Farmers Cooperative West, a grassroots group from Western Bushmanland that was developing along the lines of the original NNFC of Eastern Bushmanland and has since become the N=a Jaqna Conservancy. This meant that more than one Bushman language was involved, and thus more time had to be allocated for translation. Languages used and carefully translated included Ju/'hoansi, Vasekela, Nama (Khoekhoegowab), Afrikaans, Herero, and English.

The meeting, which lasted for three days, was jointly chaired by a representative from the NNFC and another from the MWCT. This fact contributed to the particularly cross-cultural flair and genius of both the agenda and the consensus process. By the end of the conference, each participant had learned a great deal about the "culture of speaking" of other groups, and new respect for alternative ways of attaining planning goals was established.

Topics covered and resolutions reached included the following: local views on land use options; science from the people; wildlife management as part of a mixed land use practice; sustainable wildlife utilization; priority of concession rights; devolution of natural resource revenues; and agriculture as part of mixed land use practice. Many thorny problems heretofore unresolved between local communities and the former DNC were brought into the open, and creative solutions were sought. Since all of the participants were camping together under substantially similar circumstances, delegates had a chance to visit informally as well.

A particular point of interest was an intense dialogue with interested parties on the subject of trophy hunting, safari, and lumber concessions. Formerly remote, powerful figures that had caused local frustration from afar, the concessionaires themselves were suddenly there, hats in hand, at a meeting convened by the people. The tables were clearly turned. The NNFC leaders demonstrated a willingness to continue to work with the concessionaires, but only on NNFC terms and under the assumption that the local people were now in charge.

A second area of discussion was the inauguration of the radio collaring of problem lions by wildlife biologist Flip Stander and his Ju/'hoan trainees, so that the animals could be moved unharmed out of Nyae Nyae and could sometimes even be sold to foreign zoos to generate revenues for the NNFC. Other revenue-producing plans, such as the use of wild resources to produce salable handicrafts and community-regulated environmental tourism, were also discussed.

A third item of particular interest was the problem of low indigenous game numbers that had been brought about by SADF and tourist poaching, by the DNC's previous removal of some game from Nyae Nyae to the Etosha Game

Reserve, and by injudicious fencing. In fact, a plan was put in place to restock with animals like eland, which can be ranched, perhaps using local Ministry of Agriculture infrastructure, such as a quarantine camp at Tsumkwe.[4]

The fencing issue in general was of great concern, as there were some MWCT plans afoot to fence off the Kaudum Game Reserve from Nyae Nyae, which would further cut game migration routes. Examples from Botswana and elsewhere in which game experienced die-offs due to fences stood the Ju/'hoansi in good stead as they argued that environmental soundness should be a necessary part of any fencing plan. In general, the amount of comparative information that was handled well by the conveners impressed the government personnel present and may have had a lot to do with the structural outcomes of the meeting, which involved long-term land use planning relationships with the government.

Land Use Planning and Land Tenure

One of the most telling interchanges at Klein Dobe III involved not only multiple voices but a skein of vitally interwoven topics, including traditional and transitional social technologies of resource management, governmental participation and control, and local empowerment. Because it is a superb example of both evolving leadership style and newly empowered rhetoric, we present it here in full. The speakers are Ron Thompson, a Zimbabwean wildlife writer attending the conference on behalf of the local (expatriate) trophy hunting concessionaire, Volker Grellmann; Peter Tarr, an MWCT official and co-chairperson of the meeting; Brian Jones of the MWCT Planning Unit; Tsamkxao =Oma, past chairperson of the NNFC; Chiza Africa, an official of the SWAPO government within the Ministry of Lands; Megan Biesele, anthropologist/translator; and /'Angn!ao /'Un, then chairperson of the NNFC and, with Peter Tarr, co-chairperson of the meeting.

> Ron Thompson: Within the community living in Bushmanland—perhaps the chairman [/'Angn!ao /'Un] should answer this—is there some way they can discipline themselves, discipline other families, some way they can guarantee that their families are not going to hunt roan this year or for five years? Is there any way of self-discipline amongst the people, where that sort of idea can be enforced?
>
> Peter Tarr: That's the sort of planning which is going to take place ... Concepts like community game guards can be set up to ensure self-regulation. We wouldn't prescribe that—that must come from the community.

---

4. The first dozen eland did, in fact, eventually arrive in September 1992 as the property of the NNFC and the start of a promising experiment in fenceless cooperative game ranching.

Brian Jones: The community game guard system is being discussed in the communities at the moment.

Tsamkxao =Oma: Our old people long ago worked hard talking together to decide how to share resources. Today we are still working hard to come up with good ideas for how to use our resources under the new government. We consider part of our work to be coming up with new ideas to help the new government keep the peace among the people. The new government is listening to us as we do our work of thinking. We don't need a new government to tell us how to get along with each other. We already know this. And the new government has told us that we have authority to decide some of the things which will happen in our land. Our land is not the kind of land that can be bought and sold like a farm. This is the sort of thing we in the Nyae Nyae Farmers Cooperative sit together to talk about. We have formed a committee to talk about our resources so that we don't waste them. I'm not saying we don't have disputes: we're always telling each other that some idea is bad and will end up ruining us. We've been meeting together for five or six years on this ... At the beginning we had an uphill fight with the old government. Today with the new government we've got more encouragement for what we do, and we're more confident about our ideas.

For example, we know that there is certain veld burning we shouldn't do, because we want to keep cattle now. But because we have always managed our game and bush foods with fire, there is certain burning we still want to do. We now have our committee on resources to work with the Ministry of Wildlife and the Ministry of Agriculture on this. This committee [the EPC] is an outgrowth of the Farmers Cooperative and is operating on the same principles by which we have governed ourselves in the past.

Ron Thompson: I thank this man for his explanation.

Chiza Africa: Did this man say he didn't need the new government?

Megan Biesele (translator): No, he was referring to the fact that sometimes their own rules of government are invisible to outsiders because they aren't written down ... it's not that he is rejecting government—not at all. He's saying, "We already have some rules by which we live."

Peter Tarr: He was saying that the people here are quite capable of regulating themselves, and they have mechanisms for doing that.

/'Angn!ao /'Un (Kiewiet): Older brother, I'm now going to address you [Chiza Africa] and only you. As we two stand here, we are not people who have bought our land. Others have bought land in this country, and if you want to discuss that with me, let's just the two of us get together to talk about that. The only people here in our area who have "bought" land are the people who live very close to us here in the south [Hereros who have "bought" G/am area by means of politics] ... We're here today to talk about land that is our own: we don't need people to come here and tell us what government we live under. I know about the government, and all I'm doing today is asking this government for certain agreements.

When I think about it, I ask myself, as we two stand here, who is the government in our area of Nyae Nyae? Is it you, younger brother? When you ask me what the government is, I say, "I am part of the government." As I understand this country, it is one that gives government powers to everyone who is in it.

As we two stand here today, you can read and write. I can't read or write at all. But I do know where I live. These differences between us go back to governments: the old government is in fact the reason I can't read or write. It's the reason I'm lacking a great deal of information about how governments operate. But here in Klein Dobe, which is my land, Nyae Nyae, I don't need you to come and tell me what government I'm living under. Here I speak as part of the new government.

I thank you very much. Tomorrow we'll speak again together.

In /'Angn!ao's transition from calling Chiza Africa, the Ministry of Lands official, "older brother" to calling him "younger brother," volumes were spoken. Yet they were spoken with traditional African tolerance and goodwill, neither offending nor cutting off further dialogue. Chiza Africa, in fact, had his rather hostile question turned around completely, and he became one of the most enthusiastic workers within the Ministry of Lands for the most significant new project to come out of Klein Dobe III—the Nyae Nyae pilot project in land use planning.

By the end of the July 1992 conference, not only had the minister of agriculture commended the NNFC's EPC for its planning ideas, but he had called, within the hearing of quite a few journalists, for "a similar public consultation process to be held in every community in Namibia." The Ministry of Lands representatives offered an even more concrete affirmation of what they had witnessed at Klein Dobe III. The officer in charge of land use planning announced that the first national land use planning pilot project in Namibia would be the Nyae Nyae area. He stated that this choice was made because of the consultation process that he and his colleagues had witnessed, because the grassroots communication system was in place and functioning in the form of the NNFC, and because the NNFC had already assembled both traditional knowledge (people's science) and scientific research on the Nyae Nyae area.

Thus, the third Klein Dobe meeting not only gave public legitimacy to the people's EPC, so many years in the making, but also tied the Namibian government legally to a local planning process under local control. This fact had profound implications for both land use planning and land tenure. The groundwork had been laid for the land use planning process to revert inexorably to the Ju/'hoan *n!ore* system, which for so long had regulated the Ju/'hoan people socially as to the land and its resources. The NNFC's proposed creative use of the *n!ore* system as the basis for a mixed-subsistence system, governed by a locally and nationally recognized cooperative, could thus be enshrined in public planning and should not be ignored in land allocation. The fact that allocation was to take place under the auspices of the same ministry as the land use planning process was further cement for the fusion of the two government functions. It was clear that communications with the DNC/MWCT, which had started years before, could quickly bear fruit in an improved atmosphere after independence.

Our next chapter traces political developments experienced by the Ju/'hoan people's organization in its various incarnations (JFU and NNFC) from 1988 to independence in 1990. These developments paralleled, informed, and were informed by the Ju/'hoansi's gradual empowerment over their natural resources through their improving relationship with the DNC/MWCT.

Chapter Five

The Lead-Up to Namibian Independence in Nyae Nyae

☀️

I thank you for this talk [about UN Resolution 435 on Namibian independence], which comes to us from far away. But one thing that gives me pain is that long ago I never heard anything like this, and only today am I hearing it. Not knowing things is death. Today my heart is happy with what I have heard. News is life.

— /Ui Djo, N=aqmtjoha, 1988

The start of the independence process in South West Africa seemed sudden when it was announced in 1988, but it had been building internationally for many years. Many of the leaders of the South West Africa People's Organization (SWAPO) had been in exile all over the world, some for as long as 30 years. Although army recruitment and training took place locally, most of the fighting occurred beyond the borders of South West Africa in Angola. What had preceded the announcement of UN Resolution 435 was a mystery to many within the country, managed from afar as the event was, with the involvement of the United Nations and powerful First World countries. The process was, for those orchestrating it, in many ways less about forming Namibia and more about carrying out a small-scale "dress rehearsal" for South African independence to come four years later. Thus, it had a remoteness and a kind of unreality about it for South West Africans, particularly those who had little access to international news.

The Ju/'hoansi were an extreme example of South West Africans cut off from information about the enormous change in the making. Watching the lead-up to independence from the perspective of Nyae Nyae meant seeing the transformation of a Third World society that had been oppressed by apartheid—but seeing it through the eyes of a Fourth World people at the very bottom of the socio-economic ladder. When news of UN Resolution 435 was finally brought to the Ju/'hoansi via their fledgling political organization (at that time called the Nyae Nyae Farmers Cooperative), their response was electrifying. The informal communication system of the Ju/'hoansi, propagated through constant inter-community visits and talk, was very effective, and political consciousness grew with astounding speed within the communities. That consciousness combined with the activist stance of their NGO, the Ju/wa Bushman Development Foundation (JBDF) to pave the way for at least a brief time of Ju/'hoan participation in high levels of governmental transformation. That time started well before independence (March 1990) and included the National Land Rights Conference (June–July 1991) and many months beyond.

This chapter details the growth of political awareness in Nyae Nyae from 1988 to April 1989, when the Ju/'hoansi definitively allied themselves with returned SWAPO exiles and started off with them on the road to independence. Two main intertwining stories chart this growth. One is a story about increasing change on the national level in South West Africa as external processes leading to independence came ever closer, eventually centering on Windhoek, the capital. The other is an account of the NNFC's struggle to provide an internally cohesive representation of Nyae Nyae communities and a voice to be reckoned with nationally in the social transformation at the moment of independence. One of the most demanding aspects of change for the Ju/'hoansi and their organization was the struggle within their communities to meet the challenges of establishing a mixed-subsistence economy.

Militarization and Politicization

In the late 1970s, outside politics had begun to be an inescapable factor in Ju/'hoan life. As previously discussed, attempts were made at that time by the South African Defence Forces (SADF) to recruit Ju/'hoan and other San trackers for their war against SWAPO. Military camps were set up at Tsumkwe and at several places in Western Bushmanland, and several hundred Ju/'hoansi took jobs in the army, little realizing what kind of "work" they were getting into or what the political consequences of collaborating with an enemy of the possible future government might be. The relatively enormous army salaries created income differentials that led to conflict within the Ju/'hoan communities. They also made it possible for dangerously large amounts of money to be spent on liquor by inexperienced young soldiers, with chaotic and sometimes violent results.

These social effects of militarization were an added incentive, beyond the reduction of Ju/'hoan land, that led to the formation of the Ju/wa (Ju/'hoan) Farmers Union (JFU). Started in 1986 with the encouragement of John

Marshall's Cattle Fund and the goal of tackling Ju/'hoan community problems, the new organization hoped, as we have stated in earlier chapters, to establish a self-determined, mixed subsistence based on more than hunting and gathering. Together, the members of the JFU struggled to combat problems such as the cattle predations of an artificially large lion population, the destruction of water installations by elephants lured into the area for safari tourists, and the hostility of administration officials who did not believe that the Ju/'hoansi were capable of managing their own communities. The JFU represented the *n!ore* groups from Tsumkwe who went back to their own land, and it also worked to enable dispossessed Ju/'hoan groups from other areas, such as the Gobabis farming district to the south, to settle on available land along the old *n!ore* lines of use and sharing of resources.

The most important work of the JFU, which became in 1988 the Nyae Nyae Farmers Cooperative (NNFC), was communicating new understandings and skills that were needed to re-establish the Ju/'hoan communities at this time of great political change in southern Africa. Traditionally, the Ju/'hoansi did not have an overarching political organization larger than their localized kin-based living groups. To meet the challenges of becoming self-sufficient and of developing a voice to speak in external forums about land rights and development, they began to explore a broadening of their familiar, tolerant, and egalitarian way of governing themselves into a version of representative democracy that would support the interests of the region as a whole.

The NNFC also discussed the relation of their land rights struggle to the independence process, as South West Africa at last became Namibia. NNFC leaders accomplished, prior to independence, an extraordinary public-awareness program, which carried to the far-flung villages of Nyae Nyae the knowledge of UN Resolution 435, the meaning of SWAPO's war for liberation, and the challenges and opportunities they would face as new citizens of a non-racist state. Men, women, adults, and children alike assembled in these communities to hear the news, expressing their profound gratitude at being included at last in the loop of information about what was to happen to the government they had been living under. By the time of the first free election in 1989, a large proportion of the Ju/'hoan population turned out as informed voters.

While political awareness was growing for the Ju/'hoansi, they were also consolidating their communities economically. With the combined help of the NNFC and the JBDF, the people of Nyae Nyae drilled boreholes for water, built stout kraals for small cattle herds, started dryland and in some cases small irrigated gardens, began selling their handicrafts on an expanded basis in Windhoek, and developed plans for community stewardship of their natural resources.

These improvements did not come without some turmoil within the communities. The once egalitarian Ju/'hoansi, whose economic activities centered on individually initiated pursuits such as hunting, had to face new challenges, both in leadership and in the organization of cooperative work and its rewards. They had to find ways of adapting the strengths of their reliable sharing system to new demands. They also had to adapt their face-to-face method of relating in small groups, where each person had a say in decisions, to the concept of decision-making by representatives charged with community trust. In the process of solving these cultural problems, the creative ideas that came forward during this tumultuous pre-independence time seemed hopeful indicators that the Ju/'hoansi were making steps toward an organic change in their polity—one that grew from within by consensus, rather than being imposed in top-down fashion by outside sources.

Debating Leadership and Representation

An exchange between G/aqo =Oma and Tsamkxao =Oma at a meeting about UN Resolution 435, Djxokhoe, 9 September 1988, went as follows:

> G/aqo =Oma: Swanie [Johan Swanepoel, the South West Africa Commissioner of Bushman Affairs] says he is the leader of Bushmanland, but he is not acting like a leader. He wants to take Ju/'hoansi *n!ore* and give it to other people! Ju/'hoansi have no idea where they'll be in the future.

> Tsamkxao =Oma: My brother, I ask you one thing. This "leader" of ours, can you name one thing he's done for us?

> G/aqo =Oma: When you talk to him he doesn't listen. He hasn't helped at all. John Marshall has helped.

> Tsamkxao =Oma: Swanie—is he a person who's ever gathered together white people *and* Ju/'hoansi to talk together? No, he just speaks to other Afrikaners. They all get together up at the Nature Conservation camp to talk. McIntyre [a former commissioner stationed at Tsumkwe] got Ju/'hoansi and white people together, but Swanie doesn't. Am I lying?

Because their own interactions with each other took place on an informal basis and their leadership was based on ad hoc, sapiential authority, the Ju/'hoansi at first dealt with government officials as individuals. Names such as Swanie, McIntyre, Ben Beytel, Dirk Mudge, Marnie Muller, Gaerdes, Loots, and Wessels—all South West Africa officials who touched their lives—peppered their talk in the pre-independence years. Outsiders were often extended a kind of fictive kinship as a way to include them politely in local communications. It was only later that the Ju/'hoansi began to realize that the actions of South West Africa Administration (SWAA) officials were representative of, and constrained by, institutional decisions and rules made far from the Ju/'hoan area and often in defiance of Ju/'hoan opinions and needs. They became aware that they had to be careful about treating officials as individuals who could be trusted to act in friendship.

About the same time, JFU officials were hashing out what it could mean for the Ju/'hoansi to have members of their communities represent them at meetings and then report back to them. Earlier, their consensus-based decision-making had made them wary of any meeting that did not include anyone who wanted to attend. The Ju/'hoansi have a strongly entrenched ethic of not speaking for others and insist on including everyone, young and old, in the loop of communication in order to avoid hard feelings. They also feel strongly that to minimize possible mistakes in judgment on the part of a few people, the larger the number of people involved in decisions, the better. Thus, the one who leads best is actually the best facilitator of group decision-making. =Oma Tsamkxao, Tsamkxao =Oma's father, who was said to have "stopped the feet" of the /Aotcha people at that *n!ore* and to have begun the repatriation of the Ju/'hoansi to their remaining land in Nyae Nyae, was a prime example of a facilitative leader. To this day, the most effective Ju/'hoan leaders are those who make sure that everyone's voice is included.

However, around 1988, outside pressures combined with practicality to make it necessary for the JFU to develop more effective representational and membership structures. Its original Constitution, written in 1986, had provided for a Management Committee, which was to be elected by JFU members. But membership requirements were not formalized until 1988, when the JFU was transformed into the more formal NNFC. This institutional change was deemed necessary when it became clear that some Ju/'hoansi from Botswana and from the Gobabis farms area to the south of Nyae Nyae wanted to join the Nyae Nyae Ju/'hoansi in settling, and thus helping to protect, the land. That is why the new Constitution defined membership candidates as "All persons who speak Ju/'hoan and call themselves Ju/'hoansi and are over the age of 18." Another criterion for membership was residency: people who had lived in the area for 10 years could become members. Lastly, membership was extended to others who could apply formally to the council. This provision allowed not only Ju/'hoansi living outside Nyae Nyae to apply, but also people from other ethnic groups in the country, some of whom had established long-term relationships of goodwill with the Ju/'hoan community.

There were long deliberations in the NNFC about what it meant to open membership to non-Ju/'hoansi. Having lived so long under apartheid isolation, many NNFC members feared being overrun by relatively richer settlers from outside the Nyae Nyae area. They worried that the integrity of their environment could be quickly compromised if pastoralists, for instance, were to arrive with unsustainable numbers of cattle. Others, however, emphasized the importance of establishing their willingness to work toward the open, democratic society that they understood Namibia would become. They eventually decided that using their traditional social sanctions to control the number of cattle that any group of people could graze in Nyae Nyae would keep problematic outsiders uninterested. This strategy, in general, worked to protect the environment until the Nyae Nyae Conservancy, the successor to the NNFC, was established in 1998.

At the other end of the scale, outsiders who might pose problems because they were too poor and thus might prove too great a drag on local resources were deterred by a separate strategy. This approach involved the NNFC deciding about the "viability" of any group that proposed to settle and farm in Nyae Nyae. Viability involved the physical strength, skills, numbers, and social organization of the groups. If they came as individuals or in small, fragmented groups without prior experience of the hard work and rough living that they would encounter, they would be respectfully turned away. This strategy, too, had the general effect of protecting Nyae Nyae from a flood of economic refugees from other areas of Namibia.

Formalizing the Nyae Nyae Farmers Cooperative

As previously recounted, the structure of the NNFC was formalized in 1988 with a Constitution written in both Ju/'hoansi and English. Each of the communities in Nyae Nyae elected two representatives to the Representative Council of the NNFC to act as voices for their communities on matters of *n!ore* allocation, *n!ore* group viability, cattle allocation, and the organization of farming labor. A first leadership structure was formalized, as well. Ongoing debate and refinement of this structure have since provided continuous opportunity for the engagement of community members in the creation of their own local and regional rules.

The Representative Council of the NNFC was to include two people from each community in Nyae Nyae, including the "municipal area" of Tsumkwe. Every six months, council members were to have meetings lasting at least three days. It was felt that the distances the representatives would have to travel, combined with the large number of issues that they would have to discuss and of people from whom they wanted to hear at each meeting, necessitated these lengthy interactions. In the first few years of the meetings, before any Ju/'hoansi had obtained driver's licenses and before their organization owned any vehicles, the transport of representatives was organized by the JBDF. This, along with the provision of food and sometimes shelter for the duration of the meetings, was a massive and expensive job for the JBDF. It soon became clear that logistical support for the meetings, which allowed the Ju/'hoansi to establish an effective decision-making body and a regional voice for themselves, was perhaps the single most important function that the Ju/'hoan people's supporting NGO provided in those years. At the early meetings, the council members selected a chairperson and representatives for an Executive Committee, to be made up of persons from "each quarter of Nyae Nyae" (JFU 1986: Article 22). It should be noted, however, as pointed out in chapter 3, that since there was still uncertainty in 1988 over the status of land in the western part of Nyae Nyae, representatives on the Executive Committee came only from the north, south, and east. The Executive Committee thus consisted at that time of a chairperson, a secretary, and three "quarter" representatives.

The NNFC debated heatedly and in detail on regional matters, from land allocation for farming or other purposes to drilling boreholes and installing water facilities. It decided on the applications of new groups for *n!ore* water points and materials to build infrastructure, the best way to interact with local government entities, and the need for NNFC members to support each other in questions about new settlements by outsiders, who might not agree to abide by the organization's rules. It emphasized that the health of the land would be preserved only by careful limitation of the numbers of introduced stock, such as cattle. It made provisions relating to conservation and resource management, including the authority to limit or prohibit the hunting of certain species of animals and to prevent the setting of bush fires. It disseminated information about the availability of community services, including health care, schooling, and vocational training, and it kept members abreast of national and international news that was likely to have an effect on the communities. As a legally constituted body, the Representative Council had the authority to initiate legal action and to receive and manage funds from the government and other sources.

The JBDF's role in the meetings of the NNFC was not limited to logistical facilitation. JBDF mentors helped the NNFC officials establish and keep to the agendas of important discussions and decisions. At first, this help was very necessary. The early meetings, before rules about speech length, precedence, and holding the floor could be established, looked chaotic from an outsider's perspective. They went on for many hours and days, sometimes threatening to end without having covered important agenda items. Unwilling to interrupt long-winded speakers, the delegates were, at the same time, very insistent on having their own say, as they would have in their traditional small groups. It was only gradually that some of the rules of parliamentary procedure were adopted. That change came about through sheer necessity and the tireless efforts of the new Ju/'hoan leaders.

A further important task carried out by JBDF staff at these meetings was documentation. At the NNFC's request, Megan Biesele made audiotape records of most of the meetings of the JFU/NNFC from 1988 to 1993. Part of the extensive Nyae Nyae Tape Archive, these audiotapes have been digitized for long-term storage and eventual dissemination with the permission of the Nyae Nyae Conservancy, the organization that has succeeded the JFU and NNFC. Some of the meetings were also filmed by John Marshall or his film team, and selections from them appear in Marshall's (2003a) last and most comprehensive film, *A Kalahari Family*.

External Political Meetings in 1988: The Struggle to Keep a Marginal Group on a Changing National Agenda

Preparations for the JFU to become the NNFC, with the organizational and representational issues that this change entailed, were made during 1988 in a series of meetings that took place outside of Nyae Nyae. These meetings were the following:

- A conference in Cape Town, called "Struggle for Land in Namibia," organized by South African activist filmmaker Cliff Bestall. Here, John Marshall and two Ju/'hoan delegates met SWAPO representatives for the first time and discussed the possible fate of communal lands if independence should in fact be achieved in Namibia.[1] Danny Tjongarero, a SWAPO friend whom the Ju/'hoansi met at that time, was then the director of communications for the Namibian Council of Churches, one of the main organizations inside South West Africa (SWA) that was active in resistance to apartheid.
- A meeting in Lusaka, Zambia, between Marshall and exiled SWAPO leader Hage Geingob, Namibia's future prime minister, set up by Hifekepunye Pohamba, Namibia's future minister of home affairs (and current president), and Tove Dix, program officer of World University Service Denmark, an organization providing aid to Namibians exiled in Angola.
- A meeting in Rehoboth, SWA, attempting to convince the Ju/'hoan people to join the Bevryde Demokratiese Partei (Liberation Front), along with the Original People's Party and other small, marginal groups that were intent on preserving the relatively privileged "colored" status that they enjoyed under the apartheid social structure. This meeting was convened by the Rehoboth

---

1. The status of SWAPO officials in Namibia before independence was complex. Some of them were in jail, while others were working undercover for fear of arrest. Some SWAPO activists served in positions in other organizations, including the Council of Churches of Namibia (CCN) and the National Union of Namibian Workers (NUNW). SWAPO activists were also working in townships around Windhoek, such as Katutura, and in the fish-processing plants of Walvis Bay. SWAPO officials traveled surreptitiously throughout Namibia, meeting with representatives of organizations or individuals, seeking support and sharing ideas and information.

Baster leader Kaptein J. G. A. Diergaardt in what was quickly revealed as a political move to increase numbers aligned with the Basters.[2]
- A meeting in Windhoek with SWAPO officials. The Ju/'hoan delegates had met some of these officials, who had been present at the Cape Town land rights meeting. This meeting was held immediately after the Ju/'hoan delegates walked out of the meeting in Rehoboth in disgust at the way that they were being co-opted by the Baster agenda.

The scattered and various nature of these meetings illustrates the confusion experienced by both the Ju/'hoan people and their NGO friends during these years. At first, they did not know where to turn politically. It was indeed a chaotic time, in which all concerned had a sense of "flying by the seat of their pants," turning this way and that in search of a good path forward for the Ju/'hoansi. Many meetings were more the result of chance occurrences than of a strict adherence to a sensible political agenda.

In the following section, we describe some of these meetings in more detail and show how they led to the Ju/'hoansi's eventual, important alignment with SWAPO. That alliance occurred many months later when SWAPO officials were finally, under cover of night, able to travel to Nyae Nyae to cement understandings about the Ju/'hoan political and economic future.

The trip to Cape Town in early May 1988 was an enormous eye-opener for the two Ju/'hoan delegates, Tsamkxao =Oma and G=kao Petrus, who flew there with John Marshall. Neither of them had been farther out of Nyae Nyae than Windhoek, let alone thousands of kilometers away in a vast city under an enormous mountain by the southern Atlantic Ocean. At the meeting, convened at the University of Cape Town, a key issue was Ju/'hoan alienation from mainstream politics in the country then struggling to become Namibia. During talks at the conference, SWAPO leaders, academics, and many observers learned that, far from being the fierce foes of SWAPO that they had been made out to be by the conservative Democratic Turnhalle Alliance (DTA), the Ju/'hoansi constituted only a small fraction of the SADF's "Bushman battalion," that they had been misled by the SADF as to the meaning of the war, and that they were in fact fighting for survival in their remaining corner of South West Africa's Bushmanland. It became very clear that the general claim that all San were supporters of the

2. The Basters, who are also known as the Rehoboth Basters after the place where they settled in central Namibia in the early 1870s, today are a group of some 35,000 people who are descendants of Dutch settlers and Africans, some of them Khoekhoe (Barnard 1992: 195–196). They are very proud of their identity and have long sought autonomy and self-determination, establishing their own system of government and leadership in the nineteenth century and continuing into the new millennium. Like San peoples, the Basters maintain that they are indigenous Namibians (see http://www.rehobothbasters.org).

SADF and would vote for the DTA was false. The consensus after the conference, following a round of critique in the newspapers and in reports of the various organizations involved (Community Education Resources 1988; JBDF 1988a, 1988b; Weinberg and Bestall 1988), was that the Ju/'hoan struggle for Bushmanland was part and parcel of the wider struggle for Namibia. As Tjongarero said, "We have all been dispossessed and suffered at the hands of colonial rule" (Weinberg and Bestall 1988: 3). G=kao Petrus summed up the Ju/'hoan delegates' own feelings about the meeting this way: "Speakers here have said that we are all Namibian, but no one has ever told us that before. We are going to change this and take what we have learnt today home to our brothers and sisters."

Along this same line, attempts were being made inside Namibia to set up a meeting on behalf of the Ju/'hoansi between Marshall and other SWAPO leaders still in exile. Here is an excerpt that Tove Dix provided from her notes:

> Having close contact with SWAPO and knowing their attitude toward the San on account of the latter's collaboration with the South Africans, I was grateful to have the opportunity to meet John Marshall. During our meeting we discussed his project, the Ju/wa Bushmen Farmers [*sic*], and I carefully introduced the political aspect of the San-issue vis-à-vis the Namibian liberation struggle. Later I brought up the San's relationship to SWAPO, the supposed future government of Namibia, and the necessity of improving it. John was adamant, however, that his project and the Ju/wa had nothing to do with politics. Nevertheless, John did concede that it would be useful for him to meet the SWAPO leadership in exile.

The meeting with SWAPO leader Geingob took place in Lusaka in mid-1988. Marshall brought with him the expert American negotiator William Ury, co-author of *Getting to Yes* (Fisher, Ury, and Patton 1981). Afterwards, Ury told the JBDF and the NNFC that the SWAPO officials, in line with their support of grassroots democracy, had stressed to Marshall the importance of adhering to cooperative principles in the formation of people's groups during the run-up to independence. So although no Ju/'hoan delegates went with Marshall and Ury to Zambia, their grassroots organization benefited greatly from the meeting.

The invitation to participate in the Liberation Front meeting, to be held 2–3 September 1988 in Rehoboth, and the Ju/'hoan meeting with SWAPO in Windhoek, which followed closely on its heels, were the result of even more unlikely circumstances. When the invitation to the Liberation Front meeting arrived in Nyae Nyae, leaders of the NNFC were uncertain about its import, as was Biesele, recently arrived as project director for the JBDF. No one seemed excited about the meeting, but it was also hard to know what it would mean to ignore the invitation, as it included several other marginal groups with whom the Ju/'hoansi hoped to establish solidarity. At the time of the invitation, South African activist photographer Paul Weinberg, who had been at the Cape Town conference, was visiting Nyae Nyae to take pictures for a future book. Marshall being absent, Weinberg agreed to help Biesele accompany the Ju/'hoansi, who went as observers to the Liberation Front meeting so that they could judge it for themselves. Here is an excerpt from Weinberg's notes for the JBDF about the meeting and the diplomatic (and very understated) response supplied by the Ju/'hoan attendees:

> [The United Nation] asked other countries to help in seeing that free and fair elections take place and that the people of Namibia control their own country. [But] this meeting [in Rehoboth] felt that Namibians in the country had been left out. The parties at this meeting were neither for SWAPO nor South Africa nor the DTA [SWAPO's major political competitor]. They agreed on a set of principles. However, the Ju/wasi Farmers Union decided to withdraw from the meeting because it felt it was not a political party and that they were concerned mainly with the land issue and administration of their land. In general the representatives, !Xashe, Tsamko, and N!ani, felt that this was a learning process. They saw politicians in practice and made up their own minds and took decisions. They also saw that people will make decisions for them and that they need to tell politicians what the needs of the Ju/wasi are.

While still in the capital area with the Ju/'hoan observers, Weinberg offered to take them, along with Biesele, to SWAPO headquarters in Windhoek. After the stifling, coercive atmosphere of the Rehoboth meeting, the three Ju/'hoansi said they felt genuinely welcomed in the SWAPO office as fellow countrymen. Moreover, the staff in the office knew of them and their efforts to develop and definitively settle the remote part of the country that they had come from. They again greeted SWAPO official Tjongarero, discussed their mutual aim of cooperation, and quickly made a plan for SWAPO representatives to visit Nyae Nyae to meet with the NNFC whenever they possibly could. The delegation from Nyae Nyae then headed back on the long road home with light hearts, feeling they were on the right track at last.

A Decisive Road Trip

News of the upcoming implementation of UN Resolution 435, with free elections to follow in November 1989, had startled the Ju/'hoansi into a realization of the magnitude of possible changes. In September 1988, soon after the return of the delegation that had gone to Rehoboth and Windhoek, members of the NNFC went on the road to take the news to the far-flung *n!oresi*. To reach the almost 500 people who had by then left Tsumkwe and resettled on the land, they ranged for days along many miles of bumpy, pot-holed, sandy, muddy, and sometimes impassable tracks, bringing the news of the international peace talks and the trip to Rehoboth and Windhoek to the Nyae Nyae communities, not one of which at that time had a radio.

During the trip, the NNFC visitors were greeted by increasingly excited groups of Ju/'hoansi at the first nine *n!ore* communities that had been established, including N//oaq!osi, Djxokhoe, !Ao='a, and N=aqmtjoha. There was a feeling of intoxication in the air that had nothing to do with alcohol and everything to do with the Ju/'hoan people's new sense of validation. There was a belief that their own, deeply held social values could have new life in the Namibian society that was to come, as reflected in records of people's commentaries at the meetings. During the meeting at //Auru on 13 September 1988, Di//xao =Oma, one of the first women *n!ore* representatives, explained as follows:

> When someone says, "You Bushmen have no government," we'll say that our old, old people long ago had a government, and it was an ember from the fire where we last lived which we used to light the fire at the new place where we were going ... I *know* this place where my fathers and mothers gave birth to me and nourished me, and I grew up to be like I am. But we don't know where these Afrikaners were born or who their fathers were: where are their fathers' and mothers' *n!oresi*? What do these people know about carrying embers to start a new fire? Have they ever picked up an ember and gone forward with it? We say, "Don't hold us back: we want to lift ourselves up." We have our own talk: it isn't other people's talk. Long ago when we went to our new camps, we brought embers from our old camps. When has this government ever come to *us* with an ember?

Di//xao =Oma's brother, Tsamkxao =Oma, the first chairperson of the NNFC, spoke of the way that they would now be able to protect the *n!oresi*, which they held so dear. "Your father's father's *n!ore* is a place you do not leave," he said. In his speeches he began to extend the word *n!ore* to encompass regions far beyond Nyae Nyae—to cities, states, and even countries as large as the United States. "America-*n!ore*," he said, is where the decision to send UN troops to Namibia was made. Tsamkxao =Oma referred to these peace-bringing UN troops, which were painting all the khaki South African army vehicles white, as "the army of understanding rather than anger."

At the community of N//oaq!osi, the information meeting was held in the shade, near a circle of small huts recently made of sticks and freshly dried grass. N!ani Kxao, one of the men who had gone with Tsamkxao on the trip to the capital, said:

> All those things we heard at the meeting—they were heavy things. We have to think about it: if things are going to change this way, how are we going to react to them? There were many things we saw there: there are so many different kinds of people. Black people spoke, white people spoke, one person and then another ... They said everyone was alike and that no one's speech would be ignored, that everyone was a person like everyone else. They told us we should throw our hearts into the talk. They said we should listen and later ask ourselves what we should do about this tomorrow. We said we wanted to live and die where our fathers and mothers are buried.

The travelers, trying to explain elections to people who had no word for them in their language and had never even heard the Afrikaans word for election, *Verkiesing*, put it as follows: "An election means to come to an understanding about a *n!ore* ... An election means that you give praise to the person who will sit in the chair of leading, the head person ... An election is where you plant your feet and stop."

The talks about elections and other democratic concepts were mostly held outdoors, with a tree or a shelter of sticks and leaves for shade, or underneath a pole framework with sliced wild melons drying overhead. People sat on old blankets or skins or on the silver-gray sand. One day, when sand was blowing violently, making conversation impossible, the travelers were forced indoors into tiny mud houses, where entire communities sat on top of each other to hear the news.

At Djxokhoe, Tsamkxao =Oma said, "The Farmers Cooperative is coming into government things much later than everyone else. The Boers took hold of things first. Now it's very late, and we have to get going." He went on to outline the recent trip to Windhoek, during which he and the other two delegates saw Dirk Mudge, then minister of finance and economic planning, along with the head of police and the administrator-general of South West Africa, Louis Pienaar, on television. They had been discussing recent peace talks and UN Resolution 435. Tsamkxao also told everyone about two confounding discussions in the same morning with government officials, one of whom told the Ju/'hoansi that they were now responsible for defending against elephants the government-installed wind pumps of the Nyae Nyae area, while the other reiterated that the Ju/'hoansi had no legal right to control any of the government's actions there. Such infuriating exchanges had become familiar to the Ju/'hoansi. Tsamkxao put his head in his hands and sighed. Then he said simply, "Let's think together and talk together. People should take hold of each other's hands."

A young man named G/aqo, wearing an SADF cap and boots, asked to be recognized. He spoke not only Ju/'hoansi but also Fanagalo (the *lingua franca* of the gold mines), which he learned during his time in Johannesburg with the Witwatersrand Native Labor Association. His wider perspective on personal and group rights and his communication skills came into play as he explained to his relatives the laws by which the Ju/'hoansi had lost so much control over their lives. A young mother, /Asa, said that it was time for all the communities to work together to protect the Nyae Nyae area. "Didn't our fathers and their fathers die here? How can we let these unmannerly people step on their graves? We have to cry out for our *n!oresi!*" A middle-aged man, who sat by in ragged shorts, with several toes poking out of his shoes, was quiet until his turn came to talk. He then revealed his anger that no help and no hearing seemed to be forthcoming from local or national officials. "They are employed to be the 'owners of helping,' and we trust them at first. But soon they come to seem like jackals, sneaking around behind us instead."

Tsamkxao was aware that he had a huge job ahead of him to convey to the isolated inhabitants of Nyae Nyae the nature of the new opportunities and challenges that awaited them in the coming independence. He realized that UN Resolution 435 and free elections and the final end of apartheid would suddenly overtake them, and many of the Ju/'hoan people would not know what these events actually portended: "We who were first have come to be last. We are behind. Now we must work fast to catch up. If there's going to be a new government, we still don't know what we, Ju/'hoansi, are going to do. If Namibia will become an independent country and if Namibian people will all get together to discuss things, we still don't know how to be part of it. We should let all our people know, all talk about what to do. A new day is coming. There is a new law coming. We are going to start a new law." He was also aware that the Ju/'hoansi had lived through decades of administrations whose communications somehow missed them, not only because of isolation, but because, being egalitarian, they did not have identifiable "chiefs": "They say we have no government and we agree, asking what help we have ever gotten from any government ... But today things are changing. The government of this country is changing too. Other countries like America-*n!ore* have spoken and said the government must change. America-*n!ore* says that Namibia should have its own say, that all of us in Namibia should have our say."

Suddenly, in 1988 and 1989, the Ju/'hoansi faced both the challenge and the opportunity of taking part in a political process that was being watched eagerly by the eyes of the world. Their friends in the JBDF and around the globe asked, though, whether a small minority with a hunting and gathering heritage, a history of under-education and exclusion from affairs that concerned them, and a problematic situation of economic under-development and militarization could transform itself quickly enough to make the most of this turn of events. Would the Ju/'hoansi be able to hold onto some of their ancient territory and also take advantage of the new national opportunities of freedom?

Leadership and Propaganda

As at the South African Cape three centuries earlier, when leaders were called into being among San groups battling for their lives with the Dutch colonists (Marks 1972), the Ju/'hoansi were beginning to create strong leaders to meet the challenges of the present. As one of them put it, "At first we had no leaders, but now we're making leaders because these days we're getting strong. We're learning not to take the suggestions of just anybody about what we should do. We'll elect someone who comes from our own *n!ore*, to work for our interests ... This cabinet [of the interim government], which has told only a few people what it's doing, not everybody, works that way in order to put its own people into office. They're looking for people they can run as they like, people whose brains are short."

The DTA interim government was supported in part by the military opponents of SWAPO, who engaged in last-ditch propaganda efforts. In March 1989, huge armored vehicles swept into /Aotcha, a tiny Nyae Nyae village of mud huts, and stopped, towering over the people like dinosaurs. Effectively silencing the usual village hubbub, uniformed men with submachine guns announced that they were there to hold a "public relations" meeting. The SADF was then pulling out of northern Namibia, and as it went it was stumping for the DTA party, SWAPO's main opposition. "Watch out for the hyena (SWAPO)" and "Vote for the eland (DTA)" were the condescending slogans that the soldiers offered. "The eland is the animal without deceit: you are the people of the eland."

The Ju/'hoan hunters' sign for eland antelope horns is the letter "V," formed with the fingers. This also happened to be the adopted "victory" hand sign for the DTA. In a further ironic twist, which the soldiers could not have known about, but which made the puzzle even harder for the Ju/'hoansi to unravel, "Eland" is an ancient clan name for many Ju/'hoansi in the area. Some people were taken in by this overwhelming symbolism, but others remained skeptical. "SWAPO's never done anything to us. Why should anyone call them hyenas before hearing what they have to say?" asked Tsamkxao.

The soldiers next attempted to get the /Aotcha community to practice ("play") voting on mock ballots drawn up for non-literate people, to which Tsamkxao said, "Why should we 'play' with something as important as the election?" Ultimately, the public relations meeting was a bit of a rout because the officer in charge refused Tsamkxao's request to tape the session. The message brought by the SADF that day was hardly secret, but since it and the people's responses could not be taped as a public record, the people regarded the communication as a "theft."[3]

The nuances of strong symbolism further backfired on the SADF during the last feverish days of election campaigning in Nyae Nyae. Dabe Dam, the NNFC representative for //Auru village, criticized the DTA's use of the eland hand sign to represent its party. Having observed violent drunkenness and clear intimidation of potential voters by DTA campaigners, he said, "Today my shame is piled high. My people's name from long ago, 'the people of the eland,' has been rubbed in the dirt and stolen by politicians who will never do anything for us. All they want is to give other people our land." Later that day in the same village, people spoke of the loss of the actual eland on which they

3. Unfortunately for the SADF, it did not know that the Ju/'hoansi call tape cassettes =*xusi*— their word for oracle disks. These disks are traditionally made from eland hide and are thus associated with the eland's herd sociability and supposed guilelessness. Taping the meeting on =*xusi* would have established that it was an open event without hidden agendas.

once depended. Many adults remembered a time when eland were abundant in their area, a time before game fences restricted their migration and before armed hunters, some of them soldiers from nearby SADF camps, had greatly reduced herd sizes.

> Trucks with hunters shooting from them have chased away the animals we had here, trucks and the fences that have been built. Long ago you saw all the animals here, including eland. But today there's not a single eland. You don't even see ostrich eggs, because the ostriches too are stopped by the fences. We don't want this. We want the fences taken down so that wild animals will come back and be close to us as before ... Long ago the eland used to cross Nyae Nyae according to the season, but one season the fence was closed on them and on their calves, and they haven't returned. (N=amce, at the N=aqmtjoha meeting, 15 October 1989)

Issues of theft and deception were major themes during discussions of the Ju/'hoansi's unwitting involvement in the SADF's war with SWAPO in Angola.

> We thought our young men were being offered a job of work, like any other job, by the SADF. The only difference was the salaries were much bigger. But we came to see it was a job of anger and of killing and of deception. The SADF said that they were helping us against SWAPO, but we found out that we were helping them instead. SWAPO never did anything to us. Most of us have asked our children to come home. (Kaqece G/aq'o, at the !Ao='a meeting, 15 September 1988)

Only a handful of Ju/'hoan soldiers were involved in the external civil war, compared to the many Angolan San trackers who, having lost their land to years of war there, had few other options. The situation of San who went into the army was like that of the Montagnard people of Vietnam in the 1960s. Out of economic need and due to ignorance of the wider implications of the war there, the Montagnards participated as a way to feed their families. Later, the Ju/'hoansi saw the broader significance.

> We knew nothing about the war and were just sitting around and saw it come. Now we have to have our own meetings, to come to an understanding about this. We are people who do not fight like that. It was something our fathers and mothers didn't know. We only wanted to talk about our *n!oresi*, not about the fighting. We didn't want fighting. (Kaqece G/aq'o, at the !Ao='a meeting, 15 September 1988)

SWAPO Visits the Ju/'hoansi

At the very end of March 1989, the long-awaited visit of SWAPO officials to Nyae Nyae occurred at /Aotcha. The officials had to travel by night so as not to be questioned by the military police, since SWAPO was still considered an illegal organization by SWAA. Their arrival was a joyous occasion, a reunion of sorts because of shared political views, although most of the Ju/'hoansi were meeting them for the first time. The assembled NNFC representatives and the people of /Aotcha, who had gone to sleep hours before, got up immediately and started a dance of welcome that lasted until dawn.

The following day, the meeting of SWAPO with the NNFC, which lasted all day, carried an air of profound relief and excitement. With the two groups sitting in the grass in a rough circle of about 40 people, including onlookers, the NNFC presented a document stating its goals regarding land and representation. Written in Ju/'hoansi and translated into English, the statement called for a democratic national system with regional autonomous government in Nyae Nyae, based on current and long-term residence. The Ju/'hoansi reiterated, and the SWAPO visitors acknowledged, their unbroken contact with the fragment of land that was still theirs. They spoke not just of the land but of their *ties* to the land as their main resource: "Where your mother and father are buried is where you have your strength."

The NNFC delegates knew it was still an open question whether Ju/'hoan concepts of belonging to the land could influence national thinking after independence. The SWAPO delegates invited them to participate in the difficult tasks that lay ahead and in the national meetings and conversations that would determine the nature of the new democracy. SWAPO representatives spoke of their hopes for a truly multicultural state and the eventual dissolution of the old "native location" slums like the one outside of Windhoek, where non-white workers lived to serve the white population of the capital. Called Katutura in the Herero language, the name of this location had meant, all during the struggle against apartheid, "A Place We Do Not Stay." Tsamkxao, his sister Di//xao, and the other NNFC representatives responded that they look on Ju/'hoan *n!ore*, where their ancestors are buried, as "A Place We Do Not Leave."[4]

After this historic meeting, the political tide began to turn in Eastern Bushmanland against the DTA, which was increasingly seen as a retrograde party of the old order, in favor of SWAPO and its promise of democratic participation for all in "the new Namibia." During the year left before independence was celebrated in March 1990, DTA campaigners, scrambling for every vote, fought hard for the hearts and minds of the Ju/'hoansi, but they ultimately lost out to the people's desire for change.

---

4. The quotes and details in this chapter are taken from a manuscript by the same name, written by Biesele, which is a chronicle of the meetings held at the nine *n!oresi* after the announcement of UN Resolution 435 and its implementation.

Nyae Nyae community meeting at N=aqmtjoha to discuss the United Nations Resolution 435 on Namibian independence. Tsamkxao =Oma speaking, Megan Biesele recording, September 1988. Courtesy of Paul Weinberg.

Nyae Nyae Ju/'hoan woman by her fire with soldier husband and child. Tsumkwe, 1984. Courtesy of Paul Weinberg.

Ju/'hoan woman at the government-subsidized bottle store, Tsumkwe, 1984. Courtesy of Paul Weinberg.

Ju/'hoan woman bringing water to !Ao='a village beneath a baobab tree, 2003. Photograph by Catherine Collett for Kalahari Peoples Fund.

≠Oma Tsamkxao, the leader "who stopped our feet" (from wandering) and settled his extended family at the permanent /Aotcha waterhole, 1987. Courtesy of Paul Weinberg.

Ju/'hoan man and steer share cattle trough, /Aotcha, 1987. Courtesy of Paul Weinberg.

Ju/'hoan boy watching cattle, /Aotcha, 1987. Courtesy of Paul Weinberg.

Ju/'hoan girl at /Aotcha watching mounted SADF patrol, 1984. Courtesy of Paul Weinberg.

Tsamkxao =Oma and N!ani Kxao speaking at meeting on behalf of Nyae Nyae, Cape Town, 1987. Courtesy of Paul Weinberg.

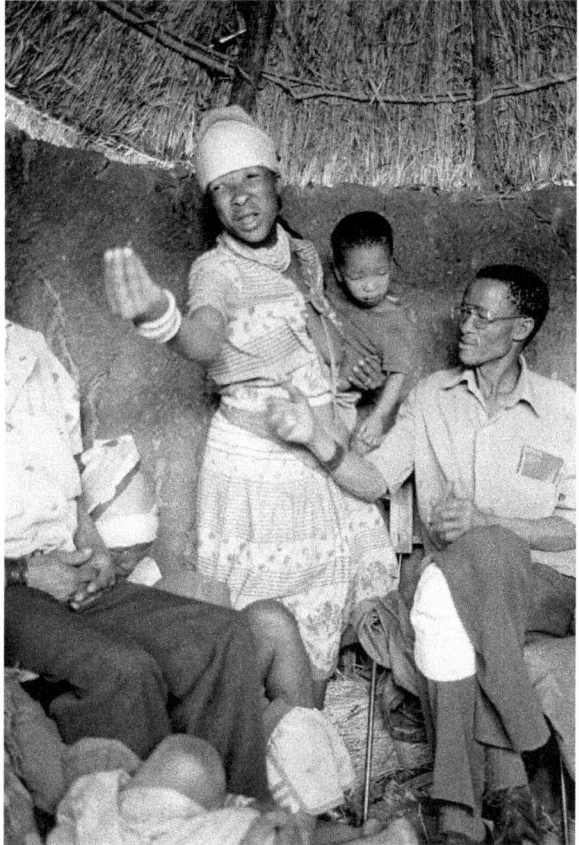

Di//xao =Oma and G=kao Dabe, representatives of their communities for the NNFC, speak about the need to protect the Nyae Nyae *n!oresi* on a road trip to discuss UN Resolution 435, September, 1988. Courtesy of Paul Weinberg.

SADF Casspir on patrol, /Aotcha, 1988. Courtesy of Paul Weinberg.

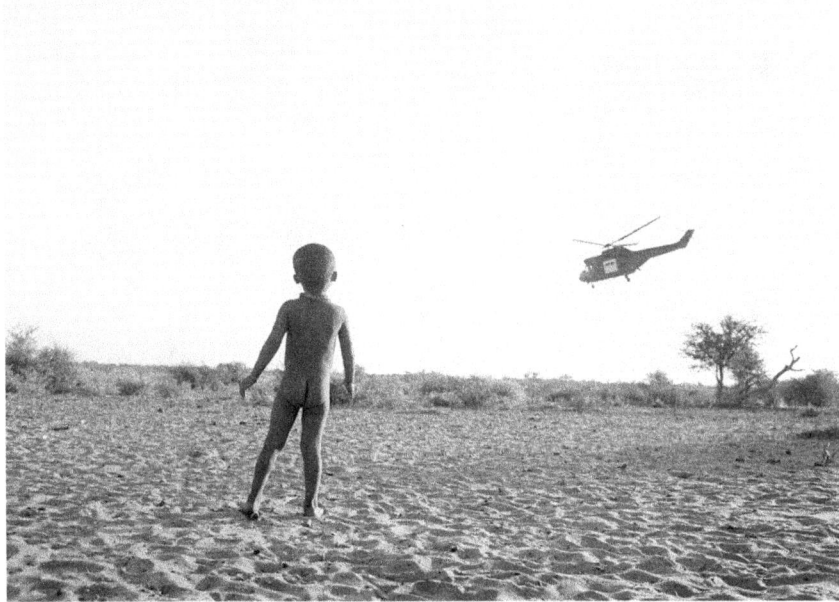

UN helicopters drop off ballots for the elections, //Auru, 1989. Courtesy of Paul Weinberg.

Tsamkxao =Oma and a visiting SWAPO supporter dancing down Tsumkwe's street at a SWAPO rally, November, 1989. Photograph by Claire Ritchie.

Headquarters of the Nyae Nyae Conservancy, Tsumkwe, 2003. Photograph by Catherine Collett for Kalahari Peoples Fund.

Laptop computers were donated to the Village Schools Project during the filming of the update by Daniel Riesenfeld to *The Gods Must Be Crazy* by Jamie Uys. Baraka, Nyae Nyae, 2003. Photograph by Catherine Collett for Kalahari Peoples Fund.

Transcription trainees Tsamkxao Fanni /Ui and /Ai!ae Fridrick /Kunta working at the Captain Kxao Kxami Community Learning and Development Centre, Tsumkwe, 2006. Photograph by Catherine Collett for Kalahari Peoples Fund.

Chapter Six

Independence
The Years of Hope

❦

Thanks to the Ju/wa Bushman Development Foundation (JBDF), the Nyae Nyae Farmers Cooperative (NNFC) was able to establish close contact with officials of the United Nations Transition Assistance Group (UNTAG), who set up a small station in Tsumkwe. With UNTAG's help, the Ju/'hoansi learned to rebut the anti-liberation propaganda of the departing South African Defence Force (SADF). NNFC communities were enabled to vote at polling booths that were helicoptered into their remote area. Being part of the process that brought about the absolute end of the repressive, Afrikaner-dominated South West Africa (SWA) regime—and ended petty apartheid in their area for good—made a permanent change in the consciousness of the Ju/'hoansi. They discovered that their own efforts could make a difference, both locally and nationally, and after that, although often constrained by circumstances, they grew freer and freer to speak their own minds. The Ju/'hoansi were very excited about what it would mean to be citizens of a free—and hopefully more equal—nation at last.

Preparations for Independence

The registration process and the campaign rallies themselves were part of the learning process for the Ju/'hoansi. They saw electioneering that ranged in tone from measured, informative meetings, like those they had with the South West Africa People's Organization (SWAPO), to the Wild West-like efforts of the Democratic Turnhalle Alliance (DTA), which were complete with young men driving drunk around the villages in light trucks, shooting guns out the windows into the sky. The latter drew crowds partly because they dispensed T-shirts and sometimes food. Many Ju/'hoansi, particularly children, eagerly accepted the T-shirts because they had few other clothes. "I needed a shirt," one SWAPO supporter said simply.

On 1 April 1989, the plan under UN Resolution 435 to monitor voter registration, political campaigning, and the process of voting for a new government went into effect. Encouraged by the JBDF, UNTAG established an office in a portable building in Tsumkwe and in June began a series of informative meetings built around voter registration at the Nyae Nyae villages. The JBDF played a notable and rather indispensable role in UNTAG's effectiveness by arranging for Benjamin /Ai!ae /Aice, a Ju/'hoan translator who was adept at English, to work for French UNTAG official Claude Echard at these meetings. It was necessary for Benjamin to travel from Botswana, because up to that point the only second language available to the few Ju/'hoansi who had obtained schooling in Namibia was Afrikaans. An excellent translator, Benjamin became for a time the busiest person in Tsumkwe, as UNTAG personnel of all nationalities came to rely on his English as their *lingua franca* with the local population. Other educated Ju/'hoansi, who had been limited to learning Afrikaans, felt cheated that they could not help with translations at this historic time and bitterly blamed the SWA school system for holding them back in this critical way. Many wanted the future government to make English the national language, and this was one of many factors that began to turn them away from uncritical acceptance of the DTA.

Language and education were especially highlighted as rights issues in Nyae Nyae at this time because of the arrival in May 1989 of linguist Patrick Dickens. Ironically, Dickens joined the JBDF in answer to an ad for a horticultural instructor and only later mentioned modestly that he had some knowledge of Khoesan languages, commonly known as "click" languages. Dickens set to work, not only on starting dryland farming, facilitating the NNFC's agricultural programs, and teaching several NNFC staff how to drive, but also on transforming the Ju/'hoan-Afrikaans dictionary work of Jan Snyman (1975) into what became the authoritative *English-Ju/'hoan, Ju/'hoan-English Dictionary* (Dickens 1994). Along with this work, Dickens taught English and literacy in their own language to a group of Ju/'hoan youth, who became the first teachers of the Village Schools Project (chronicled in chapter 10). From that point on, in the minds of the Nyae Nyae people, the revitalization of the Ju/'hoan language and learning English became inextricably linked with obtaining control of their land and with their rights as citizens of the new Namibia.

As information that was more relevant to them began to become available, some Ju/'hoansi took a critical stance toward the complex of oppressive military and economic forces that had been held in place by the DTA, the political party in power. The DTA pulled out all stops in trying to keep the supposedly passive Ju/'hoan population, which was small but numerically significant in the country's overall modest population, under their aegis and to persuade them to vote against SWAPO. Compared to the reasoned, issue-filled information distributed by SWAPO in Nyae Nyae on 12 July 1989, the DTA's sloganeering about "building houses for all Namibians" seemed empty and beside the point. DTA election rallies were circus-like affairs, as reflected in John Marshall's film record of that era. The Ju/'hoan mouthpiece for the DTA, Kaqece "Geelbooi" (Afrikaans for "yellow boy," a pejorative), who had houses in both Tsumkwe and Katutura (the Windhoek "native location"), appeared ever more disconnected from his community. To the members of the NNFC, who had been honing their political awareness over several years by then, he seemed embarrassingly puppet-like. Marshall's film of a DTA rally held in Tsumkwe on 15 July 1989 shows how the chaotic, near violent, and politically desperate nature of DTA campaigning ultimately caused most of the Ju/'hoansi to vote for SWAPO.

Nyae Nyae on the International Stage

From June until late November 1989, when it was announced that SWAPO had won the election, the JBDF and the NNFC were inundated by international visitors of all kinds. Namibian independence became the darling of the world's media in that half-year, and political figures, development workers, researchers, and activists from all over the world made pilgrimages to visit this once shuttered domain of apartheid. Prominent on the travel map—despite their remote locations that were several days' hard drive on bad roads from Windhoek—were the exotic Fourth World San of the country, of whom the most accessible were the Ju/'hoansi. The Ju/'hoansi were accessible because their communities were not fragmented like those of many other dispossessed Namibian San: they still held on to a fragment of their ancestral land. Importantly, through the exertions of their people's organization, the NNFC, they began to get international press about their goal of forming a democratic body where none had existed before, so as to represent their interests as a regional group. Marshall was filming and writing, along with other JBDF members, about their efforts to do this. Meanwhile, the critical drilling of boreholes for community water went on under the auspices of the NNFC and the JBDF, and visitors could see with their own eyes how determined the Ju/'hoansi were to occupy their land and make a dignified living there.

Extracts from a diary of the second half of 1989 written by Dickens give the flavor of this breathless period of visits: it seemed a different group of nationalities visited every day. Most of the international visitors ended up at the JBDF headquarters in /Aotcha, which consisted at that time of a mud-and-stick kitchen with an outdoor cooking and washing-up area, a few tents, and two small derelict trailers. In one of Dickens's entries, we learn that at the JBDF camp on 1 July 1989, "Mrs. Ahtisaari washe[d] the dishes." Her husband, Martti Ahtisaari, was the UN special representative heading UNTAG and later served as president of Finland. At first, the JBDF was excited that the Ju/'hoansi and their projects were receiving so much international attention. Later, it became positively overwhelming. The daily challenge for the JBDF staff was to figure out how to accommodate the needs of those travelers whose missions were critical to the Ju/'hoansi's future, while remaining polite to those whose missions were less so. The staff members were acutely aware of the intense pressure that these non-stop visits were putting on the Nyae Nyae communities and especially on those NNFC leaders who lived at /Aotcha. The leaders and the JBDF staff were, by turns, exhilarated and worn to exhaustion by the spotlight shining so brilliantly on Nyae Nyae in those months. Matters were not helped by the fact that the rains had been excessively good that year, with a subsequent explosion in the mouse population. Mice ate their way into JBDF supplies and equipment, including the cables of the radiotelephone that was the JBDF's only connection to the outside world at that time.[1]

JBDF Activities and Headquarters

This period of intense activity cemented the JBDF staff's collaboration as no other experience could have. Bound not only by the diverse commitments that had got each person involved, but also by the rigors, challenges, and extraordinary circumstances that they collectively endured, the still small JBDF staff became a closely cooperating and mutually respectful team. Claire Ritchie, among her many other tasks, continued her pioneering work of documenting the composition of the *n!ore* groups to facilitate cattle ownership and the allocation of tools. Megan Biesele honed her Ju/'hoan language skills by helping Benjamin /Ai!ae /Aice with translations at meetings, assisting Dickens in the preparation of the new dictionary and Ju/'hoan language curriculum materials, and accompanying NNFC chairperson Tsamkxao =Oma as his personal facilitator for meetings protocol, agendas, and documentation. Marshall and his film crew at the time (John Bishop, Peter Baker, and Pitchie Rommelaere) made visual records of drilling, agricultural activities, and political meetings, which were used to raise awareness nationally and internationally of what the Ju/'hoansi were doing to keep their land and develop their voice as citizens in an independent nation.

---

1. Marshall's film crew, during time off from their relentless work of chronicling the lead-up to independence, made an underground film, *Mousebusters*, with the JBDF staff under the direction of John Bishop. As yet unreleased, the film was a team-building exercise for sure.

At this time, the JBDF board, a group of Namibians with whom Marshall and Ritchie had begun the organization,[2] met in Windhoek and requested that thought be given to building a more permanent and useful headquarters than the camp at /Aotcha. Board member Robert Camby pointed out that the JBDF would not want to leave a dilapidated camp like its /Aotcha headquarters as its physical legacy to the soon-to-be independent country. Marshall and Ritchie accordingly located a Windhoek architect, who began work in September 1989, following extensive discussions between the JBDF and the NNFC about where to locate the new headquarters. It was agreed to move north and east from /Aotcha in order to be more centrally located among the various Nyae Nyae *n!ore* communities. The reason for this decision was that jealousy was simmering over the perceived historical privileging that /Aotcha had received from the JBDF. Because of Marshall's long relationship with the /Aotcha people, the JBDF had naturally located itself where his family had begun its work in the 1950s.

It was true that travel to the *n!oresi* farthest from /Aotcha was difficult, time-consuming, and costly, due to fuel and vehicle repair expenses. The eventual move to a place called Baraka (named not for the word "peace" in Arabic but for an SADF army barracks once located there) would put the JBDF camp much closer to the better road between Tsumkwe and the Botswana border. It would also make it possible for others besides the /Aotcha people to have more equal access to training, jobs, driver's licenses, and other benefits available through the JBDF. This, at least, was the theory. The way that it worked out in practice was different and quite problematic, as detailed in chapters 8 and 9.

Independence and the Formal End of National Apartheid

The long-awaited Namibian independence celebrations took place all over the country on 21 March 1990, and they were indeed exhilarating. So many large international jets bearing dignitaries from all over the world arrived at the small Windhoek airport that they had to be parked in neighboring countries. Although John Marshall was not in Namibia at the time, his film crews took footage of two aspects of the festivities: the Ju/'hoansi watching the national parade in downtown Windhoek, and Tsamkxao dancing down the main road of Tsumkwe with Namibians of other ethnic groups. Nonetheless, there was a strange air of disconnectedness to the proceedings, an uncertainty, especially for residents of communal lands such as the Ju/'hoansi. Could a society so long distorted by apartheid change enough to make a positive difference in their lifetimes?

2. These Namibians included Beatrice Sandelowsky, Olga Levinson, Charles Hartung, Clive Cowley, Zach Kazapua, Kuno Budack, Robert Camby, and June Horwitz.

Many apartheid social relations and formal political structures were in the process of being liberalized about a decade before South West Africa became Namibia in 1990. Even so, racial and ethnic stratification persisted strongly until independence, when the incoming SWAPO government challenged itself to generate quickly new democratic relations from a complex colonial legacy. The Ju/'hoansi and other San, treated as a "bottom rung" even below other non-whites on the apartheid ladder, were one of 11 ethnic groups that a new multi-racial democratic ethic was going to have to include, at least according to SWAPO rhetoric and international expectations. Even long after formal independence actualized many real democratic gains, there remained a deep underlayer of economic structuring in Namibia that was racial in nature. At its core was an enormous disparity between commercial and communal land rights. The national percentage of what was considered commercial land was about 60 percent. Located in the most fertile areas of the country, it had long before been sequestered to white land ownership. A mere 5 percent of the Namibian population lived on commercial land. All inhabitants of communal lands and landless squatters lived on the remaining 40 percent of the land—the least productive in the country.

Security of Communal Tenure Rights and Regional Cooperation

Between independence and the 1991 Namibian National Conference on Land Reform and the Land Question held in Windhoek, in which the Ju/'hoansi participated, the unclear status of communal lands in Namibia was in the forefront of the minds of everyone in the NNFC and the JBDF. Rumors flew about plans for pre-emptive government land allocations that would not take seriously either community organizations or longevity of tenure. It was a time of great insecurity for the Ju/'hoansi, who had little faith, despite their long history in Nyae Nyae, that they would be treated any differently from marginalized, already dispossessed Namibians. In January 1991, the new government did in fact make surprise land allocations around the former military base in Western Bushmanland that caused an outcry among the Ju/'hoansi of Eastern Bushmanland. The Ju/'hoansi were justifiably afraid that a model of 5-hectare allocations to heads of families (all to be male) would destroy their communal, egalitarian *n!ore* system overnight. An information meeting was called in late January at Aasvoelnes, a mixed San community at a former SADF base on the border between the eastern and western portions of Bushmanland.

NNFC leaders stood in the heat, among straw blown from the disintegrating grass huts of former San soldiers, and asked why they had not been informed about the allocations. "But they *were* informed about the allocations. It was on TV!" remarked a white Afrikaner, who was then schoolmaster of the tin-roofed Aasvoelnes school, at a time when only 2 of the 2,000 Ju/'hoansi of Nyae Nyae had ever seen a television, and then only rarely on trips to Windhoek with John Marshall. The Ju/'hoansi additionally learned that certain land "allocations"— prior to any articulation of policy or legislation—had indeed been quietly made by the new Ministry of Lands, Resettlement, and Rehabilitation (MLRR) to inhabitants of Western Bushmanland. The people living in this area were for the most part ex-soldiers and Khwe and Vasekela Bushmen who had worked for the SADF against SWAPO. They were literally starving after the departure of the SADF—and, like the Ju/'hoansi, they had very few televisions. Allocations in fact did occur in the form of 5-hectare plots to male heads of households. Many of the Western Bushmanland people had gone along with the allocations, thinking that they were being given garden plots to use in addition to "the bush" in general, never dreaming that these plots might be both their first and final chance to have and use land in Namibia. The distress felt by the Vasekela people of Western Bushmanland over this issue led to their eventual participation, along with the NNFC, in the National Land Conference in mid-1991.

For the moment, it remained unclear whether the allocation model used in Western Bushmanland would apply to other communal lands in Namibia. This uncertainty gave added impetus to the NNFC's preparation for the National Land Conference. Later, during the conference and its aftermath, this allocation model was called into question by local groups and by NGOs. They argued that time-tested, traditional, land use patterns and extended family distribution of resources were much more likely than this model to produce a living on Kalahari sand. They pointed out that the MLRR may have been generalizing from a Namibian model, but it was one that presupposed a riverine environment, such as the Okavango far to the north. They asked for long-used subsistence activities, such as hunting and gathering, to be given status as recognized forms of land use. They also pointed out the social and gender implications of the 5-hectare policy and asked for attention to varying ethnic family arrangements in land allocation.

In the Western Bushmanland case, as in many other cases for potential allocation in Namibia, this model was inappropriate for at least four reasons. The San groups there and to the east in Nyae Nyae shared social characteristics of complex, rather than atomistic, extended family relationships to land, and of gender—and general—egalitarianism. They had in common a general economic background of extensive, rather than intensive, land use (based at least partly on foraging), of relative mobility of lifestyle, and of collaborative, interlocking patterns of land use founded on local resource territories (*n!oresi*) with environmental specificity. "How could we find our food if our neighbors fenced it off from us?" one resident of nearby Eastern Bushmanland (Nyae Nyae) protested. "We have to know the land well and be able look for our food when it ripens—if necessary, in all directions."

The gender implications of the 5-hectare policy were particularly inappropriate for the Ju/'hoansi, described in anthropological literature as some of the 'least sexist' people known (Draper 1975). Ju/'hoansi living just east of the Khwe and Vasekela were incensed at the idea that this policy might be extended to them, and awareness of the threat it posed to their society spread quickly just before the 1991 National Land Conference. Because of the protest which arose at that time, the first wave of allocations was not allowed to proceed farther east toward Nyae Nyae.

Other Effects of Independence in Nyae Nyae

Between January and June 1991, when the National Land Conference was held, events in Nyae Nyae reflecting the changes brought by independence came thick and fast. After the Aasvoelnes meeting, the JBDF and the NNFC were fully involved in a groundbreaking survey of community resources and opinions mandated by the Department of Nature Conservation and facilitated by environmental activist Garth Owen-Smith and anthropologist Margaret Jacobsohn. Owen-Smith and Jacobsohn's Integrated Rural Development and Nature Conservation (IRDNC) project had pioneered similar surveys for appropriate development in the Kaokoveld with the Himba and in West Caprivi with the Khwe San and their neighbors, the Kavango.

In February, Patrick Dickens met in Windhoek with other linguists, who had worked for the South West Africa Administration, in order to discuss the new orthography he had written for the Ju/'hoan language. He successfully argued for the official adoption of this practical, streamlined, but linguistically professional Ju/'hoan orthography, which had been crafted so that the language could be written on any typewriter or computer and learned quickly by native speakers. The previous orthography, written by linguists of the Dutch Reformed Church to be used for Bible study, had an unwieldy number of special marks that made it both hard to write and to learn. As a result, no Ju/'hoansi had ever learned to write more than their names in their own language. Dickens's new orthography allowed Ju/'hoansi to be writing their language literally within weeks. Its adoption by both the Namibian government and the NNFC paved the way for the Village Schools Project, for entry into the literate national and international worlds with associated political advantages, and for a general revitalization of the Ju/'hoan language, which continues up to the present day. These developments are discussed in chapter 10.

The Regularization of Nyae Nyae Leadership

In February 1991, a new chairperson was elected by the NNFC. Tsamkxao =Oma, who had led the NNFC since its inception in 1986 as the Ju/wa Farmers

Union, had carried the organization through the challenges of independence, which had put him under a great deal of strain. It was particularly hard on a Ju/'hoan person, coming from the egalitarian background of a foraging society, to withstand the pressures of leadership. Tsamkxao was hardly the first leader to show signs of stress. Concerned about him, other NNFC leaders conferred and came up with the idea of shared leadership—essentially, "leadership by committee," which reduced the enormous pressure on Tsamkxao and allowed him to remain an effective leader. When /'Angn!ao /'Un, known also by his Afrikaans nickname "Kiewiet,"[3] took office, his style of working with the outgoing Tsamkxao was one of respectful collaboration. For a long time after Kiewiet's election, he and Tsamkxao effectively co-chaired NNFC meetings and traveled together, for instance, to Botswana to carry news and perspectives to Ju/'hoansi on the other side of the international fence. Together, they faced challenges in Nyae Nyae that included disputes among the different *n!oresi* and the threat of settlement by Herero pastoralists from adjoining, overgrazed areas to the south in Namibia and to the east in Botswana.

Other key events that took place in Windhoek in early 1991 involved the JBDF's advocacy of the NNFC at the national level. The Swedish ambassador, Sten Rylander, invited JBDF officers to meet at a dinner at his residence with Marco Hausiku, then the minister of lands. Rylander felt that perhaps the MLRR was not paying attention to the wisdom of the NNFC or the JBDF regarding Ju/'hoan communal land rights and wanted to give all parties a chance to communicate. Axel Thoma, who had arrived in Namibia from Germany that very day to start as program manager of the JBDF, and Megan Biesele were able to give and explain in person the map of the Nyae Nyae *n!oresi* to Minister Hausiku. This meeting in genteel surroundings was later to have important repercussions in recognition of Ju/'hoan land rights in a series of conferences in southern Africa, organized by Sweden and other Nordic countries, and in financial support for the NNFC's development programs.

Plans for the Namibian National Conference on Land Reform and the Land Question, to be held in mid-1991, were already in the air as well. Filmmaker Richard Pakleppa had been asked to travel to all the communal areas of Namibia to make a film especially for the conference. He shot the final section of his film in Nyae Nyae, consulting with John Marshall for visual editing advice, and with Biesele for subtitle translations. Pakleppa felt it especially important that something also be available for viewing at the conference from Marshall's major film then in the making (at that time to be a trilogy, provisionally called *Death by Myth*; this project is what became the five-part series *A Kalahari Family*). In the US at the time, Marshall sent out a short film titled *To Hold Our Ground* that

---

3. /'Angn!ao, a small but strong leader fluent in six languages, was named by Afrikaners for a small bird, the kiewiet (Crowned Plover).

dramatically presents the Ju/'hoansi's attempts to retain control of some of their ancestral land. Despite Pakleppa's and Biesele's earnest backstage attempts to have Marshall's film shown at the conference, it was blocked by the conference chairperson, Prime Minister Hage Geingob. But Geingob did allow Pakleppa's footage from Nyae Nyae to be shown, including its conversations about invading Herero pastoralists who were later effectively turned away by the NNFC, portraits of Ju/'hoansi from Gobabis who wanted to make farms in Nyae Nyae, and a fine speech by Tsamkxao =Oma about the *n!ore* system, how it works, and its meaning to the Ju/'hoansi. This film, called *Voices from the Land*, not only became one of the high points of the conference but also made Tsamkxao and others in it nationally recognizable political figures.

In early 1991, there was also national discussion about so-called traditional authorities becoming de facto local government entities for liaison with the new Namibian government. This discussion went hand in hand with deliberations on what geographical entities would replace the old apartheid ethnic homelands. These new national processes of geographical delimitation and the establishment of regional representation were particularly alarming to communal lands dwellers like the Ju/'hoansi. Two commissions, one on delimitation and the other on the role of chiefs and headmen, were established to study and recommend on these topics. Although attempts by these commissions over the next years to consult with local communities were themselves laudable, the results were patchy and confusing. In the end, decisions from on high were handed down to a mystified population. These decisions took few environmental and ethnic realities into account and have been criticized as serving the prominent national majorities. Real regional representation long eluded both Eastern and Western Bushmanland, despite the years of discussion and meetings on this topic between people's groups and government officials that had led to vibrant expectations of a worthwhile outcome.

The delays in regional and leadership restructuring did allow time for politicization among a number of "bottom rung" groups, such as the Ju/'hoansi, and for both intra- and intergroup organizing to take place. This process was led, to some extent, by the example of the NNFC, which had been one of the first grassroots groups in Namibia to organize. The NNFC managed to gain a voice in local and national forums and to inform itself substantially about participation in, and securing of, government services. This process has been in line with the contemporary realization by other world indigenous peoples that they can, and must, demand their political rights by becoming vocal on their own behalf. The 1991 National Land Conference, held 25 June to 1 July, was the first in a series of national and international venues to include prominently Namibian San peoples and their concerns. Hanging in the balance was the very real post-independence possibility that the Ju/'hoansi would lose their land through national communal land allocation.

The JBDF, now known in post-independence as the Nyae Nyae Development Foundation of Namibia (NNDFN), made contributions to the conference in two important ways. First, it took literally months of pressure applied by NNDFN members Biesele and Thoma on the office of the prime minister, who was responsible for putting on the conference, to make sure that the Ju/'hoan delegation would be included at all.[4] Second, NNDFN members Biesele and lawyer John Ford wrote, with Legal Assistance Centre lawyer Dianne Hubbard, a paper about issues in Ju/'hoan land tenure (Biesele, Ford, and Hubbard 1991), which was incorporated into the permanent government records of the National Land Conference. An important paper by John Marshall (1989) on communal lands and the national economy was also submitted as a background paper for the conference.

Alternative Land Use Models and the Land Conference

Thus, a year after independence, in 1991, the Ju/'hoansi were able to raise their newfound political voice to good advantage at the important Namibian National Conference on Land Reform and the Land Question. NNFC representatives effectively presented their case for security of communal land tenure. The leaders of the NNFC were accompanied by their own translators, written materials describing their traditional *n!ore* system of land stewardship, and the knowledge that the people they represented fully trusted them to present the regional case for communal rights.

The Ju/'hoansi of Nyae Nyae had a well-prepared delegation that came to Windhoek with effective speeches and even graphics to illustrate their suggestions. Their presentation at the conference of a map of their *n!oresi* resources and habitation areas did have an impact, partly because it was clear that the Ju/'hoansi were advancing a creative, not simply conservative, approach to their own, very old resource rules. Citing their *n!ore* map, the Nyae Nyae delegation made the following points at the conference:

- Land in Nyae Nyae is not overgrazed because Ju/'hoan settlement patterns support the health of the land.
- The Ju/'hoansi will use the *n!ore* system creatively, not just conservatively.
- There are over 300 named *n!oresi* in Nyae Nyae, reflecting the availability of, and intricate Ju/'hoan knowledge of, bush foods, breeding game, water, soils, vegetation types, and hydro-geology.

---

4. Because they were not able to make similar advance arrangements, the Hai//om San delegation, brought to Windhoek from nearly as far away as Tsumkwe by anthropologist Thomas Widlok, had to sit outside on the steps.

- Development can build creatively: aid funds have provided additional water points and income-generating activities.
- Sustainable development and a logical mixed subsistence can expand the number of families that can be supported on the same land area.

Delegates went on to explain the environmental matters that were topics of discussion in their grassroots group, and these concerns struck some responsive national chords. Here is one of the conference statements by then NNFC chairperson /'Angn!ao /'Un (Kiewiet): "Pastoralists in one area of communal land, such as Hereroland, should not think in the new Namibia that they would be able to expand into other people's traditional areas and proceed to ruin them with large cattle herds." This sentiment endeared the Nyae Nyae delegation to the legions of post-independence overseas consultants and the media-conscious politicians whom they were influencing, even while angering pastoral interests, which had been covertly eyeing Nyae Nyae's unspoiled grazing. It also underscored the need for the participation of traditional local authorities in the regulation of new settlement and carrying capacity issues.

The National Land Conference thus provided the Ju/'hoansi and other minority peoples an unparalleled chance to have their voices heard on the specific topic of alternative land use models, and some of their materials were incorporated into consultable records. These opportunities were much valued by the delegates. Those from Nyae Nyae, especially, rose to the occasion by paring down their usual volubility to observe Prime Minister Geingob's "three-minute rule" for each speaker and translator. Knowing in advance about this stipulation, the NNFC delegates and their onstage translator, Kxao Royal /O/oo from Botswana, spent many long hours beforehand in proverbial smoke-filled rooms, making sure that their main points could be expressed within the time limit.

The following points were made on the first day of the conference by Kiewiet and Tsamkxao:

- People should not overgraze their own land and then ruin someone else's.
- Namibia is now a free country, but people wanting to move to another area should ask permission of the residents.
- It is not good for the land to have too many cattle. People should rather take good care of a few cattle by selling off some of their cattle and using the money to drill boreholes.
- The land is too small, so we must protect it. People who live in a place and know it are the best ones to protect it.
- Taking care of the land means that some of it must be set aside for animal breeding and some for wild plant collection for food.
- If we protect our land, it will support our people, including those who went to Gobabis and South Africa and now want to come back.

At the end of the communal lands alphabet was Vasekela, the San group living in Western Bushmanland. Vasekela leader Alvita Victor, originally from Angola, who had been invited by the NNFC to take one of their precious allocated spots at the conference, stood up and said that his people supported all that Tsamkxao and Kiewiet said about *n!oresi*, but that he and his people were unhappy about the division of land that had already taken place in their area, because the 5-hectare divisions were too small.

Tsamkxao's first point about overgrazing was taken up by the conference and quoted at least twice by other speakers. On the last day of the conference, after the land rights video that ends with Tsamkxao's impassioned speech about *n!oresi* and the need for communication among Namibians, Tsamkxao had a final three minutes to speak. He said that he spoke not only for his own people but for others in the country who as yet had no voice. He explained that the Ju/'hoansi had a cooperative to protect their land, a constitution that provided against overgrazing, and plans to resettle suffering farm workers back from Gobabis. As Chairperson Geingob raised his hand to announce the end of his three minutes, Tsamkxao delivered through the microphone his final word— a Ju/'hoan word containing a resounding click—a flourish that brought him great applause. The applause was repeated when his speech was translated into English. Shortly thereafter, Victor stood up again and said that he now saw that the land allocation that had already taken place in Western Bushmanland was illegal in the understanding of this conference. Then he said "Ek is ontevrede!" (I am dissatisfied!), which he repeated loudly three times. After his speech was shown on national television that evening, Victor was transformed overnight from a silent, church-attending military refugee to an international firebrand.

The Ju/'hoan delegation found out later that they had also appeared on television every single night of the conference, and each time they were seen speaking eloquently, listening intently, or conferring passionately among themselves. At the same time, Pakleppa's video became a kind of reference point for speakers at the conference, who began saying things like "Even in the video it was said…." Tsamkxao's and Kiewiet's faces became familiar to people, and they were recognized in the streets of Windhoek.

Marshall's paper on communal lands was also very well received; it was serialized in *The Namibian* newspaper during the conference and distributed by the NNDFN in photocopied form. Several conference speakers referred to Marshall's phrase "Communal land is the poor man's farm." Common cause was recognized at the conference between the Ju/'hoansi and people like the Himba, who were quoted in Pakleppa's video saying "Land cannot be bought or sold: it is against our religion" and "Pigs will eat anything, but people need each other."

Moses Garoeb, the head of the SWAPO party, invited the Nyae Nyae delegates to lunch at his home on Sunday, 30 June, during the conference, saying that he wanted to be in better touch with his fellow countrymen. Garoeb said that he knew of Tsamkxao's role in getting out the SWAPO vote in DTA territory. He had seen the video, the legal paper by Biesele, Ford, and Hubbard, and the *n!ore* map, and he remarked that the statements of the Ju/'hoan conference delegates had impressed him. Kiewiet asked Garoeb about local government elections and representation in the future. He was told that in about a year a second house of Parliament, to be called a council, would be elected. Garoeb said that he wanted to see the faces of leaders of the NNFC there, not those of DTA leaders Dirk Mudge or Geelbooi, claiming to represent the Ju/'hoansi. Garoeb then called President Sam Nujoma and arranged lunch for the Ju/'hoan delegation at the State House for the next day, the close of the National Land Conference. Through Biesele, he thanked the NNDFN for the long years of preparation that made possible translations and meaningful communication between fellow Namibians, so that they could now talk to each other post-apartheid.

High points of the State House lunch with Nujoma included the president's emphasis that special protection would be given to San land rights. He said that local traditional authorities would have say over immigration into their territories. He was glad to hear about the NNFC's initiative in asking the Hereros who wanted to settle in Bushmanland to leave, through the agency of the acting commissioner in Tsumkwe, Rafael Siteketa. Plans were laid for a channel of communication leading to a request for the Herero would-be settlers to depart from Nyae Nyae in the weeks after the conference.

The National Land Conference had indeed acknowledged the Ju/'hoansi's presentation by resolving to grant special protection for the land rights of their communities. At the end of the conference, the Nyae Nyae delegates were rewarded by hearing from Minister Hausiku that their own *n!ore* system—along with its gender egalitarianism—would be used as the model for allocation in their area. Hausiku stated that full support would be given to the Ju/'hoan people's own traditional land use patterns in the context of national development. He asked that the NNDFN and the NNFC be available for consultation on all future steps to be taken concerning land allocation in Eastern Bushmanland, Western Bushmanland, and West Caprivi. He ended by giving his enthusiastic support to the start of the proposed series of "Nordic initiative" conferences that would bring together San peoples for discussion of mutual issues.

Observers noted at the time that the active intervention of outsiders like Marshall, Ritchie, Biesele, Thoma, and Swedish Embassy officials had combined with Ju/'hoan activism to produce quite positive results for the indigenous stakeholders. Yet the euphoria was short-lived. Soon afterwards, Hausiku went to another ministry, and his successor's team proved resistant to the idea of alternative models. For a long time, no local alternatives were seriously considered, despite efforts to diversify thinking on environmental and social grounds. Some of these proposals were derailed as "romantic anthropological conservatism"; others were just plain invisible, due to being mounted by ethnic groups with little clout.

Further, the hopes of the Ju/'hoansi and other San in the areas east and west of Tsumkwe to have the Delimitation Commission consider their local needs were dashed in 1992 when the commission's report came out. And when a new system of national regions was delimited, the former Eastern and Western Bushmanland both became part of a region, known as Otjozondjupa, that was dominated numerically by the powerful pastoralist Herero population. Although for population reasons neither Western Bushmanland nor the Nyae Nyae area could have hoped for regional autonomy, the very different land use and leadership patterns of Herero pastoralism posed a kind of ultimate challenge to San enfranchisement in local politics. San groups in other new Namibian regions created at the same time also experienced difficulties in establishing local political voices. Not only do the San have very low populations relative to their neighbors in the same regions, but there is also the language factor. Khoesan or "click" languages are widely regarded as unlearnable by other Namibians and are consequently rarely chosen as languages for inter-ethnic communication. In addition, San speakers often have very modest cultural styles of making their voices heard through representative leadership and so were often regarded by Namibian government officials as ineffective or unwilling leaders.

Mixed Outcomes from the National Land Conference

For most of the decade of the 1990s, thus, it was questionable whether the environmental, social, and gender dimensions of land tenure pointed out at the time of the National Land Conference had informed the thinking of Namibian ministries to any practical extent. For all intents and purposes, ongoing attempts at a uniform policy for communal lands were still modeled on agricultural and fishing communities along rivers in Namibia's north. There, high rainfall, river irrigation, fish supplies, and the familiar stratified social structure and agricultural work ethic of the Ovambo population majority combine to make a reliable subsistence possible. For other areas of the very arid country, however, this model may be regarded as an inappropriately imported one.

What has transpired since independence is the inevitable working through of the drama between these two opposed sets of interests—sustainable environmentalism and uncontrolled pastoralism—and the tale is far from told, even yet. To a great extent, marginalized peoples in Namibia have been, and will continue to be, passive observers of this high-stakes drama. But the new government's democratic ideals, commitment to consensus on a national level, and inclusion of splinter groups in consultative planning has stimulated local attempts at organization in important ways. To understand not only the high expectations but also the questions with which people like the Ju/'hoansi left the National Land Conference, let us look back at the assurances that they were given there in 1991.

The conference resolutions can be consulted on the one-page document that appeared in *The Namibian* newspaper dated 2 July 1991. Of most interest to the NNFC were the following:

- No. 2: "Ancestral rights." Restitution in full of ancestral land rights was felt impossible by the conference because of the historical complexity of the issue.[5]
- No. 4: "Government control of 'underutilized land' applied only to commercial, not communal, land." This was a relief to NNFC members.
- No. 13: "Disadvantaged communities." Special protection for "San" land rights was unanimously adopted by the conference.

However, the NNFC decided that, in giving input to the MLRR and the "technical committees" in charge of considering options for land use and administration, it should make sure that this special protection could not be co-opted by some future government for reasons of economic expediency. They pointed to the disappointing example of Botswana, where game reserves and special statuses fell prey to pressure from commercial ranching, mining, and tourism. Legislation would eventually take place, it was clear, but the NNFC felt that the specifics of these "protected" land rights must be put down in writing. The belief was that these special protections should make communal land rights as secure as those being accorded to other Namibians; otherwise, San peoples would in effect remain "wards of the state." Security of tenure, they pointed out, should not depend on politics. In addition, the NNFC stressed that the concepts of "their land rights," "the San," and "special protection" should be carefully defined. These two problems were mentioned personally by the delegation to Garoeb and to President Nujoma. Everyone in the NNFC, it was felt, should be aware of these issues and should speak actively in order to help resolve them.

At the time, the results of the National Land Conference seemed the closest that the Ju/'hoansi could get to consolidating their right to occupy the land that was formerly theirs. The participation of the NNFC, a grassroots group, in the

---

5. The NNFC decided not to ally itself with the more conservative forces—such as Rehoboth—that were calling for full restitution. Clearly, the conference was aware that San peoples have the most extensive ancestral rights, and it applauded the stance of the NNFC in making modest demands based on historical realities and population numbers. The NNFC was rewarded for its creative, not conservative, promotion of the *n!ore* system, and there was national recognition of the fact that Nyae Nyae is not overgrazed, unlike adjacent areas.

conference helped to pave the way for clear recognition of the need for partnership between local leaders and the Namibian government in communal lands issues. In fact, one year after the conference (in July 1992) and largely due to their participation in it, the Nyae Nyae people had become the pilot group for a national project in local land use planning (as we saw in chapter 4).

In actuality, none of the above assurances and clarifications amounted to much for the Ju/'hoansi or other minority groups. This disappointment has been of a piece with other failures in Namibia to realize early dreams of an equitable cultural and environmental mosaic to be built on the ashes of a complex ethnic diversity that had been strangulated by apartheid. To be sure, new ethnic awareness has flourished in the exuberance of the removal of overt racial strictures, but it has been increasingly suppressed in practice by the various balancing acts that were seen as necessary to both national and international politics.

Nyae Nyae after the National Land Conference

While political awareness was growing for the Ju/'hoansi in the latter half of 1991, they were also consolidating their communities economically. With the combined help of the NNFC and the JBDF, which had changed its name to the NNDFN when it became a registered organization in the new nation (see chapter 7), the people of Nyae Nyae established water points, built kraals for their small herds, started small gardens, sold crafts in Windhoek, and began environmental planning on a committee basis. Some of these activities became possible only after the apartheid government's lid on local initiative was removed and the new Namibian government sought at last to support self-help efforts. At NNFC meetings and meetings with government officials, Ju/'hoan voices began to enter directly into the global dialogue on the cultural survival of minorities within existing political structures. Land and leadership became entwined in a "new" democratic language that is, for the Ju/'hoansi, age-old. Their voices, far from demanding only the rights and standards of mainstream living, formed a fresh chorus of creative suggestions and possibilities.

However, President Nujoma's visit to Nyae Nyae on 18 August 1991 proved a foreshadowing of land use problems to come. The NNFC had awaited his visit with high hopes of a reiteration of government support for the *n!ore* system. Yet when Nujoma looked out over the unspoiled grazing of Nyae Nyae, he spoke of a vision of fenced farmland supporting many more Namibians than the present population of 2,000 Ju/'hoansi. The NNFC leaders sighed anxiously, with stiff smiles, until Nujoma and his retinue departed.

The very next day, 19 August, Tsamkxao, Kiewiet, and other NNFC officers went to the quarantine camp that the Hereros returning from Botswana had built at the border fence. With Richard Pakleppa again filming, and Beata

Botlhoko Kasale from Botswana translating, the NNFC used the authority and communication channels that it had built at the National Land Conference to resist politely the would-be settlers' wishes to remain with their herds in Nyae Nyae. The Hereros were soon on their way south to G/am.

Despite quiet triumphs like this, between 1991 and 1993 communal lands dwellers like the Ju/'hoansi often witnessed the dismaying spectacle of land-hungry people from other marginalized communal lands, as poor as themselves, traveling around the country looking for land. Such people perforce had to bypass completely the 60 percent that was set aside as "commercial" land and search through the remaining 40 percent of less desirable land. Thus, communal lands inhabitants and landless squatters were pitted against other communal lands inhabitants on an already impoverished resource base. Until the MLRR and President Nujoma were challenged to put teeth into their assurances of reasonable protection for local authority on new settlements, local civil unrest over illegal land seizure and occupation spiked in the "free-for-all" atmosphere.

Six Conferences Sponsored by the Nordic Countries

The nominal success achieved by the NNFC at the National Land Conference and its practical aftermath at the Botswana border did give impetus to the organization's participation in five conferences underwritten by the Swedish, Norwegian, and Finnish aid agencies operating in Namibia.[6] Building upon visits to Nyae Nyae by both the Swedish and Norwegian ambassadors to Namibia, as well as on intense communication with their aid agencies and those of Finland by NNDFN staff, the idea of a series of international conferences to bring together San peoples from all over Namibia and Botswana took shape. The rationale behind these "Nordic initiative" conferences was that a chance to discuss mutual problems and to develop a regional voice would enable scattered San groups to deal more effectively with the national governments under which they were living. NNFC, seen as one of the most experienced San organizations, played a pivotal role in these conferences, held between October 1991 and September 1993, as follows:

- Preliminary conference, Baraka, Nyae Nyae, Namibia, October 1991
- Preliminary conference, Mangetti Dune, Western Bushmanland, May 1992
- Regional Conference on Development Programs for Africa's San Populations, Windhoek, Namibia, June 1992
- Klein Dobe III conference, Nyae Nyae, Namibia, July 1992

6. One of these conferences, Klein Dobe III, which was held in Nyae Nyae in July 1992 and involved only the NNFC communities and their near neighbors, has already been discussed in chapter 4.

- Preliminary regional meeting, Mangetti Dune, October 1993
- Regional Conference on Development Programs for Africa's San/Basarwa Populations, Gaborone, Botswana, October 1993

The Swedish International Development Cooperation Agency (SIDA) and the Norwegian Agency for Development Cooperation (NORAD), as well as the Namibian embassies of Sweden, Norway, and Finland, gave visionary support for this remarkable series of conferences on development and resource management issues facing the San peoples. Centered in Namibia, the conferences managed to reach out to other countries in southern Africa with San populations—chiefly Botswana, but also Angola and Zambia. They paved the way for later conferences that took place in South Africa and included San from Zimbabwe. Taken together, they represented a major departure in both national policies and international human rights perspectives concerning the San peoples. For the first time in history, the voices of these silent and marginalized minority groups were heard internationally, both in their own languages and in respectful and informed translation.

The preliminary conference at Baraka on 14–15 October 1991 brought together San peoples from Botswana in a meeting with the NNFC to explore mutual concerns. These concerns ranged from the fundamental one of differing problems and strategies on land rights in the two countries, to adverse hunting laws and control of natural resources, to issues in regional and national governmental representation. Languages used at the Baraka meeting included Ju/'hoansi, Naro, English, and Afrikaans, and translation was carefully done so that all could understand. For many of the Botswana participants, it was the first time in their lives that they had heard about the concept of cooperatives or had had a chance to speak up at a public meeting. It appears from later reports that this was an empowering experience for many of them, as they went on to raise their voices at important Botswana forums.

Kxao Moses =Oma, Tsamkxao =Oma's younger brother, greeted the Botswana visitors and explained that, as the NNFC secretary, he was the one who took care of the writing jobs:

> Some people know well what our cooperative is, but some who have come from far away may not know so well. It has people who lead it, like /'Angn!ao here, who is chairman, and Tsamkxao off to the side over here, who is now president ... I take care of things like checking whether the money we have will last for the things we want to do, or seeing if one truck especially uses a lot of petrol and is using up the money, and other work. For instance, if a head of stock is to be bought, or if there's a little money to pay for fuel, or if there needs to be repairs on vehicles—that's my work, to see to that money.

Then Tsamkxao spoke:

Do you understand the meaning of the words [for our cooperative], "N//oaq!ae //Koa//kae" (Nyae Nyae Working Together)? Do you understand that this means we hold fast to each other and that way we have strength? … At the National Land Conference we learned that we have to get our friends together and come to good agreements. I say don't just wait for the government to come and help you. When a government says it is helping you, someday it will later come and chase you away from the things it says are not yours. But if you build up your own place, the government can't chase you away from it. Today we'll stay in our *n!oresi* … Government money can burn your hands. Don't think about clothes if you have none: a loincloth was good enough for your father. Take care of the old things.

Xumi from /Kae/kae in Botswana explained how difficult it had been for the Ju/'hoansi in Botswana to form a cooperative:

We haven't been able to do anything [since Tsamkxao and Kiewiet went to visit in 1989]. We have meetings, but they're convened by the Tswanas. They say they want us Ju/'hoansi to take care of ourselves. They've given us … food for indigents. I asked what kind of people qualify for this food? … They said it was for *tengnyanateng*—those who have nothing.[7] People of many different languages are *tengnyanateng*, but all are like ostriches still closed up inside their eggs: they can't see. For instance … I can't write. The Tswanas write down their own speech at our meetings, but they don't write my speech. I have papers from the meeting last week, but I haven't found anyone to read them to the /Kae/kae people yet. They say the Land Board will give you land to farm on. I want a farm on my own place, where my father's father was born. They say that people on *n!oresi* will get the money of the *n!oresi*. Now, this is what I'm telling you—this is the deceitfulness of the Tswanas. They expect us to believe all this! [Instead], the Land Board is the way the government has gotten our land away from us.

G=kao Petrus, an NNFC representative, spoke of political differences between Namibia and Botswana: "They told us that if you're in SWAPO politics, you don't *fail* to have meetings! If we hadn't been holding meetings, we wouldn't be on our farms today. We have to have our own meetings to lift up our *n!oresi*. Our young children must be told where our land is."

A second preliminary conference, held in Western Bushmanland in May 1992, was convened to set the issues for the agenda of the international meeting to take place the following month in Windhoek. It was held in Mangetti Dune, where many Vasekela and other San had been resettled following the departure of their former employer, the SADF, in order to underscore the needs and goals that the peoples of Eastern Bushmanland (Nyae Nyae) held in common with those of the West. In addition to several San peoples, this conference

---

7. *Tengnyanateng*, which translates literally as "deep within the deep," refers to remote area dwellers (Mogwe 1992).

brought together the Norwegian ambassador to Namibia, Bernt Lund, and government and development workers involved in the newly formed Environmental Planning Committee for Bushmanland.

The major issues discussed at this second preliminary conference, which started the agenda-setting process for the international ("regional") conference to be held in June in Windhoek, included local grassroots organizing and communication; border and mobility concerns; land rights communications and legislation; the comparison of the *n!ore* system of settlement in Nyae Nyae with other forms, for example, village settlements, in the West; new ex-military San arrivals from Kuruman, South Africa; new Nyae Nyae settlers from the Gobabis farms; the most participatory way to coordinate East and West development; and the election of delegates for the June conference. Government personnel, donors, and NGOs played only a facilitation role at this conference, since its purpose was to hear the concerns of San peoples and make sure that they were the ones structuring the agenda. Languages translated at the Mangetti conference included Ju/'hoansi, Vasekela, Khwe, English, Afrikaans, Nama, and Herero. Again, many delegates had the chance to speak out for the first time.

The Regional Conference in Windhoek, held in June 1992, was a landmark in international understanding of marginalized minorities. It brought together San representatives from Namibia and Botswana, as well as government delegates from two other countries, Angola and Zambia. Without the foresight of the Nordic countries involved, such an event would have been unthinkable. It was fortunate that this conference took place under the auspices of Scandinavia, an area of the world long committed to human rights, especially those of indigenous peoples. For one thing, the way that the catchword "nomadism" is sometimes used in ignorance to justify discriminatory and even oppressive policies in certain countries was exposed with the intelligent mediation of the Nordic official delegates, and better perspectives were suggested. For another, the commitment of the Nordic countries to land rights as the basis for all meaningful human rights provided a dignified and practical bottom line for the conference as a whole. Languages used at this three-day conference included Ju/'hoansi, Nama, Naro, Khwe, Vasekela, Setswana, Herero, Afrikaans, and English. Not only did many people who had never spoken out at a public meeting participate actively, but also many who had never spent a night in a hotel or shared coffee on a terrace in an atmosphere of goodwill had a chance to do these things and thus perhaps came to trust more in the process of international understanding. The conference (which was attended by both authors of this book) covered the following ambitious agenda:

- Land and resource issues, including legislation, subsistence resource rights, recognition of hunting and gathering as a land use, participation in land allocation, specific rights in communal lands, provision of local water

committees, monitoring of water quality, emergency reservoirs, more official border posts, local liaison between communities, devolution of resource
benefits to communities, and wildlife utilization and management

- Education issues, including educational facilities provision, teaching in
the mother tongue, school fees, non-formal education, technical education, and vocational training
- Tourism and environmental issues, including control of tourist revenues,
trophy hunting, and the community game guard system
- Cultural and political rights, including local and regional representation, action against exploitation and undignified practices, retention of
cultural identity, and local language radio broadcasts
- Health and citizens' rights issues, including community-based primary
health care, community health worker training, traditional medicine in
the health system, government health facilities, waiving of health fees,
old age and disability pensions, easing access to identification documents, affirmative action employment in government posts, minimum
wage legislation, and provision of transport and communication

Perhaps most importantly, the LIFE Project, a collaboration between USAID
and the Government of the Republic of Namibia, was planned at the conference.[8]
One of the target areas was the Caprivi region and a second was Nyae Nyae.

The Regional Conference on Development Programs for Africa's San/Basarwa
Populations, held in Gaborone, Botswana, in October 1993, had as its theme
"Common Access to Development." The two main Ju/'hoan delegates to this
conference were /'Angn!ao /'Un, the second chairperson of the NNFC, and Seg//ae
Kxao, the woman who represented the *n!ore* community of N=aqmtjoha. Their
presentation ranged across a number of Nyae Nyae issues, including the unsuit-
ability of much of the land for arable agriculture and the danger of overgrazing;
advocacy of a community-based management approach to wildlife; control of
tourism; and employment discrimination. The conference as a whole adopted
a comprehensive set of resolutions in six main areas: education and culture;
land (including a formal agreement with the consensus of the 1991 Namibian
National Conference on Land Reform and the Land Question); health and social
welfare; employment and economic opportunities; water; and communication
(MLGLH 1993; Saugestad 2001).

The initiative taken by the NNFC to re-establish sound roots in their Nyae
Nyae area also received ongoing support from the Nordic governments that
were active in development in Namibia. Sweden and Norway together agreed
to fund further efforts by the NNDFN and the NNFC to secure a sound

---

8. This collaboration between USAID and the Government of the Republic of Namibia is
discussed in detail in chapter 9.

future through education, training, and communication. Funded programs were intended to support life skills and literacy work, in cooperation with the Namibian Ministry of Education; livestock and game management; environmental planning; and horticultural and vocational training.

What the NNFC learned from these conferences and from its own experiences at home during its formative years had repercussions far beyond Nyae Nyae for other San peoples. After ethnic boundaries were dissolved in Namibia following independence, there was a call for organizational help made to the NNFC and the NNDFN by other groups living on communal lands. Again with the help of the Nordic governments, the NNFC began a new period of outreach to other areas such as Western Bushmanland and Botswana, where groups of San peoples and others had not yet received support and assistance. The NNFC, with the help of the NNDFN, became not only a learning body within Nyae Nyae but also a teaching organization for other areas, basing its lessons on its very sound achievements in the years surrounding and immediately after independence.

Chapter Seven

The Nyae Nyae Development Foundation of Namibia

The Nyae Nyae Farmers Cooperative (NNFC) had developed in tandem with the non-governmental organization that mentored it. Founded in 1981, John Marshall and Claire Ritchie's non-profit foundation was one of the earliest established NGOs in Namibia. Originally called the Cattle Fund, the !Kung San Foundation was officially incorporated in December 1982, although development work had already started in March 1981. The Ju/'hoan trustees appointed (by the founders) were /Ui /Ai!ae (N=aqmtjoha), G=kao Debe (/Aotcha), Kxao /Ai!ae (N=anemh), and N!ani Kxao (Gura). In September 1982, the University Centre for Studies in Namibia (TUCSIN), based in Windhoek and founded by archaeologist and educator Beatrice Sandelowsky, among others, agreed to become the umbrella organization that would administer what was then still called the Cattle Fund. At the first meeting of these groups, in December 1982, the name of Marshall and Ritchie's NGO was changed to the !Kung San Foundation. For some time, the Foundation rented office space from TUCSIN and paid Martha van Neel and Jacobus van Neel to do secretarial and bookkeeping work, respectively. In the early years, office space was shared with TUCSIN because it was the administrator. Later, the Foundation established its own office elsewhere.

In April 1983, the board of trustees for the !Kung San Foundation consisted of Marshall and Ritchie (founders), Robert Camby (chairperson), Clive Cowley (secretary/treasurer), Anton Lubowski, Olga Levinson, and Brown Neels. Affiliations were with TUCSIN and with the American NGO Cultural Survival, headquartered in Cambridge, Massachusetts. TUCSIN undertook the responsibility of fieldwork—for example, organizing and putting up pumps—and of administering funds left in Namibia by Marshall during the periods when he was back in the US. Cultural Survival took on public relations work and acted as a conduit of funds.

In 1984, Beatrice Sandelowsky joined the board. Hartmut Ruppel was the Foundation's lawyer, and the accountant was W. H. Schmidt of Deloitte, Haskins & Sells. Americans Anne Edwards and John Payne joined as project directors/field officers in October of that year. It was at this time that the Foundation officially changed its name to the Ju/wa Bushman Development Foundation (JBDF). In 1985, Kuno Budack, Charles Hartung (secretary), and Zach Kazapua joined the board, and Clive Cowley replaced Robert Camby as chairperson. The Ju/'hoan trustees were /Ui /Ai!ae, /Kaece Martin =Oma, Kxao Debe, Kxao Tekeni /Ai!ae, and Tsamkxao =Oma. In 1986, board members also included Paul Tew as treasurer and Rakuu Murangi as education officer. June Horwitz was also asked to join. By 1988, Adrian Strong had joined the board.

The first 10 years of Marshall and Ritchie's foundation—initially as the Cattle Fund and then as the JBDF—saw the consolidation of local organization (the NNFC) and land tenure, with this period ending after the National Land Conference in 1991. Applying the lessons learned during this time, the foundation underwent reorganization and expansion in the early 1990s. For its second 10 years, the JBDF planned the diversification of training and education programs and local income production, projecting 2001 as the year for the takeover of programs by the Ju/'hoansi themselves or by Namibian government agencies. Much good was to come of the changes that the JBDF was anticipating, but many difficulties also, as this chapter will show.

Like the NNFC, the JBDF sought to "Namibianize" itself after independence. In the course of two board meetings held in May 1991 at Baraka and in Windhoek, the name of the foundation was changed to remove the possibly discriminatory word "Bushman" and to emphasize its regional focus in Nyae Nyae. Although it was first called the Nyae Nyae Development Foundation, the words "of Namibia" were eventually added, and it became the Nyae Nyae Development Foundation of Namibia (NNDFN). This action was taken at the suggestion of new board member Moise Tjitendero, since the Nyae Nyae region extends into Botswana as well. Also in May, board member Joshua //Hoebeb, who later became Namibia's ambassador to South Africa, replaced Megan Biesele as chairperson of the foundation (JBDF 1990).[1]

These changes were part of a shift in the foundation's strategy for effectiveness on behalf of the Ju/'hoansi—a shift away from isolationism and toward growing involvement in the national affairs of Namibia. This was a move directly in contrast to the route that co-founder John Marshall would have liked to take, had

---

1. New JBDF/NNDFN board members after independence included Moise Tjitendero, Joshua //Hoebeb, and John Ford.

he been present, but it was much in keeping with the participatory spirit newly alive in Namibia. Like other NGOs in the country at this time, the NNDFN registered itself as a national non-profit organization and began to participate in conferences and form alliances with other like-minded organizations. The NNDFN was keenly aware that it needed to move increasingly away from expatriates for its board and staff and toward the inclusion of Namibian citizens, not only Ju/'hoansi, as before, but also people from other ethnic groups, such as Damaras, Namas, and Hereros.

Even so, in the first few years after independence, expatriates dominated the NNDFN for several reasons. First, Namibian development projects were suddenly favored targets of the international philanthropic world, with European, North American, and Australian governments and non-governmental aid agencies vying with each other to fund projects, such as those that the NNDFN had planned with the Ju/'hoansi. With overseas funding came a demand for qualified staff to carry out projects, and, due to educational and vocational training systems that had been crippled by apartheid, qualified Namibians were few and far between. Second, in the belief that little good could come of cooperating with government entities or agendas, the NNDFN had for so long operated with an isolationist philosophy in Nyae Nyae that it took some time for other Namibian citizens to wish to become involved with its activities.

NNDFN Staffing and Funding in Its Second Decade

During 1990 and 1991, there was a great expansion in the NNDFN staff working in both Windhoek and Nyae Nyae. Although it is not possible to name everyone involved in NNDFN projects, staff members and associates in those years included (alphabetically) Megan Biesele, American, as director; David Cole, South African, working in income generation; Patrick Dickens, South African, as Village Schools Project (VSP) instructor; Frikkie Farrell, Namibian, as pump and vehicle repair instructor; Elizabeth O'Neill, Australian, as coordinator of primary health; Rosie Pauly-Kurz, German-Namibian, working in the Windhoek office; Piet van Rooyen, Namibian, managing the cattle project in Nyae Nyae; Adrian Strong, British, as horticultural instructor; Axel Thoma, German, as program manager and later foundation director; and Wendy Viall, South African, managing the Windhoek office. Others associated later, in 1992–1993, included Thor Boe, Canadian, student volunteer; Magdalena Broermann, German, as education coordinator; Murray Dawson-Smith, Australian, working with the NNFC; Jean Guernier, Zambian, who had worked previously in Australian Aboriginal education; Holly Payne, American, environmental worker (and sister of John Payne, who had worked with the foundation on water development prior to 1987); Joachim Pfaffe, German,

VSP coordinator; Flip Stander, South African, wildlife biologist radio-collaring lions for study/control/sale; Mark Spoelstra, Dutch, as NNDFN program manager; Eric Wood, Canadian, student researcher on local resources; and Froukje Zwaga, Dutch, medical anthropologist.

International funding for various NNDFN programs, although still hard won, was relatively abundant after independence. Besides private donors, the 26 generous donor agencies included the following (in alphabetical order): Brot für die Welt, Catholic Agency for Overseas Development (CAFOD), Canadian High Commission, Commission of the European Community, DanChurchAid, Development and Peace of the Catholic Christian Outreach (CCO) of Canada, Deutsche Welthungerhilfe/German Agro Action (DHWW/ GAA), Diakonia, Christian Aid and the British Council of Churches, Evangelical Lutheran Church in Namibia (ELCIN), Ford Foundation, Health Unlimited, Interchurch Organisation for Development Co-operation (ICCO), Interfund, Konrad Adenauer Stiftung, Ministry of Education and Culture (Namibia), Misereor (German Catholic Bishops' Organisation for Development Cooperation), NORAD (Norwegian Agency for Development Cooperation), Our Lady of the Wayside (Britain), Oxfam Canada, Oxfam UK, Rössing Foundation, SIDA (Swedish International Development Cooperation Agency), Stichting Hivos (Humanist Institute for Development Cooperation), United Nations 1 Percent for Development Fund, and USAID (United States Agency for International Development).[2]

In the years 1991–2001, the NNDFN planned to implement programs to continue its ongoing mission as established during its first 10 years. The mission was summarized as protecting the legal security of the Nyae Nyae land base and assisting with a healthy and productive stewardship of Nyae Nyae's natural resources in a social context of empowerment and dignity. The NNDFN increasingly saw itself as the "employee" of the NNFC, as well as its adviser. The principles on which it was to operate were defined as follows:

- Strategic support to economic self-help initiatives
- Provision of options and information for decision-making
- Community empowerment for decision-making
- Devolution of financial authority to the NNFC
- Gradual training of the NNFC for takeover of all program activities
- Fostering of communicational and organizational skills
- Provision of help toward self-sufficiency rather than handouts

---

2. Only 2 of the 26 agencies, the Ford Foundation and USAID, were American, despite many applications sent to US organizations. This imbalance was a source of embarrassment to both John Marshall and Megan Biesele, and it may have accounted for some of the anti-American feeling that arose in the NNDFN at this time.

- Provision of training and education felt necessary by the community
- Responsible media communication regarding development initiatives
- Developing income-generation potential for the NNFC and individuals
- Supporting environmental sustainability and resource benefits
- Providing a forum for exploration of community development issues

The program of integrated educational and training projects that the NNDFN undertook was aimed at a viable mixed subsistence in Nyae Nyae, the health of the land and the people, and participation of the San in the national life as Namibian citizens by the end of the foundation's second decade.

At the start of the decade, the NNDFN's basic activities were summarized as follows in organizational and program information made available to donors:

Aid provided by the NNDFN to communities in the Nyae Nyae area takes several forms. First, infrastructure needed to develop the mixed local economy (small stock-keeping and dryland gardening in addition to hunting and gathering) are supplied to groups of people able to supply the labor of their installation. This infrastructure includes boreholes and hand or wind or solar pumps to which roads are built by community labor; fencing wire for kraals and cattle crushes whose poles are cut by community labor; small lots of cattle, all of the work of which depends on community labor; and vehicles which make possible the convening of NNFC meetings from all 30 of the established communities at a central point. In addition there is handicrafts marketing. (NNDFN 1992: 1)

At that time, the NNDFN had a staff of 16 Namibians and 7 expatriates residing at a camp at the Baraka Training Centre in Nyae Nyae. The office manager/accountant and the education coordinator lived in Windhoek. The staff was in the process of expanding the original Integrated Rural Development Program (IRDP) to include educational and training projects to facilitate the takeover of the entire program in 2001 by local people. These educational projects encompassed adult and child literacy and life skills, community-based health education, and vocational training.

The expatriate staff positions were designed to complement each other, and in most cases the expatriates' salaries received topping-up by the respective foreign governments. The NNDFN did not want to increase much beyond the existing seven expatriate positions, as it did not want to overshadow local staff numbers. Instead, expertise needed in different sections such as wildlife management, agriculture, and horticulture was requested from the various government departments already working in the Nyae Nyae area. The expatriate positions in Nyae Nyae were as follows: foundation director, program manager, VSP coordinator, researcher on local resources, education consultant, coordinator of primary health, and medical anthropologist. Local staff positions were as follows: marketing coordinator and assistant, office manager (accounting), borehole maintenance technician and assistant, livestock manager, horticultural advisers (2), workshop technicians (2), cooperative facilitation team (4), and needlework advisers (2).

Practical input to this team by the NNFC leadership (the president, chairperson, secretary, and two representatives in each of 30 *n!oresi*) was substantial. For instance, the operating costs of any NNDFN vehicle turned over to the NNFC were secured by income-generating projects, such as the NNFC shop, a mobile service that bought crafts and sold necessary food items on the same trip; the marketing of natural and agricultural products; and educational tourism/wildlife management. Future income from tourism and wildlife in Nyae Nyae was estimated at the end of 1991 at ZAR500,000 (US$181,500) per annum by the Directorate of Nature Conservation. The NNDFN had four vehicles at the end of 1991. In addition, the NNFC had one vehicle for its exclusive use. All of the vehicles and their running costs were paid for by the various donors to the IRDP. The NNDFN vehicles were used for the Windhoek office, purchasing, and administration; the program manager and foundation director; local resource assessment and the educational consultancy; and extra timeshare for NNDFN staff and the NNFC.

The NNDFN's good reputation and first decade of hard work resulted in increasingly available international funding after independence and helped to create a national atmosphere that was more supportive of both grassroots efforts and nationally registered NGOs like the NNDFN. This gave the organization a high-profile reputation for success with donors. In calendar year 1991, the NNDFN's donors gave an unprecedented total of ZAR702,863 (US$255,140) to the IRDP, ZAR379,979 (US$137,932) to the building and operating costs of the Baraka Training Centre, and approximately ZAR190,000 (US$68,970) to the community health education program.

By late 1991, large international donors like NORAD and SIDA, the Norwegian and Swedish aid agencies, had approached the NNDFN with funding offers and began working closely with the NNDFN to plan program coordination. It was a heady time of enormous promise. Shortly before Biesele left the job of foundation director to return to the US, NNFC chairperson /'Angn!ao /'Un said to her, "With the team and plans we have now, our two organizations will continue to do great work together."

Ironically, an abundance of funding for the NNDFN—and the growth in diverse international staff that this made possible—eventually created communication and coordination challenges in what had previously been a tightly bonded organization. By mid-1992, when Biesele returned as education consultant, problems had arisen in the NNDFN that were a source of grave concern, not only to the NNFC, but also to the donors. Each of the NNDFN's programs after independence could have an entire book written about it; the interactions among the programs were equally complex. In what follows in this chapter, thus, we confine ourselves to a focus on events that affected the NNDFN as a whole up through 1992 and on some lessons to be drawn from them.

The Foundation's Move from /Aotcha to Baraka

Between 1981 and 1991, the number of Ju/'hoan groups leaving Tsumkwe and the army bases to re-establish themselves at their old *n!oresi* rose from 3 to 30. These 30 communities were flung all over the broad map of Nyae Nyae. Marshall and Ritchie's foundation, then known as the JBDF, which had established its original base camp near the /Aotcha community and waterhole in the southern half of Nyae Nyae (where long before the Marshall family had begun their association with =Oma Tsamkxao and his family), was hard put to maintain equal contact with all the new communities. Jealousy arose over the close relationship between the /Aotcha community and the foundation. The foci of resentment included paying jobs that were given by the foundation to members of the /Aotcha community; transport and requested shopping for /Aotcha people by foundation staff; training (especially learning to drive) and help with obtaining driver's licenses; and the foundation's nearby presence for trouble-shooting in terms of medical emergencies, problem predators, and invasive outsiders, such as tourists.

This jealousy was especially disruptive because the Ju/wa Farmers Union, and later the NNFC, were intended to represent the interests of all the new *n!ore* groups, but in fact they were dominated by the same prominent associates of the Marshall family at /Aotcha. Despite attempts to make sure that the growing number of communities each played an active part in the NNFC, sentiment grew that /Aotcha was favored and that the JBDF was neglecting the interests of the widespread, larger group of communities, about half of which were north of the road from Tsumkwe to the border and thus geographically remote from /Aotcha.

Even as early as the late 1980s, it became apparent to the JBDF that something would have to be done to even out the influence of its programs among all the Nyae Nyae communities. After Megan Biesele joined as project director in 1988 and Patrick Dickens as horticultural and linguistic instructor in 1989, a decision was made to increase the JBDF staff by a number of positions that would be offered exclusively to non-/Aotcha Ju/'hoansi. Two young men from other communities were taught to drive and helped to get their licenses by Dickens, and both they and two others (also not from /Aotcha) became part of an experimental education program in the Ju/'hoan language, assisting Dickens in the writing of a practical orthography, a dictionary, and curriculum materials. Other young people were incorporated as NNFC trainees under Tsamkxao =Oma and as mechanics' assistants under the direction of Frikkie Farrell, the JBDF's maintenance supervisor. Still others received training in borehole siting, as drillers' assistants, in water infrastructure maintenance, and in dryland and irrigated gardening. Until 1991, these trainees lived at the /Aotcha community, getting home leave only sporadically due to limited transport. The /Aotcha people provided hospitality all this time to the live-in trainees, who swelled the size of the community considerably.

However, local criticism of both the JBDF and the NNFC continued to increase due to envy over the close connections with /Aotcha. Marshall and Ritchie impressed upon the newer staff the necessity of thinking seriously about a move to neutral turf, so that the commitment to all the NNFC villages would be underscored and the opportunity for training would be spread more widely. It was also at this time that the JBDF began thinking about more convenient accommodations in order to attract and hold the necessarily professional staff of the future. Further, the temporary collection of small tents, mud-walled houses, and caravans that composed the JBDF's two camps at /Aotcha pan did not seem the sort of legacy that the foundation would like to leave to a newly independent country. The JBDF was committed to a vision of the future that involved a clear pull-out date in favor of the Nyae Nyae people's own continuing authority over a development plan that they themselves had helped to create. Leaving behind a rural slum in the middle of Nyae Nyae was not an option; instead, the JBDF wished to bequeath a functional, flexible, and attractive training center, where both local Namibian and overseas staff members could work in a comfortable setting in all weathers. Accordingly, in 1989, Ritchie and Biesele wrote into their major JBDF funding proposal the start-up construction costs for such a center, calling it "Gura Community Centre" after the area then favored for the relocation.

The NNFC and the Gura *n!orekxaosi* (the traditional "owners") formally agreed to the plan to relocate. However, road conditions around Gura and the presence of an important game resource—the Nyae Nyae roan antelope—at the waterhole there led to a rethinking of the location of the site. Eventually Baraka, near the center of Nyae Nyae and much more accessible by road, was chosen as the site for the new training center and JBDF headquarters. The NNFC and the Baraka *n!orekxaosi* met and formally allocated the *n!ore* with its new borehole, drilled by the JBDF, to these purposes. Baraka was not at this time inhabited by local people, as its *n!orekxaosi* were already located at N//oaq!osi, Makuri, and in Botswana at !'Ubi, just across the border. One reason given for supporting Baraka as the site for the foundation's work was that the JBDF, unlike Ju/'hoan groups in Nyae Nyae, was not planning to raise cattle. The JBDF was supposed to use Baraka only for educational, training, and administrative purposes, not as a place to settle any group of people. This fact became important later when conflict arose over the favoritism to /Aotcha that was thought to be continuing in the way that jobs were allocated at Baraka.

In February 1991, after almost all of its staff had made the move to Baraka, the JBDF held a meeting to consider the matter of rotating jobs away from the /Aotcha over-representation that had so long characterized the employment roster. This over-representation extended to the NNFC as well, due to the ambiguous position of Tsamkxao =Oma, who had recently been replaced as chairperson. Although he had chaired the fledgling NNFC since 1986, Tsamkxao had never been properly elected by the Nyae Nyae people. There was widespread admiration of him, but also a sense that he had been "placed" in his position by John Marshall. The election of Kiewiet (/'Angn!ao /'Un) in February 1991 by due process of the NNFC, as required by its new statutes, had been a landmark event that was recognized by all as the start of a more genuinely participatory era for all the NNFC communities, de-emphasizing the pioneering leadership of /Aotcha. For some time, as mentioned previously, there had been talk about the stresses of leadership beginning to tell on Tsamkxao, and in fact "leadership by committee" had already been in place for some time, with *n!ore* representatives /Ui of Maxamesi, G/aqo of //Aqri=ah, G=kao Petrus of =Habace, and N!ani of N//oaq!osi joining with Kiewiet of Com!ao to help Tsamkxao with the chair's responsibilities. It was in fact Kiewiet who, before his election, inaugurated the idea that the chairperson's power should be shared. It seems that his election may have reflected the support of the Ju/'hoan people for this egalitarian, yet practical, solution to some of the leadership problems.

At the JBDF's February 1991 meeting in Baraka, the issue of rotating employment to people from other *n!oresi* was discussed in relation to the new problem of transport for Ju/'hoan employees living far from Baraka. This problem had been minimal when most of the foundation's employees lived within walking distance at /Aotcha. Baraka, in contrast, was over an hour's drive by truck from /Aotcha, although it was closer by far to the northern communities, which had felt cut off from the activities of both the JBDF and the NNFC. Further, many of the /Aotcha staff members had received training that was felt by some JBDF staff to be indispensable to the continued smooth operation of the foundation's projects. The argument was further supported by the unanswerable question, "what have these people been trained for, if only to go back to their *n!oresi* and have their skills disappear?" The Ju/'hoan staff members were understandably anxious at the prospect of suddenly being off the payroll with no job prospects. The reasons for the move from /Aotcha, however, remained uppermost in the minds of Biesele and other JBDF staff, who argued that the purpose of establishing the new base would not be fulfilled if new job opportunities and training activities were not found for people from *n!oresi* other than /Aotcha.

A Critical Decision

A decision, later seen as a critical turning point in relations between the NNDFN and the NNFC, was made by the foundation to retain the current Ju/'hoan staff even with the move to Baraka. Transport to /Aotcha was to be made available to them on weekends. The prospect of increasing rosters of trainees in several fields (village health workers, teacher trainees, agricultural trainees, NNFC leadership trainees, etc.) made it seem as though the emphasis on /Aotcha staff would soon diminish in people's minds and would not continue as a problem. Other reasons for the decision included the following: (1) the move of both the JBDF (soon to be the NNDFN) and NNFC staff to Baraka was of a phased nature, and, encouraged by some of the newer expatriate staff, some old Ju/'hoan staff had already established themselves at the new camp before the issue could be discussed generally; (2) there were new social challenges posed by a rushed plan for expatriate and Ju/'hoan staff to live together in one community, with equal access to housing, office space, ablution facilities, and a communal kitchen; and (3) new expatriate NNDFN staff were not properly apprised of the cultural and historical perspectives on the move that might have made it more successful.

Unfortunately, this decision did not reckon with the multiplication factor implicit in visits of extended families of staff at Baraka. Ju/'hoan sociability makes it impossible for people to refuse the visits of such relatives or the imperative to share materially with them. The presence of many /Aotcha staff soon meant a preponderance of /Aotcha visitors. Eventually, the charge was being laid by some in other *n!oresi* that Baraka was no longer a training center and NNDFN camp but in fact a *n!ore*, meaning that people were living there. Buried feelings about the long uninhabited *n!ore* in which Baraka was situated began to surface among those with kin ties to that *n!ore*'s dead. Jealousy was focused on both the /Aotcha visitors and the /Aotcha staff. The tide of feeling against the /Aotcha people resulted in several visits from disgruntled former *n!orekxaosi*, including a woman named N/haokxa from !'Ubi in Botswana and N!ani Kxao from N//oaq!osi, north of Baraka. Both expressed strong aversion to the way that Baraka was becoming a living place for /Aotcha people, and at one angry moment N!ani declared that the /Aotcha people at Baraka should "fall on the ground so that their stomachs split open" (a rather serious curse). Shortly after this, !U'u, the elderly mother of Tsamkxao and the whole /Aotcha group, contracted a debilitating diarrhea and very nearly died during an extended visit at Baraka. Many other people were also sick at Baraka during this time, and since many of them were /Aotcha people, it began to look as though there was something significant going on with regard to their presence. Although all of the sick eventually recovered, explanations were sought partly in the spiritual realm, as will be seen below.

Emergence of a Privileged Group at Baraka

The problems experienced by the /Aotcha people were part of a larger social problem surfacing at Baraka. In the view of many of the NNFC *n!oresi* and of the Tsumkwe residents, including both Ju/'hoan inhabitants and government representatives, Baraka was becoming the bastion of a growing privileged class with access to some of the best housing in Nyae Nyae, water and sanitation facilities that were far better than elsewhere, training, jobs, transport, communication opportunities through the NNDFN and its radiotelephone, up-to-date information on local and regional developments, and material benefits, such as food, clothing, and even alcohol, shared more or less frequently by some NNDFN staff or purchased and transported for employees on request. More and more often the complaint was heard that Baraka had actually never been intended as a training center but rather as a living community. These complaints were rarely aimed at the NNDFN per se (probably because there was widespread recognition that it was practically "the only game in town" for upwardly mobile Ju/'hoansi in Nyae Nyae). Instead, they were leveled at the /Aotcha community and others who had secure jobs at Baraka. In June 1992, several *n!ore* representatives at other villages said that the NNFC leaders could not be seen as real leaders (*g/a'an!angjuasi*) because they were no longer taking care of their own *n!oresi* but living in salaried comfort at Baraka.

In another expression of jealousy, Tsamkxao =Oma's non-official status as a driver came under fire from people of other *n!oresi*. Tsamkxao, who was then still chairperson of the NNFC, was perceived as helping only his own family with transport. Overwhelmed by the numbers, distances, and pressing need to feed his own family, he was also accused of not fulfilling his duties of maintaining regular contact with all the NNFC *n!oresi* and instead running a route to Tsumkwe from Baraka that involved drinking or unfair numbers of trips to the store. It was certainly difficult to reach all the *n!oresi* (by then numbering more than 30) on a regular basis, but each *n!ore* expected equal treatment.

The presence of a select Ju/'hoan community in residence at Baraka and the social disruption that their presence caused reflected other issues that were being experienced within the Ju/'hoansi's own organization. Some of these were the reasons for a quite necessary reorganization of the NNFC (discussed in detail in chapter 8), which was looming because of all the new *n!ore* communities. This too had an effect on the broader Ju/'hoan community's opinion of Tsamkxao and of the /Aotcha people.

Community Health and Governance

During 1992, a number of NNFC leaders became ill. When Ju/'hoan *n/omkxaosi* (traditional healers) were consulted, they said that the sickness was a result of the fact that a long-ago *n!orekxao*, Old Komtsa, buried beneath the Baraka baobab, had spoken up and said that he did not want people living at Baraka. Some of those who were ill had, like !'U'u, Tsamkxao's mother, come originally from /Aotcha. Because in the Ju/'hoan worldview causes of physical illness can include community dissension, ill will, and envy, it is possible that this illness reflected serious problems in the Nyae Nyae community as a whole that cen-tered on the relative historical privileging of the people at /Aotcha. Certainly, it made many in the NNDFN aware of the profound spiritual dimensions of the *n!ore* concept and its relationship to the equally profound Ju/'hoan concept of egalitarianism. It is possible, in fact, that the eventual wholesale departure of the /Aotcha people from Baraka back to /Aotcha on 9 August 1992 may in fact have had illness as a factor at its core.

A meeting between NNDFN staff and /Aotcha people living at Baraka was held just before this move was effected. Following some months of conflict over related issues, this meeting showed that enough consensus had been reached to make the move possible under certain agreed conditions of salary, transport opportunities, and guaranteed return (for some employees) after a period of time spent concentrating on the *n!ore* issues at /Aotcha. It was acknowledged that too much conflict had come into the NNDFN's and the NNFC's activities because of the Nyae Nyae community's perception of favoritism to the /Aotcha people. Too many of the /Aotcha people had suffered illnesses and other problems since living at Baraka for the people to continue to feel secure. Their relatives back in /Aotcha were pressing them to return and solve some problems connected with their non-arable location. There was also a feeling that the /Aotcha community was vulnerable to Herero invasion when its leaders were gone, a feeling expressed strongly in !U'u's request for a "piece of paper" to keep at /Aotcha, stating that even when Tsamkxao was not present, any outsider wishing to water cattle there or use the kraal must first get his permission.

A rallying point for the consensus was a return to the original purpose of Baraka as a training center and NNDFN camp rather than as a living area or even a center of NNFC operations. In general, the feeling was that even the highest levels of NNFC leadership should center their living at their *n!oresi* and that transport should be provided to meetings and other important activities, although housing at Baraka would still be available for part-time occupation. Negotiations got underway about drivers, driver's licenses, authority over the few working vehicles, and the ways to get the non-working vehicles repaired or replaced. After Tsamkxao's departure, Kiewiet took the position that, due to petrol considerations, most of his own time would have to be spent at Baraka rather than in his own remote *n!ore*, Com!ao. But he recognized the mutually pro-active stance toward *n!ore* responsibilities that had resulted in Tsamkxao's decision to take his family home to /Aotcha.

This move by the /Aotcha people was felt to be a difficult but necessary step in the establishment of a fully participatory and fair people's movement. The NNDFN, for its part, discussed and acknowledged some of its mistakes, including, for example, its too-rapid growth and a lack of clarity on the way that Baraka was intended to be used. However, it maintained that some of the decisions that had been made were historically necessary at the time due to the press of national politics, particularly in regard to holding the land base. History has borne out the rightness of this view. The course correction accepted by the /Aotcha group, in returning to their *n!ore*, has proved to be an important part of the longer process as well.

Contrasting Development Philosophies and Some Lessons about Ju/'hoan Society

Conflicting development approaches within the NNDFN soon compounded the problems of rapid organizational growth and the ill-planned move to Baraka. The conflict was expressed in two arenas—first, that of the policy on "handouts" of any kind and, second, that of authority relationships and communication between the NNDFN and the NNFC. The NNDFN's program manager, Axel Thoma, was following a long-established NNDFN policy of self-help, in which any food aid or other handouts were seen as creating dependency and were thus to be avoided. Some of the NNDFN staff, on the other hand, felt that handouts were justified in certain circumstances, for instance, in the case of TB patients or the aged. Both sides were passionately committed to their positions, and, as a result, staff communication deteriorated sharply over this issue.

The issues concerning communication with the NNFC and the devolution of authority for decision-making were perhaps even more pressing, however, and eventually led to a major rift within the staff of the NNDFN. One view held that NNFC members were in general not yet ready to carry out new development tasks and make decisions, even on a day-to-day basis, and that a "mentoring" relationship with the NNFC should be provided by the NNDFN liaison with the NNFC—in this case, with Thoma, the program manager. In contrast, Thoma's view, which was supported to some extent by others in the NNDFN, was that the NNFC should have the leeway to make many of their own mistakes. It was later acknowledged by both sides in this controversy, however, that the distance between Baraka and Windhoek, along with the increasing demands on the program manager's time in the capital city, made it imperative that another post be created for a full-time mentor to work with the NNFC at Baraka. The compromise eventually arrived at was a more realistic assessment of the degree of mentoring that was necessary.

The NNDFN: Dilemmas of Development

The situation of the NNDFN in mid-1992, when problems began to compromise its post-independence promise, has been fully documented in an evaluation of the NNDFN-NNFC relationship made for the Ford Foundation and the

NNDFN by Robert Hitchcock (1992). Readers wishing more detailed information are encouraged to refer to this evaluation. In this section we offer ideas toward an analysis of this problematic situation and show how the problems in the NNDFN affected the NNFC in the years of the mid-1990s, leading up to the formation of the Nyae Nyae Conservancy. We take an analytic perspective precisely to avoid falling into the trap of what the NNFC's Kxao Moses called "blame-*akhoe*," a compound neologism with the Ju/'hoan portion denoting mutuality, meaning "blaming each other"—an activity, he told the NNFC, that would never get them anywhere. Laying blame for an organizational failure, even a temporary one such as occurred within the NNDFN in the mid-1990s, seems much less important than understanding it and trying to avoid similar events in the future. Other participants in this painful time in the NNDFN's history may have perspectives differing from ours. This book has been written partly to get discussion going again among a group that has been little able to communicate about this experience. Of necessity, we offer the following from the point of view of only two of the people involved in a complex process that, once begun, spiraled quickly out of control.

The too-rapid growth of NNDFN staff and programs meant that problems related to different development approaches multiplied too quickly to be dealt with. New staff members hired in 1990–1992 could not be fully oriented to the specifics of the history of the NNDFN or to the Ju/'hoansi's much longer history of trying to keep the peace among themselves while attempting to protect their land. Polarization emerged between older, more experienced NNDFN staff members and the newer ones in areas of gender, political correctness, and approaches to development mentoring. The different languages and cultural backgrounds of the expatriate staff were further barriers to cooperation. Other than a few who took no side and attempted instead to hold the organization together, a general split developed between staff members who spoke English as their first language and those who did not.

Perhaps the single most egregious problem was the new staff's lack of background on Ju/'hoan society and the ways in which it had been stretching itself in recent years, growing organically into an effective form for dealing with the radically changed circumstances of the new Namibia. Instead, these new staff called for Ju/'hoansi employed by the NNDFN to be given unrealistic benefits with their jobs, thus further alienating them from their extended families because these benefits could not be easily shared along lines that the families expected. The politically correct background from which many of the new staff came stressed the rights of the individual in ways that the Ju/'hoan community, with its ancient but thriving mechanisms of social leveling, could not tolerate. The new staff also stressed an urgent need for Ju/'hoan women to stand up against male oppression—not recognizing that these people had long been the most gender-egalitarian in the world. There were, indeed, instances of male-female aggression occurring among the Ju/'hoansi, notably in alcohol-related contexts and the competitive atmosphere of Baraka, but there was a sense that some of the models for thinking about gender were inappropriately imported and caused confusion, particularly in the community education project.

Gender activism, as it was used to justify resistance to the status quo exemplified by certain individuals, also caused a significant split in the NNDFN staff. Those individuals—including then director Biesele and program manager Thoma, despite and perhaps even because of the fine record, good plans, and promising funding that they had helped to establish by that time—were seen as using "top-down" methods. This assessment was in turn used to justify a move that signaled an irreversible crisis in the viability of the NNDFN. Rather than negotiate effectively about this issue, the critics took news of the split that they had identified (and perhaps caused) to the NNDFN's major donors. As a result, funding was suspended pending investigations, which were carried out by parties who clearly had already made up their minds. Amid accusations and counter-accusations, the NNDFN, for a period, ceased to function effectively.

Ju/'hoansi, both young and old, were amazed at the bad feeling that had erupted in 1992 in their NGO and started earnest efforts to heal the splits. /'Angn!ao /'Un, in particular, was outraged at the lack of communication and coordination among the NNDFN staff, whom he had come to regard, with their agreement, as "employees" of the NNFC. He brought the NNDFN staff together at a meeting in Baraka and spoke passionately to them about the need to stop criticizing and to start working together again. The older staff, including Biesele and Thoma, were sure that things would get better after /'Angn!ao's speech. They knew the power of the Ju/'hoan community healing system, in which careful levels of talking, as well as dancing and singing together, can very effectively heal discord (Katz, Biesele, and St. Denis 1997; L. Marshall 1961, 1976, 1999). But this aspect of Ju/'hoan culture was regarded as "anthropological" and thus discounted by the newer staff. The year 1992 came to a close with many of the NNDFN staff angrily alienated from each other or already departed for foreign countries. The NNFC's confidence in its once-trusted partner decreased drastically.

The NNDFN's problems of 1992 were eventually resolved, but not for a few painful years, during which time scapegoats were sought and little healing took place. Some of the difficulties and transitions experienced by the NNDFN mirrored issues being confronted at the same time by the NNFC, to which we now turn.

Chapter Eight

The Nyae Nyae Farmers Cooperative after Independence

Some longer processes of change unfolding in Nyae Nyae during the middle years of the 1990s centrally challenged long-operative Ju/'hoan notions of social equity.[1] These challenged notions evolved, as we saw in earlier chapters, both in the context of the local community, as represented by the Nyae Nyae Farmers Cooperative (NNFC) and its development projects, and in the wider Namibian context of land and local governance policy issues. They also developed in a matrix of continued involvement with the NNFC's NGO partner, the Nyae Nyae Development Foundation of Namibia (NNDFN), itself experiencing growing pains and questions about its mandate to continue in a mentoring relationship to the NNFC.

Whether the NNFC would gain national representative legitimacy was one problem; its internal legitimacy in Nyae Nyae was quite another. Since 1986, this organization had been growing in a way closely coterminous with social change in Ju/'hoan society as a whole. Thus, its equity and authority debates closely mirrored those taking place in all of Nyae Nyae. One debate in the 1990s, for example, was about whether the name of the Nyae Nyae Farmers Cooperative should be changed to the Nyae Nyae Residents Council. The NNFC had become the local authority, but since not everyone who desired political and legal representation was in fact farming or intending to farm,

---

1. In this chapter, the word "equity" (rather than "equality" or "egalitarianism") is used intentionally. Many internal rules can go into a cultural definition of equity, whereas so-called egalitarianism can easily become a Procrustean bed. Debating the concept of egalitarianism itself is beyond the scope of this book. Nevertheless, the ways in which Ju/'hoan foraging history impacts the society today are numerous and pervasive, and many of them have been assembled in the

some Nyae Nyae residents wanted the organization name to be more inclusive. The proposed name change never actually came about, but the debate revealed concerns in the Nyae Nyae community about equity issues, economic planning for the future, and the change in Ju/'hoan decision-making from a process of all-inclusive consensus to selective democratic representation that had taken place.

These underlying issues revealed themselves in a change in the way that the NNFC regarded the NNDFN and other outside agencies, such as hired consultants. Wishing to present a united front in the new national context, the NNFC adopted a more formal, distant stance toward outsiders. This was especially true of outsiders who might, in the course of their work, learn about conflicts and jealousies within the Nyae Nyae community. An anthropologist or development consultant hired specifically to do something about community disagreements was thus faced with an ethical dilemma. Bringing attention to these inequities was easily seen by community members as laying blame on individuals. Yet a sense of ethnographic honesty rebelled at being asked to suppress such issues in reports both to a wider world of readers and to the NNFC itself, which had hired the consultants to help in the first place. As a compromise, more and more Ju/'hoan individuals spoke under condition of anonymity. The fact that some quotes in this chapter are given without attribution is in itself revelatory of the massive social changes occurring.

Securing the Land of Nyae Nyae after Independence

After independence, the NNFC continued its major local administration and economic work, as well as its outreach to San in adjacent areas. It oversaw the drilling of more boreholes and the allocation of more livestock to communities, represented the Ju/'hoansi in meetings at the regional and national level, and helped to mediate in intra- and inter-community disputes in Nyae Nyae.

Between 1988 and 1991, the NNFC held at least four internal meetings of its representatives per year and was often also involved in external meetings with other San communities, government representatives, donors, legal assistance workers, and other entities. One of its most important activities during this period was keeping local police aware of the continuing threat to the

---

past under the rubric of studying the "egalitarianism" of Ju/'hoan and other San peoples. We draw on this research but emphasize the necessity for detailed ethnographic understanding of the specific community at Nyae Nyae, especially with regard to recent rapidly escalating change. To understand the changes, we must take a close look not only at the NNFC and the Nyae Nyae community but also at their continued involvement with the NNDFN, which was itself changing radically during the years after independence and the National Land Conference.

environment from Herero pastoralists. Traditionally, Hereros, like Tswana pastoralists in Botswana, regarded Ju/'hoan and other San people as serfs, not as owners of cattle or land. A letter written on 9 May 1989 by the NNFC to the United Nations Transition Assistance Group (UNTAG) and the Tsumkwe police force helped to solidify the NNFC's position as Nyae Nyae's traditional authority two years later when Hereros made inroads deep into Nyae Nyae:

> We of the Nyae Nyae Farmers Cooperative wish you to be informed about a possible situation of trouble in the Tsumkwe area. Herero people from G/am have told us they intend to move in here with their cattle and take over our grazing. But we do not wish them to come. Our *n!oresi* are small, and there are many Hereros. We are few. We want our cattle to have good grass, so we do not want the Herero cattle to come here.
>
> We want everything to be discussed publicly, because we Ju/'hoansi are people like everyone else. It's important to have understanding. We want it to be known that we do not want the Herero people here. They think they can come here because they have a government and we don't. They must wait [for a decision on entering our area] until all Namibians have a new government. Our *n!ore* is small. We pray that you help us.

In a similar letter to Namibia's president, Sam Nujoma, dated 1 April 1991, the NNFC wrote:

> Our land is very small, so we don't want many cattle, goats, horses, and other stock because we want to use our land correctly. If we have many cattle, then they will cause soil erosion. Also there will be a lack of grasses, and on the other hand the cattle will destroy our bush food.
>
> The other problem is that we have heard that Hereros will come into our area at a very large number, so we are very upset about it. We are writing you this letter because it seems as if the minister of lands doesn't want to listen to us because today there are some Hereros staying in our farms without our permission.
>
> We want a meeting so that we can come to an agreement on doing things, for example, like dividing the land and letting people get our permission for staying in the area.

The Ju/wa Bushman Development Foundation (JBDF), as the NNDFN was then known, helped facilitate these communications with officials by translations and transport. Similarly, it assisted with the NNFC's own meetings by making transportation and accommodation arrangements. In these early first years of the NNFC's activities as an autonomous organization, both the NNFC and the JBDF members felt that the latter's assistance and activities at the meetings were necessary and welcome. Both organizations had the sense that they were making and documenting history together.

By mid-1991, however, it was clear that an NNDFN presence might be less desirable at some of these meetings, particularly when delicate issues, such as disputes among *n!ore* communities, were at issue. In May, NNDFN staff members were told that it would be better if they did not attend an NNFC meeting to be held at the Xamsa community. At Xamsa, as at Djxokhoe and several other *n!ore* communities, Herero pastoralists from G/am were trying to settle so that their cattle could use the water and pasturage. They pursued an approach to individual *n!ore* owners that put those *n!ore* owners at odds with the NNFC's united stand against overgrazing. At this historic May 1991 NNFC meeting, the NNDFN was told later, the NNFC leadership attempted to convince the *n!ore* owner at Xamsa, known as Kxao Xamsa, that all the communities must stand together against the Hereros' desire to graze their cattle in Nyae Nyae. Kxao was convinced that his own group's life depended on the milk that would come from taking care of Herero cattle. Knowing that if the Herero cattle were allowed in by special arrangement with one *n!ore*, they would soon overgraze the rest of unfenced Nyae Nyae, the NNFC leaders regarded this meeting as a particularly significant and fraught occasion. The agenda also included discussion on how to evict, politely and effectively, the Herero pastoralists who had brought their cattle from Botswana into Nyae Nyae without the NNFC's permission.

Present at the meeting was a Herero man from G/am, Seth Joseph Tjipopa, whom Kxao and other men of Xamsa wanted to have as their patron. John Marshall had emphasized, as an important part of his film record, problematic Ju/'hoan relationships with the Hereros, who, for bride wealth and other social purposes, were seen by the Ju/'hoansi as often keeping larger numbers of cattle than the land could support (although this point is something that many Hereros would disagree with). But Marshall was not in the country at the time, so asking him to refrain from filming the meeting did not become an issue for the NNFC. In an important milestone, for the first time NNDFN staff were not invited to attend the meeting. However, the NNFC secretary taped the meetings for Megan Biesele to include in the Nyae Nyae Tape Archive as part of the ongoing record. The meeting included these words from Tsamkxao =Oma:

> This place is not the territory of one person, but is the territory of the government and of all of us here. All that is done must be done by all of us … Don't think only of your own food but of everyone's food and how far away it is … If one person gets cows, everyone should get cows. You shouldn't just do something by yourself, but by laws … Don't you all remember when we went to the border and saw how the Hereros had taken over [in Botswana], and we said to ourselves, we're not going to experience this same pain? Let's not kill ourselves, let's not kill each other.
>
> Don't think the independence of Namibia is complete. There has been one election but there will be many more. Since elections are many, you must use them to ask for the right law … There will be a meeting on land rights in Windhoek soon, and we have made an application to be there. We will ask where the Hereros have gotten the agreement to come here.

G/aq'o =Oma added:

The men who agreed to the Hereros didn't even agree beforehand whether they would be paid. All they got was milk to drink. What kind of a thing is that? ... Hereros and Kavangos ... Long ago I worked for Hereros in Botswana and still ended up wearing a loincloth. Then I came to Tsumkwe and worked for Kavangos and am still wearing a loincloth. If you work for these people, you end up running around in nothing but skins with skin tails hanging down behind. So now that these two peoples are taking over the government, you won't see anything but loincloth-wearing from now on. So I say the NNFC representatives should throw their hearts into our having trousers instead of loincloths.

G=kao Dabe voiced a similar argument: "Is it right that we should still be wearing loincloths? Milk is a good thing, but it doesn't mean our women should have to expose their stomachs and buttocks again by wearing skin clothing ... Today we've gathered to explain to Kxao Xamsa that we're looking for a new law, not going back to the old one ... Today we're talking about our own law."[2]

In June–July 1991, a month after this meeting, the National Land Conference took place with Ju/'hoan representatives attending. As we saw in chapter 6, a time of uncertainty about the status of communal lands in Namibia soon ensued, and Nyae Nyae was not exempt from it. In August 1991, pressure due to Herero pastoralists from G/am was augmented by the sudden arrival in Nyae Nyae of other Hereros who had settled in Botswana after the colonial wars with the Germans in 1904–1907. These Hereros, with ties to those already settled at G/am in the 1980s, came with tools and materials to build large fenced enclosures near Ben se Kamp at the Namibia-Botswana border.[3] The Hereros—from G/am, Okakarara, Windhoek, and Botswana—informed the Ju/'hoan community that they had come merely to build quarantine pens for Herero cattle from Botswana that were purportedly on their way to G/am. They did not ask permission, stating that they were there under orders from a Herero tribal body. The Ju/'hoansi were incensed. Hereros were at Xamsa, Djxokhoe, and now the border. Even if they meant only to trek their cattle through Nyae Nyae on the way to G/am, as some of them claimed, the NNFC believed that many animals would inevitably go astray and that the Hereros would end up

2. In April 2009, Tjipopa and other Hereros from G/am again brought large numbers of cattle into Nyae Nyae, along with guns to protect them. The Nyae Nyae Conservancy (NNC), the successor to the NNFC, collaborated with Namibian authorities to have the cattle confiscated and is still (as of September 2010) in the process of bringing the Hereros to justice and seeking legal support for land and resource rights. The young Ju/'hoansi of the Ju/'hoan Transcription Group have transcribed for their elders in the NNC the digitized six-hour record of the historic meeting in Xamsa in May 1991. In August 2010 they began transcribing proceedings of further meetings with the G/am farmers that took place in June–July 2010 (see chapter 10).

3. Ben se Kamp was actually the Ju/'hoan community G!ukon!aqo. It had been informally named for Ben Badenhorst, the police officer who had helped Ju/'hoansi many times in the past in their skirmishes with Hereros and their cattle.

establishing a foothold on Nyae Nyae land, not to mention the possibility of spreading disease due to the quarantine pens.

In late August 1991, shortly after the visit of President Nujoma to Nyae Nyae, the NNFC and the NNDFN brought a quickly assembled delegation to the quarantine camp to speak to the Hereros. The NNFC delegation included the leaders /'Angn!ao /'Un and Tsamkxao =Oma. The NNDFN delegation included Axel Thoma and Megan Biesele. Accompanying the delegation were the filmmaker Richard Pakleppa, who had made the *Voices from the Land* film, and the Setswana translator Beata Botlhoko Kasale, who facilitated understanding with the Hereros who had been living in Botswana.[4] At a few points, Afrikaans was the only *lingua franca* that made sense for the exchange. Five languages were used in the complex communications that took place in those few days.

Tsamkxao =Oma and /'Angn!ao /'Un reported to the inhabitants of Ben se Kamp that the problem of Herero cattle coming in from Botswana had been raised with President Nujoma during his visit. Tsamkxao said, "Long before Namibia's first election, Chief Riruako of the Hereros stated that he wanted to cut the border and bring all the Hereros across from Botswana. But these days you don't meet a single person who believes they can do this without permission." Tsamkxao went on to say that they asked the president about what the Hereros were doing, and Nujoma had said, "Uh-uh! No, they can't do that." Tsamkxao finished by saying that "at the National Land Conference there was not a single opinion expressed about allowing Hereros to cross the border with cattle. If there had been, then all would know."

The following day, the delegation traveled to Djxokhoe, one of the other *n!oresi* where Hereros had moved in and were watering their cattle. /'Angn!ao /'Un asked the assembled Ju/'hoansi and Hereros, "Were any of these Herero men over there at Tsumkwe on Saturday when the president was speaking? I told them they should be there. What did they say when they came back?" Kaqece /Ukxa, one of the Ju/'hoan men at Djxokhoe, replied, "The Hereros didn't tell us anything. Also the only translators there were Ju/'hoansi, and those Hereros don't understand Ju/'hoansi." At that, one of the Herero men spoke up and said that nevertheless they had understood a little. He said, "Namibia is now free, and Bushmanland has no Hereros, no white people, no black people. All these kinds of people should be here." /'Angn!ao /'Un then said to the Djxokhoe people: "Here's what I have to say to you here at Djxokhoe: protect your own water. No one else is going to protect it for you. Once it was water belonging to the Department of Nature Conservation, and they were going to make a game reserve here. But we stopped that, and the water was given back to the people ... These days

4. The filmmakers were later able to obtain the services of an Otjiherero translator, Elizabeth T. T. Tjaronda.

people have to help themselves. If this were a game reserve, you'd have to pay for every tree you wanted to cut down."

The delegation then proceeded to Tsumkwe, where they informed the police commander, Rafael Siteketa, that Hereros were building kraals inside Namibia and intended to cross the international border with their cattle. At first reluctant to accompany the delegation to the border, Siteketa eventually agreed to go, apparently understanding more thoroughly his own relationship to the communication process that was going on by the time that they reached Ben se Kamp. The Hereros building the quarantine pens told Siteketa and the delegation that the Democratic Turnhalle Alliance's member of Parliament for Tsumkwe, Kaqece Geelbooi, had reached an agreement via letter with Chief Riruako that a Herero quarantine camp should be built at this spot. The police commander responded by reading out a more recent letter sent by the regional commissioner, John Mutorwa, to the effect that the Herero plan was illegal. It stated that the National Land Conference had decided that newcomers could not settle without the legal permission of the local traditional authorities—in this case, the NNFC—and the endorsement of the Ministry of Lands, Resettlement, and Rehabilitation. No illegal crossing of cattle and people from Botswana into Namibia would be allowed.

Siteketa explained the situation as follows:

> These people must first go to the government for the approval of the cattle from Botswana into Namibia. There are certain ministries that they must face. And then certain letters must be obtained by them from those ministries … The law does not allow at this stage for them to build a kraal here for the cattle that must come from Botswana. They must first go to those ministries and get some authorization letters. Otherwise, the local people are going to chase them away right here, not maybe today, but TODAY! Because they are not even legal to stay in Bushmanland! … They have not informed the traditional leaders of this place why they are in Bushmanland! These people here are the traditional leaders of this place … that's the main point. That's why they have raised the thing to the president himself. It's not me who is chasing [the Hereros], NO!

Pakleppa captured on film this growing realization by Siteketa of the gravity of his police role in upholding the authority of the traditionally recognized authorities of Nyae Nyae, the Ju/'hoansi. It was dawning on him that the Ju/'hoansi were people who had turned, in a few short years, from wards of the state or serfs into citizens living under the law like other Namibians. This same realization dismayed the Hereros, who had expected that their longer recognized traditional authority would allow them to settle anywhere after independence without seeking permission.

As the meeting concluded, Tsamkxao said:

Don't people first have to go to the law and ask who the leaders are, find out who the *n!ore* owners are, find out that it's the Nyae Nyae Farmers Cooperative? ... /'Angn!ao and I are the local leaders because we have been elected to be the chairperson and the president of the Farmers Cooperative. Geelbooi was not elected by the people here, so if you say you have spoken to him, he is not our leader. But we are not the ones who could give or withhold authority for the building of that kraal. We were not informed about it, and have no authority to give that permission. It's a matter of law ... This isn't a police place, and it's not a Herero place. It's our place, a Ju/'hoan place. Did they ask anybody if they could start such a thing here? I also voted for Namibia to be "opened up." But have [the Hereros] come to an understanding with people? Do they just do things on their own? ... I don't say that the police should drive them out for us: this should be our work for our own land.

/'Angn!ao then translated into Afrikaans the last thing Tsamkxao said: "Shouldn't we tell them that it may be three or four years before the border is opened? It still isn't opened now. Even though you hear that 'Namibia is open,' it doesn't mean that just anyone can walk in anywhere." The Herero spokesman then threw up his hands in a gesture of defeat, saying in Afrikaans, "Geen politik, asseblief!" (No politics, please!). Needless to say, this was an amazing reversal in the history of Ju/'hoan-Herero relationships. Communicating effectively via film and television clearly played a role in this moment of transformation.

Fighting Fire with Fireworks

Pakleppa's footage of this meeting was made into a 24-minute film for the new Namibia Broadcasting Company and widely seen on television in Namibia. Titled *What the Baobab Heard: A Land Dispute*, the film successfully condensed the decades-long struggle of the Ju/'hoansi to keep Herero cattle herds out of Nyae Nyae. Its final scene takes place under the baobab tree at Baraka, by then the headquarters of the NNFC. Ben Uhlenga, deputy minister of wildlife and the South West Africa People's Organization member of Parliament for Bushmanland, had viewed the illegal quarantine camp and informed a meeting of the NNFC that it was impossible that the Hereros should come into Bushmanland in this fashion without the NNFC's permission.

The success of the film as a communication device mirrored the profound effect that the interchange it recorded had on relations between the Ju/'hoansi and the Hereros. Both the confident resistance of the Ju/'hoansi and the success of Pakleppa's film as an instrument of national consciousness-raising built on the foundation of resistance that John Marshall had fostered through his foundation's support for the NNFC. The Ju/'hoansi were having the opportunity to observe the powerful effects of film that they had begun to learn about from Marshall. In short, they began to view film as action, not just as documentation. Increasingly, they saw film, radio, and other media as rhetorical means to make things happen. Their chief objectives included adding to the awareness and empowerment of Ju/'hoansi within Nyae Nyae and, to a small extent, increasing useful national exposure in Namibia.

By December 1991, the eviction of the Herero settlers from Xamsa and from Djxokhoe took place in an orderly and cordial manner. These groups of Herero people, who had long looked at the unspoiled grazing of Nyae Nyae as the next big arena for expansion of their cattle herds, were persuaded to take their herds to G/am, with its good waterhole, south of the Nyae Nyae area. Choosing to "Namibianize" themselves, rather than persisting in isolation, the Ju/'hoansi had invoked the new law of the land by which their duly constituted group had acquired this kind of resource control. They had quietly asked the Namibian police, whom they had long ago made cognizant of the situation, to stand by in case of trouble. Thus, they effectively and without incident escorted the group of Hereros and their cattle on their way to the south. John Marshall, had he been present, would have been very happy at this outcome. Yet Tsamkxao =Oma, watching the departure of the Hereros with satisfaction, said, "We could never have done this if John Marshall had been here." Too polite to say it directly, he nevertheless implied that Marshall's methods, which often became confrontational in person, might have resulted in a less favorable outcome to the negotiations.

Other NNFC Activities in Nyae Nyae after Independence: Reorganization

The NNFC's sense of empowerment, which emerged from their successful and dignified negotiation with and eventual removal of the Hereros, carried over into many of the activities and new programs that they pursued through 1991. The 1992 evaluation of the NNFC and the NNDFN carried out for the Ford Foundation and the NNDFN found that "[t]he members of the cooperative have the ability to make their own decisions on matters relating to land and resource allocation ... The NNFC has the flexibility to deal with issues that come up and to respond to them in innovative ways. Overall, it is evident that the NNFC is a relatively effective body from the standpoints of 1) external contacts and representation, 2) program implementation, and 3) internal communication" (Hitchcock 1992: 48).

By 1992, the NNFC had expanded the number of its *n!ore* communities to 31 and was increasingly involved in land use planning, with an eye toward securing legal access to land and resources in the Nyae Nyae area. During 1991–1992, it was reorganizing itself with a management team consisting of a chairperson, a president, a manager, and an assistant manager, who worked primarily among themselves on a committee basis. The team operated in conjunction with a cooperative made up of two representatives, called *radasi*, from each of the farming communities. Technically, all adults in the villages (*tju/hosi*) were members of this *n!ore* cooperative. There was also an executive body made up of five district leaders, or *!'haotzijuasi* (side people), who were selected to represent sections of the area. In theory, the running of the NNFC was a participatory process in which everyone in the Nyae Nyae area had a right to take part. The revamped organizational and administrative structure of the NNFC leadership was as follows:

Chairperson   President
District Leaders
N!ore Representatives
Villages
Individuals

The members of each of the farming communities elected its two representatives to the *n!ore* cooperative. The members of the Representative Council of the NNFC, in turn, selected the district leaders, one of whom served as the assistant manager.

The day-to-day running of the NNFC was the responsibility of the manager, who was chosen by the Executive Committee of the Representative Council. The manager's duties were to supervise the four program sections of the NNFC (i.e., technical services, production services, social services, and income generation), and also included accounting, payroll, purchasing, general administration, and public relations. In addition to an assistant manager, there were also individuals serving as program facilitators. The structure of the NNFC's program implementation unit was as follows:

Manager
Assistant Manager
Programs
Program Facilitators

The management team took the lead in implementing programs, while the NNFC leaders, including the district leaders and *radasi*, established the guidelines and provided direction for the various activities. The economic development, fiscal management, and training activities of both the NNFC and the NNDFN were aimed at ensuring the self-sufficiency and independence of the NNFC in the future.

Part of the NNFC's mandate was to oversee development activities designed to increase the well-being of the people of Eastern Bushmanland. Many of these activities (e.g., the NNFC Education Program) were initiated at the request of community members. Others were introduced because there was expertise available locally (e.g., a sewing group trained by Jessie Hartung, wife of Charles Hartung, and by Huey Min Wood, wife of Canadian volunteer Eric Wood). Still others (e.g., drip irrigation gardening) were suggested by members of the NNDFN, consultants, or visitors to the area.

The reorganization of the NNFC also saw the introduction of a whole new set of activities. Besides its ordinary duties, the NNFC was now involved in matters as diverse as running a cooperative shop and distributing government drought relief food. It also attempted to provide community services, ranging from health care to education.

The four program sections of the NNFC were structured as follows:

1. technical services: overseeing the installation, maintenance, and repair of village water systems, physical infrastructure (e.g., roads), and a mechanical workshop and furnishing supplies;
2. production services: providing supervision and technical support for the livestock and agriculture activities in the villages;
3. social services: implementing educational, training, health, and legal services; and
4. income generation: running the mobile cooperative shop, purchasing and selling crafts, and planning for tourism and an eventual butchery in Tsumkwe.

At the time, these services were provided by the NNFC working in tandem with the NNDFN. It was planned that these services would eventually be provided by the NNFC itself or would be taken over by government institutions, for example, the Ministry of Education and Culture, the Ministry of Health and Social Services, and the Ministry of Home Affairs. In 1992, a dozen program activities had been set up and were in various stages of operation:

- boreholes, water pumps, and drip irrigation
- livestock purchase, distribution, and management
- agriculture, including crop production and horticulture
- Baraka Training Centre management and maintenance
- brick making, construction, and thatching
- mobile cooperative shop
- handicraft purchasing and sales
- knitting and sewing
- poultry and beekeeping

- wildlife management, land use planning, and resource conservation
- liaison between Eastern and Western Bushmanland
- administration and management of the NNFC

In the six years since the NNFC's inception, the organization's role had expanded greatly in planning and implementing what became a complex and multi-faceted Integrated Rural Development Program (IRDP) for the vast majority of Nyae Nyae's inhabitants. Over time, it added to the original goals of economic development and land settlement a series of human resource development activities, ranging from community-based health education to child and adult literacy programs, such as those listed above. Recordings of the Ju/'hoan language and culture were undertaken, and the results were incorporated into the school curriculum (discussed in detail in chapter 10) and into the overall planning of the various NNFC programs.

The reorganization, most of which took place after the arrival of Axel Thoma as program manager in April 1991, regularized Tsamkxao's position as the paid "president" of the NNFC in recognition of his pioneering work as its first chairperson. It was envisioned that Tsamkxao would work alongside /'Angn!ao /'Un (Kiewiet) as a sort of elder statesman, and an avuncular working relationship was established between the two men during this transitional time. It is noteworthy that due to Tsamkxao's ambiguous status (and the question as to whether he should be paid by the NNDFN or the NNFC), the newly elected chairperson, Kiewiet, did not receive, nor did he request, any salary for some months until the reorganization of the NNFC was in place.

This, combined with the fact that Tsamkxao's house at Baraka was finished early on and he was able to make his family comfortable at Baraka, whereas Kiewiet's house was not finished until months later, produced the sense in Ju/'hoan onlookers that the /Aotcha people were once again being favored. Kiewiet, however, seemed to gain in stature at this time for his modest way of moving into his new office, deferring as he did to Tsamkxao in public speaking. Kiewiet eventually emerged as the genuinely acknowledged new leader of the NNFC. Naturally, however, he in turn has had to take up the challenge of facing the pressures leveled at anyone in Ju/'hoan society who is placed, or places himself, in an elevated position of any kind.

At this time, in mid-1991, both Kiewiet and Tsamkxao made a strong move, supported by the NNDFN, to encourage younger district leaders (the *!'haotzijuasi*) to become involved and to define their roles. It was a direct action in favor of decentralizing the NNFC's authority, and it helped to rectify people's view that NNFC leaders had more power than they should. Furthermore, the position of Kxao Moses =Oma as the NNFC's manager became clarified. Literate, experienced, and trusted by all, Kxao was seen as the most likely candidate to work closely with Thoma as the link between the NNFC and the NNDFN. Unfortunately, Kxao's very capability involved him in the complex demands of a fast-growing program and staff, and he experienced immense amounts of pressure.

As the NNFC's manager, Kxao was often put in the awkward position of receiving contradictory communications, and he felt the confusion keenly. He also bore much of the brunt of community ill will against the seemingly privileged /Aotcha group at Baraka. Like Tsamkxao, Kxao was accused of being stingy with transport, when in fact he was trying to limit the numbers of passengers in order to comply with the carrying capacity of the vehicles and thus to extend their life. Kxao worked in the purchase of crafts as well, and this too involved him in accusations of stinginess at many *n!oresi*. Since funds were limited, he had to use his discretion about how much to purchase from any one group.

Older and Younger Leaders of the NNFC

All in all, it was a busy decade that followed the 1986 founding of the NNFC (then known as the Ju/wa Farmers Union). A great deal had happened in that time, including the defeat of the South West Africa government's plan for a game reserve in Nyae Nyae, the end of the liberation war fought by the South West Africa People's Organization against the South African Defence Force (SADF), the coming of UN Resolution 435 and Namibian independence, the National Land Conference, several major regional conferences on Bushman development, the reorganization of the NNFC structure and functioning, the provision of basic infrastructure and services to 30 or more Nyae Nyae communities along with training programs of all kinds, the start of a comprehensive education program in the Ju/'hoan language and teacher training of the first group of Ju/'hoan teachers (the Village Schools Project discussed more fully in chapter 10), the testing of new Namibian policies on local control of settlement in communal lands, the establishment of an Environmental Planning Committee, and the beginning of local land use planning, to name some highlights. These events taxed the ingenuity and social resourcefulness of NNFC leaders and communities alike, and it is not surprising that some strains emerged in the NNFC leadership and between the NNFC and the NNDFN. Some of these strains included tension between the original leaders of the NNFC, most of whom were men and women in their fifties and sixties, and none of whom had had the opportunity to become literate, and the younger leaders, many of whom had had schooling and were in their twenties and thirties in the early 1990s. Disputes arose between these two groups about the direction of local leadership.

Between 1987 and 1993, younger leaders were actively sought by the older leaders so that guidance for the NNFC and the communities could continue when they retired. Young leadership was thought desirable throughout this process by both the NNDFN and the NNFC, but neither wanted it at the expense of community solidarity. Nonetheless, in the first half of the 1990s, many older leaders in the NNFC were being challenged by the younger people about the worth of their work. Some observers worried about the fragmentation that this challenge might bring about in the community. Yet in retrospect, it is possible to look more deeply into the quiet wisdom of the collective community in order to understand the social dynamics of what was going on. It seemed that there was a self-correcting process in place whose mechanisms were mysterious to outsiders: only time has told its positive outcomes, as new balances have been found. What seemed surprising to outsiders at the time was that the older leaders did not appear to combat the criticism of their juniors but rather "stood aside" passively while the younger people presented their views. They did criticize the younger people privately at times, but in public their tolerant, consensus-based social code prevented them from speaking out. It also seemed that their lenient approach to child-rearing meant in this context that older people should have patience while younger people learned.

Meanwhile, the viewpoint presented by the younger people seemed much less idealistic and community-oriented than that of the earlier leadership. It seemed to be more concerned with job security and personal advancement than with the earlier, larger vision of a cooperative group of *n!oresi* working together to hold on to and develop their land. The new spirit was "revolutionary" in that it tried to overthrow older leaders by leveling charges of supposed "corruption" (i.e., using NNFC vehicles for private trips, drinking, or failing to contact all communities in outlying areas). But it was also "conservative" in that it emphasized individual rights and advancement, secure jobs, and easy food supplies for individuals rather than for whole communities. In those years outsiders often asked why the older people did not stand up for their original communal vision and what they knew to be right for the land.

In partial answer to this question, we could look again at what anthropology has gleaned of the more "traditional" Ju/'hoan society and how it governed itself, which was generally through varying consensual practices. Like many other hunter-gatherers, the Ju/'hoansi had moral or sapiential, rather than formal, leadership, preferring to make sure that each person had some say in decisions (see Biesele 1978). This was a society without ageism, sexism, or coercive structures as the First World knows them. "Each one of us is a headman over himself," is what one Ju/'hoan told Richard Lee (1984: 89) in the 1960s. As we have stated previously, the idea of indirect representation—of "speaking for another"—was anathema to the Ju/'hoansi. This idea extended to relationships between old and young as well. Although there was a certain informal moral authority exercised by elders due to their experience, older people would never presume to speak for younger people. As late as 1991, one heard, and probably still could hear today, the comment that each and every person has to be consulted about community decisions, "otherwise someone might get sick."

This extremely tolerant social style has deep roots in Ju/'hoan child-rearing practices, which survive today despite great change. In the face of opposition or stubbornness, Ju/'hoansi have been taught to shrug and say that each person is entitled to her or his own opinion. Obviously, it is hard to make quick social decisions (or "progress," as Western societies see it) in such a situation, and outsiders would be unrealistic in expecting that of Ju/'hoansi. Older Ju/'hoan people have for many generations done what they had to do and waited tolerantly while younger people were going through the process of "learning sense."

In this case, there were several added factors that conspired to make the old leaders step aside and let the younger ones do what they would, even if they did not agree with them. One was the literacy issue, and the other, related issue was the ability to get driver's licenses. Driving and mobility convey enormous status in Ju/'hoan society, which does not even have draft animals, and many NNFC decisions became de facto the province of the younger people, because they controlled the vehicles and thus could decide where the daily efforts of the NNFC would be concentrated. Then, too, awareness of the power of the printed word, especially in transactions with the government, safari operators, donors, etc., had a depressing effect on those older leaders who had had no access to schooling and who therefore had to defer to the younger, literate leaders.

Problems of Core and Periphery

In the 1990s, one began to hear general comment among the Ju/'hoansi about a privileged class of younger leaders based at the Baraka Training Centre. Most of these young leaders never had to "make it" in the bush, having grown up with wage work for the government or the NNDFN or the NNFC, and their relatively higher standard of living had become a necessity for them in less than a generation. Older people appeared intimidated, baffled, and unable to join in the rapid changes. Their social response to these feelings appeared, at least superficially, to be passivity. In May 1995, an older village representative (*rada*) made an illustrative statement. Shaking his head over the ways that the younger leaders were taking over the decision-making process, he said: "Even in the villages, you see young people who hold aloof from their elders, refusing to speak to them. But this is especially true at Baraka."

In some ways, the emergence of a relatively privileged class at Baraka can be seen as a "core-periphery" problem that affected the equity not only of information flow within the Nyae Nyae community but also of access to development benefits. As such, its human rights implications were internal to the Ju/'hoan community. In the mid-1990s, the NNFC addressed this very issue of full enfranchisement of all community sectors in the development process. As the then program manager, Murray Dawson-Smith (1995: 8), wrote in an NNDFN report at the time, "The NNFC acknowledges there are not only communal aspirations and goals, but also individual, family, *n!ore*, district and group goals which must also be recognized and efforts made to meet these goals, within the context of broad community progress." In the development context, the NNDFN also addressed the issue of the social appropriateness of the younger leaders' relatively high expectations of living standards. Never wishing to deny them the right to better themselves as individuals, the NNDFN also did not wish to ignore the problems of social equity that were involved. Questions of sustainability and equity asked at that time included the following: Will Nyae Nyae ever be able to produce, for all inhabitants, equitable economic advancement of the kind aspired to by the younger leaders who have been living on temporary international aid? Should a large proportion of the population have to keep up their hunting and gathering skills (some people doing so reluctantly), so that a small fraction can have wage labor and store-bought food and clothes? Will the cohesion of the society manage to persist in the face of such inequity?

These were hard questions, ones asked not only by analytic outsiders but also by Nyae Nyae community members. In 1995, some Ju/'hoansi, while not making direct accusations, mused aloud about whether or not the material advantages that they observed in the lives of some of their young leaders might have been bought by "skimming the cream" from eco-tourism deals in their area. One older man said, "I'm not saying I know that this is happening: I just wonder. I don't know enough about money or how the deals have been made. But I do know that our community did the work [of hosting tourists], but we never saw a profit from it." Another illustration of such equity problems involved driving privileges. At the same time that younger people were achieving disproportionate prominence as leaders, the driving privileges of some of the NNFC staff came under fire. It was admittedly difficult to reach all of the *n!oresi* (by then more than 30) on a regular basis, but there does seem to be justification for the people's sense that some leaders were visibly self-aggrandizing. A mute but poignant comment on the envy about driving privileges was to be seen in the toy wire trucks being made and pushed about—not only by children but also by unemployed men in some of the communities.

Also at this time, the much-needed reorganization of the NNFC was looming, and this too affected the community's view of its original "privileged" leaders. These leaders (who were, not surprisingly, mostly men and mostly from the same extended family) had not been elected, as was pointed out in chapter 7, but took leadership roles by historical accident. Later, the younger leaders—even elected ones—experienced similar pressures, and their diplomatic skills were taxed to the utmost. Observers felt great sympathy for these young leaders, caught as they were between older, traditional social expectations and the current necessity to have effective spokespersons and new, more "efficient" rules for deciding things and taking action.

Older NNFC leaders, supported by the NNDFN, continued their policy of choosing younger district leaders and working with them to define their roles. This was a direct move in favor of NNFC authority decentralization, and it had important consequences in how the NNFC was viewed by all. It went hand in hand with continuing experimentation with variants on the theme of "governance by committee" rather than concentrating power in individuals. After a period of misunderstandings, the proposed reorganization began to yield substantial beneficial effects.

Problems of numbers, communication, and conflicting agendas overtook, for a while, the sincerely intended attempt by the older leaders to enfranchise the younger people. Also, for a period, certain individuals were put under dysfunctional amounts of stress by the central roles that they had courageously taken on. But by 1995, several observers (Dawson-Smith 1995; Hitchcock 1996; Wyckoff-Baird 1996) found encouraging signs that participatory, rather than merely representative, democratic practices were being established in the community—to the evident relief of all concerned. These practices had apparently resulted from lengthy debates within the community about evolving changes in consensus and leadership.

A conversation between two older Nyae Nyae residents that Biesele recorded in 1995 gives some insights into these debates:

Speaker 1: Long ago our older people had authority over younger people. Younger people were supposed to keep quiet and learn. But today this situation has been turned upside down at Baraka, and younger people do not listen to older people, and think they themselves should have all authority. The worst thing is that this attitude is now being taught to *all* our young people.

Speaker 2: The problem is that now one family has all the power. It started with one person, and then it was his brother, his sister, his wife, his son, his nephews, and many others. In the next generation I think that even the tiny children of that same family will grow up way beyond the rest of us, and soon be as "tall" as that baobab over there.

Speaker 1: The old people used to have the say over the animals, over the grass, and over all the things in the *n!oresi*. But no longer. I think that the policies of the Coop have maybe caused this to happen. That and the fact that most of the jobs are held by people from one *n!ore*.

Back when the Foundation and Coop were based at /Aotcha [prior to 1991], there was no question of young people running things. They listened to their elders. But once they moved to Baraka, suddenly there were a lot of *//aehasi* [powerful people/self-aggrandizers].

Speaker 2: It's not just Baraka, but all of Nyae Nyae, especially Tsumkwe.

Speaker 1: This is a good example of young men taking over power from older people. It began at Baraka.

Themes of compromised social equity—such as the conflict between old and young, perceptions of unequally growing privilege, and the incipient formation of an elite—are strong in this quotation. Such conversations are by no means rare in Nyae Nyae, even now, more than 15 years later. But the rules about them are very strict: the presence of anyone at whom criticism is leveled will keep conversations like this from occurring. Informing others by indirection and avoiding escalations of conflict through avoidance of direct confrontation are long-term tenets of Ju/'hoan social life that have persisted, even in changed contexts.

Further, in Ju/'hoan society it is hard for someone to enjoy achieving something that distinguishes her or him from others. As one Ju/'hoan told anthropologist Polly Wiessner (pers. comm.), if he stands tall, "he will bump his head against the sky." In other words, asserting oneself incurs the jealousy of other community members. Ju/'hoan people, including those currently grappling with recent chances at unequal privilege, are only too aware of this strong feature of their society. They ask themselves whether gaining special benefits is worth losing status as an ordinary member of their society. In the 1990s, they were weighing literacy, vehicle access, and salary privileging against the familiar comforts of fair sharing and the security and "anonymity" it still conveyed.

These and other issues of social equity that were surfacing in the process of development at the time may have been natural side effects of too-rapid growth. As such, they were nobody's fault, yet everyone's concern. The fast-paced advance of development projects in small societies brings on many of the same problems of size and structure as in large-scale societies. The ambitious IRDP, undertaken by the NNFC with its partner the NNDFN, was no exception. There were sound historical and environmental reasons why Ju/'hoan society had long remained stable as a collection of decentralized but carefully articulated small groups with controlled relationships to the land and its resources. The reasons why the society later experienced social and economic disruption were equally sound: they were the retrospectively predictable results of too-rapid change from a deeply socialized human pattern without the benefit of effective resocialization or data-based resources planning.

Effective resocialization and new communicative structures were earnestly undertaken, it must be stressed, by the NNFC. But it seems that both the NNFC and the NNDFN may have underestimated the time that it might take for people of all ages in all of the Nyae Nyae communities (numbering 35 by 1995) to become informed about and motivated to support a substantially new set of social goals. Basic organizational skills that outsiders might take for granted were simply lacking, as were new economic skills that were needed to make this complex transition. Worse, despite attempts by the NNDFN to provide data on which to base estimates of the viability of the economic changes under discussion, full information on available resources and carrying and productive capacities was not assembled at the time that it was needed. This information was not available until later, from Polly Wiessner's work in 1996–1998 and afterwards.[5]

A main mistake, it seems, was the assumption that something which could be socially effective on a small scale—as at the start of the "back to the *n!oresi*" movement of the three original communities—could be easily expanded to a much larger scale. There was lack of foresight with regard to the escalating communicational demands and problems necessarily attendant on the movement's growth in size and scope. Unbearable pressures were put upon NNFC leaders and NNDFN workers alike to "treat all communities fairly" in a no-win situation of difficult transport and long distances to cover. Each one of the sub-projects within the IRDP experienced agonizing decisions and perceived failures due to the difficulty of traveling to reach the entire widespread population of about 2,000 Ju/'hoansi.

Unfortunately, internal struggles within the NNFC over these growth issues became acute so quickly that they could not be remedied through judicious analysis and strategic downscaling. The situation was then ripe for ideology mongering, and this happened in a most confusing interplay of opinions and claims to authority between the NNFC and the NNDFN, surfacing visibly in early 1992. A great deal of the confusion centered not only on the relationship between the NNFC's older and younger leadership and on the controversy over the privileged versus the less-privileged communities, but also on the entire issue of participation versus representation, which continued to be seen as problematic throughout this period.

Participation versus Representation

> We never wanted to represent our communities. That was a white people's idea in the first place.
>
> — Kxao Moses =Oma, 1994, as quoted by M. Dawson-Smith
> (pers. comm., 1994)

Understanding the emerging new polity in Nyae Nyae during the 1990s involves seeing that some of the long-established Ju/'hoan social rules, such as those covering internal discipline and participatory decision-making, were themselves in a state of change by that time. In an important move, a Management

---

5. Polly Wiessner's relevant data are summarized in chapter 9.

Committee, which was intended to streamline the everyday activities of the NNFC, was also set up. In many ways, the NNFC board was posing a direct challenge to the importation of the concepts of American-style democracy, favored by John Marshall and others, and was taking a step back so as to build organically upon the Ju/'hoansi's own traditional, well-understood social rules. But the application of an international model of leadership and community management in the Ju/'hoan area had been a long and subtle process—one that was not easily undone.

It is fairly easy to see the roots of institutional dilemmas that, by early 1995, had become painfully obvious in the Nyae Nyae community. Barbara Wyckoff-Baird (1996), a periodic observer working closely at that time with the NNFC on a USAID/World Wildlife Fund natural resources management project (Living in a Finite Environment—LIFE), wrote about the re-empowerment of the Ju/'hoansi as social actors. She stressed that the focus of the early NNDFN-NNFC approach (roughly during the decade of the 1980s) was "on the *products* of democratization (i.e., representative institutions) rather than on the *process* of democratization (i.e., indigenous people choosing and achieving their own appropriate models)" (ibid.: 19; italics added).

A man from Djxokhoe, an outlying community, said to Biesele in June 1995 that "the 'Ones-Who-Know' [the Management Committee at Baraka] say that the old =*xanu* [dispensation] has died and the new one is being born." This statement reflects the pro-active approach of the reorganization that had been taken in order to democratize the committee in early May (the previous month), but the marginalization still felt by the Djxokhoe resident was evident in the sarcastic way that he styled the committee's name. Wyckoff-Baird's (1996: 4) analysis concurred:

[T]he Management Committee, reduced from five to four members, had become an isolated decision-making body, often speaking on behalf of the community, making decisions for them, and rarely communicating the results back to the community. The Management Committee had ceased seeking the ideas and inputs from the community for planning and implementation of the development program. Visits by the Management Committee members to the *n!oresi* had become all but nonexistent by early 1995. Interviews in January 1995 revealed that most community members were not aware of the activities in which the Committee was currently engaged. Community members had become dissatisfied with the Management Committee, frequently stating that the members should be replaced ...

Interviews during this time also revealed that, while a representative structure might be in place, changes in culture and social organization necessary to make these structures effective had not occurred. Community members who were interviewed continued to believe that no one could speak on their behalf ... In many *n!oresi*, there was no sense of one person having been selected to perform a representative role on the Council and several *n!oresi* were represented by a different individual at almost each meeting. As one RADA representative characterized the situation, "Whoever is in the *n!ore* when the transport arrives jumps on the truck and goes to the meeting …"

Furthermore, the roles and responsibilities of the various parties in a representative structure were not clearly understood. Community members did not see themselves as having rights to demand information and accountability from their representatives. Similarly, only one of the members of the Representative Council interviewed, out of six, had held a village meeting prior to the last Council meeting to elicit opinions and issues. Only half of the members of the Representative Council interviewed had reported back to the villagers on the last Council meeting. In discussions with 10 members of the Representative Council, all agreed that they were not sure how to perform their roles and that they required training in representative governance.

For more than a decade these communities and leaders had been in a substantial bind, however, because insistent outside forces (such as Namibian government ministries) continued to regard the representative structure as the only one with which they could do business. The bind persisted due to both the imported Euro-American models of democracy (on which the Namibian Constitution was based) and the sheer logistical difficulty of getting the Representative Council together on short notice when action needed to be taken. As Wyckoff-Baird (1996: 19) went on,

> [B]y early 1995, the NNFC seems to have evolved from a facilitative organization built upon a tradition of decision-making by consensus, to one centralized at the Management Committee level with little or no participation of community members … [T]he imposition of a representative structure, as a symbol of democracy, also contributed to this evolution by concentrating authority in a few select individuals, a concept [that is] anathema to the Ju/'hoansi. Given that this structure was not of their own making, the Ju/'hoansi did not have the insights or resources necessary to modify and adjust the model to changes in their world …

The concentration of authority in a few individuals resulted in enormous bad feeling that the Nyae Nyae community attributed in a general way to the Baraka Training Centre. A constant refrain heard in mid-1995 was that young *Barakakxaosi* (owners of Baraka) made all the decisions but showed poor judgment in doing so. It was said that their poor judgment was proven by their non-appearance at outlying communities, their preference for working at communities near Baraka, their habit of using community trucks for personal errands and for drinking in Tsumkwe, and their extremely bad track record with regard to road accidents. In other words, the same social pressures that affected the older generation influenced the choices of the younger one.

Furthermore, Baraka drew a crowd of idle young people who were attracted to its supposedly more sophisticated lifestyle but who could not afford the commodities that they saw employed people enjoying. As a non-traditional community in Nyae Nyae, Baraka did not benefit much from the older social rules, for instance, regarding sharing, many of which were still in place in the smaller communities. People from these communities, observing competition, anomie, and a decline in traditional morals at Baraka, linked these problems to the presence there of the NNFC and to its structure, which had become top-heavy and socially problematic.

Gender Issues in the NNFC

The centralization of the NNFC at the Management Committee level also con-tributed to a visible marginalization of women, despite their pro-active work. This was true both in NNFC politics and in Nyae Nyae economic development in general. Ju/'hoan women, especially the older ones who became *radasi*, had an expectation of substantial gender equality in both of these areas, and by 1995 it was clear that these expectations were not being met. No women were on the Management Committee, and no women had paid jobs at Baraka, in contrast to approximately 20 male workers and NNFC spokespersons there.

In 1993, at the preliminary regional meeting in Mangetti Dune (a former SADF camp), which was held before the international conference in Gabo-rone, Botswana, the all-male leadership of the NNFC was publicly criticized by other San groups for not including a woman in their delegation. The NNFC rapidly and sheepishly organized a passport for Seg//ae Kxao, an older female *rada* (only 3 out of 35 were women at the time), and she was able to fly with them to Botswana. But by June 1995, this token inclusion in the affairs of men was being openly challenged by all three women *radasi*. One of them, Di//xao =Oma, told Biesele that Nyae Nyae women were fed up with the fact that the NNFC had no paying jobs for women and that, as a result, they were protesting the newly initiated Community Game Ranger program supported by USAID and the World Wildlife Fund. "This is just one more project that will benefit men only," she said.

From an outsider's perspective, Di//xao =Oma's angry activism seemed somewhat misplaced: none of the *radasi*, men included, received salaries for being representatives. Furthermore, the Community Game Ranger program, then in its infancy, was abundantly supplied with gender-conscious plan-ning and motives. But she did identify an inequity that disturbed her, and she expressed it in the ways available to her. Much of her anger centered on the Baraka community and a whole range of social inequities she saw developing. There was not only unequal economic opportunity but also unequal access to transport, which was linked to literacy and thus also limited women's options. She also fumed about the kinds of sexism that she saw operating in the Village

School at Baraka (one of five experimental lower-primary schools that the NNDFN set up in Nyae Nyae). Although the school at Baraka was the flagship school of a community-based education project, although the teacher was a Ju/'hoan person teaching his own people, and although there was no problem of inter-ethnic bullying, such as that known to take place at the government school in Tsumkwe, this woman's daughter had had to leave school because "the boys there were ripping the girls' clothes off. The boys also twist the girls' arms at the school at Baraka." She continued: "This doesn't happen at the smaller villages. This isn't a matter of early sex but of violence."

This woman *rada* was also experiencing some of the same ageist attitudes that were troubling her male counterparts—but from younger men, not from younger women. Apart from a few recently instituted affirmative action roles, there were few younger women in either leadership positions or employment. Thus, the older women *radasi* were doubly marginalized by the sexist and increasingly ageist realities of their situation. As among the Himba (Jacobsohn 1995: 183–184), younger Ju/'hoan men are increasingly dismissive of women, especially older women, and this also is linked to the loss of political power and economic clout among women. Many of these issues, related partly to inappropriately imported models of governance, were exacerbated by interactions with conflicting development approaches within the NNDFN.

The Social Implications of Centralized Leadership

Using the same approach that they offered the NNDFN in 1992—resolving conflicts through better communication—the Ju/'hoansi tried to heal the splits emerging in their own new polity. During 1992, the aforementioned issues swirling around the NNFC-NNDFN headquarters at Baraka, combined with the growing tide of resentment against the concentration of large numbers of people there from a single *n!ore* (/Aotcha), were coming to a head. Most of the envy involved was grounded in traditional Ju/'hoan attitudes toward sharing. Strain was experienced because the possibilities and rules for sharing were changing—and at different rates for different individuals and *n!oresi*. New social attitudes and models were competing for a hearing.

How the Ju/'hoan people of the Nyae Nyae area were to relate to each other in such changing times was coming to depend partly on models that they were learning from the outside. These included new organizational structures, communicational modes, hierarchical concepts of authority, delegation of responsibility, and concepts of political representation. But to a great extent, the way in which the Ju/'hoansi related to each other was still based on expectations and social patterns from the past. These patterns were self-evident to the Ju/'hoan people, and they were continually surprised that outsiders involved in mentoring them did not know of their special ways of thinking and modes of behavior. Many problems arose merely because diverse communicational and relational cultures were unknowingly at cross-purposes with each other.

For instance, cultural rights and communication were increasingly at the core of problems being addressed by the Nyae Nyae communities and their leadership. The charge that "*Barakakxaosi* are running everything" implied the failure of the original decentralized model that had been shared by the NNFC and the NNDFN. This model, in which a number of re-formed *n!ore* groups would build a mixed-subsistence economy based on land, resources, and social rules that they were familiar with, appeared to have been compromised (at least temporarily) by what Baraka had become.

One might characterize the leadership problem evident at Baraka at that time as one that favored "vertical" politics over the "horizontal." For one thing, the emphasis placed upon Baraka as the headquarters failed to take into account the cognitive need of the 34 other communities, spread out "horizontally" over the land, to see themselves as equals. For another, the difficulty of maintaining Baraka as a training center rather than a living area was underestimated, and practical problems, such as leave, transport, wealth discrepancy, differential access to training and schooling, and the sheer unfamiliarity of Western-style housing and sanitation, were not adequately addressed. The NNDFN may have made a serious Utopian mistake in assuming that the idea of creating a different kind of village, one for training and administration, would be practical in Nyae Nyae. Chief among the related missteps was failing to insist on personnel rotation for NNDFN jobs so that people from all of the communities would have equal access to training and wages.

But the Ju/'hoansi who lived at Baraka in the 1990s and whose families became dependent on the NNDFN and its programs, including its support of the NNFC, were caught in a hard-to-break cultural and economic bind. The development process ended up pitting them against their extended families in the less privileged outlying *n!oresi*. It also gave them a feeling of reduced, rather than augmented, subsistence options. In one example, when their peers began to label foraging knowledge as "uncool," fewer young people expressed an interest in learning and honing the intricate, traditional environmental skills that they would still need to fall back on in a mixed economy.

One of the worst problems may have been the enforced idleness of young people, whose aspirations brought them to Baraka but who found "nothing to do" there. Many young people felt somehow that the NNFC owed them work and relentlessly pressed its leadership to create jobs. The NNFC was hard put to manage this social challenge, and observers got the sense that it was apologizing for this insufficiency. But job competition was palpable, and the organization had little experience or wherewithal to create fulfilling, remunerative, and cost-effective jobs. It managed to create a few jobs for young people, but even when they were employed by the NNFC, much of their time was often unoccupied. Meanwhile, other essential work in the *n!oresi* went undone and was not aspired to.

The employment issue was one of the large social processes in development that would have become problematic in any changing context, and it became one of the starting points for factionalism among both the Ju/'hoansi and the staff of the NNDFN. It also seemed that continuing factionalism in the NNDFN, as described in chapter 7, had the effect of further dividing the Nyae Nyae people along lines that would not have separated them, had they not witnessed their mentors' lack of unity. Whether or not this assessment is fair, problematic exposure to the competitive Western model that values "individualism" and "getting ahead" over communal values *has* been an unintentional side effect for the Ju/'hoansi, stemming from their close relationship with outside development organizations. In mid-1995, a tourist in Nyae Nyae, seeking help with a punctured tire, made this observation after a brief stop at Baraka:

> When I went to [the NNFC manager]—I had been told who to go to—I got the feeling that he was trying to impress me with his authority, as well as sincerely trying to help me. But he pointed his finger, saying, "You, go help him!" to [an assistant]. [The assistant]'s response was as if he'd been picked on in front of his peers. From what I had heard from everyone about [the Ju/'hoansi], it was a different type of situation from what I expected. It was more like something you'd see in a developed country. When I thought about it a little, though, it was similar to what you see when someone first gets a job with a little authority: they haven't yet learned how to handle it.

Competitive models unwittingly fostered by development efforts may have had the effect of polarizing the Nyae Nyae community along the lines of age, sex, and activity preference. Wanting Third World people to share in a First World competitive value structure can be culturally imperialistic and quite destructive. The mercenary focus of this approach is often deeply shameful to people for whom traditional sharing has long been the key to happiness. Participating in it sets up irresolvable contradictions for them and sometimes results in being shunned by their communities.

It seems that unequal authority and competition, so thoroughly guarded against in the traditional Ju/'hoan scheme of social and spiritual values, posed enormous cognitive problems in the 1990s for those Ju/'hoansi who wanted to "better themselves." They had to ask themselves, "Is this the only way to get ahead?" If the only models they saw were divisive, and if the only available answer to their question was "yes," the result was bound to be growing social dislocation. Yet, as we will see in our final chapter, the Ju/'hoansi continued to find creative ways to extend their own social ideas organically into a new context. In their own socially effective way, the Ju/'hoansi began to reject the idea that there could be only "one way" to proceed in what the world regards as "development."

The NNDFN and the NNFC in 1994: Finalizing *A Kalahari Family*

Perhaps the most profound lesson offered by the story of the Ju/'hoan people is that as long as there are feelings of dissension, consensus has not been reached and the talk around an issue should therefore not cease. Instead, their view is that community conversation should always be open, with room for second thoughts and slept-upon deliberations to keep it moving in creative ways.

John Marshall, who was not in Nyae Nyae during the worst of the NNDFN's problems in 1992, presented his view of the 1994 consequences of those problems when his five-part film, *A Kalahari Family*, was released in 2003. The fifth and last part of the film, *Death by Myth*, presents a moment in 1994 that was deeply rethought by members of the Ju/'hoan community after it was filmed. Yet because it was fixed in film, the conversation on the incident was in some ways closed, to the embarrassment of NNFC officers and Ju/'hoan community members. In this episode, the NNDFN's director, Axel Thoma, is portrayed being fired ("chased away") at a meeting of the NNFC. This meeting is referred to in a quote from an older Ju/'hoan leader that was tape-recorded in 1995:

> When we had the meeting where [Axel was] "chased away," I told the young men that it was not our way to "chase away" … people so quickly without discussing it. I said that instead it was important to talk with them, tell them our concerns about their work. I told them we should wait with Axel, because earlier we had worked well together. But the young people refused. They said that they were following white people's ways now, and that white people's custom is not to stop in the middle of chasing someone away. White people's custom is to do it all at once.

Also in 1995, another Ju/'hoan witness to the meeting, who like the first wished to remain anonymous, said that five to seven young men, two of them teachers from Botswana and not involved in the NNFC management, were going through the crowd at the meeting, shouting, "Get these useless Cooperative leaders fired!" They were interrupted by Marshall, who said, "No, no, I don't mean the Cooperative leaders. I was talking about Axel." Then the young men turned around, shouting, "The white faces have to go!" Two young men shouted, "We do it in the white man's way and do not stop halfway!" This sudden shift in emphasis does not appear in the film.

No one questions that Marshall's camera saw what he has presented. But it is clear that there were other things to see that were not presented, other things to hear that were not translated; his points are made with selective evidence. This is, of course, true for any expressive presentation, including the present chapter and book. But it is important to recognize possible bias and to maintain openness to reinterpretation, given new evidence. This is one very important lesson of Ju/'hoan culture that, as we have seen, the NNDFN neglected in the mid-1990s at its peril.

Social Equity Lessons of Ju/'hoan Society: Learning from Mistakes

Others have made the argument that the dislocations and confusions that the Ju/'hoansi have experienced—even those tied directly to the Ju/'hoansi's relationships with outside agencies—are all part of the process of "democratization" and must be allowed to proceed unhindered. It did seem that the Ju/'hoansi embarked on a series of necessary "course corrections" for themselves in the 1990s, based partly on the problems that they observed arising in the NNDFN. However, certain mistakes made by all of us who were associated with that organization shook the foundations of long-established Ju/'hoan community stability and may also have threatened Ju/'hoan credibility on the Namibian national level. Thus, we should take responsibility for, at the very least, an analytic understanding of our errors and try to avoid them in future. In chronicling the experiences and lessons gained from them, we may also perhaps offer people in similar situations a chance not to make the same mistakes.

In particular, it became evident as the 1990s progressed that the major democratic model under which Nyae Nyae had been operating, due to unexamined external paradigms and problematic power relationships, actually victimized leaders as well as members, caused elitism problems, and enhanced gender inequities. This realization prompts an important observation on dilemmas facing any responsible ethnography on post-foragers—that is, the critical importance of paying attention to local communicational conventions.

Cultures of Communication

Much Third World development work is today carried out under the banner of "coming from the people," but without recognition that community opinion is an elusive commodity. As social scientists and people who have personally lived in a small-scale society know, community decisions are hard to make, and joint opinion is almost impossible to characterize, even through "accepted" representatives. Opinion is rarely unitary. Too often, instead, facile statements are made by outsiders, each one claiming privileged knowledge about "what the people want." These statements may become the basis of decisions and plans that actually reflect First World projections.

Local "cultures of communication" are thus vitally important to understand. Mentoring to effect real communication may involve years of standing back, watching and listening, participating passively or actively in discussions and re-discussions, and understanding how the people involved relate *to each other*. Without knowing the social expectations, for instance, that Ju/'hoansi have of each other, one cannot know the expectations that they have of outside help, or what exactly is meant when they ask for it. Failure to gauge communicative expectations has meant more than two centuries of broken treaties and trust between peoples such as the Maori, native North Americans, and colonial and post-colonial governments. Development workers and anthropologists should not make the mistake of ignoring such an obvious lesson of history.

Communicational culture, moreover, vitally includes concepts of relatedness and power sharing. Traditional cultures have deeply embedded techniques and practices for maintaining agreement about how power is to be shared, often through leveling mechanisms. In Ju/'hoan concepts of equity, for example, talk and communication are regarded as commodities that must be carefully regulated by some of the same rules that regulate the flow of goods and food. Thus, when NNFC spokespersons began in the 1990s to travel within Namibia and internationally on behalf of their organization, their biggest challenge came at the report-back when they returned home. When the NNFC's manager returned from an international conference in Copenhagen in 1993, his first trip outside of Namibia, he said that he would have to tell his community only small bits of the story of his journey from time to time, and that the whole story might take six months to come out. This was because he felt he had to avoid self-aggrandizement (Axel Thoma, pers. comm.).

The failure to recognize this relentless emphasis on careful self-presentation and sharing in Ju/'hoan culture has too often led development workers to urge Ju/'hoansi to self-promote and to act in other competitive ways that are not in keeping with their culture. Many of the entrenched conflicts that became visible in Nyae Nyae can be traced to uneven empowerment given to NNFC leaders through the well-meaning but misguided influence of the NNDFN. This uneven empowerment gave unusual energy to conflicts between individuals that would ordinarily have been resolvable through traditional means. On reflection, it seems that the NNDFN may have been guilty of outmoded "trickle-down" thinking when it assumed that training a first cadre of leaders would *not* cause problems of social equity.

Unless the danger of projecting First World assumptions is vigilantly guarded against, development mentoring and anthropological documentation both can tend to import divisive problems. Mentoring demands tightrope walking of a most delicate sort: it is all too easy to cross the line from being facilitative to being suggestive—or even paternalistic. To ensure meaningful development, it must constantly be asked whether a step or a program or an idea will have the effect of promoting social equity or the reverse, perhaps even destroying an old equilibrium that existed in ideological and spiritual realms, as well as in economics.

It is particularly important to ask such questions in social-structural areas where there are marked differences between an indigenous people's tradition and First World social conditions. We should not assume, for example, that the gender and age splits now fragmenting Western societies are replicated in indigenous societies and require the same activism or remedies. From experience in Nyae Nyae, it seems that assuming that a high degree of gender activism is appropriate there creates counterproductive distance between the sexes. Yet, clearly, some sort of gender activism is both needed and taking place. Possibly, we might see outside pressures not as causing but as *enabling* processes that are already inherent in the dynamism of the society itself.

Similarly, promoting individualism at the expense of cooperation and progressivism for youth at the expense of family and community solidarity have had far-reaching and deleterious consequences in Nyae Nyae. By and large, those young people who have had the most access to literacy and employment have begun, in a few short years, to form an envied and pressured elite. Traditional Ju/'hoan leveling mechanisms still batter them, but the investments that they have made in the fruits of the local equivalent of "white-collar" jobs force them to try to ignore this pressure and the distance that it creates between them and their extended families.

Older people, too, have been marginalized as a group. Even the pioneers who had the vision to create the NNFC in the first place have taken a back seat to young people. These youths, mostly male, are literate, which allows them to obtain coveted driver's licenses and jobs. As salaried, driving community leaders, their mobility effectively allows them to make far-reaching decisions about community priorities. Yet their Western-influenced lifestyle, involving not only highly problematic access to alcohol but also store-bought food, clothing, and materials for shelter, lacks the fail-safe of being able to make a living with traditional local knowledge.

In the 1990s, these younger people faced nutritional deprivation due to impoverished diets, and their newly sedentary lifestyle, with its lack of exercise, imposed a health burden. Their geographic mobility put them at risk for AIDS and other STDs, while their social mobility reduced their ability to rely on spouses and in-laws. Sharing with them became problematic because they were perceived to have superior resources. Spiritual support tied to economic mutuality evaded them more and more. The erosion of individual ties to the land exposed the community resource base to the cupidity of expansionist non-San neighbors.

These young leaders were individuals undeniably at risk, and because of the divisiveness that their lifestyle was creating, their society as a whole was put at risk. But development is supposed to *reduce* risk for individuals and societies. In the decade of the 1990s, Ju/'hoan people, both young and old, reached a point of bewilderment about the effects of development that they saw around them, particularly those stemming from new models that they had been asked to embrace less than a decade before. With the formation of the Nyae Nyae

Conservancy (NNC) in 1998, there was evidence that the tide was beginning to turn, in terms of both active and passive cultural resistance. But the new equilibrium that was to be created would look little like the equity to which older Ju/'hoansi, still the nominal decision-makers, had become accustomed. In the following chapter, we outline the steps by which the NNFC transformed itself into the NNC and how that transformation has affected the way in which the Ju/'hoansi regard their future. In particular, we address in chapter 9 the sustainability and equity questions that the Ju/'hoan community and its supporters continue to pose up to the present.

Chapter Nine

Community-Based Natural Resource Management and Other Development Models

In June 1998, the Nyae Nyae Farmers Cooperative (NNFC) became the Nyae Nyae Conservancy (NNC), the first conservancy on communal land in Namibia. This chapter describes the lead-up to the establishment of the NNC, starting in 1992, and the way its policies and procedures have been worked through and refined up to the present.

In the period between 1992 and 2010, there were many events that significantly affected the well-being of the Ju/'hoansi in Nyae Nyae. Some were related to the NNFC/NNC organization and its decisions about the use of Nyae Nyae's natural resources. Others involved the work of the Nyae Nyae Development Foundation of Namibia (NNDFN) in assisting the people's organization. There were also external pressures on the people and habitats of Nyae Nyae, some of them coming from the government or from groups and individuals who wanted to immigrate to the area and bring their livestock with them. Visits were made to Nyae Nyae by safari companies who hoped to be able to use Tsumkwe and other places as bases for their hunting and photo-tourism operations. Deliberations among the Ju/'hoansi focused on how they could face these external pressures but still sustain themselves and their environment.

A major event that occurred across the border in Botswana and that affected the Nyae Nyae region both directly and indirectly was an outbreak of lung plague (contagious bovine pleuropneumonia, CBPP) among cattle. This disease outbreak occurred in the Kaudum area of North West District

(Ngamiland) of Botswana in February 1995. The Botswana government moved quickly to deal with this crisis, cutting off all livestock movements, establishing quarantine areas, and killing all of the cattle in the district, some 320,000 head.[1] Some individuals tried to move their livestock out of Ngamiland to protect them from the mass killings. There were also rumors to the effect that a few Ngamiland cattle owners, some of whom were Herero, were talking to local and national government officials in Botswana and to residents of Namibia about the possibility of moving across the border and establishing themselves and their herds in Nyae Nyae and areas to the west and south. Both governments were reluctant to allow this, given the possibility of spreading the disease to new areas.

In the 1990s, the government of Namibia played a relatively important role in the lives of the people of Nyae Nyae. Namibian government assistance took the form of educational support, water development, veterinary work, and some agricultural advice. There were also statements made by government officials regarding the land tenure status of Nyae Nyae, some of which were contradictory. The Namibian government was providing pensions to the elderly, and food and other goods were distributed to people in need during droughts, although the frequency of the food provision was somewhat variable. There were also mineral exploration activities in the Tsumkwe area, some of them carried out by Mount Burgess Mining, an Australian company that employed several dozen Ju/'hoansi at various times.

An important trend in the late 1990s and into the early part of the new millennium was a substantial increase in the population of Tsumkwe, with many of the people coming from the surrounding *n!ore* villages. At Tsumkwe, there were sometimes disagreements between people, and alcohol consumption was a severe problem, as was disease, including tuberculosis. Conflicts between groups occurred, and there were cases where severe physical abuse occurred, including one incident in Tsumkwe District West in 2004 involving an elderly woman and a baby (WIMSA 2005: 68). The lack of follow-up by Namibian government authorities in these cases motivated the people to seek legal advice and help from non-governmental organizations (NGOs), such as the Legal Assistance Centre and the Working Group of Indigenous Minorities in Southern Africa.

With regard to the Nyae Nyae region, much of the planning that was carried out by government officials in the 1990s revolved around community-based natural resource management and the establishment of what came to be known as conservancies. As we discuss below, conservancies are areas of land in which local communities have the right to make decisions about the use of wildlife resources and to engage in wildlife-related enterprises, including tourism.

---

1. For a discussion of this set of events, see Hitchcock (2002b).

Community-Based Natural Resource Management in Southern Africa

In the 1980s and 1990s, significant strides were made in what came to be known as community-based natural resource management (CBNRM) projects, sometimes also described as integrated conservation and development projects. These projects were based on a number of assumptions. First, it was assumed that southern African governments would be willing to devolve authority over wildlife resources to the local level and would enact legislation to make this possible. A second assumption was that local people would be willing to participate in community-based conservation and development. Third, it was assumed that government authorities and NGOs would be willing to consult local people and have them be involved in planning and decision-making. A fourth assumption was that if local people had the rights over wildlife resources and got the benefits from them, they would work to conserve them. Fifth, since CBNRM combines wildlife conservation and rural development, it was assumed that both human and wildlife populations would benefit (Borgerhoff Mulder and Coppolillo 2005; Child 1995; Fabricius et al. 2004; Getz et al. 1999; Hulme and Murphree 2001; Marks 1984; Neumann 1998; Suich, Child, and Spenceley 2009). In order to make CBNRM possible, then, governments have to devolve responsibility over wildlife resources to local communities and at the same time allow those communities to benefit directly from the wildlife resources.

Some of the ecologists and social scientists working on CBNRM projects realized that the promotion of biodiversity conservation could have significant impacts on human populations. An increase in the number of large mammals, such as elephants and lions, was not viewed all that positively by the Ju/'hoansi. As has been noted, there were incidents in Nyae Nyae where lions preyed on people's livestock and elephants destroyed water points and gardens. One of the positions taken by the Ju/'hoansi was that if the government of Namibia was going to promote CBNRM in Nyae Nyae, then efforts would have to be made to compensate people for wildlife-related damages.

CBNRM projects became very popular in southern Africa in the latter part of the twentieth century and into the new millennium (Gibson 1999; Hulme and Murphree 2001; Nelson 2010). A characteristic feature of some of these projects was that local people were able to get some cash income, employment, and, in a number of cases, meat from animals that were obtained in their areas. In some places, local communities could contract out the rights to wildlife to private companies, who then paid them for the right to bring in hunters or tourists. These companies would sometimes employ local people as guides or safari camp assistants, paying them in cash. The clients of the companies would also purchase locally made products, including handicrafts, thus enabling the local people to generate some income.

CBNRM projects have also had their downsides. There were situations where safari operators took advantage of local people and did not provide the agreed-upon benefits. Concerns have also been raised about the equity and gender impacts of CBNRM projects (see, e.g., Hunter, Hitchcock, and Wyckoff-Baird 1990; Nangula 2004). In addition, some of the CBNRM projects in southern Africa saw the benefits flow to district-level authorities rather than local communities (Gibson 1999; Patel 1998). Moreover, the establishment of conservancies for specific groups sometimes led to resentment on the part of other groups in nearby areas who felt that unfair advantages were being accorded to those groups who were able to set up conservancies.

CBNRM and the LIFE Project in Namibia

After independence was achieved in Namibia, the Ministry of Environment and Tourism (MET) shifted its attention more toward working with local people in communal areas of the country (Jones 1996, 2010; MET 1994, 1995a, 1995b). In 1991, personnel from the MET worked with NNDFN members and the Ju/'hoansi on socio-ecological studies of the Nyae Nyae region (Biesele and Jones 1991). There was a whole series of meetings between the MET, the NNFC, and the NNDFN in 1992, many of them aimed at coming up with recommendations on how best to implement CBNRM and tourism activities.

The idea of working with safari companies was not something new to the people of Nyae Nyae. The Ju/'hoansi had done so for a number of years, notably with Anvo Hunting Safaris, owned by German-Namibian safari operator, Volker Grellman. Grellman hired local Ju/'hoansi to serve as hunting guides, and some Ju/'hoansi earned income through sales of crafts and doing odd jobs for the safari company's clients. In the mid- to late 1990s, after the departure of Anvo Hunting Safaris, some of the safari operators who visited Nyae Nyae brought in outsiders to serve as guides, causing bad feeling locally.

In 1992, the government of Namibia entered into an agreement with the United States Agency for International Development (USAID) in a development effort known as the Living in a Finite Environment (LIFE) Project (USAID/Namibia 1992). This project was the result of extensive work by the MET, consultants, development workers, and local people, including the Ju/'hoansi in Nyae Nyae. Initially, the LIFE Project was designed to work on a national scale in Namibia, but it was ultimately determined that the project would have greater impact if it focused its efforts on a limited number of target areas. The three target areas chosen early on were Caprivi, Tsumkwe District East (Nyae Nyae), and a portion of the Etosha pan catchment area (ibid.). During the assessment process in the period between 1992 and 1995, criteria were delineated to determine if interventions were appropriate for a particular community within the target areas. These criteria were as follows: homogene-ity of the population, number of potential beneficiaries, number of institutions ready for CBNRM, viability of the wildlife resource base, time frame for the establishment of conservancies, livestock competing with wildlife, tourism potential, and income-generating potential from natural resources.

Grassroots work by LIFE Project personnel placed substantial emphasis on gaining an understanding of the structure, organization, and workings of communities and community institutions. The LIFE Project team, which was made up of members from both international and Namibian NGOs (notably, the World Wildlife Fund US, the Rössing Foundation, and Management Sys-tems International) and the Directorate of Environmental Affairs of the MET, learned quickly through fieldwork, workshops, and discussions that commu-nities in the rural areas of Namibia were internally differentiated and complex and could not be easily defined.

In the case of Nyae Nyae, the LIFE Project team could draw on the substan-tial amount of work that had already been done by anthropologists, ecologists, development workers, and others. What they found was that even though vari-ous communities seemed homogeneous, when they examined them carefully, there were internal differences along gender, age, occupations, interests, and a number of other dimensions. They also found that there were traditional, culturally distinct kinds of roles in societies that varied not just from group to group but from area to area.

At the time of its initial conceptualization in 1992, the LIFE Project aimed to provide broad-based capacity-building to a variety of different Namibian NGOs involved with environmental issues. It was assumed at the outset of the project that Namibian NGOs possessed the institutional capacity and knowl-edge to provide assistance to communities in CBNRM. During the course of the LIFE Project implementation, it was discovered that there were relatively few NGOs with the necessary human resource capacity and experience in nat-ural resource issues. The LIFE team determined that there was a widespread need for intensive assistance in the organizational development of Namibian NGOs. As a result, LIFE Project staff invested considerable time and energy in institutional strengthening and were more directly involved in program implementation at the local level.

One of the most crucial aspects of initiating change in rural communities is the presence of strong and active communication channels that allow for a two-way flow of information. Formalization of the communication channels and the use of appropriate approaches for conveying information are necessary. During the LIFE Project, information flow was facilitated through discussions and direct contacts with people living and working in communities, includ-ing those in Nyae Nyae. The LIFE Project team sought to increase commu-nity awareness and knowledge of natural resource management opportunities and constraints through a number of mechanisms, including participatory implementation of natural resource inventories and surveys (with the direct involvement of community members); dissemination of the results of such inventories and surveys to the wider community; and holding public meetings and workshops, during which community members were updated on the policy developments that had implications for community resource management rights and return of benefits.

The LIFE Project had a sizable number of personnel and of consultants working with them.[2] The NNDFN had its own staff, some of whom also worked on CBNRM issues. In 1993–1994, for example, Niall Powell was working with the NNDFN as a community liaison officer. As part of his work, he collaborated with the Ju/'hoansi in carrying out surveys of natural resources and doing land management assessments in Nyae Nyae. Powell (1994: 37) noted that the land use systems of the Ju/'hoansi were in a state of flux, and he identified some of the constraints that were affecting the ability of the NNFC to implement community-based conservation and development programs. The LIFE Project team reviewed the findings of Powell and other NNDFN personnel and attempted to build on them when designing and implementing project activities. One undertaking of the LIFE team was to try to gauge the sentiments not only of people working in the NGOs but also those living in the communities. The project personnel had numerous meetings in Nyae Nyae to explain the ideas behind the project and held workshops in which they encouraged people to put forth their views.

Admittedly, these processes worked in fits and starts. There were times when the people in the various Nyae Nyae communities were involved with other things. As one Ju/'hoan woman put it, "We had to earn a living. We didn't have time for all those meetings." Another woman said at a meeting of NNFC management and project staff held in August 1993, "The NNFC management does not understand our needs." Between July 1993 and September 1994, there was only one Representative Council meeting, and the NNFC management did not make any visits whatsoever to its members in the Nyae Nyae settlements (Powell 1994: 35).

In November 1993, the Ministry of Lands, Resettlement, and Rehabilitation (MLRR) began a land use planning exercise in the Otjozondjupa region. The Ju/'hoansi in Nyae Nyae expressed concern that the baseline study done of the region (MLRR 1994) would not contain sufficient detail on which to base land use and management plans for their area. As it turned out, the baseline study was very useful, but additional data were necessary in order to come up with comprehensive plans. Some of these data were collected by NNDFN personnel and some by LIFE Project members. Consultants who were brought in to Nyae

2. For a list of many of these individuals, see Berger et al. (2003: 10–11).

Nyae looked at diverse issues, such as range ecology and water development. In addition, researchers visited the area, and some of the materials that they produced were helpful in enabling the NNFC, the NNDFN, and the LIFE Project to come up with a viable project proposal and set of plans for Nyae Nyae.

It was not until 1995 that the first LIFE Project grant was made available to the NNDFN. The grant was called Integrated Natural Resource Management Program in Nyae Nyae and covered the period from June 1995 to January 2000. A second grant was made available to the NNDFN from February 2000 to October 2002. The total amount of funding was N$6.9 million (US$917,252), with a matching grant from the World Wildlife Fund (WWF) of N$1.6 million (US$212,696) (Berger et al. 2003: 7).

The LIFE Project provided organizational facilitation, technical assistance and training to help the Nyae Nyae communities organize themselves and assess their resources. It also assisted the NNDFN and the NNFC with training opportunities in basic aspects of institutional development, such as the fundamentals of holding formal meetings, roles and duties of management body officers, group decision-making, group problem identification and prioritization, project management and administration, simple record-keeping, accounting, conflict resolution, communication, and a range of other basic skills. The LIFE Project personnel sought to provide community members with information on the costs and benefits of the various options, thereby allowing the members to make more informed and rational choices about the kinds of activities that they wished to pursue.

The LIFE Project partners realized that a crucial aspect in assisting local communities is to make sure that the agencies working with them listen to the people's needs. There have to be active channels of communication that facilitate the easy flow of information from the bottom up and, conversely, from the top down (Cernea 1991; Chambers 2005; Holland and Blackburn 1998). These communication channels can be formal, such as official meetings held between government officials, NGOs, and local people. Alternatively, they can be informal, such as discussions between individuals at the local level and people working hand in hand with members of local communities, as was done, for example, by an MET researcher, Flip Stander, who conducted work on lions with the Ju/'hoansi in the Nyae Nyae area in the early 1990s (Stander, //Ghau et al. 1997; Stander, Kaqece //au et al. 1997). It is necessary to use both formal and informal systems of communication, especially in cases like that of Nyae Nyae, where people were not used to getting together in large groups and hearing information presented in a different forum, often in languages that they did not understand.

The personnel of the LIFE Project used local translators, who worked closely with staff members of the NNDFN and the NNFC. Nevertheless, information about the implications of forming a conservancy and about the impacts of greater engagement with tourists and the market in southern Africa was difficult to interpret, and Ju/'hoan spokespersons said frequently that they were confused by much of what they were hearing. A great deal of time was spent by MET personnel and members of various NGOs in Nyae Nyae explaining the goals and objectives of CBNRM and the implications of the LIFE Project for the people, wildlife, and habitats of the Nyae Nyae region.

One objective of the LIFE Project was to assist the process whereby responsibilities to and rights over natural resources were shifted from the state to local communities. In order to make this possible, the MET's Directorate of Environmental Affairs drafted legislation for review by the attorney general and the Parliament of Namibia that would allow for the establishment of conservancies in communal areas such as Nyae Nyae. Doing so would give local people some decision-making power vis-à-vis wildlife and tourism. In Namibia, conservancies were defined as locally planned and managed multi-purpose areas on communal land in which land users have pooled their resources for wildlife conservation, tourism, and wildlife utilization. The conservancy members were granted wildlife resource rights under an amendment to Namibia's Nature Conservation Amendment Act of 1996. Conservancy formation required a representative conservancy committee to be elected by the group's members, who also had to produce a land use and management plan and a constitution that was acceptable both to local people and to the attorney general of the country.

Once the Nature Conservation Amendment Act of 1996 was in place and the LIFE Project team was working in the Nyae Nyae area, the Ju/'hoansi grappled with the issue of selecting a representative community committee. In many ways, this process mirrored past efforts to create a board to oversee the work of the NNFC. As discussions focused on the process of selecting appropriate committee members, local people suggested that conservancy committee members should be drawn from all 35 communities in the area. What this meant was that project meetings, just as in the NNFC's early years, had to be held in places scattered across thousands of square kilometers of the Kalahari. It also meant that people had to be brought to the meetings, something that was far from easy, given the transport constraints in both the NNFC and the LIFE Project.

During debates about the "representativeness" of the conservancy committee, some people argued that the committee had to include traditional authorities (*n!orekxaosi*), and one person suggested that the committee had to have at least one *kxao n!a'an* (big owner), referring to traditional kin-based ownership. Still others insisted that the committee should include people who had been to school and who spoke at least minimal English. Quite a few people (and some members of the NGOs working in Nyae Nyae) said that both women and men should be on the committee. The committee that was finally arrived at consisted of men and women, some educated and some not, and a number of people who had served in the past in positions of significance with the NNFC. A frequent complaint about the representativeness of the committee by local people and by NGOs related to the low number of women on the conservancy committee and in the Ju/'hoan traditional authority, an issue that continues to be remarked on by observers (see, e.g., Susser 2009: 186–187, 196).

In 1997, the LIFE Project team, the NNFC, and the NNDFN worked together to document the existing situation in Nyae Nyae and to come up with a management plan for what was to become the NNC. Once the conservancy committee was in place, a constitution was drawn up and agreed upon by the committee and the communities, and it was sent to the government for review. An aerial survey of the wildlife in the area was carried out in 1997, and additional wildlife data were obtained by community members who had been trained by the MET, the NNDFN, and the LIFE Project. This information was used to help in the formulation of the management plan for the Nyae Nyae area. The *radasi* approved the constitution, management plan, and benefits distribution plan in 1997 (Berger et al. 2003: 12). Attention was also paid to the issue of water supplies, and an inventory was made of the various water points in the region. The water points survey took into consideration ownership, current condition, degree of damage from elephants, and maintenance requirements. A drilling company was contracted to drill new boreholes, which were to be located in the northern and southern parts of the Nyae Nyae area. In addition, local people were trained in tourism through the Namibia Community Based Tourism Assistance Trust.

The Nyae Nyae Conservancy

In June 1998, the Nyae Nyae region became the first conservancy on communal land in Namibia (for data on communal conservancies established in Namibia, see table 5). Some of the relatively unique features of the NNC included the following: (1) its membership was made up almost entirely of people from a single ethnic group, the Ju/'hoansi; (2) the community members had been involved in natural resource management and development activities together for an extended period of time prior to the establishment of the conservancy; (3) the area in which the conservancy was established contained a rich and diverse assemblage of wildlife, unusual habitats (e.g., the pans of the area), and a human population that was itself of considerable interest to tourists, researchers, and development workers; and (4) there was an existing community-based organization with which the government and NGOs could work.

As part of its work in Nyae Nyae, the LIFE Project trained individuals to serve as game guards and community resource monitors. Game guards, who were titled community rangers and who tended to be men, were involved primarily in monitoring wildlife. They were not "classic" game guards in the sense

Table 5 Conservancies in Namibia's communal areas

Name	Region	Size (sq km)	No. of Members	Date Registered
African Wild Dog	Otjozondjupa	3,824	5,500	September 2005
Anabeb	Kunene	1,570	337	July 2003
Doro !Nawas	Kunene	4,073	430	December 1999
Ehi-Rovipuka	Kunene	1,975	500	January 2001
//Gamaseb	Karas	1,748	495	July 2003
//Haub	Kunene	1,817	364	July 2003
=Khoadi //Hoas	Kunene	3,366	1,600	June 1998
!Khob-!Naub	Hardap	2,747	429	July 2003
Kwandu	Caprivi	190	1,800	December 1999
Marienfluss	Kunene	3,034	121	January 2001
Mashi	Caprivi	297	718	March 2003
Mayuni	Caprivi	151	1,500	December 1999
N=a Jaqna	Otjozondjupa*	8,547	1,344	July 2003
Nyae Nyae	Otjozondjupa*	9,003	752	February 1998
Okamatapatu	Otjozondjupa	3,096	3,000	September 2005
Okongundumba	Kunene	1,131	448	July 2003
Omatendeka	Kunene	1,619	374	March 2003
Orupembe	Kunene	3,565	132	July 2003
Oskop	Hardap	96	20	February 2001
Otjimboyo	Erongo	448	148	March 03
Otjituo	Otjozondjupa*	6,133	9,000	September 2005
Ozonahi	Otjozondjupa	3,204	5,500	September 2005
Ozondundu	Kunene	745	173	July 2003
Purros	Kunene	3,568	85	May 2000
Salambala	Caprivi	930	4,000	June 1998
Sanitatas	Kunene	1,446	76	July 2003
Seisfontein	Kunene	2,591	437	July 2003
Soris Sorris	Erongo	2,990	380	October 2001
Torra	Kunene	3,522	450	June 1998
Tsiseb	Erongo	8,083	950	January 2001
Twyfelfontein-Uibasen	Kunene	400	61	December 1999
Uukwaluudhi	Omushati	1,437	25,000	March 2003
Wapuro	Caprivi	148	1,700	December 1999
Total	7 regions	84,614	67,824	

Note: * signifies conservancies with majority San membership. It should be pointed out that there were 59 communal conservancies as of October 2009, according to the Namibian Association of CBNRM Support Organisations (NACSO) (http://www.nacso.org.na/SOC_profiles/conservancylist.php). For a discussion of the evolution of communal conservancies in Namibia, see Jones (2010).

Source: Data obtained from the Directorate of Environmental Affairs, Ministry of Environment and Tourism (MET), Namibia. See also NACSO (2006).

that they did not patrol areas to prevent poaching. Rather, they monitored the game itself, reporting on wildlife numbers and distributions. They did not have powers of arrest, nor did they want to have them. In some instances, the community rangers worked with people who served as fencing attendants and who were part of the technical water team that was set up in Nyae Nyae. These teams focused on setting up fences and other kinds of barriers around water points to prevent elephant damage (Berger et al. 2003: 13–14). The MET game warden based at Tsumkwe assisted the NNC by helping to cover the cost of rehabilitating 10 water points, using cement, wooden posts, and wire, in order to protect village water supplies.

From 1998 through the end of the LIFE Project in 2002, a sizable number of different wild animals were brought in to the Nyae Nyae area in order to expand the wildlife populations in the region. Some of these animals were paid for by the safari company that had obtained the lease to hunt in the area, while others were contributed by donors. Wildlife purchases and translocation costs were also covered by the LIFE Project. In the late 1990s, the NNFC generated N$17,400 through photographic safari operations and N$5,000 through game ranching that had a tourism component (at that time, US$1=N$7.5). One safari company based in the northern part of the Nyae Nyae area, Namibia Adventure Safaris and Tours, charged clients N$350 for a full day of traditional hunting. Only a small portion of those funds went to the two or three adult male hunters who took part and who were paid approximately N$40 apiece. Traditional dancing paid N$25 per person, with most of the funds going to women, but these dances were held infrequently and often under demeaning circumstances.

In 2001, the NNC brought in the most money of the 10 existing cash-earning conservancies in Namibia at that time: N$341,011 (Berger et al. 2003; Jon Barnes, Ministry of Environment and Tourism, pers. comm.). Benefits to individual members of the NNC totaled N$59,000. Some of the funds went to cover operating costs and the translocation of wildlife into the Nyae Nyae area. In 2001, for example, 250 red hartebeest were brought into the area by the LIFE Project from a conservancy in central Namibia, and 48 gemsbok were purchased with NNC funds. The animals, which local people were not supposed to hunt, were placed at first in a holding pen at Nyae Nyae pan and later released, after orange ear tags had been applied. La Rochelle Hunting and Game Farm, a Namibian safari company that had won the contract to operate in the Nyae Nyae pan, provided some employment, food, and other goods to the Ju/'hoansi.

In 2002, the NNC generated N$956,500 (Berger et al. 2003). Of this, N$477,672 was distributed as benefits to the 770 adult members of the conservancy, amounting to N$620 per person. The safari operator that had obtained a concession from the NNC, African Hunting, employed 26 men and 2 women (Weaver and Skyer 2003). As a side benefit, the meat from animals that had been killed by safari clientele was distributed to residents of Nyae Nyae. While a few Ju/'hoansi noted that the meat represented an important contribution that helped fill some of the protein needs of their households, there were also those who pointed out that most of the meat was from elephants, which few Ju/'hoansi ate.

In the period from 1998 to 2002, many issues arose in Nyae Nyae, ranging from conflicts with the safari operator concessionaire over the way that employees and community members were treated (Berger et al. 2003: 16) to concerns about restrictions imposed on subsistence hunting by the government and the LIFE Project staff. There were also debates about the impact of tourists and safari hunting clients in the Nyae Nyae area. While tourism returns represented only a small percentage of the income of the households in the Nyae Nyae area in 2002 (Wiessner 2004: 154, table 4), the social and environmental effects of tourism on the Nyae Nyae region caused great concern in many of the villages and were brought up in discussions with LIFE Project members.

Members of the NNC came up with a set of tourism regulations that they hoped would be enforced by the government of Namibia, private companies, and NGOs working in Nyae Nyae. These regulations included the following:

- The NNC and the management board should be consulted prior to the initiation of any tourism activities in Nyae Nyae.
- The number of tourists in Nyae Nyae should be controlled.
- Tourists are requested to treat people with respect.
- Tourists should greet people in villages prior to making camp or taking photographs.
- Tourists should not drive off the existing tracks.
- Tourists should camp in designated areas, and tour operators and tourists should obtain their firewood at least 5 kilometers from existing villages and from tourist concessions.
- Large campfires are to be avoided so as not to frighten game on which people depend and so as not to waste fuel.
- Tourists should not enter villages and photograph people without seeking permission beforehand.
- People in the villages should not be requested to remove their clothing for photographs.
- Tourists may not swim or bathe in people's village reservoirs.
- Tourists should pay a designated amount of money for specific activities in which they take part (e.g., camping close to a village, accompanying people on gathering or hunting trips)
- The NNC has a recommended set of prices that should be paid for all activities and overnights in villages.
- All litter should be carried out of the area.
- Liquor, beer, or wine should not be given to local people in exchange for goods or services.

- Fair prices should be paid for all craft items.
- Only local people should be used as guides.
- People should not camp directly on or adjacent to pans so that game will not be frightened away and the surface of the pan affected.
- Alternative tourism (sustainable, ecologically friendly tourism) is preferred to other types of tourism.
- Villages where tourism activities occur should receive the benefits.
- A levy should be paid by tourism companies and individual tourists per person for visits to Nyae Nyae.
- Local communities under the auspices of the NNC will have discretion as to whether tourists have complied with the above guidelines.

A major concern with tourism in Nyae Nyae was that it was highly dependent on a very fickle international market, and the benefits from tourism generally reached only a small proportion of the Nyae Nyae population, exacerbating social tensions. A few of the communities in the Nyae Nyae region engaged directly in tourism activities, contracting with individual tourists who wished to learn, for example, about the processes of wild plant collecting or game tracking and organizing dances for tourist groups (Berger et al. 2003; Garland 1994; Garland and Gordon 1999; Schalken 1999). The number of tourists was relatively small, and they came to Nyae Nyae only occasionally. The perspective of at least some Ju/'hoansi was that tourism was "a necessary evil." As Wiessner (2004: 154) notes, "The Ju/'hoansi are not willing to be regular players in a service oriented industry."

One of the benefits of tourism, according to some of the local people, was that tourists bought crafts from the Ju/'hoansi. While the market for crafts was not as strong as many people hoped it would be, craft production was seen as important and useful. Several people remarked not only that crafts were beneficial as a way of generating income, but also that the production of crafts kept culturally important skills at the forefront, ensuring that knowledge of plants and other resources that are important in craft manufacture would be passed on. Crafts were socially valuable items that could be used for gifts and for exchange with other people. In 2002, the sale of crafts generated N$302,000, or 14 percent of the total income earned by the Ju/'hoansi in Nyae Nyae (Wiessner 2004: 153–154, table 4). Some residents of Nyae Nyae took part in the collection and sale of devil's claw (grapple plant) tubers, an activity that generated N$30,000 in 2002, 1.5 percent of total income earned in Nyae Nyae. Berger et al. (2003: 29) estimated that 225 women throughout the conservancy were making and selling crafts in the early part of the new millennium.

It is interesting to note that much of the rhetoric about the value of CBNRM related to the supposedly significant returns from safari hunting. When one examines the returns from safari hunting as compared to other kinds of activities in Nyae Nyae, one finds that these returns are relatively low. The safari operator employed three Ju/'hoansi in its trophy hunting operations, and they received N$43,200 in 2002, or about 2 percent of the total cash income in the Nyae Nyae area (Wiessner 2004: 154; cf. Berger et al. 2003: 28). The majority of funds generated in Nyae Nyae came from government-related employment (N$774,764, or 36 percent of the total) (Wiessner 2004: 154, table 4). Most of the cash that was earned in Nyae Nyae was spent on food, cooking oil, tea, sugar, clothing, tobacco, and alcohol (Wiessner 2004: 154–155; Wiessner and N!aici 1998). As Berger et al. (2003: 27) note, the NNC's total income over the period from 1997 to 2002 was approximately N$3,635,000, of which N$2,000,000 went to individual members and the balance to the NNC.

With the exception of 2001, the amount of funds generated has gone up over time, although it is far from certain whether this trend will continue. The conservancy income for trophy hunting in 2002 was N$845,798, whereas household-level income generated through employment, camp sites, and craft sales was N$306,327. Two important points should be made about these figures. First, the conservancy generates funds that it either uses for its own purposes or gives to its members in the form of annual payouts. Some of the conservancy members say that larger proportions of the NNC's income should be paid out to its members. Others say that the conservancy management board should expend funds on activities that are of benefit to the population as a whole. Some people were outspoken about the amounts of money spent on translocating game animals into Nyae Nyae, especially in light of the fact that they could not hunt these animals. As one man put it, "They were reserved for rich hunters from other places."

Second, while the conservancy was a source of employment and income for some people, it did not represent the most important source of income in Nyae Nyae, which was from government-related pensions and jobs. In May 2002, there were 61 people employed in various capacities in the NNC. A common opinion among many Ju/'hoansi was that the NNC should employ more people—something that was not easy to do, given budgetary constraints. Another concern expressed by a number of Ju/'hoansi, both men and women, was that only two full-time jobs and four positions on the management board of the conservancy were held by women, which they felt was insufficient.

A member of the NNC's management board said that even though the amounts of money generated by the conservancy may seem high for a place that has long faced poverty and hunger, the funds given to individuals have not made much of a difference in enabling people to procure their basic needs, particularly "the urgent need for food" (Berger et al. 2003: 27; Wiessner 2004: 153–154). From the perspective of many Ju/'hoansi, while they appreciate the conservancy, it has yet to meet their most important concerns: having sufficient food and having security of land tenure. To address the problem of food access, the NNDFN and the NNC, in conjunction with the Namibian government, the LIFE Project, and other donors, placed greater emphasis on three major areas: the provision of water, the promotion of sustainable systems of agriculture and livestock production, and diversification of the economic systems in the region. Another option under consideration was to seek increased inputs from international donors, although there were internal disagreements about whether this was an appropriate way to increase self-sufficiency.

Livestock, Agriculture, and Employment in Nyae Nyae

Some of the Nyae Nyae Ju/'hoansi have owned or have managed livestock for a substantial period of time. Europeans who came through the Nyae Nyae area in the nineteenth century had cattle that needed tending (L. Marshall 1976: 58). A number of Ju/'hoansi had migrated to the farms of Grootfontein or Gobabis in order to seek employment as herders, and some of them had been paid in the form of livestock. There were also people who obtained livestock and livestock products from other groups. At the time of the Marshall family expeditions in the early 1950s, however, few, if any, Ju/'hoansi in Nyae Nyae owned cattle.

By the 1990s, there were Ju/'hoansi who had cattle of their own, and several of them managed sizable herds of cattle belonging to other people. For that work, they received the right to drink the cattle's milk and sometimes to eat the meat of animals that had died. Some of these people were paid cash for their labor. Some Ju/'hoansi were given livestock in the form of long-term loans by other people—often Hereros but sometimes Kavangos. In this system, the herders were responsible for managing the animals. They watered the cattle at pans and boreholes. During the day, they either released the cattle to graze on their own or took them to places where the animals could graze. Theoretically at least, people were supposed to watch over the cattle so that nothing happened to them, especially if there were predators or poisonous plants in the area. Cattle, goats, and other domestic animals were penned up at night in the villages so that they would not stray or be exposed to predation.

The Ju/'hoan herders also took care of the health needs of the animals, tending their wounds and providing them with medicines, if they had them. Some people in Nyae Nyae worked with the veterinary assistants from the Ministry of Agriculture, Water, and Forestry (MAWF), collecting the animals so that they could be immunized and helping to dip them in insecticides to rid them of ticks. Some Ju/'hoan herders also provided the animals in their care with minerals in the form of licks (blocks of salt and other minerals).

Unlike some other herding peoples in southern Africa, the Ju/'hoansi generally did not move their animals from one grazing area to another on a seasonal basis. Rather, they kept their animals in one place, usually in locations where there was permanent source of water. A few Ju/'hoansi noted, however, that they did sometimes move their animals from place to place in a kind of rotational grazing pattern. They did this, they said, in order to take advantage of fresh grazing and to allow areas to recover from grazing pressure.

There were (and continue to be) a number of constraints that have affected livestock production in the Nyae Nyae area. The most important has been water availability. Droughts were common in Nyae Nyae in the 1980s and 1990s, and some of them were extremely serious, resulting in the deaths of a substantial number of animals (Sweet 1998). There are only a limited number of permanent water points in the region, and borehole drilling is extremely expensive and often unsuccessful. Elephants, which have risen in number from 200 in the 1980s to well over 1,000 now, are responsible for the destruction of numerous water facilities in the Nyae Nyae region. They have also been known to injure and even kill cattle, especially when they are competing for water at boreholes and troughs.

A major constraint is the presence of predators, including lions, leopards, hyenas, and black-backed jackals, which sometimes attack calves and small stock (sheep and goats). Elizabeth Marshall Thomas (2006: 157–159) points out that the Ju/'hoansi did not hunt lions in Nyae Nyae, in contrast to the situation at /Kae/kae in Botswana, where the Hereros, who had guns, went after lions that killed their cattle. She notes that =Oma Tsamkxao told her and her family that where lions were hunted, they were dangerous to people, but where they were not hunted, they were not dangerous (ibid.: 157). Thomas describes a situation in which a Ju/'hoan hunter purposely did not shoot an arrow into a lion that had killed a cow and a calf at /Aotcha in 1986, in spite of the urging of an outsider who worked for a local NGO. The reason, she suspected, was that the Ju/'hoansi did not want a wounded, angry lion marauding around the area (ibid.: 159).

Another factor affecting livestock production in Nyae Nyae is livestock disease, including, at various points in the past, rinderpest, which occurred, for example, in 1896–1897; East Coast fever; foot-and-mouth disease; and lung plague. Tick-borne diseases have proved to be a problem in Nyae Nyae. An additional drawback is that some of the grazing in Nyae Nyae is phosphorous-deficient, meaning that cattle have to be provided with licks for supplementing their minerals and nutrients. Yet another constraint that livestock keepers face is bush fires, which have been known to kill cattle and to destroy the grasses and shrubs upon which cattle depend. Also affecting the health and safety of livestock is the presence in some areas (notably, in Tsumkwe District West) of *maqen*, also known as *gifblaar* or *mogau* (*Dichapetalum cymosum*), a plant that is poisonous to cattle, causing deaths particularly in the early spring and during drought periods.

Livestock represent an important source of investment for a number of Ju/'hoansi, who keep them for several purposes. In some cases, they rely on the milk of their animals and use their dung as fuel or fertilizer. They prefer, if at all possible, not to sell, slaughter, or give away their livestock, although sometimes social pressure is brought to bear by relatives who want an animal to be killed so that they can share the meat. When livestock are killed, the Ju/'hoansi make use of the various byproducts, including meat, hides, horns, hooves, and bones. Cattle and sometimes goats and sheep are exchanged with other people. A few young Ju/'hoan men said that they had given livestock to their prospective fathers-in-law in a kind of bride wealth arrangement. Bride wealth (*otjitunja* in Herero) is livestock that is pledged to the family of the bride by the family of the groom. In neighboring Ngamiland, Botswana, bride wealth among Hereros was often three cows, or sometimes a combination of cows, calves, sheep, goats, and cash (Pennington and Harpending 1993: 141–142).

It is interesting to look at livestock numbers and distributions over time in the Nyae Nyae region. In the 1950s, at the time of the Marshall expeditions, there were relatively few cattle in Nyae Nyae. In 1951, 20 cattle had been brought to G/am by the relatives of a Tswana livestock owner from Botswana. As Elizabeth Marshall Thomas (2006: 58–59) notes, the Ju/'hoan residents of G/am either may have given them permission to use the water and surrounding grazing, or they were too polite (or intimidated) to refuse the request.

In 1973, 40 Ju/'hoansi men in Tsumkwe obtained cattle through a program sponsored by the South West Africa Administration that was overseen by Claude McIntyre, the commissioner of Bushman Affairs. Over time, most of the animals were sold, killed by predators, given away, or slaughtered so that the meat could be shared with other people. In 1981, there were 101 cattle belonging to 30 Ju/'hoansi living in the Tsumkwe settlement (Marshall and Ritchie 1984: 126). When three groups of Ju/'hoansi moved away from Tsumkwe in order to establish themselves in their *n!oresi* in 1981, they had a total of 58 cattle (43 at /Aotcha, 9 at N=aqmtjoha, and 6 at N=anemh). From 1981 through the mid-1980s, Ju/'hoansi obtained cattle and other domestic animals through a combination of purchase, gifts, inheritance, and allocation through the Cattle Fund (the original name of the foundation initiated by John Marshall and Claire Ritchie), and the NNFC. In 1986 there were 115 cattle at three settlements, nearly half of which were milk-producing cows (Payne and Edwards 1986: 11). The total number of cattle in 1986 in Nyae Nyae was 628, according to NNDFN records.

In 1987, when Robert Hitchcock undertook an assessment of the activities of the Ju/wa Bushman Development Foundation (JBDF), the precursor of the NNDFN, and the Ju/wa Farmers Union (JFU), the precursor of the NNFC, there were 330 cattle in 10 settlements. By 1988, a total of 478 cattle were owned by 188 families in 23 settlements. From June 1989 to June 1990, the number of livestock in the communities increased to 510. In that year, 84 calves were born and 88 died. The losses were due primarily to slaughter for consumption by people (67 percent), predators (9 percent), and disease (5 percent). The cause of death could not be established in 20 percent of the cases, according to NNDFN records. In 1992, we were told by MAWF personnel that there were 500 cattle in the Nyae Nyae region.

Changes occurred over time in the ways that the JFU/NNFC and the JBDF/ NNDFN dealt with livestock management and distribution. In 1986, as new settlements were established, cattle were distributed to people for free by the JBDF and the JFU. Initially, new communities were given six pairs for free and were loaned six pairs by the JFU, according to a plan that it had worked out. Two representatives from each of the settlements were supposed to decide who received the cattle. It was agreed that the animals were to be given only to those people who wanted to begin farming, who did not already have cattle, and who agreed to look after them carefully.

The allocation process for JFU cattle became somewhat complicated over time. Some animals were given directly to groups that were moving out of Tsumkwe in order to resettle in their *n!oresi*. Others were loaned to them in a *mafisa* or agistment type of arrangement. Still others, notably bulls, were held by the JFU itself, although people in the settlements were allowed access to them for a limited period of time. The JFU stipulated that the members of the group could keep the cattle after a year, on the condition that they kept up with the livestock-related work and that they managed the animals well. The JFU retained the right to remove cattle at any time during that year, if it felt that the cattle were needed, for example, to assist another group. One difficulty was that sometimes people could not identify whose animal was whose, resulting in conflicts over cattle management and milking.

Cattle that had not been distributed by the JFU made up what came to be known as the "endowment herd." These were watched over at various places, called cattle posts, by individuals who received payment for their work (at a rate of R25 per week). Payment receipts and the files on the cattle were kept by the staff of the JBDF. Later on, there were major problems with the *mafisa* and the "looking after" cattle. The system, according to Ritchie (1992: 19; pers. comm., 1992, 1995), became overly complex and confusing. This was due in part to the fact that livestock ownership widened as people gave offspring of the animals that they were managing to their relatives and friends. In 1990, the NNFC decided to change the system of cattle distribution to one in which cattle were sold to people instead of being given to them outright. This policy shift had the advantage of reducing the complexity of cattle ownership and management.

From 1991 onward, the NNDFN bought cattle from the MAWF agricultural farm at Tsumkwe. Between 1992 and 1995, 170 cows and 25 bulls were purchased by the NNDFN and provided to people in the various settlements.

In 1993, there were 601 cows and calves in 25 settlements. The provision of Sanga bulls enhanced the breeding process, and some of the Ju/'hoansi said that the progeny of these bulls provided more milk and that more calves were born. The MLRR and the Social Science Division of the University of Namibia reported that there were 150 livestock owners in Nyae Nyae in 1993 (Botelle and Rohde 1995). According to John Marshall (pers. comm., 2003), there were fewer than 60 livestock owners in 2003, the numbers having declined, he said, because the NNDFN and the NNC were not emphasizing livestock production and because the water points were not being maintained. As was noted previously, some of the water points had been destroyed by elephants.

The Nyae Nyae Environment and Its Carrying Capacity

A question raised by some government agriculture personnel, range management specialists, and development consultants related to the environmental impacts of the cattle and other domestic animals in the Nyae Nyae region. MAWF personnel argued that overgrazing was occurring because "there were too many animals on the land." The Ju/'hoansi responded, saying that the number of cattle in any one place was relatively low, rarely over a few dozen head. They maintained that their herd management systems were such that the range resources were not being overexploited.

One of the problems pointed out by the Ju/'hoansi is that livestock eat some of the same foods that people do. When there are sizable numbers of cattle and other domestic animals in a settlement, the degree to which foraged wild plants make up a portion of the diet tends to decline. This is in part because there are significant overlaps between what cattle consume and what people use for food and other purposes. It is also because cattle have significant impacts on the local environment through trampling, grazing, and browsing, although this point is contentious, and both scientists and Ju/'hoansi argue that the environmental impact of livestock in Nyae Nyae is relatively low.

John Marshall (pers. comm., 2003) argued that the NNFC and the NNDFN lessened their support for livestock production over time, especially in the mid- to late 1990s, in part because the emphasis shifted to wildlife and tourism-related activities. Another factor was the substantial increase in the number of elephants in the area and the concomitant increase in elephant damage to water points. In spite of the fact that fewer people own livestock today than was the case in the mid-1990s, many Ju/'hoansi still wish to obtain livestock. The principal reasons that they give are that they wish to have milk and meat for their families and that they want to be able to generate income through sales of animals. They also say that "Ju/'hoan women and men like meat." Some people want to use cattle as draft animals for plowing and planting fields. And there were those individuals who saw livestock as a good source of long-term investment, in spite of the risks and social pressures brought to bear on livestock owners.

Like livestock production, crop production in Nyae Nyae has also been on the decline, at least until recently. Part of the trend is due to problems with water points, some of them caused by elephants and some resulting from breakdowns and lack of spare parts. Although the Ju/'hoansi complain bitterly about the weather and about animals that destroy their fields, many of them continue to plant at least some crops. Some people have put up fences, many of them made out of thorn brush. A few households have even erected wire fences, in spite of the high costs of fencing materials. Seeds are distributed to people by extension agents of the Namibian government and by the NNC.

Most of the crops planted in the area are dryland ones (i.e., they are rain-fed), but irrigated gardens can be found in some communities as well. The staple grain crops are maize (*Zea mays*), which is susceptible to drought, and pearl millet (*Pennisetum typhoides, omahangu*), which is well-adapted to dry conditions. Sorghum (*Sorghum bicolor*) is also grown. Other crops include cabbage (*Brassica oleracea*), beans (*Phaseolus mungo*, mung bean, and *Phaseolus acutifolius*, teppary bean), pumpkin (*Cucurbita pepo*), sweet melons (*Cucumis melo*), cowpeas (*Vigna unguiculata*), and, in a few cases, tobacco (*Nicotiana tabacum*). People plant by hand, using hoes and digging sticks. Land is cleared using fire and axes. A small proportion of Ju/'hoan households cultivate their fields using plows that are pulled by teams of oxen or donkeys.

In Nyae Nyae, agriculture is a complex cycle of production, involving planting, cultivating, weeding, bird-scaring, and harvesting. Post-harvest work (e.g., threshing) is done mainly by women. People in the area pointed out that the Kalahari sands are generally deficient in minerals and organic nutrients, and they become waterlogged rapidly in the rainy season. In good seasons, fields can yield as much as 200 kilograms of grain per hectare. Such yields are achieved, however, only through the expenditure of considerable amounts of time, labor, and capital.

The Problem of Hunger

Today, an important component of the diet of many of the people of Nyae Nyae is food relief provided by the government of Namibia and by NGOs (Suzman 2001b: 46–48; Wiessner 2004: 151; Wiessner and N!aici 1999, 2005). In the early part of the new millennium, four different programs have been ongoing. First, food was provided by the government's Emergency Management Unit for drought relief purposes. Second, food was given to vulnerable groups (pregnant and lactating mothers, children under 5 years old, the elderly, and the physically incapacitated) under the Vulnerable Group Feeding Program of the UN's World Food Programme. Third, there was a Food for Work program of the Namibian government , in which people received food in exchange for labor, for example, clearing roads. Fourth, there was a School Feeding Program of the Namibian government that provided food for school-going children. One of the problems with the food relief programs was that they were sometimes erratic in their delivery, and people would go for lengthy periods without provisions. At these times, people would fall back on foraging, craft sales, and temporary employment in order to supplement their subsistence and incomes. As Wiessner (2004: 151–153, table 1) notes, the food situation in Nyae Nyae in the latter part of the 1990s and the early part of the new millennium was bleak, and hunger was a huge problem.

The LIFE Project, the NNDFN, and the NNC attempted to cope with the hunger problem in a number of different ways. One strategy was to increase the number of jobs in Nyae Nyae. The two largest employers in 2002 were the government of Namibia and the NNC. As shown by Wiessner (2003: 152–154, table 4), income from government employment in Nyae Nyae was substantial, making up some 36 percent of the total income for people in the region. Government pensions, at N$250 per month in 2002, generated N$153,000, or 7 percent of the total income. The NNC was also an important source of employment and income, providing jobs for 26 men and 2 women and generating 8 percent of total income in Nyae Nyae, according to Wiessner (ibid.: 153–154). Berger et al. (2003: 29) said that the NNC provided employment for people in 21 of 27 villages in Nyae Nyae in 2002–2003, where data were obtained. Figure 4 presents the organizational structure, programs, and staff of the NNC in 2002–2003. It can be seen that there were Ju/'hoansi employed in the management committee, the board, and as staff members in the various programs of the conservancy.

Another source of employment in Nyae Nyae in 2002 was the Australian mining company, Mount Burgess Mining, which was carrying out mineral surveys in the area. There were 26 Ju/'hoansi employed by the mining company in 2002, and together they received N$580,000 (US$77,102) in wages and benefits, approximately 27 percent of the total income in Nyae Nyae (Wiessner 2004: 154, table 4). Given this situation, it is not surprising, perhaps, that at least some Ju/'hoansi were in favor of commercial mining operations in the Nyae Nyae area. But mining, like tourism, can be very unpredictable. As mineral prices declined and exploration became more expensive, Mount Burgess opted to close its operations in Nyae Nyae. As a result, the Ju/'hoansi are having to find other sources of employment and income.

Debates about Development Models in Nyae Nyae

In his film *A Kalahari Family*, John Marshall (2003a), argued persuasively that the Ju/'hoansi are shrouded in myth. He said that the people of Nyae Nyae were all too often perceived as "foragers" who did not need land. Marshall believed

NYAE NYAE CONSERVANCY

Board: Nyae Nyae Development Foundation of Namibia

Paul Vleermuis
Evonne
NNC: Manager (K. Moses)
NNC: Chairman (Kiewiet)
NNC: Dist. Rep. (Seg//ae)

Nyae Nyae Development Foundation of Namibia

2 staff:
Windhoek Coordinator, Assistant (half-time)

Support

technical assistance; training support; financial mgmt. assistance; fundraising/coord. of donor support; communication

Nyae Nyae Conservancy (Management Committee)

Manager
Asst. Manager
Chairman
Senior Field Officer

total full-time salaried staff = 35 persons

Administrator

Oversight & Guidance

management supervision; program approval; policy; program implementation

Nyae Nyae Conservancy Management Board:

Manager (Kxao Moses)
Asst. Manager (Tsamkxao Moses)
Chairman (Kiewiet)
Senior Field Officer (Andreas)
District Representatives,
North (3)
South (3)
Central (3)
West (3)

Programmes:	Natural Resources Management	Tourism	Crafts	Agriculture	Village Schools	Technical Workshop	Public Health Programme
Managers:	Kxao Moses Andreas	Kxao Moses Tsamkxao Moses	Tsamkxao Moses	Kxao Moses Tsamkxao Moses	Kiewiet	Kxao Moses Tsamkxao Moses	Kiewiet
Staff:	Community Rangers (11) Half-time Boma Assist. (2) Daily labor. Water Team (10)	Field Workers: (2 positions) Dam Jo/o	Crafts Coord. (1); Crafts Assist. (1)	Ag. Assist. (1) /Aice Gardner (1) vacant	Senior Student Teachers (5) Junior Student Teachers (5)	Shopworker (1) Sunrise	- program is not directly managed through conservancy structure

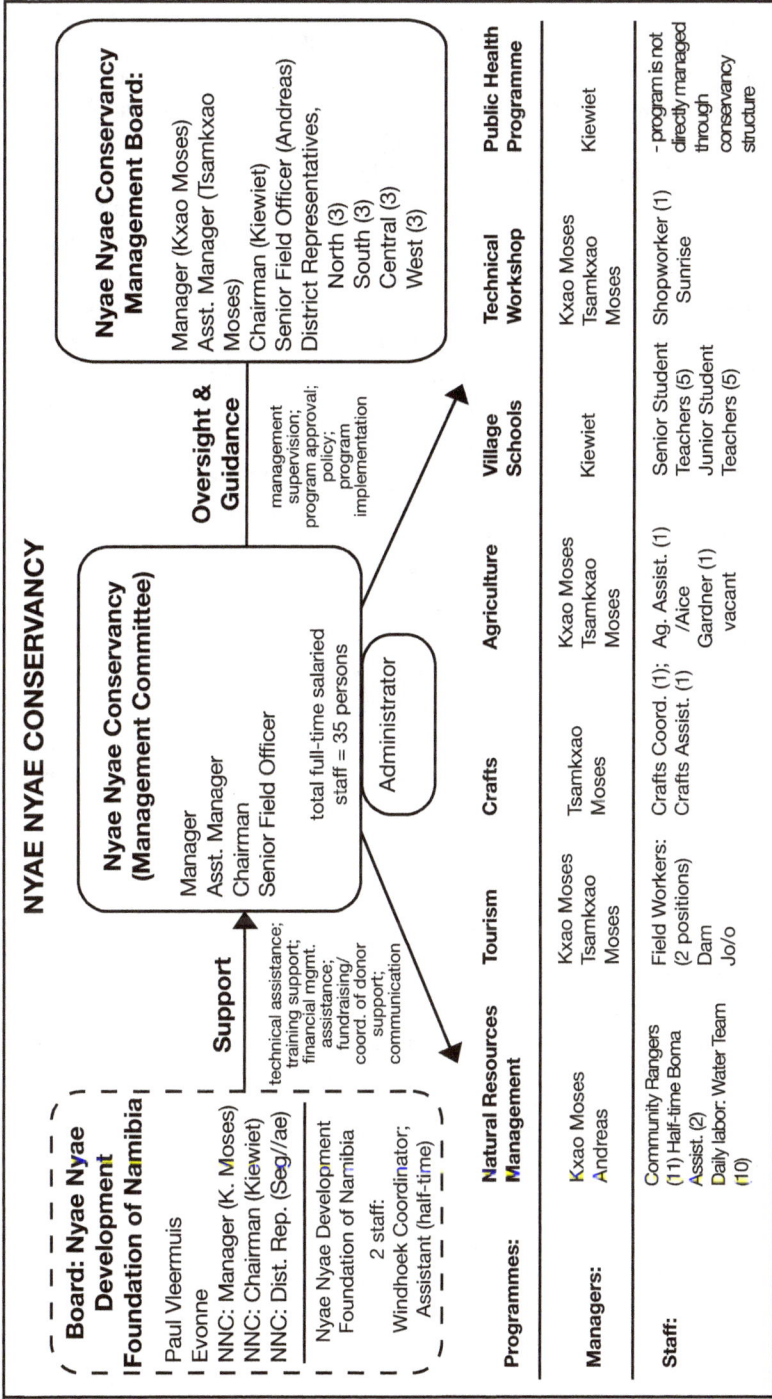

Figure 4 Nyae Nyae Conservancy, showing organizational structure, programs, and staff as of 2002–2003

that, as he put it in *Death by Myth*, the fifth segment of his film, "Ju/'hoan land rights had nothing to do with wildlife management." The idea of establishing a conservancy and promoting tourism in the Nyae Nyae area was anathema to Marshall. He viewed game reserves and cultural tourism as relegating San to what he aptly termed "a plastic Stone Age" (Marshall 1984: 14). As Marshall asked, "Who would want to go back to 'the old life'?"

Marshall's question arose in part from what he felt to be the difficulties facing hunter-gatherers: it was a hard life, one characterized, he believed, by hunger and strenuous work. Marshall recorded Ju/'hoansi who said, "We don't have food. We don't have grazing for our cattle. We don't have land." The best way for the Ju/'hoansi to meet their subsistence needs and to get rights to their land, according to Marshall, was for them to raise cattle and grow crops. In order to make this possible, the Ju/'hoansi had to have more assistance in water point provision and maintenance, agricultural advice and training, tools, seeds, and veterinary supplies.

Marshall complained that the LIFE Project provided few funds for water development or for agricultural training, instead investing considerable funding in the transfer of wild animals into the Nyae Nyae area. The idea for game translocation derived from the notion that tourism would be the primary source of income for the Nyae Nyae area, which, as noted previously, is not the case. Marshall felt that tourism would do more harm than good. He also questioned the idea of the Ju/'hoansi contracting with film companies who wanted to shoot films in the Nyae Nyae region. He reacted against the idea of some members of the NNFC "going around the world telling people that bush foods are important."

In the early part of the new millennium, the Ju/'hoansi continued to worry about the impact of elephants on their water points and gardens. With help from various sources, including anthropologists, the LIFE Project, the government, the Kalahari Peoples Fund (KPF), and the NNDFN, the Ju/'hoansi endeavored to protect their water sources by constructing walls made of rocks, cement, and railway sleepers (Berger et al. 2003: 14, 39–42; Thomas, 2006: 297–298; Polly Wiessner, pers. comm., 2006, 2007). In the early 1990s, rocks were placed around water points to discourage elephants (reportedly, elephants have soft feet). In addition, electric fences powered by solar batteries were constructed around water points. The Nyae Nyae elephants have worked out ways to get around some of these constraints, dropping logs on electric fences to cut the power. They have also pushed their way into areas where the fences were anchored in loose, sandy soil. Another strategy used by the NNC, the LIFE Project, and the MET was to open up new water points to draw elephants away from the villages (Berger et al. 2003: 29). As one Ju/'hoan man put it, "We have our land and waters, but now we have to protect them from both people and animals."

In *A Kalahari Family*, a cooperative plan was outlined by Marshall and /Ui Chapman, a Ju/'hoan resident of the Nyae Nyae area who had relocated from the Gobabis farms. Marshall and /Ui Chapman argued that establishing Ju/'hoansi as farmers and livestock herders in Nyae Nyae was crucial to their livelihoods and to their land tenure security. They believed that each homestead should be a family farm, and that people in the area should raise livestock and engage in agriculture. While this approach is desirable in theory, in practice it is somewhat problematic. Crop yields in the Kalahari are notoriously variable and, in many cases, are quite low on a per-farm basis. Crop farmers in Nyae Nyae face numerous problems, including recurrent droughts (which in the Kalahari may be as frequent as every third or fourth year), periods of too much rainfall (which causes flooding and saturation of the soil), pests, and crop diseases.

In 2003, Marshall did a survey of activities in 18 Nyae Nyae communities to get an idea of the issues that they had to deal with. Data that he obtained ranged from water availability to the presence of gardens and the size of livestock herds. Marshall's (2003b) results indicated that some Nyae Nyae communities had functioning water points and gardens while others did not, and that the distribution of livestock of various kinds was also highly variable. Only 5 of the 18 villages had cattle, with a total of 105 (at an average of 21 per location). A conservancy herd, located at !'Obaha South, numbered 19 head.[3] Marshall's major complaint was that people were getting too little support in livestock production and agriculture from the NNDFN and from the government. He pointed out that people in all of the communities that he visited said that they wanted the NNC to invest in water development, agriculture, and community development (ibid.: 2). As Marshall says in *A Kalahari Family*, the Ju/'hoansi were "ever more dependent on trickle down [of funds]." This income, he said, was controlled by outside donors. The purpose of the NNDFN, Marshall argued, was "to help people help themselves."

In 2005, Polly Wiessner and /Aice N!aici (2005) held discussions in all of the Nyae Nyae villages with the exception of Tsumkwe and Apelpos. When asked about the positive and negative aspects of the conservancy, they found that "few positives were mentioned" (ibid.: 1). While it could be pointed out that "complaint discourse" was highly developed among the Ju/'hoansi (Rosenberg 1997), there is no question that the Ju/'hoansi to whom Wiessner and N!aici spoke were very critical of the NNC.

When pressed, people did say that they appreciated the fact that the NNC distributed cash benefits to people, that water points were protected, that elephant meat was distributed to the villages, and that some jobs were available through the conservancy. Communication between the NNC and the communities was very poor in 2005, and Wiessner and N!aici found that 13 of 29 villages had been visited only once by conservancy committee members since 2004, while 16 had not been visited at all. According to Wiessner and N!aici (2005: 1–2), people in

3. A conservancy herd is one from which animals were drawn when the NNC wanted to establish a new community with water, livestock, and tools.

26 of the 29 villages said that they had brought problems directly to the NNC, but that little had been done to address them. The response of some of the NNC committee members generally was that there were insufficient funds and that there was no transport available to enable them to get out to the villages. Problems mentioned by villagers ranged from hunger to elephant damage and from land and resource conflicts to problems with tourists and film crews. People in all of the villages pointed out that NNC management had declined significantly in recent years. The food situation in three villages surveyed in detail was such that people were living largely on bush food, supplemented with food bought with income earned from craft sales to tourists and church craft buyers and pensions (Wiessner and N!aici 2005: 6–8). The nutritional situation was exacerbated by elephant damage to wild foods in some places, and hunger was a serious problem.

In recent years, disagreements have arisen between members of the NNC and the WWF and the government of Namibia. The WWF and the MET are concerned about the fact that some villages have been established by Ju/'hoansi south of Tsumkwe at Daupos and Mountain Pos. The placement of these communities, which are relatively close to the Nyae Nyae pan, is not seen as appropriate and is said to be out of line with the conservancy zoning plan. According to WWF and MET personnel, it is leading to overhunting. There are also concerns on the part of the NNC and the other villages of Nyae Nyae that the placement of the two villages near Tsumkwe gives them disproportionate access to revenue from tourist-related activities of Namibia Country Lodges, a tourism company that took over Tsumkwe Lodge in 2007. Namibia Country Lodges is considering evening out the situation by setting up an "academy" to train Ju/'hoan guides from all over Nyae Nyae to help them get jobs in the tourism industry (Stacey Main Alberts, pers. comms., 2008–2010).

The NNDFN in 2007–2010

In 2007–2010, the NNDFN was providing support to the NNC and the people of Nyae Nyae in three major areas: protection and sustainable use of environmental resources; income generation and food and water security; and organizational and health training. Projects in the environmental area include supporting the application of some Nyae Nyae communities to become a Community Forest. This designation will increase the security of the area, since the MAWF will protect it, along with the MET. The NNDFN is promoting field conservation activities in Nyae Nyae—such as game counts, fire break maintenance, and ranger training—through logistical support and funds for training and uniforms. Lastly, it encouraged good relations with the trophy hunting concessionaire to ensure awareness and preparation for hunts, so that meat can be readily distributed to villages.

The income generation and food/water security projects of the NNDFN during this period included securing funding to support devil's claw harvesting and to make this activity sustainable for the future. In 2007, 195 harvesters earned N$160,000 (US$21,270) individually, and the NNC earned N$34,000 (US$4,520). In reviewing and relaunching the crafts project, the NNDFN aimed to get more ostrich eggshell into the area, so that there can be more output and more quality control training; to perform a tree survey in order to assess the impact of woodcarvers; and to promote new products that do not deplete increasingly scarce resources. In addition, the NNDFN was funding the development of 10 gardens in Nyae Nyae and 10 in neighboring Tsumkwe District West, where the N=a Jaqna Conservancy, established in February 2003, is located. The NNDFN was in the process of carrying out a tourism feasibility study of the two conservancies to assess the potential for additional camp sites, lodges, and other ventures that would create more jobs and income for the area. Funds were also being raised to purchase blankets, warm hats, and supplementary food for children enrolled in area schools. The last and perhaps most important NNDFN activity in this area, one to which the KPF and Polly Wiessner have made contributions, was the protection of water sources from destruction caused by elephants.

The other major threat to the people and habitat of Nyae Nyae was the presence of livestock owners and their herds from G/am that had entered the Nyae Nyae area in 2009 (Hays 2009). While efforts were made to get government support to remove the herders from the area, with the result that some of them were jailed and subsequently released, there were still sizable numbers of livestock present in 2010. The NNC and the Ju/'hoan traditional authority, with advice from the NNDFN and other NGOs, were seeking legal assistance and support to require the livestock owners and their herds to vacate the Nyae Nyae conservancy area.

As of this writing (August 2010), the G/am farmers who cut the veterinary cordon fence in April 2009 are still living in Tsumkwe. Their numbers have increased from the original 32 to nearly 300. Although their cattle have been confiscated, they have large numbers of horses, donkeys, and small stock within the Tsumkwe municipality, where stock is illegal. They are paying no fees for water, sanitation, or electricity; hence, the local residents are in effect subsidizing their presence. These settlers are putting pressure on water and sanitation in an already overtaxed and struggling small town, and it appears that there may even be a public health danger. Regarding them as "refugees," the Red Cross has provided the G/am settlers with substantial tarpaulins to cover the houses that they have built in Tsumkwe, thus making the settlers' houses much better protected than those of the majority of Ju/'hoan inhabitants. Ju/'hoansi in both the municipal area and the surrounding conservancy have had their resources decimated and have been intimidated by theft and violence, in one case having their huts burned down.

The current approach of the settlers is that they are poor people, too, and they are asking the Ju/'hoansi to "please share what you have. Anyone can make a mistake [cutting the fence illegally]. Next time it could be you." Meanwhile, during the second week of June 2010, the fence was cut at least three more times, according to the State Veterinary Office in Gobabis.[4] Another tactic used by the settlers is not to recognize their own Traditional Authorities. Instead, they say that they recognize only Tsamkxao =Oma (known as "Chief Bobo") as their Traditional Authority—at the same time that they disregard his instruction to leave the area.

The Namibian government announced in July 2010 that the G/am farmers would be recompensed for the loss of their cattle. The farmers are now requesting that this recompense be paid in Tsumkwe itself. The response of Tsamkxao =Oma as Traditional Authority, as well as of the NNC leadership, is that the recompense must be paid only after the settlers return to G/am. The settlers have also asked that their drought relief rations be given to them in Tsumkwe, but Tsamkxao and the NNC are refusing to allow this precedent to be set. It is unknown, however, what the Namibian government will do about these two sets of payments. Between June and August 2010, a set of seven relevant meetings took place involving the Ju/'hoan and Herero leadership, Namibia's Legal Assistance Centre, NGOs, and government officials. The only outcomes of these meetings have been a missed deadline (9 August 2010) for the settlers to return to G/am and another postponement (to late October 2010) of the criminal case against the 32 settlers who originally cut the fence in 2009.

In Nyae Nyae, traditional authority and NNC opposition is still strong, but the Ju/'hoansi fear they will get little help from local courts and officials. The NNDFN is currently looking at building an alternative approach. News media have been generally supportive of the Ju/'hoansi. However, both the Ju/'hoansi and supportive NGOs, such as the NNDFN and the Working Group of Indigenous Minorities in Southern Africa (WIMSA), fear that media fatigue may be occurring in this long-drawn-out affair.

Meanwhile, in addition to its activism with regard to the G/am settlers, the NNC continues its work of looking after the wildlife resources and water security of the conservancy area surrounding Tsumkwe. Early in 2010, its second chairperson, /'Angn!ao /'Un, retired and was replaced by /Kaece Ghau from //Aqri=ah near the Botswana border. Unfortunately, as soon as Ghau took office, he was diagnosed with multi-drug-resistant tuberculosis and is now at the Grootfontein Hospital for at least six months. The acting chairperson is /Ui Hartman. At the

---

4. See "Letter from Dr. E. Hikufe, Gobabis State Veterinarian to G/am Community Traditional Leaders and Farmers Unions," dated 14 June 2010, in the records of the Ministry of Agriculture, Water and Forestry, Republic of Namibia, State Veterinary Office, Directorate of Veterinary Service, Gobabis, Namibia.

August 2010 *rada* meeting of the NNC, a new Executive Committee was put in place, consisting of three men and two women, some of whom are experienced in the job and some of whom are new to it. A new manager is currently being sought by the NNC. One of several applicants is Kxao Royal /O/oo, a recently retired member of the Namibian Parliament.

The KPF continues to support the NNC's activities in Nyae Nyae. During 2010, it raised funds to drill three boreholes at Nyae Nyae *n!oresi* and to shield them from elephants, and it is providing ongoing maintenance funds for water protection. In July 2010, the KPF took part in a comprehensive evaluation of the Village Schools Project conducted by the Namibia Association of Norway's San Education Project. The KPF is active in working with other stakeholders to provide much-needed reliable Internet communications at the Captain Kxao Kxami Community Learning and Development Centre (CLDC) in Tsumkwe. The Ju/'hoan Transcription Group (JTG) that the KPF started in 2002 is now Ju/'hoan-run and operating year-round. It was invited by the National Institute for Educational Development to investigate registering itself as a community-based NGO, so that it can obtain translation work from Namibian ministries and other entities. These and other activities of the KPF are carried out in close collaboration with both the NNC and the NNDFN.

In the area of organizational support and training, the NNDFN undertook several main projects during this time frame. For example, it provided HIV/AIDS training in all workshops for craft producers, gardeners, and water protection teams. This training was intended to supplement health information available over the solar radios that the NNDFN has already provided to every *n!ore* community. The NNDFN also supported the NNC management committee in handling its staff, planning, funds, and reporting, and in ensuring that governance issues were taken care of.

The NNDFN is currently raising funds for a number of future projects that include the following: training two local hunters so that the own-use quota can be fully utilized to provide food for all villages; hiring a gardening specialist to help improve garden productivity; providing assertiveness and negotiation training for NNC staff so that they are better able to negotiate with filmmakers, hunters, etc.; running a pilot poultry project in several villages to investigate other ways of improving food security; and providing ongoing water protection. The NNDFN is also raising funds for a grazing specialist to assess whether livestock introduction can be done sustainably and to investigate alternatives. In addition, efforts are being made to set up a forest management committee, tied to the conservancy management committee, which will deal with forestry-related issues in Nyae Nyae, including the establishment of a Nyae Nyae Community Forest that will be announced by the government of Namibia after mapping and documentation take place. The exploitation and management of forest products have long been important strategies of the Ju/'hoansi. This program has the potential of expanding benefits available to Ju/'hoan community members and, at the same time, of promoting conservation.

When asked about desired economic options, many Ju/'hoansi say that they would like to be able to farm, but they would also like to have jobs that pay cash wages, to receive rations from the government, to take part in tourism and craft production, and to have the option to hunt and gather. It should come as no surprise that the Ju/'hoansi are concerned about the future of the conservancy and how it is functioning. The household benefits given to people periodically are appreciated, but more important to the Ju/'hoansi are the ways in which the NNC and the NNDFN operate. They want to see more people employed, more communities provided with services, more development activities, and greater transparency on the part of the conservancy. They appreciate the work of the NNC and of the NNDFN, but many Ju/'hoansi feel that their lives have improved only marginally, if at all, and they want to see greater attention paid to equitable, sustainable, and community-driven development.

Chapter Ten

Nyae Nyae Conservancy Programs and the Future

※

The previous chapter brought our chronicle up to date regarding the continuing attempts of the Nyae Nyae Conservancy (NNC) to foster environmentally appropriate economic development in Nyae Nyae. In this chapter, we describe three more of the NNC's main programs, those in the areas of health, education, and community heritage conservation. We use the history of these three programs to explore answers to questions posed throughout the book about the future of Nyae Nyae.

The Nyae Nyae Health Program

Background

The Ju/'hoansi, like other indigenous peoples, are undergoing major changes in health and nutrition (Jenkins 1994; Ohenjo et al. 2006; Stevens et al. 2005; Wiessner and N!aici 1998). When they were hunter-gatherers, Ju/'hoansi had very low serum cholesterol, low blood pressure that did not increase with age, and little in the way of heart disease (Nurse and Jenkins 1977; Nurse, Weiner, and Jenkins 1985). Many Ju/'hoan adults were very active, going on forays for foraging and visiting purposes, carrying infants, and engaging in extensive work activities, both in their camps and in the bush. Their nutritional status varied seasonally and over the longer term (Lee 1979a: 435–436; Wilmsen 1982: 105; 1989: 235–237, 304–305). The plants and animals in their diets provided vitamins and nutrients. There were always recurring periods, however, when people went hungry, especially during the late dry season, and under-nutrition was a serious problem at times.

As noted by Professor Trefor Jenkins (pers. comm., 2005) of the South African Institute for Medical Research in Johannesburg, malaria sometimes sweeps the Kalahari in epidemics, depending in part on the rains. In some instances, entire Ju/'hoan communities come down with malaria to the point that the residents have difficulty collecting sufficient food or performing agricultural and domestic work. Until recently, little in the way of medical malaria prevention or treatment was available to Ju/'hoan communities. However, psychic help was available for malaria and other illnesses: a fairly significant number of Ju/'hoansi in the past were proficient *n/omkxaosi*, or traditional healers (L. Marshall 1976, 1999). Ju/'hoan psychic healing is efficacious, well-known, and still practiced today (Katz 1982; Katz, Biesele, and St. Denis 1997). The Ju/'hoansi also use a substantial number of plants for medicinal purposes, including Hoodia, a thirst and appetite suppressant (Leffers 2003: 8; L. Marshall 1976: 92; van Heerden et al. 2007).

Over the past several decades, the Ju/'hoansi, like other San people, have experienced physiological changes as a result of the major socio-economic and demographic transformations that accompany the shift from nomadic foraging to sedentary crop and animal raising (Biesele and Hitchcock 2000; Draper and Howell 2006; Howell 2000; Lee 2003). Ju/'hoansi are taller and heavier now than they used to be (Tobias 1962, 1975; Wilmsen 1982: 107–108; 1989a: 305–312). The disease environment is worse for Ju/'hoansi living in stationary settlements than it was when they engaged in mobile foraging (Draper and Howell 2006: 84–85). On the other hand, the availability of Western medicine, periodic inputs of government-provided food, and the transition from what one elderly Ju/'hoan woman described as "the tough life of the past" have resulted in some positive changes in terms of Ju/'hoan well-being.

It is a fact, however, that the diet of the Ju/'hoansi has deteriorated substantially, with a greater emphasis on carbohydrates and highly refined sugars (Hansen et al. 1993; Wiessner 2004). There are indications that adult-onset diabetes is on the increase, a process not dissimilar to that among Native American populations after the establishment of reservations and the provision of government food. In addition, cardiovascular disease is more common today among the Ju/'hoansi and other San than it was in the past. The Ju/'hoansi are suffering increasingly from the "diseases of development"—cancer and heart problems—although this has been offset to some extent through their access to health services and medicines. Some Ju/'hoan people interviewed in Tsumkwe by health workers during the 1990s noted that gastroenteritis was a problem for some of the infants and young children, particularly at times of the year when seasons changed. Many of the people said that they were hungry. As one man put it in an interview with Robert Hitchcock in 1992, "Look at us. We are thin. We are dying from hunger."

Southern Africa is the global epicenter of HIV/AIDS in the new millennium, and major efforts have been made to curb the spread of the disease (Susser 2009). In Nyae Nyae, the HIV/AIDS prevalence rate was formerly relatively low, but this situation has changed substantially in the past decade (Lee 2007; Lee and Susser 2006; Mijlof 2006; Susser 2009). Efforts are being made by government health officials and NGOs such as Health Unlimited to provide anti-retroviral drugs to people with HIV. Food is also provided to those people who are HIV positive and who are under-nourished. Another critical health problem in Nyae Nyae is tuberculosis, with multi-drug-resistant strains of the disease on the rise (Richard Lee, pers. comm., 2009). Food availability and nutritional adequacy are linked closely to the tuberculosis and AIDS epidemics. As Richard Lee (pers. comm., 2009) notes, "Undernourished people have increased vulnerability to initial infection, the course of the illness is more rapid, and without adequate nutrient intake, drug treatment regimes are less effective, driving up rates of non-adherence to treatment protocols. Non-adherence in turn fosters drug resistance in patients, necessitating resort to second-line drug treatments and sharply poorer prognosis." Food security is a critical issue in Nyae Nyae, and there is an urgent need for additional information on this topic to add to the fine baseline data obtained by Wiessner (2004; see also Wiessner and N!aici 1998, 2005).[1]

The Ju/'hoansi have also continued to face alcohol-associated problems. Medical personnel from the South African Institute for Medical Research and anthropologists working in Nyae Nyae during the 1980s noted that the fairly high prevalence of folate, thiamine, and iron deficiency in the population may be related in part to alcohol consumption (Fernandes-Costa et al. 1984). Alcohol was sold not only in Tsumkwe but also in the settlements in the Nyae Nyae region. Even after the return to the n!oresi, alcohol-related violence has been responsible for injuries to women, children, and men. Alcohol continues to be sold in Tsumkwe at unlicensed shebeens and at people's homes, although efforts have been made by the Ju/'hoan traditional authority, the NNC, local churches, and NGOs to have the shebeens closed and the sale of hard liquor declared illegal (Susser 2009: 186, 195). Alcohol consumption is seen by medical personnel and NGOs as a factor affecting the health and nutritional status of local people in the Nyae Nyae area.

As in many San communities in southern Africa, alcohol in Nyae Nyae has contributed to spousal and child abuse and is a major cause of social conflict (Felton and Becker 2001; Sylvain 2006). Statements of concern about the alcohol problem were made at a 1989 meeting of the Nyae Nyae Farmers Cooperative (NNFC), the precursor of the NNC, and alcohol-related issues were raised in numerous interviews with Ju/'hoansi over the years. There were

---

1. Richard Lee and his students are currently engaged in collecting information on food and health issues in the Nyae Nyae region. Polly Wiessner and her colleagues collected superb data on nutritional, economic, and health issues in the 1990s and early part of the twenty-first century.

expressions of dissatisfaction that alcohol was being sold in Tsumkwe, up to at least 2009, by both residents and visitors. It has long been felt that having a culturally sensitive intervention program for substance abuse that not only treats the symptoms but also addresses some of the root causes would go a long way toward ameliorating the lives of people in Nyae Nyae.

The JBDF's Response to the Health Issues

To describe the health program that was eventually set up in Nyae Nyae, we return briefly to its roots within the Ju/wa Bushman Development Foundation (JBDF), the precursor of the Nyae Nyae Development Foundation of Namibia (NNDFN). In 1988, Claire Ritchie began background work for the program by arranging for Jenkins to liaise with the Witwatersrand University Department of Community Health on a health assessment of the Nyae Nyae communities. She also coordinated a visit and feasibility study for a rural primary health care program by Toos van Helvoort, a health educator from the Netherlands who was working in Ovamboland.

In 1989, a proposal written by Ritchie for a community health education project was funded by a grant from Christian Aid, Oxfam (UK), Development and Peace (Canada), and CAFOD (UK). Oxfam (UK) then sponsored her in Namibia for a three-month assessment of the needs of the project and ways to coordinate health authorities, personnel, and funding. Health Unlimited (UK) was chosen as the organization to provide staff to the project, to be carried out in partnership with the NNFC and the JBDF.

In October 1990, the project undertook mass X-ray screenings for tuberculosis. Ritchie also conducted a survey of the Nyae Nyae communities (33 by then) to discuss traditional health practices and the project's needs with the Ju/'hoan people and to identify possible health worker trainees. Ritchie was assisted by Ju/'hoan translators Kxao Royal /O/oo and Tshao Xumi, both from Botswana and thus already schooled in English. Kxao Moses =Oma gave an AIDS education workshop in many communities, using the first AIDS pamphlet in Namibia written in a local language—one that Patrick Dickens and Megan Biesele had developed with the Ju/'hoan dictionary trainees.[2]

Also in 1990, the NGO Swiss Disaster Relief (SDR) signed an 18-month contract with the new Namibian government and placed Dr. Melitta Bosshart at a hospital at the old military base at Mangetti Dune. A series of SDR nurses staffed the small clinic in Tsumkwe and made mobile clinic visits to outlying Nyae Nyae communities.[3] SDR left in 1992, but "Doctor Melitta," as she is known, stayed

---

2. The language and literacy work of the education program is further described below.

3. Previously, the nearest hospital or nurse was in the town of Grootfontein, a drive of three and a half hours from Tsumkwe.

on as director of health services in the area for the Ministry of Health and Social Services (MHSS). Based in Mangetti, she is responsible for running the hospital there and the clinic in Tsumkwe. As of 2010, Health Unlimited (now independent of the NNDFN and the NNC) is still providing health care in Tsumkwe District in collaboration with the MHSS and Doctor Melitta. The work of SDR has greatly improved the relationship between the Ju/'hoansi and medical workers and has increased the Ju/'hoansi's willingness to go to clinics and hospitals. Some of the work of Health Unlimited has included training Ju/'hoan grade school teachers about AIDS prevention (Susser 2009: 182). Health Unlimited personnel, along with government health care services, have also helped substantially in increasing awareness among the Ju/'hoansi about HIV/AIDS transmission and ways to reduce the spread of HIV, an area where the autonomy of Ju/'hoan women has played an important role (Lee and Susser 2006; Mijlof 2006; Susser 2009: 171–198).

The JBDF (which in 1990 became known as the NNDFN) and SDR collaborated on promoting immunizations, sputum tests for TB, delivery of TB medication, TB X-rays by mobile team, and the identification of other health problems in outlying communities. After Health Unlimited started its work, two Ju/'hoansi were trained as community health workers/medics, and they, in turn, were responsible for training and coordinating with resident health monitors in each of the Nyae Nyae villages. The program occasioned a great deal of excitement and pride in the Nyae Nyae communities as trainees were chosen and got their teaching materials and first aid kits.

Villagers had a very positive response to the project, which was presented as a learning opportunity, not just as "handing out medicines." Many people surveyed wanted to learn about birth spacing and contraception and how to assist women in childbirth. As Ritchie (1990: 7) wrote in her report at the end of 1990, "They were enthusiastic about the idea of having a person in their own village who would monitor TB patients, hand out simple medicines and know how to do first aid." Although they were very respectful of the strength of their (mostly older) traditional healers, they were also adamant that new medical knowledge be brought to their communities by young people who were literate.

A medical glossary and a primary health care primer were translated into Ju/'hoansi by a group of students in the health project. Ju/'hoan-language health care posters were also produced. There were discussions about HIV/AIDS, alcohol abuse, and the causes and transmission of disease in the Nyae Nyae villages and in Tsumkwe. In 1991, full funding for Nyae Nyae's Community Health Program was secured through the Overseas Development Agency (UK), and personnel from Health Unlimited were hired. In February, the Community Health Program, based at Baraka, got underway with staff members Elizabeth O'Neill and Froukje Zwaga.

Health Unlimited worker Ingrid Mijlof (2006) wrote a thorough history of the program's operation from 1991 to 1995. She identified several problems, many of which are common to similar programs worldwide. These included the difficulty of locating suitable volunteers, the disappointment that training did not lead to wages or other employment, and, in the case of the Ju/'hoansi, the strong egalitarian ethos, which meant that even volunteering was regarded as self-aggrandizement. Mijlof found that it was difficult for a Ju/'hoan health worker to tell another person what was wrong with him or her and how her or his behavior should be changed, because that would be taken as aggression. Another problem was that a mobile clinic with curative services "turned into dependency on expatriates with medicine and in the long run undermined the [MHSS's] credibility" (ibid.: 31).Tuberculosis control was more effective. The entire population was screened, and 90 people were put on treatment for a period in the mid-1990s, with a success rate of 84 percent. Malaria control interventions in the form of mosquito nets also produced substantial progress (ibid.: 34).

Perhaps most important to remember in the Nyae Nyae case is that poverty and nutrition are closely linked with disease (Detels and Breslow 2002; Lee 2007; Lee and Susser 2006). Good nutritional status supports a strong immune system that puts the body in a better position to fight against diseases like tuberculosis and HIV. When their hunter-gatherer lifestyle came to an end, the Ju/'hoansi experienced a nutritional transition with a shift in diet (from one high in complex carbohydrates and fiber and low in saturated fat) and a change from the high activity levels of hunting and gathering to a diet less varied and a lifestyle less active (Popkin 2002). The shift away from traditional bush foods resulted in a decrease in the consumption of plant foods and therefore in important micro-nutrients.

A study undertaken in 1996–1997 by Wiessner and N!aici (1998) showed that hunting was by then providing only 19 percent of caloric intake, while gathering was even smaller with 9 percent. The majority of calories came from food bought in stores (34 percent) and from government rations (37 percent). Bought food consisted mainly of tea, sugar, and alcohol, with healthier corn-meal and flour bought only secondarily (Wiessner 2004; Wiessner and N!aici 1998). The Ju/'hoansi have also received food aid on and off since 1993 under the government of Namibia's emergency drought relief program (Suzman 2001b), which stopped them from gathering healthier food at certain times. Survivorship among elderly Ju/'hoansi in Botswana improved in the 20-year period between 1968 and 1988, in part because of sedentism, increased access to medical assistance, permanent water supplies, and government-provided food (Draper and Howell 2006: 90–95), something that appears to us to be the case in Namibia as well.

Mijlof (2006: 39–40) concluded her assessment of the health situation in Nyae Nyae in this way:

The San living in Tsumkwe … have a worse health status than the other population groups in Namibia, and there are many factors that contribute to the situation. In most of the health indicators they are worse off, except in their life expectancy. It seems as if they are living longer than the average Namibian, and that might be due to their still low HIV/AIDS prevalence … The San of Tsumkwe, however, have now more opportunities to improve their health, social and economic situation than ever before. They have political representation nationally and also regionally. They have had foreign aid to help them to set up Conservancies that give them control over the land they are living on and from which they can generate income. They have a health NGO that partnered with them in improving their health and also many opportunities for the children to go to school and finish their education … [The San] are going through a transitional period and are confused on how they want to develop. Often, when they are offered alternatives, they have no experience … and therefore no possibility to make informed decisions. And they are faced with many questions: Where do they fit into Namibian society? The world? They want to become part of the "Western World," but does that mean losing aspects of their culture that they still value greatly today? It is essential that development be tempered to the nature and pace of change that they choose for themselves.

The Nyae Nyae Education Program

Background

Many of Mijlof's observations can also be applied to Nyae Nyae community education projects that began under the auspices of the NNDFN around the same time as the Community Health Program. The problems due to remoteness and the painful legacy of apartheid combined in Nyae Nyae to create an educational crisis that was deeply worrisome to the leaders of the NNFC. As the 1987 quote below from the then chairperson, Tsamkxao =Oma, shows, looking forward to the time of independence, the JFU/NNFC was very much motivated to tackle it:

When I look into the future to see what [my children] will see, one thing I see is that my children have come to fear schooling. They fear it because they fear being beaten. So they've all separated, left school, and gone off in all directions. Every time I'm in Tsumkwe I see kids who aren't in school. They say they're tired of trying. They got along all right with the earlier teachers, but now there's no understanding with the new ones. All [that the children] see is pain. And that's why they go about avoiding school these days. They don't want to be there.

A while back we went to the [school administrator] and asked, "If beating a child makes him leave school, what good does that do?" And all he said was "Mmm." So we said, "Misbehaving is one thing. If a child acts badly on many occasions, and the teacher discusses it with the parents so they understand each other, well, okay, go on and hit the child. But don't just beat him as an ordinary thing!" Sometimes they beat them for very small things. They don't even tell the child why. They don't even speak to the father about it.

[We said,] "If the child learns some things but doesn't learn others, you shouldn't just beat him, but tell him what he hasn't learned. You say, 'This is the name of this,' and you teach him along, teach him along, and then finally you ask him if he has learned the thing … If instead you go around beating the children, pretty soon you'll see they'll all be gone." This is how we tried to talk to the school administrator. But he persisted and finally we gave up.

But if the children *did* get good schooling? Some of them could get work in hospitals, medical work, and some could teach children in schools, and some could be police, and some could work in offices and do secretarial work. There'd be men's work and women's work. Or they could have shops, or some could learn to work on machines, machines that build trucks, or [welding] machines that work with fire, because these days people don't just do one thing but do lots of kinds of things. Some are truck people and others are welders and some work on truck machines and others keep hostels for schoolchildren. Some could go to work for the government in another area, maybe in waterworks, or some might be in agriculture, and many of them might want to work in water detection and borehole drilling.

If they had a chance to learn these things, they'd know how to do them. My heart burns for them to learn. That's how our work would go forward.

Education in Nyae Nyae after Independence: The Village Schools Project

During 1991, the newly independent nation of Namibia made a commitment to support minority-language education for the first three years of school. Partly this commitment was made because of an internationalist perspective on ethnicity fostered by the leadership of the South West Africa People's Organization on its return from exile. Partly it was made because of the historical circumstances of separate development during the period of South Africa's illegal mandate over South West Africa: at the time of independence fully 11 "national" languages were in use. Ironically, however, it also owed at least something to lessons learned from an opposite educational policy in Botswana.

At the time of independence, the new Namibian director of USAID/Namibia, Richard Shortlidge, who was transferred to Windhoek from Gaborone, shared with other involved parties an express mission to foster minority-language education in the new Namibia. In Shortlidge's view Botswana's educational language policies had contributed to increased marginalization for minorities. This view meshed well with that of the Namibian education minister, Nahas Angula, who opened the way for the Ju/'hoansi to form one of several recognized national language pilot projects in education.

About the same time, the Ju/'hoan people themselves were growing aware of the power of the media and of their own need for the tools of literacy. World literacy experience has affirmed that the most effective approach is learning to become literate in the mother tongue and then, after the first three or four years, generalizing this skill to a national language. Around the time of independence, English was taking the place of Afrikaans in Namibia, and the Ju/'hoansi, like many other minority groups, were anxious to develop both aptitude in English and a written form of their own language.

The pilot program called for the participation of the Ju/'hoan communities in deciding what features of their own traditions would be included in literacy materials as enrichment for their children's curriculum. A starting class of 16 teachers from these communities was trained to teach at five local schools. The schools were located in villages that were strategically chosen to maximize familial help from relatives of the students. This and other ideas about the Nyae Nyae Village Schools Project (VSP) were worked out in consultation between USAID/Namibia and Nyae Nyae community members. The Ju/'hoan people concurred with educators, who had identified the unfamiliar cultural and linguistic environment of the few schools formerly available to Ju/'hoan children as the single greatest factor contributing to the high dropout and failure rates.

The VSP began officially in 1991, but was rooted much earlier in the community's desire for a meaningful education program for young Ju/'hoansi. Tsamkxao =Oma's statement in 1987 reflected some of the social problems with the government school at Tsumkwe, which since 1978 had been increasingly staffed with white South African military personnel as teachers. A high dropout rate resulted from corporal punishment, punitive rote instruction in Afrikaans, terrible sanitary conditions in the hostel, and a national cap on San education levels, which meant that even the Ju/'hoan students who finished school there could not obtain jobs. The permissive (yet efficacious) traditional child socialization and hands-on learning system that the Ju/'hoansi enjoyed in the *n!ore* community context was the opposite of what the government system offered at Tsumkwe under apartheid.

The NNDFN, following repeated requests from Nyae Nyae community members and the NNFC, determined to explore the possibility of a more appropriate educational system that would be based in the *n!oresi*, where children could live with relatives and keep learning the traditional skills that their elders still wanted to teach them, along with becoming literate and possibly employable. Assessment of the educational situation of San peoples in Namibia, including in Nyae Nyae (Biesele, Lambert, and Dickens 1991), revealed a most dire need for relevant educational options to be made available. Ulla Kann (1991: 3) echoed this assessment in an in-depth Swedish International Development Agency (SIDA) consultancy on San teacher training and literacy needs, describing the situation as "an educational crisis."

But because the NNDFN believed that it needed to promote agricultural activities for food security first, in 1989 it created a post for a horticultural instructor, which was filled by Dickens. After he was interviewed and hired,

Dickens, a linguistics student at the University of the Witwatersrand who had done fieldwork with !Xoo (another San language) in Botswana, let it be known that he had some facility with Khoesan languages and would like to learn and eventually teach Ju/'hoansi at the development project in Nyae Nyae.

The result was the ambitious and effective Village Schools Project, which has become an example for appropriate, community-based, mother-tongue education projects in other parts of southern Africa. Throughout the three years remaining in his life, Dickens worked tirelessly to render Ju/'hoansi a professionally documented and professionally taught language. Basing his work on that of Jan Snyman (1975) of the University of South Africa, Dickens (1991) produced a practical, streamlined orthography that met international linguistics standards. His *English-Ju/'hoan, Ju/'hoan-English Dictionary*, whose manuscript was completed by the time he died of AIDS in October 1992, was published in 1994. It has become an indispensable tool of literacy and scholarship for the Ju/'hoan community and for linguists of the Khoesan languages. The NNFC advanced the Ju/'hoan agenda of effective national and international communication by formally adopting Dickens's orthography for educational and political purposes.

Dickens also trained four young Ju/'hoan men, who already had some schooling in Afrikaans, to read and write Ju/'hoan using the new orthography. Dickens worked with these four men and the Nyae Nyae community on the Ju/'hoan language materials while employed by the NNDFN as a horticultural trainer. The NNFC, as the NNDFN's partner organization, became the community custodian of the linguistic work and the education program it made possible. The VSP education program may be seen as a pioneer of the creation of a "self-literate" population, helping to design curriculum communally in a newly written language.

The Namibian Ministry of Education and Culture accepted Dickens's orthography as the official one for Ju/'hoan schools. Biesele, at that time still the director of the NNDFN, was able to promote Ju/'hoan education by explaining the concerns and goals of the Ju/'hoan community to some of the government agents and donors who were stakeholders in their future. At the same time, Biesele and Dickens were preparing texts in the Ju/'hoan language for the NNFC's requested school curriculum.

It is important to realize that if the Ju/'hoansi had not had their community-based education program already underway by the time of independence, their minority language concern might have gone unnoticed in the general clamor of many groups for recognition after independence. Not only did the Nyae Nyae community have a people's organization already well-formed and operative, but they had mobilized both a Namibian NGO and overseas interest and funding in support of their education program. Partly they were able to do this because literacy and early childhood education were integrated as goals into their overall community development program. Overseas funders and Namibian government agencies alike saw this integration in a most positive light.

The NNFC and the NNDFN could afford to set the precedent for scholarly input into Ju/'hoan education because those who began it volunteered their spare time to the development program. It would have been difficult for the new government—either then or since—to lay the groundwork on its own for language education. But the Namibian Ministry of Education was receptive to the work done in this case because the Ju/'hoan people themselves, via their own community organization, their NGO partner, and international funding, had a language and literacy program virtually ready to go.

Self-Literacy and the First Phase of the VSP

One of the most exciting original intentions of this project was community collaboration in the preparation of materials for what international educators referred to as "self-literacy." Curriculum work in Ju/'hoan has directly involved materials developed by scholars working within the NNDFN, local people within the NNFC, the education team of the VSP, and local teachers in the pilot project. These materials include orthography and dictionary updates, folktales, oral history, song texts used in readers for the primary school grades, and a numeracy booklet. The student teachers made tape-recordings of older community members telling stories and then transcribed the stories as group exercises in Ju/'hoan literacy. Also, creative writing in Ju/'hoan was promoted via workshops, which were met with great enthusiasm by the student teachers.

The first phase of the VSP (about 1989–1992) was characterized by the challenge of bringing relevant learning experience and literacy to a group of people whose own educational system is integrated into all aspects of life—a people, thus, with high educational standards. The VSP took into account the need to communicate with the many villages of Nyae Nyae about the social, as well as linguistic, bridge that the VSP plan could provide in answer to the people's expressed needs. It also undertook to demonstrate to national educational entities that the Ju/'hoansi were a people who had a robust educational system of their own, one that had previously sufficed for their lives. With changing times, however, the Ju/'hoansi became aware that they needed further education to allow them to participate in the wider society. At the same time, the VSP planners, both community workers and development workers, felt that it was imperative to retain the very great strengths of the Ju/'hoan oral learning system, which involved hands-on experience and emphasized the learning and creativity of groups rather than of individuals alone.

The challenge of dovetailing with the developing educational system in Namibia arose after independence. It was approached via an innovative set of pre-school pilot projects carried out for the NNDFN on a volunteer basis by

Melissa Heckler, a US educator and librarian specializing in early childhood. Based on Heckler's work and on the success of previous projects that incorporated high-level community involvement and holistic education in the mother tongue, a general proposal was written for Ju/'hoan education to the Namibian Ministry of Education (Biesele, Dickens, and Beake 1991). Under the premises of this proposal, groundwork was laid for the eventual accreditation of the five village schools and of the local teachers. Two Ju/'hoan teachers were hired by the national school system on an in-service training basis, and they began lengthy careers in the Tsumkwe Junior Secondary School. Dialogue between the two nationally employed teachers and the teachers (also local Ju/'hoan) eventually employed in the five Nyae Nyae schools was most important in the eventual national acceptance, in 2001, of the VSP as a bona fide part of Namibian education.

This outcome grew directly from substantial contributions to the VSP by the late Ulla Kann, a Swedish consultant to the Namibian Ministry of Education who had also worked extensively among remote area dwellers (mostly San) in Botswana. Kann's 1991 consultancy on the VSP for SIDA and for the NNDFN covered the interlocking issues of language and orthography, primary education and adult literacy, teachers and teacher training, curriculum and materials production. Titled *Where the Sand Is the Book: Education for Everyone in the Nyae Nyae Area—A Challenge*, Kann's (1991) report focused on the importance of local language education in the development of critical thinking and the consequent upcoming need for the training of local teachers. Kann concluded from her research that the VSP must strive to prepare Ju/'hoan children and adults to participate in the national education system. "The intent is *not*," she wrote, "to develop a separate education system for the Ju/'hoansi."

Also very important in making the bridge between the VSP and the national Namibian system was the position of education coordinator, which was created within the NNDFN. This post, filled by Magdalena Broermann starting in 1991, ensured that the necessary liaison work would be done with the Ministry of Basic Education and Culture and with donor agencies, as well as with other NGOs, colleges of education, and other schools working along the same lines. At the start of her work, Broermann collaborated with Lesley Beake, an award-winning South African writer of books for young people who co-authored the original VSP proposal to the Namibian government, to produce samples of desktop-published curriculum materials for testing in the first phase of the VSP. Broermann was instrumental in arranging the lengthy participation of the Bernard van Leer Foundation (of the Netherlands) in funding the start of the Ju/'hoan-language curriculum with materials produced by Dickens, Biesele, and the Ju/'hoan teachers and trainees. Together with Joachim Pfaffe, the village schools coordinator, Broermann also prepared proposals to SIDA that ensured continuous funding for the VSP.

Perhaps most critical in Broermann's work as education coordinator was the lobbying she did for equivalent accreditation for the student teachers. She was also responsible for continuing, with Jean Guernier and Pfaffe, the extensive program of training young Ju/'hoansi from the villages to act as teachers for the village schools (see Guernier 1992a, 1992b). From a starting class of 16, 5 eventually filled the school posts. With the participation of the student teachers, Pfaffe produced a series of training modules called *TEACH!* (Biesele and Pfaffe 1993).

The five pilot schools of the VSP were enthusiastically received by the Nyae Nyae communities. Even before Dickens's death in 1992, the VSP was praised by southern African educators as a very successful San community education project. Although for many years the project remained a struggle—practically, politically, and philosophically—by March 2008, it was clear that this ambitious pilot attempt had borne fruit as a model in the wider area of southern Africa. In a major poster exhibit on the VSP created by the staff and students at !Khwa Ttu, a San people's learning center in South Africa, the Village Schools Project was said to be "perhaps the most progressive and best-known minority education initiative in southern Africa."

Community Heritage Conservation in Nyae Nyae

The Ju/'hoan Transcription Group

A decade later, in 2002, a project in cultural heritage preservation, language development, and linguistics training for local people developed as a spin-off from the VSP. At this point, the Kalahari Peoples Fund (KPF), a US-based NGO, began to support projects made possible by the linguistics work and the VSP. Tired of the few flimsy mimeographed and desktop-published curriculum materials available in Ju/'hoan, the VSP teachers and other Namibian educators called for attractive published schoolbooks in their own language. Biesele, with funding from the National Science Foundation and National Endowment for the Humanities (United States), as well as the Wenner-Gren Foundation, the Jutta Vogel Foundation, the Firebird Foundation, the Hans Rausing Endangered Languages Documentation Project at the School of Oriental and African Studies of the University of London, and other donors, collaborated with the Ju/'hoansi on a digital heritage conservation project called the Ju/'hoan Transcription Group (JTG) to provide them with printed curriculum and archival materials drawn from their own culture. Some of these materials were contemporary essays written by the teacher trainees in a creative writing course that Biesele facilitated in 1992. The project has continued to offer authoritative materials to the Namibian government's National Institute for Educational Development (Pfaffe 2003, 2006), such as the book produced under Trafford Publishing's First Voices Publishing Programme in British Columbia, Canada (Biesele, /Kunta et al. 2009).

There are so far very few text collections of San languages, either in the original or in translation, that are annotated or glossed and thus easily usable by either anthropologists or linguists. In response to this need, the ongoing project is a long-term effort to transform an extensive "legacy collection" of audio textual material in Ju/'hoansi into digital texts and sound files, enabling the responsible posting of the material to Internet archives. The texts, gathered between 1970 and the present, range from folklore, dreams, and narratives of trance healing to political meetings and oral history. Later, interviews and conversations about the NNC, focusing on the environment, land rights, and new issues in governance and representation, were recorded as well. Transcribed and translated with precision by a collaborative team containing computer-literate native speakers trained originally by the VSP, these texts are not only valuable research tools for anthropologists, archaeologists, and linguists, but also valuable archival materials for the Ju/'hoansi themselves. They contribute to a movement now developing among indigenous people in many parts of the world to document and develop their own culture and language for educational, political, and economic purposes.

The JTG uses an innovative workshop format for processing authoritative texts, one made possible not only by new technology but by the "old" technology of collaborative learning that was traditional among the Ju/'hoansi and other San. The JTG has become a comprehensive, contextualized, and critical language project, building as it has on the original work of Dickens and his Ju/'hoan students and on Biesele's collected materials, now fully digitized. At first carried out only when Biesele and her technical assistants could be in Tsumkwe, since 2006 it has been ongoing throughout the year under local supervision at the Tsumkwe Community Learning and Development Centre (CLDC), established by the Namibia Association of Norway (NAMAS). NAMAS has an ongoing San education project based at the CLDC, and this project works closely with both the KPF and the NNDFN to foster community education in Nyae Nyae.

The uniquely productive and authoritative heart of this work is its collaborative workshop format, which continues to be used up to the present day. To add to the project's efficiency, the NGOs involved were able to construct by April 2008, at community request, a high-speed Internet connection at the CLDC in Tsumkwe, to allow for the exchange of sound files and translation drafts between the trainees and scholars outside of Namibia. This connection will be used to speed the preparation of language materials to be vetted by local experts for both publication and online dissemination. To date, over 250 collected stories and other texts (estimated at roughly one-ninth of all materials collected and to be collected) have been transcribed and/or translated, and some of them have been published Several additional book contracts are under discussion and will be completed in coming years, and Web site outlets for the materials have been prepared.[4]

4. For more information, see Biesele, /Kunta et al. (2009) and the KPF's new Web site, the KPN (http://www.kalaharipeoples.net), edited by Lesley Beake and soon a San editorial board.

As a part of the JTG, Ju/'hoan trainees Kaqece Kallie N!ani and Dam Kim Dabe received training in computer literacy, language preservation, and linguistic techniques, including interlinearization training from German linguist Tom Güldemann. By 2010, the number of experienced transcribers has risen to six, all dedicated and keen to continue the work of their predecessors. What the trainees have learned from the JTG may be regarded as a substantial contribution to the development of human resources for the study of Ju/'hoansi and other San languages. The Ju/'hoan language—especially in Nyae Nyae, as enabled by the VSP, the JTG, and a new Namibian commitment to minority radio—can genuinely be said to be experiencing community-based revitalization.

The final goal of the JTG is a lasting, publicly available collection of Ju/'hoan texts that is easily navigable; allows indexing by—and thus can be searched from—outside search engines; conforms to the standards of the Open Language Archives Community; and provides linguistic annotation of the text that is informative and useful in a readily accessible format for both large-scale computational processing and manual examination. This development is in line with those of similar projects in indigenous communities around the world. So recently an isolated and unwritten language, considered exotic and unlearnable even by its closest neighbors, Ju/'hoansi will become a world language. The knowledge it contains will become available as far as the World Wide Web can carry it.

The data from both audio recordings and isolated word recordings will be registered and deposited according to international guidelines and archived locally at the CLDC in Tsumkwe. Two full sets of backups will be preserved outside of Tsumkwe, one at the KPF's office in Austin, Texas, and another on the KPF's Web site. These resources will support not only research but also ongoing community language development. In 2009, the KPF constructed an annex to the CLDC to house the JTG and its records, using funds donated by the Texas Chapter of the Explorers Club.

The Youth Transcription Project and the Future

In early February 2008, the JTG trainees asked to expand their program. They have now added a youth component to their work, so that younger people, especially young women, can receive training in transcription, translation, and other linguistic techniques. They do the training themselves, in the spirit of "each one teach one."

An important subsection of new work during the text project is the addition of entries to Dickens's *English-Ju/'hoan, Ju/'hoan-English Dictionary.* Biesele and her technical assistants are collaborating with linguists Amanda Miller and Bonny Sands on this project. Miller and Biesele will co-edit the reissue of

Dickens's dictionary with Ju/'hoan-speaker Hacky Kgami Gcao, who has won an essay contest in the Ju/'hoan language on the topic "The Importance of the Ju/'hoan Dictionary."

Throughout this book, many oral quotes from Ju/'hoan people have been presented. What follows is this book's first written Ju/'hoan quotation, taken from Hacky Kgami Gcao's written translation of his own essay, in Ju/'hoansi, on the importance of the Ju/'hoan dictionary.

> When I left school, I started with work. I worked at many institutions, and when I started working in the Government, I worked as a Literacy Promoter for the adults. At the Government, they sent me to go and be trained in Ju/'hoansi to come back and train the other trainers, who would then be able to read and write in Ju/'hoansi. I went and entered the schooling with them and we learned together. At Baraka, I met the main teacher with the name Patrick Dickens and the other new trainers of teachers, who needed to know how to read and write Ju/'hoansi. They were Dabe Kaqece, Tsama Daqm, N!aici Hill, Beesa Boo, G=kao Martin, G=kao Plaatjies, /Koce Chapman and her sister Kun//a, Kha//'an /Kaece, Koba G/aq'o, and N!hunkxa /Kaece. Teacher Patrick Dickens tried his level best to teach us how to read and write Ju/'hoansi. After the training, we were given a test to write. All the students were all from different areas of Nyae Nyae, and it was planned they should become teachers and go back and teach the children in their areas. We started with the Ju/'hoansi Orthography that was accepted by the Government and were taught in it. From that day I have been happy, because I'm able to read and write Ju/'hoansi language.
>
> Learning together, at Baraka, gave me skill in writing the Ju/'hoansi language. The training in Baraka was what up-graded me to be able to write the Ju/'hoansi language. From Baraka, I came back with an experience of teaching adult Literacy Promoters. In those years, I was very good in Ju/'hoansi writing and reading.
>
> I'm also attending the Ju/'hoansi Transcriptions Project. It's very important, and also a good way to learn. I'm also able to write the Ju/'hoansi language now at the computer.
>
> I think that to write and read your own language is a very important skill to teach our younger generation. Our younger generation must start early with our Ju/'hoansi language, how to read and write it. I believe that when our young children know how to read and write our Ju/'hoansi language, all will be developed and like white people and the other groups of people in Namibia.
>
> I'm very happy that we now have schools at our villages that can teach our young generation to read and write Ju/'hoansi. I think that if the children can read and write the Ju/'hoansi language, they will be able to compile books in our own language.

Thanks to the technology that has finally caught up with the enthusiasm of the Ju/'hoan people for both preserving old knowledge and learning new things, this quote, with certainty, will not be the last written quote in the Ju/'hoan language that we will see from Nyae Nyae.

A Song Called "Conservancy"

Written products are not the only ones coming out of the Nyae Nyae community heritage preservation activities. Trainees are digitally recording older people's historical stories and folktales, chronicles of how they themselves became healers, and accounts of the composition of medicine songs and how they were transmitted, by teaching and sharing, across the landscape. They are making videos of these activities as well, and these videos will go into their own archives, along with decades of sound files made in earlier years. The Nyae Nyae Tape Archive, now digitized, includes records of the early meetings of the Ju/'hoan people's organization such as the writing of its Constitution, the historic meeting with Hereros at Xamsa in 1991, and statements about further negotiations with Hereros in 2009 and 2010. The JTG is now processing these files for a permanent record. Increasingly, media projects are putting digital and video cameras into Ju/'hoan hands so that the Ju/'hoansi can tell their own contemporary stories visually as well as in writing. The Web site of the Kalahari Peoples Network (KPN) receives postings of all kinds from Nyae Nyae and other San communities.

These activities have been characterized by a high degree of collaboration between young and old. Some young people, who have had the chance to become literate, do not know the old lore and are finding the knowledge of non-literate elders indispensable to the creation of good community records. The following account of a work session with transcription trainees is a case in point.

> In June and July 2006, in Tsumkwe, Nyae Nyae, Namibia, six young Ju/'hoan trainees, trained in computer literacy and transcription of their only recently written language, were hard at work on donated laptops. They were transcribing and translating, from digital sound files, hundreds of hours of folktales, healing narratives, and other materials recorded in their language as long ago as 1970. At one point in a detailed phenomenological description of the mechanisms of traveling on the "threads of the sky" to God's village, which Ju/'hoan healers do in an altered state of consciousness, a trainee sighed, "If only /Kunta Boo [the raconteur on the old sound file] were here to help explain all this to us so we could get it written down right!" At that moment, the trainees looked toward the doorway of the community library where they were working. There stood old /Kunta himself, having trekked in from his far-off camp when he heard about the project. Without further ado, /Kunta and his wife N!ae sat down by the computers in the midst of the young people and didn't get up for two solid weeks except for breaks or to go to bed at night. They went through the sound files with the trainees word for word. Excitement erupted around this collaborative process, which, along with transcriptions, began to generate many esoteric vocabulary words for the trainees to use in updating their dictionary. The result was over 200 pages of authoritative, annotated, richly nuanced, transcribed and translated Ju/'hoan material that answers many questions outsiders have had about the people's famous, but mysterious, healing dance. When /Kunta and N!ae were leaving to go back to their village, one of the trainees was moved to

read them a speech he had written, which contained the words "We young people could never have done this work correctly without you, our elders."

An interest in producing stories, both imaginary and historical, essays, both thoughtful and critical, and images, both moving and still, of the lives of the Ju/'hoansi—these must be seen as part of the complex legacy left in Nyae Nyae by the collaboration of concerned outsiders with the ongoing Nyae Nyae people's movement. Although there is much that is challenging, difficult, and even tragic about life in Nyae Nyae today, there is also cultural revitalization, and it is far more than solely the conservation of past heritage. It is creative, engaging with enthusiasm and critique the new realities that the Ju/'hoansi face as they go forward. Their ethnographer Lorna Marshall (1999: 74–79) drew the world's attention to the fact that the Ju/'hoansi have long named their efficacious medicine songs for things that they consider "strong," such as the giraffe, gemsbok, eland, sun, rain, and honey. Little wonder, then, that when bead-bedecked Ju/'hoan women gathered recently to sing and dance a haunting song to the music of stringed instruments, handmade from oil tins and wire, they said that the name of the song was "Conservancy."

References

Albertson, Arthur. 1998. *Dobe Land Mapping Project*. Report to Kuru Development Trust. D'Kar, Botswana: KDT.

_____. 2000. *Traditional Areas (N!oresi) of the !Goshe Community*. Shakawe, Botswana: Trust for Okavango Cultural and Development Initiatives.

Bank, Andrew, ed. 1998. *The Proceedings of the Khoisan Identities and Cultural Heritage Conference*. Cape Town: Institute for Historical Research, University of the Western Cape and InfoSource.

Barnard, Alan. 1992. *The Hunters and Herders of Southern Africa: A Comparative Ethnography of Khoisan Peoples*. Cambridge: Cambridge University Press.

_____. 2007. *Anthropology and the Bushmen*. Oxford and New York: Berg.

Barume, Albert. 2010. *The Land Rights of Indigenous Peoples in Africa*. Copenhagen: International Work Group for Indigenous Affairs.

Bause, Tanja. 2007. "First San Coffin Makers to Graduate." *The Namibian*, 24 May.

Berger, Dhyani J., in consultation with Kxao Moses #Oma, Hosabe /Honeb, and Wendy Viall. 2003. *"The Making of a Conservancy": The Evolution of the Nyae Nyae Conservancy; Restoring Human Dignity with Wildlife Wealth 1997–2002*. Windhoek: Eco-Development Education and Training and WWF/LIFE Program.

Berndt, Ronald M., ed. 1978. *Aborigines and Change: Australia in the '70's*. Canberra: Australian Institute of Aboriginal Studies; Atlantic Highlands, NJ: Humanities Press.

_____, ed. 1982. *Aboriginal Sites, Rights, and Resource Development*. Perth: University of Western Australia Press.

Biesele, Megan. 1978. "Sapience and Scarce Resources: Communication Systems of the !Kung and Other Foragers." *Social Science Information* 17, no. 6: 921–947.

_____. 1986. "A Tribute to Lorna Marshall." In Biesele, Gordon, and Lee, 1986, 11–20.

_____. 1992a. "'Our Government Is a Glowing Coal': Ju/'hoan Bushman Self-Determination and Namibian Independence." Paper presented at the Allard K. Lowenstein Symposium "Evolving Boundaries of Self-Determination," Yale Law School, New Haven, Connecticut, April.

_____. 1992b. "The Nyae Nyae Farmers Cooperative and the Nyae Nyae Development Foundation of Namibia." Paper presented at the Regional Conference on Development Programs for Africa's San Populations, Windhoek, Namibia, 16–18 June.

_____. 1992c. "Integrated Environmental Development in Namibia: The Case of the Ju/'hoan Bushmen." Paper presented at the 91st annual meeting of the American Anthropological Association, San Francisco, California, December.

_____. 1994. "Human Rights and Democratization in Namibia: Some Grassroots Political Perspectives." *African Rural and Urban Studies* 1, no. 2: 49–72.

Biesele, Megan, and Steve Barclay. 2001. "Ju/'hoan Women's Tracking Knowledge and Its Contribution to Their Husbands' Hunting Success." In *African Hunter-Gatherers: Persisting Cultures and Contemporary Problems*, ed. J. Tanaka, M. Ichikawa, and D. Kimura. *African Study Monographs, Supplementary Issue* 26: 67–84.

Biesele, Megan, Patrick Dickens, and Lesley Beake. 1991. *Education Proposal for Ju/'hoan Speakers in Namibia*. Windhoek: NNDFN.

Biesele, Megan, John Ford, and Dianne Hubbard. 1991. "Land Issues in Nyae Nyae: A Communal Areas Example." In Republic of Namibia 1991, 517–544.

Biesele, Megan, ed., with Robert Gordon and Richard Lee. 1986. *The Past and Future of !Kung Ethnography: Critical Reflections and Symbolic Perspectives; Essays in Honour of Lorna Marshall*. Hamburg: Helmut Buske Verlag.

Biesele, Megan, Mathias Guenther, Robert Hitchcock, Richard Lee, and Jean MacGregor. 1989. "Hunters, Clients, and Squatters: The Contemporary Socioeconomic Status of Botswana Basarwa." *African Study Monographs* 9, no. 3: 109–151.

Biesele, Megan, and Robert K. Hitchcock. 1999. "'Two Kinds of Bioscope': Practical Community Concerns and Ethnographic Film." *Visual Anthropology* 12: 137–151.

_____. 2000. "The Ju/'hoansi San under Two States: Impacts of the South West African Administration and the Government of the Republic of Namibia." In *Hunters and Gatherers in the Modern World: Conflict, Resistance, and Self-Determination*, ed. P. Schweitzer, M. Biesele, and R. K. Hitchcock, 305–326. New York and Oxford: Berghahn Books.

Biesele, Megan, Robert K. Hitchcock et al. 1996. "Visual Ethics and John Marshall's *A Kalahari Family.*" *Anthropology Newsletter* 37, no. 5: 15–16.

Biesele, Megan, and Brian Jones. 1991. *Integrating Conservation and Development in Eastern Bushmanland*. Windhoek: Directorate of Nature Conservation, Ministry of Wildlife, Conservation and Tourism.

Biesele, Megan, ed., with /Ai!ae Fridrick /Kunta et al. 2009. *Ju/'hoan Folktales: Transcriptions and English Translations; A Literacy Primer by and for Youth and Adults of the Ju/'hoan Community*. Victoria, BC: Trafford Publishing, First Voices Programme.

Biesele, Megan, John S. Lambert, and Patrick Dickens. 1991. "Educational Policy Affecting Ju/'hoansi in Independent Namibia: Minority Needs in Nation Building Context." Paper presented to Namibian Ministry of Education and Culture and to the 6th International Conference on Hunting and Gathering Societies, "Symposium on Education and Language Policies toward Hunter and Gatherer Societies in the Context of Modern Nation States," University of Alaska, Fairbanks, May–June.

Biesele, Megan, and Joachim F. Pfaffe. 1993. *Village Schools Project/NNDFN Education Project Bibliography*. Windhoek: NNDFN.

Bixler, Dorinda Sue. 1992. "Parallel Realities: Ju/wasi of Nyae Nyae and South African Policy in Namibia 1950–1990." MA thesis, University of Nebraska-Lincoln.

Bollig, Michael, Robert K. Hitchcock, Cordelia Nduku, and Jan Reynders. 2000. *At the Crossroads: The Future of a Development Initiative. Evaluation of KDT, Kuru Development Trust, Ghanzi and Ngamiland Districts of Botswana*. The Hague: Hivos.

Borgerhoff Mulder, Monique, and Peter Coppolillo. 2005. *Conservation: Linking Ecology, Economics, and Culture*. Princeton, NJ: Princeton University Press.

Botelle, Andy, and Rick Rohde. 1995. *Those Who Live on the Land: Baseline Survey for Land Use Planning in the Communal Areas of Eastern Otjozondjupa*. Land Use Planning Series, Report No. 1. Windhoek: MLRR.

Cassidy, Lin, Kent Good, Isaac Mazonde, and Roberta Rivers. 2001. *An Assessment of the Status of the San in Botswana*. Windhoek: LAC.

Cernea, Michael, ed. 1991. *Putting People First: Sociological Variables in Rural Development.* New York: Oxford University Press.

Chambers, Robert. 2005. *Ideas for Development.* London: Earthscan.

Chenje, Munyaradzi, and Phyllis Johnson, eds. 1996. *Water in Southern Africa.* Maseru, Lesotho, and Harare, Zimbabwe: Southern African Development Community, IUCN (the World Conservation Union) and the Southern African Research and Documentation Center.

Chennells, Roger. 2002. "The =Khomani San Land Claim." *Cultural Survival Quarterly* 26, no. 1: 51–52.

Chennells, Roger, and Aymone du Toit. 2004. "The Rights of Indigenous Peoples in South Africa." In Hitchcock and Vinding 2004, 98–113.

Child, Graham. 1995. *Wildlife and People: The Zimbabwean Success.* Harare, Zimbabwe, and New York: Wisdom Foundation.

Community Education Resources. 1988. *Community Education Resources' Response to Cliff Bestall and Paul Weinberg's Weekly Mail Report on Namibia Conference* (by Catherine Kell, Ruth Lewin, and Gaby Ritchie). Windhoek: Community Education Resources.

Coombs, H. C., B. G. Dexter, and L. R. Hiatt. 1982. "The Outstation Movement in Aboriginal Australia." In Leacock and Lee 1982, 415–439.

Corbett, Andrew, and Clement Daniels. 1996. *Legislation and Policy Affecting Community-Based Resource Management in Namibia.* Windhoek: LAC.

Crystal, David. 2002. *Language Death.* Cambridge: Cambridge University Press.

Daniels, Clement. 2003. "The Struggle for Indigenous People's Rights." In Melber 2003, 47–68.

———. 2004. "Indigenous Rights in Namibia." In Hitchcock and Vinding 2004, 44–62.

Dawson-Smith, Murray. 1995. *Integrated Natural Resource Management Program in Nyae Nyae (Eastern Bushmanland)—A 24 Months Grant.* Windhoek: NNDFN.

Detels, R., and L. Breslow. 2002. "Current Scope and Concerns in Public Health." In *Oxford Textbook of Public Health*, ed. R. Detels, J. McEwen, R. Beaglehole, and H. Tanaka, 4th ed., 3–20. Oxford: Oxford University Press.

Dickens, Patrick. 1991. "Ju/'hoan Orthography in Practice." *South African Journal of African Languages* 11, no. 1: 99–104.

———. 1994. *English-Ju/'hoan, Ju/'hoan-English Dictionary.* Cologne: Rüdiger Köppe Verlag.

———. 2005. *A Concise Grammar of Ju/'hoan with a Ju/'hoan-English Glossary and a Subject Index.* Cologne: Rüdiger Köppe Verlag.

Dieckmann, Ute. 2007. *Hai//om in the Etosha Region: A History of Colonial Settlement, Ethnicity, and Nature Conservation.* Basel: Basler Afrika Bibliographien.

Draper, Patricia. 1975. "!Kung Women: Contrasts in Sexual Egalitarianism in the Foraging and Sedentary Contexts." In *Toward an Anthropology of Women*, ed. R. Reiter, 77–109. New York: Monthly Review Press.

Draper, Patricia, and Christine Haney. 2005. "Patrilateral Bias among a Traditionally Egalitarian People: Ju/'hoansi Naming Practice." *Ethnology* 44, no. 3: 243–259.

Draper, Patricia, and Nancy Howell. 2006. "Secular Change in the Persistence of Intergenerational Kin Links among Ju/'hoansi (!Kung): Speculation on the Implications of Increased Longevity with Settled Life." In Hitchcock et al. 2006b, 81–100.

Fabricius, Christo, and Eddie Koch, eds., with Hector Magome and Stephen Turner. 2004. *Rights, Resources and Rural Development: Community-Based Natural Resource Management in Southern Africa.* London: Earthscan.

Felton, Silke, and Heike Becker. 2001. *A Gender Perspective on the Status of the San of Southern Africa.* Windhoek: LAC.

Fernandes-Costa, Francisco J., John Marshall, Claire Ritchie, Susan V. van Tonder, David S. Dunn, Trefor Jenkins, and Jack Metz. 1984. "Transition from a Hunter-Gatherer to a Settled

Lifestyle in the !Kung San: Effect on Iron, Folate, and Vitamin B12 Nutrition." *American Journal of Clinical Nutrition* 40: 1295–1302.

Fisher, Roger, and William Ury, with contributions by Bruce Patton. 1981. *Getting to Yes: Negotiating an Agreement without Giving In.* Boston: Houghton Mifflin.

Garcia-Alix, Lola, and Robert K. Hitchcock. 2009. "Report from the Field: The Declaration on the Rights of Indigenous Peoples; Implementation and Implications." *Genocide Studies and Prevention* 4, no. 1: 99–109.

Garland, Elizabeth. 1994. *Tourism Development in Eastern Bushmanland: Final Report.* Windhoek: NNDFN.

———. 1999. "Developing Bushmen: Building Civil(ized) Society in the Kalahari and Beyond." In *Civil Society and the Political Imagination in Africa: Critical Perspectives*, ed. J. L. Comaroff and J. Comaroff, 72–130. Chicago, IL: University of Chicago Press.

Garland, Elizabeth, and Robert J. Gordon. 1999. "The Authentic (In)Authentic: Bushman Anthro-Tourism." *Visual Anthropology* 12: 267–287.

Getz, Wayne M., Louise Fortmann, David Cumming, Johan du Toit, Jodi Hilty, Rowan Martin, Michael Murphree, Norman Owen-Smith, Anthony M. Starfield, and Michael I. Westphal. 1999. "Sustaining Natural and Human Capital: Villagers and Scientists." *Science* 283: 1855–1856.

Gewald, Jan-Bart. 1999. *Herero Heroes: A Socio-political History of the Herero of Namibia, 1890–1902.* Oxford: James Currey.

Gibson, Clark. 1999. *Politicians and Poachers: The Political Economy of Wildlife Policy in Africa.* Cambridge: Cambridge University Press.

Gleick, Peter. 2006. *The World's Water, 2006–2007: The Biennial Report on Freshwater Resources.* Washington, DC, and Covelo, CA: Island Press.

Gordon, Robert J. 1984. "The !Kung in the Kalahari Exchange: An Ethnohistorical Perspective." In *Past and Present in Hunter-Gatherer Studies*, ed. C. Schrire, 195–224. New York: Academic Press.

———. 2009. "Hidden in Full View: The 'Forgotten' Bushman Genocides of Namibia." *Genocide Studies and Prevention* 4, no. 1: 29–57.

Gordon, Robert J., and Stuart Sholto Douglas. 2000. *The Bushman Myth: The Making of a Namibian Underclass.* 2nd ed. Boulder, CO: Westview Press.

Green, Reginald, Marja-Liisa Kiljunen, and Kimmo Kiljunen, eds. 1981. *Namibia: The Last Colony.* Burnt Mill, Harlow, Essex: Longman.

Grove, A. T. 1969. "Landforms and Climatic Change in the Kalahari and Ngamiland." *Geographical Journal* 135: 191–212.

Guenther, Mathias, ed. 2005. *Kalahari and Namib Bushmen in German South West Africa: Ethnographic Reports by Colonial Soldiers and Settlers.* Cologne: Rüdiger Köppe Verlag.

Guernier, Jean. 1992a. *Report on the Initial Literacy Course Run Over an 8-Week Period for the Student Teachers, 31 July.* Windhoek: NNDFN.

———. 1992b. *Report on the Continuation of the Literacy Course during the Last Part of July, Aug., Sept. 1992.* Windhoek: NNDFN.

Hahn, C. H. L., H. Vedder, and L. Fourie. 1928. *The Native Tribes of South West Africa.* Cape Town: Cape Times.

Hangula, L. 1995. "Communal Land Reform in Namibia and the Role of Traditional Authorities." SSD Discussion Paper No. 11. Windhoek: Social Sciences Division of the Multi-disciplinary Research Centre, UNAM.

Hansen, J. D. L., D. S. Dunn, R. B. Lee, P. J. Becker, and T. Jenkins. 1993. "Hunter-Gatherer to Pastoral Way of Life: Effects of the Transition on Health, Growth, and Nutritional Status." *Suid-Afrikaanse Tydskrif vir Wetenskap* 89: 559–564.

Harring, Sidney L. 2004. "Indigenous Land Rights and Land Reform in Namibia." In Hitchcock and Vinding 2004, 63–81.

Harring, Sidney L., and Willem Odendaal. 2006a. *'Our Land They Took': San Land Rights under Threat in Namibia.* Windhoek: LAC.

_____. 2006b. *'One Day We Shall All Be Equal': A Socio-Legal Perspective on the Namibian Land Reform and Resettlement.* Windhoek: LAC.

_____. 2007. *'No Resettlement Available': An Assessment of the Expropriation Principle and Its Impact on Land Reform in Namibia.* Windhoek: LAC.

Hartung, Charles, and John Marshall. 1988. *Ju/wa Farming in Eastern Bushmanland: Problems and Recommendations.* Windhoek: JBDF.

Hays, Jennifer. 2009. "The Invasion of Nyae Nyae: A Case Study in On-Going Aggression against Hunter-Gatherers in Namibia." In *Forum Conference 2009: Violent Conflicts, Cease-fires, and Peace Accords through the Lens of Inidgenous Peoples*, 25–32. Tromso, Norway: Forum for Development Cooperation with Indigenous Peoples.

Heinz, H. J. 1972. "Territoriality among the Bushmen in General and the !Ko in Particular." *Anthropos* 67: 405–416.

_____. 1979. "The Nexus Complex among the !Xo Bushmen of Botswana." *Anthropos* 79, nos. 3–4: 465–480.

Hines, C. J. H. 1992. "An Ecological Survey of the Vegetation of Eastern Bushmanland (Namibia) and Its Implications for Development." BSc Honors, University of Natal.

_____. 1993. "Temporary Wetlands of Bushmanland and Kavango, Northeast Namibia." *Madoqua* 10, no. 2: 57–69.

Hinz, M. O., with S. Joas. 1995. *Customary Law in Namibia: Development and Perspective.* Center for Applied Social Sciences Working Document No. 28. Windhoek: CASS, UNAM.

Hitchcock, Robert K. 1992. *Communities and Consensus: An Evaluation of the Activities of the Nyae Nyae Development Foundation and the Nyae Nyae Farmers Cooperative in Northeastern Namibia.* Windhoek: NNDFN; New York: Ford Foundation.

_____. 1996. *Kalahari Communities: Indigenous Peoples, Politics, and the Environment in Southern Africa.* Copenhagen: IWGIA.

_____. 2001. *Anthropological Study in the Potential Impact of Refugees in M'Kata, Namibia.* Windhoek: United Nations High Commissioner for Refugees.

_____. 2002a. "Coping with Uncertainty: Adaptive Responses to Drought and Livestock Disease in the Northern Kalahari." In *Sustainable Livelihoods in Kalahari Environments*, ed. D. Sporton and D. S. G. Thomas, 169–192. Oxford: Oxford University Press.

_____. 2002b. "'We Are the First People': Land, Natural Resources, and Identity in the Central Kalahari, Botswana." *Journal of Southern African Studies* 28, no. 4: 797–824.

_____. 2004. "Human Rights and Anthropological Activism among the San." In *Human Rights, Power, and Difference: The Scholar as Activist*, ed. C. Nagengast and C. V. Ibanez, 169–191. Norman, OK: Society for Applied Anthropology.

_____. 2005. "Sharing the Land: Kalahari San Property Rights and Resource Management." In *Property and Equality, Vol. 2: Encapsulation, Commercialization, and Discrimination*, ed. W. Tadesse and T. Widlok, 191–207. New York: Berghahn Books.

_____. 2006. "'We Are the Owners of the Land': The Struggle of the San for the Kalahari and Its Resources." In Hitchcock et al. 2006b, 229–256.

_____. In press. "Refugees, Resettlement, and Land and Resource Conflicts among !Xun and Khwe San in Northeastern Namibia." *African Study Monographs.*

Hitchcock, Robert K., and Wayne Babchuk. 2007. "Kalahari San Foraging, Territoriality, and Land Use: Implications for the Future." *Before Farming: The Archaeology and Anthropology of Hunter-Gatherers* 2007/3: 169–181.

Hitchcock, Robert K., and Laurence G. Bartram, Jr. 1998. "Social Boundaries, Technical Systems, and the Use of Space and Technology in the Kalahari." In *The Archaeology of Social Boundaries*, ed. Miriam T. Stark, 12–49. Washington, DC: Smithsonian Institution Press.

Hitchcock, Robert K., and John D. Holm. 1993. "Bureaucratic Domination of African Hunter-Gatherer Societies: A Study of the San in Botswana." *Development and Change* 24, no. 1: 1–35.

Hitchcock, Robert K., Kazunobu Ikeya, Megan Biesele, and Richard B. Lee. 2006a. "Introduction: Updating the San: Image and Reality of an African People in the 21st Century." In Hitchcock et al. 2006b, 1–42.

_____, eds. 2006b. *Updating the San: Image and Reality of an African People in the 21st Century.* Senri Ethnological Studies 70. Osaka: National Museum of Ethnology.

Hitchcock, Robert K., and Diana Vinding, eds. 2004. *Indigenous Peoples' Rights in Southern Africa.* Copenhagen: IWGIA.

Hitchcock, Robert K., John E. Yellen, Diane J. Gelburd, Alan J. Osborn, and Aron L. Crowell. 1996. "Subsistence Hunting and Natural Resource Management among the Ju/'hoansi of Northwestern Botswana." *African Study Monographs* 17, no. 4: 153–220.

Hohmann, Thekla, ed. 2003. *San and the State: Contesting Land, Development, Identity, and Representation.* Cologne: Rüdiger Köppe Verlag.

Hopwood, G. 2007. "Regional Development and Decentralization." In *Transitions in Namibia: Which Changes for Whom?* ed. Henning Melber, 173–189. Stockholm: Nordiska Afrikainstitutet.

Howell, Nancy. 2000. *Demography of the Dobe !Kung.* 2nd ed. New York: Aldine de Gruyter.

Hulme, David, and Marshall Murphree, eds. 2001. *African Wildlife and Livelihoods: The Promise and Performance of Community Conservation.* London: James Currey.

Hunter, M. L., R. K. Hitchcock, and B. Wyckoff-Baird. 1990. "Women and Wildlife in Southern Africa." *Conservation Biology* 4, no. 4: 448–451.

Jacobson, P. J., K. M. Jacobson, and M. K. Seely. 1995. *Ephemeral Rivers and Their Catchments: Sustaining People and Development in Western Namibia.* Windhoek: Desert Research Foundation of Namibia.

JBDF (Ju/wa Bushman Development Foundation). 1988a. *Annual Report 1988.* Windhoek: JBDF.

_____. 1988b. *Annual Report 1988 (Supplement).* Windhoek: JBDF.

_____. 1990. *Annual Report 1990.* Windhoek: JBDF.

Jenkins, Trefor. 1979. "Southern Africa's Model People." *South African Journal of Science* 75: 280–282.

_____. 1994. "Hunter-Gatherers in Southern Africa." *South African Medical Journal* 84: 10–12.

JFU (Ju/wa Farmers Union). 1986. *Ju/wa Farmers Union Constitution.* Windhoek: JBDF.

Jones, Brian. 1988a. "Bushmanland: Fate in the Balance." *African Wildlife* 42, no. 2: 87–92.

_____. 1988b. "Can the San Survive in Bushmanland?" *African Wildlife* 42, no. 6: 226–227.

_____. 1988c. "Reply." *African Wildlife* 42, no. 6: 356.

_____. 1996. "Institutional Relationships, Capacity, and Sustainability: Lessons Learned from a Community-Based Conservation Project, Tsumkwe District, Namibia, 1991–96." Directorate of Environmental Affairs Research Discussion Paper No. 11. Windhoek: MET.

_____. 2010. "The Evolution of Namibia's Communal Conservancies." In Nelson 2010, 106–121.

Jones, Brian, and Marshall W. Murphree. 2001. "The Evolution of Policy on Community Conservation in Namibia and Zimbabwe." In Hulme and Murphree 2001, 38–58.

Kann, Ulla. 1991. *Where the Sand Is the Book: Education for Everyone in the Nyae Nyae Area; A Challenge.* Windhoek: NNDFN and the Swedish International Development Authority.

Katz, Richard. 1982. *Boiling Energy: Community Healing among the !Kung.* Cambridge, MA: Harvard University Press.

Katz, Richard, Megan Biesele, and Verna St. Denis. 1997. *Healing Makes Our Hearts Happy: Spirituality and Cultural Transformation among the Kalahari Ju/'hoansi.* Rochester, VT: Inner Traditions.

Kolata, Gina Bari. 1981. "!Kung Bushmen Join South African Army." *Science* 211: 562–564.

LAC (Legal Assistance Centre). 1991. "Communal Lands in Namibia: The Legal Framework, Its Application, and Existing Practices." In Republic of Namibia 1991, 99–141.

Leacock, Eleanor, and Richard Lee, eds. 1982. *Politics and History in Band Societies.* Cambridge: Cambridge University Press.

Lee, Richard B. 1968. "What Hunters Do for a Living, or, How to Make Out on Scarce Resources." In *Man the Hunter*, ed. R. B. Lee and I. DeVore, 30–48. Chicago, IL: Aldine.

_____. 1969. "Kung Bushmen Subsistence: An Input-Output Analysis." In *Environment and Cultural Behavior*, ed. A. P. Vayda, 47–79. New York: Natural History Press.

_____. 1976. "Introduction." In Lee and DeVore 1976, 3–20.

_____. 1979a. *The !Kung San: Men, Women, and Work in a Foraging Society.* Cambridge: Cambridge University Press.

_____. 1979b. "Hunter-Gatherers in Process: The Kalahari Research Project 1963–1976." In *Long-Term Field Research in Social Anthropology*, ed. George M. Foster, Thayer Scudder, Elizabeth Colson, and Robert V. Kemper, 303–321. New York: Academic Press.

_____. 1984. *The Dobe Ju/'hoansi.* 2nd ed. New York: Harcourt Brace.

_____. 1985. "The Gods Must Be Crazy, but the State Has a Plan: Government Policies towards the San in Namibia." *Canadian Journal of African Studies* 20, no. l: 91–98.

_____. 1986. "!Kung Kin Terms, the Name Relationship, and the Process of Discovery." In Biesele, Gordon, and Lee 1986, 77–102.

_____. 2003. *The Dobe Ju/'hoansi.* 3rd ed. Toronto: Wadsworth/Thompson Learning.

_____. 2007. "The Ju/'hoansi at the Crossroads: Continuity and Change in the Time of AIDS." In *Globalization and Change in Fifteen Cultures: Born in One World, Living in Another*, ed. George Spindler and Janice E. Stockard, 144–171. Belmont, CA: Thompson Higher Education.

Lee, R. B., and Irven DeVore, eds. 1976. *Kalahari Hunter-Gatherers: Studies of the !Kung San and Their Neighbors.* Cambridge, MA: Harvard University Press.

Lee, R. B., and Susan Hurlich. 1982. "From Foragers to Fighters: South Africa's Militarization of the Namibian San." In Leacock and Lee 1982, 327–345.

Lee, R. B., and Ida Susser. 2006. "Confounding Conventional Wisdom: The Ju'hoansi and HIV/AIDS." In Hitchcock et al. 2006b, 45–60.

Leffers, A. 2003. *Gemsbok Bean and Kalahari Truffle: Traditional Plant Use by Ju/'hoansi in North-eastern Namibia.* Windhoek: Gamsberg Macmillan.

Le Roux, Willemien, and Alison White. 2004. *Voices of the San: Living in Southern Africa Today.* Cape Town: Kwela Books.

Lewis, M. Paul, ed. 2009. *Ethnologue: Languages of the World.* 16th ed. Dallas, TX: Summer Institute of Linguistics International.

Leys, Colin, and Susan Brown. 2005. *Histories of Namibia: Living through the Liberation Struggle; Life Histories Told to Colin Leys and Susan Brown.* London: Merlin Press.

Leys, Colin, and John S. Saul, eds. 1995. *Namibia's Liberation Struggle: The Two-Edged Sword.* London: James Currey; Athens: Ohio University Press.

Lindholm, Karl-Johan. 2006. *Wells of Experience: A Pastoral Land-Use History of Omaheke, Namibia.* Studies in Global Archaeology 9. Uppsala: Uppsala University.

Longden, Christina, ed. 2004. *Undiscovered or Overlooked? The Hai‖om of Namibia and Their Identity.* Windhoek: WIMSA.

Malan, J. S. 1995. *Peoples of Namibia.* Pretoria: Rhino Publishers.

Marais, Francois. 1984. *Ondersoek na die Boesmanbevolkingsgroepe in SWA (The Brand Report).* Windhoek: Development Directorate, SWAA.

Marks, Shula. 1972. "Khoisan Resisistance to the Dutch in the Seventeeth and Eighteenth Centuries." *Journal of African History* 13: 55–80.

Marks, Stuart. 1984. *The Imperial Lion: Human Dimensions of Wildlife Management in Central Africa.* Boulder, CO: Westview Press.

Marshall, John. 1957. "Ecology of the !Kung Bushmen of the Kalahari Desert." Senior Honors Thesis in Anthropology, Harvard University.

_____. 1958a. "Man the Hunter, Part I." *Natural History* 67: 291–309.

_____. 1958b. "Man the Hunter, Part II." *Natural History* 67: 376–395.

_____. 1958c. *The Hunters* [film]. Hightstown, NJ: Contemporary Films/McGraw Hill.

_____. 1979. *N!ai: The Story of a !Kung Woman* [film]. Watertown, MA: Documentary Educational Resources.

_____. 1984. "Death Blow to the Bushmen." *Cultural Survival Quarterly* 8, no. 3: 13–16.

_____. 1988. "Bushmanland: Lives in the Balance." *African Wildlife* 42, no. 6: 356.

_____. 1989. *The Constitution and Communal Lands in Namibia: Land Rights and Local Governments; Helping 33,000 People Classified as "Bushmen": The Ju/wa Case*. Windhoek: NNDFN.

_____. 1996. "The Need to Be Informed: A Reply to the Collective Letter." *Anthropology Newsletter* 37, no. 5: 15–16.

_____. 2002. *Community Development in Water, Food, Stability Restoring Balance with a Two-Year Plan: Community Development Program Proposal*. Windhoek: NNC.

_____. 2003a. *A Kalahari Family* [film]. Watertown, MA: Documentary Educational Resources.

_____. 2003b. *Water and Basic Situations in Nyae Nyae Communities*. Windhoek: NNDFN.

_____. 2003c. *Community Development in Water, Food, Stability Restoring Balance with a Two-Year Plan: Community Development Program Proposal*. Windhoek: NNC.

Marshall, John, and Charles Hartung. 1986. *Ju/wa Bushman Rural Development Project*. Windhoek: JBDF.

Marshall, John, and Claire Ritchie. 1983. *Ju/Wa Concepts of Property and Land Ownership*. Windhoek: JBDF.

_____. 1984. *Where Are the Ju/Wasi of Nyae Nyae? Changes in a Bushman Society: 1958–1981*. Communications No. 9, Center for African Area Studies. Cape Town: University of Cape Town.

Marshall, Lorna. 1960. "!Kung Bushman Bands." *Africa* 30, no. 4: 325–355.

_____. 1961. "Sharing, Talking, and Giving: Relief of Social Tensions among !Kung Bushmen." *Africa* 31, no. 3: 231–249.

_____. 1976. *The !Kung of Nyae Nyae*. Cambridge, MA: Harvard University Press.

_____. 1999. *Nyae Nyae !Kung Beliefs and Rites*. Cambridge, MA: Peabody Museum Press.

Melber, Henning, ed. 2003. *Re-examining Liberation in Namibia: Political Culture since Independence*. Uppsala: Nordiska Afrikainstitutet.

MET (Ministry of Environment and Tourism). 1994. *Policy Document: Land-Use Planning; Towards Sustainable Development*. Windhoek: MET.

_____. 1995a. *Policy Document: Wildlife Management, Utilization, and Tourism in Communal Areas; Benefits to Communities and Improved Resource Management*. Windhoek: MET.

_____. 1995b. *Policy Document: Promotion of Community-Based Tourism Development*. Windhoek: MET.

Mijlof, Ingrid. 2006. *Public Health Perspective on the Health Status of the San, Tsumkwe, Namibia*. Windhoek and London: Health Unlimited.

MLGLH (Ministry of Local Government, Lands, and Housing). 1993. *Regional Conference on Development Programs for Africa's San/Basarwa Populations, Gaborone, Botswana, 11th–13th October 1993*. Gaborone: MLGLH.

MLRR (Ministry of Lands, Resettlement, and Rehabilitation). 1994. *ELCIN San Ex-Soldier Settlement Program (1992–1994)*. Windhoek: MLRR.

Mogwe, Alice. 1992. *Who Was (T)here First? An Assessment of the Human Rights Situation of Basarwa in Selected Communities in the Gantsi District, Botswana*. Gaborone: Botswana Christian Council.

MWCT (Ministry of Wildlife Conservation and Tourism). 1992. *Namibia's Green Plan (Environment and Development)*. Windhoek: GRN.

NACSO (Namibian Association of CBNRM Support Organisations). 2006. *Namibia's Communal Conservancies: A Review of Progress and Challenges in 2005*. Windhoek: NACSO.

Nangula, Selma. 2004. *Women's Participation in Conservancy Activities: A Case Study of Nyae Nyae and //Gamaseb Conservancies*. Windhoek: Multidisciplinary Research Center, UNAM.

Nelson, Fred, ed. 2010. *Community Rights, Conservation, and Contested Land: The Politics of Natural Resource Governance in Africa*. London: Earthscan.

Neumann, Roderick P. 1998. *Imposing Wilderness: Struggles over Livelihood and Nature Preservation in Africa*. Berkeley: University of California Press.

NNDFN (Nyae Nyae Development Foundation of Namibia). 1992. *Nyae Nyae Ju/'hoan Development Program: Basic Data and Information*. Windhoek: NNDFN.

Nurse, G. T., and T. Jenkins. 1977. *Health and the Hunter-Gatherer: Bio-medical studies on the Hunting and Gathering Populations of Southern Africa*. Basel: S. Karger.

Nurse, G. T., J. S. Weiner, and T. Jenkins. 1985. *The Peoples of Southern Africa and Their Affinities*. Oxford: Clarendon Press.

Odendaal, Willem. 2006a. "The SADC Land and Agrarian Reform Initiative: The Case of Namibia." Working Paper No. 111. Windhoek: NEPRU.

———. 2006b. *San Communal Lands Contested: The Battle over N=a Jaqna Conservancy*. Windhoek: LAC.

Ohenjo, Nyang'ori, Ruth Willis, Dorothy Jackson, Clive Nettleton, Kenneth Good, and Benon Mugarura. 2006. "Health of Indigenous People in Africa." *Lancet* 367: 1937–1946.

Pakleppa, Richard. 2001. *Report on Community Consultancy and Human Rights Education Undertaken in Tsumkwe District West between 5 and 22 April 2001*. Windhoek: WIMSA.

———. 2002. *Civil Rights in Legislation and Practice: A Case Study from Tsumkwe District West, Namibia*. Windhoek: WIMSA.

Pakleppa, Richard, and Americo Kwononoka. 2003. *Where the Last Are First: San Communities Fighting for Survival in Southern Angola; Report of a Needs Assessment of Angolan San Communities in Huila, Cunene, and Cuando Cubango Provinces from 17 June to 14 July 2003*. Windhoek: Trocaire Angola, WIMSA, and OCADEC.

Pakleppa, Richard, with WIMSA Team. 2004. "Civil Rights in Legislation and Practice: A Case Study from Tsumkwe District West, Namibia." In Hitchcock and Vinding 2004, 82–96.

Patel, Heena. 1998. *Sustainable Utilization and African Wildlife Policy. The Case of Zimbabwe's Communal Areas Management Programme for Indigenous Resources (CAMPFIRE): Rhetoric or Reality?* Washington, DC: Indigenous Environmental Policy Center.

Pennington, Renee, and Henry Harpending. 1993. *The Structure of an African Pastoralist Community: Demography, History, and Ecology of the Ngamiland Herero*. Oxford: Clarendon Press.

Pfaffe, Joachim, ed. 2003. *Tales from the Nyae Nyae/N=oahn //ama N//oaq!'ae (Ju/'hoan Reader for Grades 2–4)*. Stories collected by Megan Biesele and Patrick Dickens with the Ju/'hoan Curriculum Committee. Windhoek: Gamsberg Macmillan Publishers.

———, ed. 2006. *Life in Nyae Nyae//Xoa N!anga o N//oaq!'ae ga (Ju/'hoan Reader for Grades 2–4)*. Essays written by Village Schools Project Teachers and Ju/'hoan Curriculum Committee. Windhoek: Gamsberg Macmillan Publishers.

Popkin, B. M. 2002. "An Overview on the Nutrition Transition and Its Health Implications: The Bellagio Meeting." *Public Health Nutrition* 5, no. 1A: 93–103.

Powell, N. S. 1994. *Participatory Land Use Planning: Methods Development Incorporating the Needs and Aspirations of Indigenous Peoples in Natural Resource Management. A Case from Eastern Bushmanland, Namibia*. Windhoek: WWF/LIFE.

Republic of Namibia, ed. 1991. *National Conference on Land Reform and the Land Question, Windhoek, 25 June–1 July 1991, Vol. 1: Research Papers, Addresses, and Consensus Document.* Windhoek: GRN, Office of the Prime Minister.

_____, ed. 1992. *Regional Conference on Development Programs for Africa's San Populations, Windhoek, Namibia, 16–18 June 1992.* Windhoek: MLRR.

_____. 1995a. *Sectoral and Cross-Sectoral Chapters for Namibia Development Plan 1 (Draft).* Windhoek: GRN.

_____. 1995b. *National Development Plan 1: 1995/1996–1999/2000.* Windhoek: GRN.

_____. 1996. *Namibia Nature Conservation Amendment Act (1996).* Windhoek: GRN.

_____. 2001. *National Development Plan 2: 2001/2002–2005/2006.* Windhoek: GRN.

_____. 2006. *National Development Plan 3: 2006/2007–2010/2011.* Windhoek: GRN.

Ritchie, Claire. 1986. "From Foragers to Farmers: The Ju/wasi of Nyae Nyae Thirty Years On." In Biesele, Gordon, and Lee 1986, 311–325.

_____. 1987. "The Political Economy of Resource Tenure in the Kalahari." MA thesis, Department of Anthropology, Boston University.

_____. 1988. "/Toma: A Tribute." *Cultural Survival Quarterly* 12, no. 3: 36–37.

_____. 1990. *Report on Assessment and Coordination of JBDF Primary Health Education Project, July–October, 1990.* Windhoek: JBDF.

_____. 1992. *Chronological Notes from Journals and Files, 1980–1986.* Windhoek: NNDFN.

_____. 1993. "Death by Myth: Ethnographic Film and the Development Struggle." In *The Cinema of John Marshall,* ed. J. Ruby, 195–204. Philadelphia, PA: Harwood Academic Publishers.

Ritchie, Claire, and Megan Biesele. 1989. *Ju/wa Bushman Development Foundation Programme: Integrated Rural Development Programme and Sub-projects.* Windhoek: JBDF.

Ritchie, Claire, and John Marshall. 1988. *Ju/wa Bushman Rural Development Project.* Windhoek: JBDF.

Robbins, David. 2006. *A San Journey: The Story of the !Xun and Khwe of Platfontein.* Kimberley, South Africa: Sol Plaatje Educational Trust.

_____. 2007. *On the Bridge of Goodbye: The Story of South Africa's Discarded San Soldiers.* Johannesburg and Cape Town: Jonathan Ball.

Robins, Steven, Elias Madzudzo, and Matthias Brenzinger, eds. 2001. *An Assessment of the Status of the San in South Africa, Angola, Zambia, and Zimbabwe.* Windhoek: LAC.

Rosenberg, Harriet. 1997. "Complaint Discourse, Aging, and Care Giving among the Ju/'hoansi of Botswana." In *The Cultural Context of Aging: Worldwide Perspectives,* ed. Jay Solokovsky, 33–55. Westport, CT: Bergin and Garvey.

Rotberg, Robert, ed. 1983. *Namibia: Political and Economic Prospects.* Cape Town: David Philip.

RSA (Republic of South Africa). 1964. *Report of the Commission of Enquiry into South West Africa Affairs 1962–63 (Odendaal Commission).* Pretoria: RSA.

Saugestad, Sidsel. 2001. *The Inconvenient Indigenous: Remote Area Development in Botswana, Donor Assistance, and the First People of the Kalahari.* Uppsala: Nordic Africa Institute.

_____. 2005. "'Improving their Lives': State Policies and San Resistance in Botswana." *Before Farming* 2005/4: 1–11.

Schalken, Wouter. 1999. "Where Are the Wild Ones? The Involvement of Indigenous Communities in Tourism in Namibia." *Cultural Survival Quarterly* 23, no. 2: 40–42.

Schapera, I. 1930. *The Khoisan Peoples of South Africa: Bushmen and Hottentots.* London: Routledge and Kegan Paul.

Schrire, Carmel. 2004. "The Conciliators: Bushmania and the Nightmare of Survival." *Visual Anthropology Review* 19, nos. 1–2: 160–165.

Sharp, John, and Stuart Douglas. 1996. "Prisoners of Their Reputation? The Veterans of the 'Bushman' Battalions in South Africa." In *Miscast: Negotiating the Presence of the Bushmen,* ed. Pippa Skotnes, 323–330. Rondebosch, South Africa: University of Cape Town Press.

Silberbauer, George B. 1979. "Social Hibernation: The Response of the G/wi Band to Seasonal Drought." In *Symposium on Drought in Botswana*, ed. Madalon T. Hinchey, 112–120. Gaborone: Botswana Society; Hanover, NH: University of New England Press.

_____. 1981a. *Hunter and Habitat in the Central Kalahari Desert*. Cambridge: Cambridge University Press.

_____. 1981b. "Hunter-Gatherers of the Central Kalahari." In *Omnivorous Primates: Gathering and Hunting in Human Evolution*, ed. Robert S. O. Harding and Geza Teleki, 455–498. New York: Columbia University Press.

Smith, Andrew B. 1988. "Eastern Bushmanland." *African Wildlife* 42, no. 2: 226.

_____. 1996. "The Kalahari Bushmen Debate: Implications for Archaeology of Southern Africa." *South African Historical Journal* 35, no. 1: 1–15.

Smith, Andrew B., and Richard B. Lee. 1997. "Cho/ana: Archaeological and Ethnohistorical Evidence for Recent Hunter-Gatherer Agropastoralist Contact in Northern Bushmanland, Namibia." *South African Archaeological Bulletin* 52: 52–58.

Smith, Andrew B., Candy Malherbe, Mathias Guenther, and Penny Berens. 2000. *The Bushmen of Southern Africa: A Foraging Society in Transition*. Cape Town: David Philip; Athens: Ohio University Press.

Snyman, Jan W. 1975. *Zu/'hoasi Fonologie en Woordeboek*. Communications No. 37 of the University of Cape Town School of African Area Studies. Cape Town: A.A. Balkema.

Stander, Philip E., //Ghau, D. Tsisaba, //. /Oma, and //Ui. 1997. "Tracking and the Interpretation of Spoor: A Scientifically Sound Method in Ecology." *Journal of the Zoological Society of London* 242: 329–341.

Stander, Philip E., Kaqece //au, Nisa /ui, Tsisaba Dabe, and Dam Dabe. 1997. "Non-consumptive Utilization of Leopards: Community Conservation and Ecotourism in Practice." In the proceedings of a symposium, "Lions and Leopards as Game Ranch Animals," Onderspoort, 50–57.

Stevens, Carolyn, Clive Nettleton, John Porter, Ruth Willis, and Stephanie Clark. 2005. "Indigenous Peoples' Health: Why Are They Behind Everyone, Everywhere?" *Lancet* 366: 10–13.

Suich, Helen, and Brian Child, eds., with Anna Spenceley. 2009. *Evolution and Innovation in Wildlife Conservation: Parks and Game Ranches to Transfrontier Conservations Areas*. London and Sterling, VA: Earthscan.

Susser, Ida. 2009. *AIDS, Sex, and Culture: Global Politics and Survival in Southern Africa*. Oxford: Wiley-Blackwell.

Suzman, James. 1999. *'Things from the Bush': A Contemporary History of the Omaheke Bushmen*. Basel Namibia Studies Series 5. Basel: P. Schlettwein.

_____. 2001a. *An Introduction to the Regional Assessment of the Status of the San in Southern Africa*. Windhoek: LAC.

_____. 2001b. *An Assessment of the Status of San in Namibia*. Windhoek: LAC.

_____. 2002. *Minorities in Independent Namibia*. London: Minority Rights Group International.

_____. 2004. "Etosha Dreams: An Historical Account of the Hai//om Predicament. *Journal of Modern African Studies* 42, no. 2: 221–238.

Sweet, Jim. 1998. *Livestock—Coping with Drought: Namibia—A Case Study*. Rome: Food and Agriculture Organization of the United Nations.

Sylvain, Renee. 1999. "'We Work to Have Life': Ju/'hoan Women, Work and Survival in the Omaheke Region, Namibia." PhD diss., University of Toronto.

_____. 2001. "Bushmen, Boers, and Baasskap: Patriarchy and Paternalism on Afrikaner Farms in the Omaheke Region, Namibia." *Journal of Southern African Studies* 27, no. 4: 717–737.

_____. 2002. "'Land, Water, and Truth': San Identity and Global Indigenism." *American Anthropologist* 104, no. 4: 1074–1085.

_____. 2004. "Between Rock Art and a Hard Place: Development and Display in the Kalahari." *Visual Anthropology Review* 19, nos. 1–2: 141–148.

_____. 2005. "Disorderly Development: Globalization and the Concept of 'Culture' in the Kalahari." *American Ethnologist* 32, no. 3: 354–370.

_____. 2006. "Drinking, Fighting, and Healing: San Struggles for Survival and Solidarity in the Omaheke Region, Namibia." In Hitchcock et al. 2006b, 131–142.

Takada, Akira. 2008. "Kinship and Naming among the Ekoka !Xun." In *Research in Khoisan Studies, No. 22, Khoisan Languages and Linguistics*, proceedings of the 2nd International Symposium, 8–12 January 2006, Riezlern/Kleinwalsertal, ed. S. Ermisch, 1–15. Cologne: Rüdiger Köppe Verlag.

Taylor, Julie J. 2007a. "The Politics of Identity, Authority, and the Environment: San, NGOs, and the State in Namibia's West Caprivi." PhD diss., Oxford University.

_____. 2007b. "Celebrating San Victory Too Soon? Reflections on the Outcome of the Central Kalahari Game Reserve Case." *Anthropology Today* 23, no. 5: 3–5.

_____. 2007c. "Rendering the Land Visible." *Cultural Survival Quarterly* 31, no. 4: 10–15.

Terry, M. E., F. J. Lee, and K. le Roux. 1994. *A Survey of Natural Resource Based Craft Production and Marketing in Namibia*. Windhoek: LIFE Project and the Rössing Foundation.

Thoma, Axel, and Janine Piek. 1997. "Customary Law and Traditional Authority of the San." Center for Applied Social Sciences Paper No. 36. Windhoek: CASS, UNAM.

Thomas, David S. G., and Paul A. Shaw. 1991. *The Kalahari Environment*. Cambridge: Cambridge University Press.

Thomas, Elizabeth Marshall. 1958. *The Harmless People*. New York: Vintage Books.

_____. 1994. "Management of Violence among the Ju/wasi of Nyae Nyae: The Old Way and a New Way." In *Studying War: Anthropological Perspectives*, ed. S. P. Reyna and R. E. Downs, 69–84. Langhorne, PA: Gordon and Breach.

_____. 2006. *The Old Way: A Story of the First People*. New York: Farrar, Straus, Giroux.

Tishkoff, Sarah A., Mary Katherine Gonder, Brenna M. Henn, Holly Mortensen, Alec Knight, Christopher Gignoux, Neil Fernandopulle, Godfrey Lema, Thomas B. Nyambo, Uma Ramakrishnan, Floyd A. Reed, and Joanna L. Mountain. 2007. "History of Click-Speaking Populations of Africa Inferred from mtDNA and Y Chromosome Genetic Variation." *Molecular Biology and Evolution* 24, no. 10: 2180–2195.

Tishkoff, Sarah A., Floyd A. Reed, Françoise R. Friedlaender, Christopher Ehret, Alessia Ranciaro, Alain Froment, Jibril B. Hirbo, Agnes A. Awomoyi, Jean-Marie Bodo, Ogobara Doumbo, Muntaser Ibrahim, Abdalla T. Juma, Maritha J. Kotze, Godfrey Lema, Jason H. Moore, Holly Mortensen, Thomas B. Nyambo, Sabah A. Omar, Kweli Powell, Gideon S. Pretorius, Michael W. Smith, Mahamadou A. Thera, Charles Wamhebe, James L. Webei, and Scott M. Williams. 2009. "The Genetic Structure and History of Africans and African Americans." *Science* 324: 1035–1044.

Tobias, Phillip V. 1962. "On the Increasing Stature of the Bushmen." *Anthropos* 57: 801–810.

_____. 1975. "Fifteen Years of Study on the Kalahari Bushmen or San." *South African Journal of Science* 71, no. 1: 74–79.

_____, ed. 1978. *The Bushmen: San Hunters and Herders of Southern Africa*. Cape Town: Human & Rousseau.

Tomaselli, Keyan G., and John P. Homiak. 1999. "Powering Popular Conceptions: The !Kung in the Marshall Family Expedition Films of the 1950s." *Visual Anthropology* 12, nos. 2–3: 153–184.

Tracy, Mark. 2005. "Applied Anthropology and the Ju/'hoansi San: A Meta-Critique of the Development Work in the Nyae Nyae Region, Namibia." MA thesis, University of Nebraska-Lincoln.

Tyson, P. D. 1986. *Climate Change and Variability in Southern Africa*. Oxford: Oxford University Press.

USAID/Namibia (United States Agency for International Development/Namibia). 1992. *Natural Resources Management Project Paper, Namibia, Entitled Living in a Finite Environment (LIFE) (690-0251.73)*. Windhoek: USAID/Namibia.

Uys, Ian. 1993. *Bushman Soldiers: Their Alpha and Omega*. Germiston: Fortress Publishers.

van Heerden, Fanie R., R. Martinhus Horak, Vinesh J. Maharaj, Robert Vieggaar, Jeremiah V. Senabe, and Philip J. Gunning. 2007. "An Appetite Suppressant from Hoodia Species." *Phytochemistry* 68: 2545–2553.

Vierich, Helga I. D. 1981. "The Kua of the Southeastern Kalahari: A Study in the Socio-ecology of Dependency." PhD diss., University of Toronto.

Vierich, Helga I. D., and Robert K. Hitchcock. 1996. "Kua: Farmer/Foragers of the Eastern Kalahari, Botswana." In *Cultural Diversity among Twentieth Century Foragers: An African Perspective*, ed. Susan Kent, 108–124. Cambridge: Cambridge University Press.

Vigilant, Linda, Renee Pennington, Henry Harpending, Thomas D. Kocher, and Allan C. Wilson. 1989. "Mitochondrial DNA Sequences in Single Hairs from a Southern African Population." *Proceedings of the National Academy of Sciences* 86: 9350–9354.

WCED (World Commission on Environment and Development). 1987. *Our Common Future*. New York and London: Oxford University Press.

Weaver, Larry Chris, and Patricia Skyer. 2003. "Conservancies: Integrating Wildlife Land-Use Options into the Livelihood, Development, and Conservation Strategies of Namibian Communities." Paper presented at the Fifth World Parks Congress to the Animal Health and Development Forum, Durban, South Africa, September.

Weinberg, Paul, and Cliff Bestall. 1988. "A Trip to the Cape Brings the Ju/wasi Closer to Namibia." *Weekly Mail*, 20–26 May, 10.

Werner, Wolfgang. 1989. "An Economic and Social History of the Herero in Namibia, 1915–1946." PhD diss., University of Cape Town.

———. 1991. "A Brief History of Land Dispossession in Namibia." In Republic of Namibia 1991, 43–59.

———. 1993. "A Brief History of Land Dispossession in Namibia." *Journal of Southern African Studies* 19, no. 1: 134–146.

———. 2001. "Land Reform and Poverty Alleviation: Experiences from Namibia." Namibian Economic Policy Research Unit (NEPRU) Working Paper No. 78. Windhoek: NEPRU.

Widlok, Thomas. 1999. *Living on Mangetti: 'Bushman' Autonomy and Namibian Independence*. Oxford: Oxford University Press.

Wiessner, Polly. 1977. "Hxaro: A Regional System for Reducing Risk among the !Kung San." PhD diss., University of Michigan.

———. 2002. "Hunting, Healing, and Hxaro Exchange: A Long-Term Perspective on !Kung (Ju/'hoansi) Large-Game Hunting." *Evolution and Human Behavior* 23: 407–436.

———. 2004. "Owners of the Future? Calories, Cash, Casualties, and Self-Sufficiency in the Nyae Nyae Area between 1996–2003." *Review of Visual Anthropology* 19, no. 1–2: 149–159.

———. 2005. "Norm Enforcement among the Ju/'hoansi Bushmen: A Case of Strong Reciprocity?" *Human Nature* 16, no. 2: 115–145.

Wiessner, Polly, and /Aice N!aici. 1998. *Population, Subsistence and Social Relations in the Nyae Nyae Area: Three Decades of Change*. Windhoek: NNDFN.

———. 2005. *Report on Discussions in Nyae Nyae Villages Concerning the NNC*. Windhoek: NNDFN.

Wilmsen, Edwin N. 1982. "Studies in Diet, Nutrition, and Fertility among a Group of Kalahari Bushmen in Botswana." *Social Science Information* 21, no. 1: 92–125.

_____. 1989. *Land Filled with Flies: A Political Economy of the Kalahari*. Chicago, IL: University of Chicago Press.

_____. 1999. "Knowledge as a Source of Progress: The Marshall Family Testament to the Bushmen." *Visual Anthropology* 12, no. 2–3: 213–266.

_____. 2004. "A Kalahari Family Named Marshall: 'I Want a Record, Not a Movie.'" *Visual Anthropology Review* 19, nos. 1–2: 114–127.

WIMSA (Working Group of Indigenous Minorities in Southern Africa). 2001. *Style and Typing Guide for Khoe, Ju, !Ui and Taa Languages*. Windhoek: WIMSA.

_____. 2005. *WIMSA Report on Activities, April 2004 to March 2005*. Windhoek: WIMSA.

World Bank. 1992. *Namibia: Poverty Alleviation with Sustainable Growth*. Washington, DC: World Bank.

_____. 2008. *World Development Report 2008: Agriculture for Development*. Washington, DC: World Bank.

WWF (World Wildlife Fund). 2000. *Game Re-introduction to the Nyae Nyae Conservancy, 1999–2000*. Windhoek: WWF.

Wyckoff-Baird, Barbara. 1996. "Democracy: Indicators from Ju/'hoan Bushmen in Namibia." *Cultural Survival Quarterly* 20, no. 2: 18–21.

Yellen, John E. 1977. *Archaeological Approaches to the Present: Models for Reconstructing the Past*. New York: Academic Press.

Yellen, John E., and Richard B. Lee. 1976. "The Dobe-Du/Da Environment: Background to a Hunting and Gathering Way of Life." In Lee and DeVore 1976, 27–47.

Young, Elspeth. 1995. *Third World in the First: Indigenous Peoples and Development*. London: Routledge.

Index

activism, xx, 143, 167, 189, 196, 224
Afrikaans, 88, 102, 108, 125, 131–132, 138,
    148, 150, 173, 175, 235, 236
Afrikaners, 34, 116, 124, 138n
agriculture, 1, 3, 11, 12, 27, 31, 39, 43, 46, 47,
    60–61, 68, *81*, 88, 97, 99, 108, 151, 157,
    178, 212, 217, *219*, 221, 234
agro-pastoralism, 103
AIDS. *See* HIV/AIDS
alcohol, 10, 69, 124, 163, 167, 196, 199, 211,
    229–230, 231, 232
/'Angn!ao /'Un (Kiewiet), 109–110, 138,
    141–143, 146, 149, 151, 158, 161, 164,
    167, 173, 179, 224
Angola, 1, *2*, 4, 11, *35*, 36, *38*, 49, *52*, 74, 78,
    113, 120, 128, 142, 148, 150
Angolan San, 11, 36, 74, 128, 148, 150
anthropologists, 5, 13, 14, 25, 28, 30, 67, 98,
    195, 202, 220, 229, 240
anthropology, 63, 181
anti-liberation, 130
/Aotcha, 55n, 61, 68, 69–70, 72, 83, 87, 93,
    100, 101, 117, 127, 128–129, 132–133,
    134, 153, 159–165, 179, 180, 184, 190,
    213, 214
apartheid, 15, 36, 50, 64, 65, 67, 75, 78, 92,
    99, 113, 117, 120, 126, 129, 130, 132,
    134–135, 139, 143, 146, 155, 233, 235
army, 11, 113, 114, 124, 128, 134, 159

Arnold, John, 39
arrow, 47, 57, 83, 87, 89, 107, 213

band (*n//abesi*), 9, 51–53, 57
Baraka, *41*, 134, 147, 148, 154, 159–165, 167,
    175, 179–180, 182, 184–185, 187,
    188–192, 231, 242
Baraka Training Centre, 157, 158, 178, 182,
    188
Basic Education Reform Program (BERP), xx
beads, 244
Beake, Lesley, 238, 240n
benefit distributions, 12, 208, 218, 221
blackbirding, 35
borehole, 10, 11, 13, 14, 16, 19, 21, 36, 40, 43,
    47, 66, 69–70, 71, 82–83, 86, 90, 115,
    119, 132, 141, 157, 159, 160, 169, 178,
    206, 212–213, 225, 234
Bosshart, Melitta, 230
Botswana, xxi, 1, *2*, *4*, 5–6, *7*, 8, 16, 18, 21,
    22–24, 27, *35*, *38*, 40, *41*, 42, 44, *52*, 53,
    56n, 57, 58, 65, 76, 78–80, 84, 86, 90,
    94, 103, 109, 117, 131, 134, 138, 141,
    145, 146–152, 154, 160, 162, 170–174,
    189, 193, 198–199, 213, 214, 224, 230,
    232, 234, 236, 238
bride service, 58
bride wealth, 171, 214
bush foods, 57, 66, 87, 110, 140, 220, 232

Page numbers in italics refer to figures and tables.

Bushman Advisory Council, 17, 77
Bushman Affairs, commissioner of, 10, 19, 77, 93, 116, 214
Bushman Alliance, 14
Bushmanland, 5, 10–11, 12, 17–24, 34, 35, 36, 37, 39, 40, 54, 55, 66, 67, 68, 69, 71–78, 82–83, 84, 86–87, 95, 96, 97, 98–99, 100, 102, 104, 108, 109, 114, 116, 121–122, 129, 135–136, 139, 142–144, 147, 149–150, 152, 173, 174, 175, 178, 179
Bushmen, 8, 11, 17, 22, 66, 73–74, 75, 82n3, 98, 122, 124, 136

capacity-building, 202
Caprivi region, 2, 5, 6, 11, 17, 35, 36, 38, 99, 103, 137, 143, 151, 201, 207
Caprivi Strip, 1, 5, 11
Captain Kxao Kxami Community Learning and Development Centre (CLDC), 225, 240–241
cattle, 8, 10–11, 15, 22, 23, 27, 40, 46, 47, 49, 62, 65, 67–68, 69, 70, 76, 82, 83, 85, 86–88, 89–90, 94, 95, 96, 98, 99, 105–106, 110, 115, 117–118, 119, 133, 141, 157, 160, 164, 170–174, 175–176, 198–199, 212–215, 216, 220, 221, 223, 224
  complex, 90
  posts, 8, 32, 35, 49, 86, 215
  predation, 60, 83, 95, 105, 115, 213
  project, 155
  serfs, 61, 170
Cattle Fund, 14, 19, 20, 61, 68–69, 115, 153–154, 214
CBNRM. *See* community-based natural resource management
CBPP. *See* contagious bovine pleuropneumonia
cease-fire, 21
child care, 52
child-rearing, 63, 181–182
CITES. *See* Convention on International Trade in Endangered Species of Wild Fauna and Flora
citizenship, 1, 22, 75, 115, 130, 131, 133, 151, 155, 157
civil society, 28
CLDC. *See* Captain Kxao Kxami Community Learning and Development Centre
commercial land, 34, 37, 135, 147

Commission for the Preservation of the Bushmen, 34
communal land, 12, 25, 31, 34, 37, 48, 55, 57, 65–67, 74–75, 82n3, 85, 98, 103, 120, 134–136, 138–142, 144–147, 150, 152, 172, 180, 198, 205, 206
community-based approach, 27, 102, 151, 157, 179, 190, 206, 225, 236
community-based natural resource management (CBNRM), 24, 25, 27, 151, 198–199, 200–203, 205, 207, 210
compensation, 16, 106, 200
competition, 31, 34, 82, 105, 167, 189, 191, 192, 195, 202, 213
Conference on Land Reform and the Land Question, 23, 29, 60, 72, 135, 138, 140, 151
conflict, 8, 53, 59, 69, 70, 77, 99, 160, 164, 165, 185, 195, 209, 215, 229
  inter-community, 34, 53, 59, 69, 160, 169, 195, 199, 209, 215
  interpersonal, 8, 59, 69, 70, 185, 195, 209, 229
  intra-community, 34, 69, 70, 114, 169, 185, 195, 199, 215, 229
  management, 5
  over resources, 24, 77, 222
  resolution, 51, 190, 204
conservancy, 25, 41, 61, 198, 204, 205–206, 208, 210, 211, 218, 219, 220, 221–222, 223, 224–226, 243, 244. *See also* N=a Jaqna Conservancy; Nyae Nyae Conservancy
conservation, 17, 24, 26, 28, 34, 45, 48, 62, 78, 82, 85, 91, 93, 97, 98, 100, 103, 119, 179, 200, 203, 205, 222, 226
  heritage, 227, 239, 244
constitution, 142, 205, 206
  Cattle Fund, 19
  Ju/'hoan people's organization, 243
  Ju/wa Farmers Union, 20, 72, 80, 117
  Namibian, 32–33, 37, 188
  Nyae Nyae Farmers Cooperative, 57, 80, 81, 82, 118
  South West Africa, 74
  United States, 80
contagious bovine pleuropneumonia (CBPP, lung plague), 27, 94, 198, 213
Convention on International Trade in Endangered Species of Wild Fauna and Flora (CITES), 27

courts, 16, 224
crafts, 22, 44, 45, *81*, 82, 87, 105, 146, 158,
    178, 180, 201, 210–211, 218, *219*, 222,
    225, 226
    crafts project, 223
    handicrafts, 101, 108, 115, 157, 178, 200
cultivation, 39, 46, 57, 66, 217
Cunene region, 24
Cunene River, 2

death, xx, 57, 68, 93–94, 113, 213, 215, 239
    Death by Myth (film), 138, 193, 220
    "the place of death," 10, 61
decentralization, 13, 37, 69, 70, 184, 185, 191
decolonization, 21
democracy, 14, 15, 22, 27, 63, 72, 99, 115, 118,
    122, 125, 129, 132, 135, 144, 146, 169,
    184, 187, 188, 194
Democratic Turnhalle Alliance (DTA), 12, 14,
    21, 79, 86, 121–123, 127, 129, 130–132,
    143, 174
Department of Agriculture, 18, 86–87
Department of Bantu Administration (South
    Africa), 9
Department of Nature Conservation (DNC),
    12, 18, 19, 20, 22, 62, 67, 69, 73, 77,
    78, 82–84, 86–87, 90, 91–97, 98n,
    100–105, 108, 112, 137, 173
dependency, 13, 45, 104, 165, 232
development, xx, 1, 10, 11, 12, 14, 16, 19,
    20–21, 24, 25–26, 27–28, 30, 31–32,
    36, 37, 39, 43, 46, 48–49, 50, 57, 60,
    61–62, 63, 64, 65, 66, 67, 68, 69, 71, 76,
    78, 82n3, 84, 85, 86–88, 90, 96, 98, 99,
    104, 107, 112, 115, 117, 123, 126, 132,
    133, 137, 138, 141, 143, 147, 148, 150,
    151, 153, 155, 157, 160, 163, 165–166,
    168–169, 177–178, 179, 180, 181, 182–
    183, 185, 187, 189–190, 191–192, 194,
    195, 196, 198–204, 206, 216, 218, *219*,
    220–221, 223, 226, 227, 228, 233, 234,
    235, 236, 237–238, 239, 240, 241, 242.
    See also San Development Program;
    Regional Conference on Development
    Programs for Africa's San Populations
devil's claw (grapple plant), 44, 210, 223
diamonds, 25, 32, 33, *34*, 94
Dickens, Patrick, xix–xx, 131, 132–133, 137,
    155, 159, 230, 235–236, 238–239, 240,
    241–242

discrimination, 106, 151
disease, 199, 227–229, 231–232
    animal, 27, 49, 67, 94, 173, 198, 199, 213, 215
    crop, 221
    "diseases of development," 228
dispossession, 16, 26, 34, 51, 61, 65, 67, 75, 82,
    83, 84, 99, 115, 122, 132, 135
Dix, Tove, 120, 122
DNC. *See* Department of Nature
    Conservation
driver's licenses, 118, 134, 159, 164, 182, 196
drought, 40, 43, 48, 53, 57, 62, 178, 199, 213,
    217, 221, 224, 232
dryland farming, 131
DTA. *See* Democratic Turnhalle Alliance
Dutch Reformed Church, 137

ear-tagging, 76
Eastern Bushmanland, 12, 17, 18, 19, 20–21,
    22–23, 39, 54, 66, 67–68, 69, 71–74, 75,
    76, 77–78, 82–83, 84, 86–87, 97, 98, 99,
    102, 104, 108, 129, 135, 136, 139, 143,
    144, 149, 178, 179
eco-tourism, 26, 90, 97, 100, 183
education, xx, 24, 25, 30, 71, *81*, 82, 85, 87–88,
    90, 100, 105, 131, 151–152, 154, 155,
    157–160, 167, 178–179, 180, 190, 199,
    227, 230, 233, 234–240
    under-education, 126
egalitarianism, 15, 60, 62–63, 72, 115, 126,
    135, 136, 138, 143, 161, 164, 166, 168n,
    232
elections, 14, 15, 21–22, 37, 103, 115, 123,
    125, 126, 127, 130, 132, 138, 143, 150,
    161, 171, 173
elephants, 27, 44, 45, 60, 69, 73–74, 76, 82–83,
    84, 85, 86, 90, 94, 96, 98, 105, 115, 125,
    200, 206, 208, 209, 213, 216–217, 220,
    221, 222, 223, 225
elitism, 12, 185, 194, 196
employment, 10, 25–26, 27, 32, 39, 46, 89,
    106, 107, 125, 151, 160, 161, 166, 189,
    190, 192, 196, 200, 208, 211, 212, 218,
    226, 232, 235, 236, 238
    government, 25, 26, 46, 89, 106, 107, 151,
    199, 200, 208, 211, 212, 218, 238
    private sector, 19, 25, 26, 46, 161, 166, 192,
    200, 208, 211, 212, 218, 236
empowerment, 49, 91, 97, 98n, 99, 103, 104,
    109, 112, 148, 156, 176, 187, 195

Environmental Planning Committee (EPC), 24, 106–108, 110, 111, 150, 180
ethnicity, 3, 5, 34, 35, 37, 49, 74–75, 117, 134–135, 136, 139, 144, 146, 152, 155, 190, 206, 234
Etosha National Park, 5, 6, 34, *35*, 96, 108, 201
Evangelical Lutheran Church in Namibia (ELCIN), 14, 36, 46, 156
expatriates, 109, 155, 157, 162, 166, 232
extended family, 51–53, 57, 60, 63, 136, 162, 166, 183, 191, 196

fences, 27, 33, 40, 48, 62, 79, 87, 103, 109, 128, 136, 138, 146, 171, 172, 208, 217, 220. *See also* veterinary cordon fence
film, 13, 28, 44, 66, 79, 88, 96, 120, 132, 133, 138–139, 171, 173, 174, 175–176, 193, 218, 220
filmmaking, 77, 106, 120, 132, 133, 134, 138, 146, 171, 174, 193, 220, 222, 225
fire, 46, 69, 82, 104, 110, 119, 124, 213, 217, 234
  bush management by, 46, 82, 110, 119, 213, 217
  campfires, 62, 209
  fire break, 222
  firewood, 209
Firebird Foundation, 239
foot-and-mouth disease, 213
foraging, 8, 13, 18, 27, 28, 45, 46, 51, 57, 59, 60–61, 62, 66, 70, 98, 136, 138, 168n, 191, 194, 216, 218, 227–228
forestry, 225
Fourth World peoples, 114, 132
fund-raising, 20, 76

G/am, 66, 86, 110, 147, 170, 171–172, 176, 214
G/am farmers, 172n
Gariep (Orange) River, 2, *3*
gender, 136, 143, 144, 166–167, 189, 194, 196, 201, 202
genocide, 34
geographic information systems (GIS), 56n
geographic positioning systems (GPS), 54, 56n
gifblaar (*Dichapetalum cymosum*), 40, 105, 213
GIS. *See* geographic information systems
Gobabis, 6, 74, 139, 141–142, 224

Gobabis farms, 6, 10, 20, 65, 70, 80, 115, 117, 150, 212, 220
Gods Must Be Crazy, The (film), xi
Government of the Republic of Namibia (GRN), 25, 31–33, 36–37, 39, 43, 47, 48–49, 151
government rations, 10, 11, 65, 224, 226, 232
GPS. *See* geographic positioning systems
graves, 125
grazing, 12, 18, 23, 32, 39, 48–49, 57, 59, 62, 68, 69, 86, 118, 141, 146, 170, 171, 176, 212–214, 216, 220, 225
  overgrazing, 65, 86, 106, 138, 140, 141, 142, 145n, 151, 171, 216
Grootfontein, 5, 6, 21, 26, 39, 48, *52*, 74, 95, 224, 230n3
Grootfontein farms, 6, 10, 212
guns, 74, 83–84, 95, 106–107, 127, 131, 172n2, 213

Hai//om San, 5, 6, 40, *52*, 96, 140n
hand pumps, 69, 71, 82
Hans Rausing Endangered Languages Documentation Project, 239
Harvard Kalahari Research Group, 40
headmanship (chieftainship), 64, 126, 139, 181
health, 10, 63, *81*, 87–88, 90, 93, 95, 119, 140, 151, 155, 157–158, 161, 163, 178, 179, 196, 198, 212, 213, *219*, 222, 223, 225, 227–233
  health care, 119, 151, 178, 230, 231
Health Unlimited, 156, 229, 230, 231–232
Heckler, Melissa, 238
herding, 46, 61, 89, 212, 216
Herero, 8, 15–16, 17, 20, 23–24, 35–36, 40, 49, 66, 68, 75, 85–86, 90, 108, 110, 129, 138, 139, 143, 144, 146–147, 150, 155, 164, 170–176, 199, 212, 213, 214, 224, 243
Hereroland, 35, 36, 40, 66, 74, 86, 141
Himba, 24, 100, 137, 142, 190
HIV/AIDS, xx, 196, 225, 229, 230–233, 236
Hoodia, 39, 228
household, 34, 44, 46, 136, 209, 211, 217, 226
human rights, xix, 1, 15, 26, 28, 148, 150, 182
hunger, 12, 57, 59, 60, 65, 90, 96n, 105, 211, 217–218, 220, 222, 228
hunter-gatherer, 46–47, 51, 54, 63, 88, 98, 105, 181, 220, 227, 232

hunting, 13, 39, 45, 46, 47, 51–52, 55, 56, 58, 62, 82, 83, 89, 95, 96, 100, 103, 105, 109, 115, 127, 128, 200, 201, 208, 213, 225, 226
  laws, 87, 95, 99, 105, 107, 119, 148, 208, 209, 211
  methods, 45, 51, 56, 103, 106
  overhunting, 65, 98, 222
  rights, 57, 78, 200
  safari, 27, 62, 77, 95, 96, 108, 198, 201, 208, 209, 210
  sport, 96
  subsistence, 45, 209, 232
  trophy, 23, 62, 67, 78, 82, 83, 84, 95–96, 98, 99, 101, 106, 108, 109, 151, 211, 222
hunting and gathering, 8, 40, 55, 60, 63–64, 65–66, 73–74, 78, 85, 87, 88, 89, 98, 103, 105, 106, 115, 126, 136, 150, 157, 183, 226, 232
hxaro (a gift-giving system), 54
hydro-geological prospecting, 43

identity, 5, 59, 98, 121n, 151
independence, xx, 1, 6, 10, 12, 14–15, 16, 21, 22, 28, 29, 31, 32, 36, 50, 61–62, 67, 78, 91, 95, 97, 98n, 99–104, 112, 113–116, 120, 122, 126, 129, 130, 132, 133n, 134–135, 137, 138, 139–141, 144, 152, 154, 155, 156, 158, 165, 168–169, 171, 174, 176, 180, 201, 233, 234–236, 237. *See also* post-independence period; pre-independence period
  personal, 69, 177
indigenous peoples, 4, 24, 27, 28, 97, 99, 139, 150, 227
institutions, 14–15, 38, 39, 63, 178, 187, 202, 242
Integrated Rural Development and Nature Conservation (IRDNC), 22, 137
Integrated Rural Development Program (IRDP), 14, 87, 157–158, 179, 185, 186
International Union for the Conservation of Nature and Natural Resources (IUCN), 26
IRDNC. *See* Integrated Rural Development and Nature Conservation
IUCN. *See* International Union for the Conservation of Nature and Natural Resources

JBDF. *See* Ju/wa Bushman Development Foundation
Ju/wa Bushman Development Foundation (JBDF), 13, 19–21, 46, 61, 66–68, 70–72, 76–80, 82–83, 84–90, 91–92, 94, 95–96, 97, 100, 103, 114, 115, 118–119, 122–123, 126, 130–135, 137, 138, 140, 146, 154, 159–162, 170, 214–215, 230–231
Ju/wa Farmers Union (JFU), 20–22, 60, 61–62, 63, 64, 65–67, 71–73, 76–80, 82n2, 83–85, 87, 112, 114–115, 117, 119–120, 159, 180, 214–215, 233
Ju/'hoan traditional authority, 29, 170, 206, 223, 224, 229
Ju/'hoan Transcription Group (JTG), 79n, 225, 239–241, 243

/Kae/kae, 7, 8, 42, 59, 149, 213
  Dobe-, 40, 44, 56n
  Nyae Nyae-, 42
Kalahari Desert, xxi, 6, 8, 27, 42–44, 53–54, 57, 59, 60, 90, 136, 205, 217, 221, 228
Kalahari Family, A (film), 28, 120, 138, 193, 218, 220–221
Kalahari Peoples Fund (KPF), xx, 44, 76, 79, 223, 225, 239–241
Kalahari Peoples Network (KPN), 240n, 243
Katutura, 120n, 129, 132
Kaudum National Park (Kaudum Game Reserve), 17, 40, *41*, 66, 109, 198
Kavango region, 5, 11, *35*, 36, *38*, *41*, 66
Kavangos, 9, 17, 36, 40, 49, 75, 137, 172, 212
Khoesan, xix–xx, 131, 144, 236
=Khomani, xxi, 16, *52*, 79
Khwe San, xxi, 5–6, 10, 11, 16–17, 36, 39, 99, 103, 136, 137, 150
kinship, 51–54, 56, 58, 93, 116
Klein Dobe, 20, 24, 102–105, 106–107, 109, 111, 147
knowledge, environmental, 44–45, 78, 89, 93–94, 100, 105–107, 111, 191, 196, 202, 210, 241–243
KPF. *See* Kalahari Peoples Fund
KPN. *See* Kalahari Peoples Network
kraal, 19, 69, 76, 86–87, 88, 115, 146, 157, 164, 174, 175
!Kung, xxi, 4, 9, 39
Kuru Family of Organizations, 22n, 79

kxa/ho (larger land area of Nyae Nyae),
    54–55, *56*, 57

labor, 9, 18, 33, 35, 44, 46, 47, 51, 60, 62, 67,
    87, 118, 157, 183, 212, 217, 218, *219*
LAC. *See* Legal Assistance Centre
land, 3, 9–10, 12–13, 14, 15–16, 17–20, 23–24,
    25, 29, 30, 31, 32–34, 36, 37, 39, 40, 48,
    51, 53, 54, *55*, 56n, 57, 59, 60, 61, 62,
    63, 65–66, 67, 68, 70, 71, 73, 74, 75, 76,
    77, 78, 80, 82, 85, 86, 87, 89, 92, 93, 95,
    98–99, 103, 105, 106, 107, 110–111,
    114, 115, 117, 119, 120, 123, 127,
    128, 129, 131, 132, 134, 135, 136, 139,
    140–141, 142–143, 144–147, 149, 150,
    151, 152, 156–157, 165, 166, 168, 169,
    170, 171, 172, 173, 175, 176, 179, 180,
    181, 185, 191, 196, 198, 199, 203, 205,
    206, 216, 217, 218, 220, 222, 233
    mapping, 72, 138, 140, 143, 225
    rights, 15–16, 19, 23, 24, 25, 29, 37, 51, 57,
        58, 60, 65, 66, 67, 69, 70, 73, 74, 75, 85,
        87, 92, 98, 110, 115, 121, 135, 138, 142–
        143, 145, 148, 150, 171, 172, 220, 240
    tenure, 12, 15–16, 19, 30, 33–34, 37–38,
        48, 49, 51, 56n, 57, 58, 61, 62, 63, 70,
        71, 72, 73, 75, 76, 78, 85, 87, 98, 107,
        109, 111, 117, 129, 132, 133, 135, 136,
        139–140, 144, 149, 154, 165, 176, 181,
        199, 211, 221
    use, 9–10, 12–13, 14, 16, 22–24, 29, 37,
        53, 54, 55, *56*, 73, 77, 82, 95, 98, 104,
        106, 108–109, 111–112, 136, 140–141,
        143–144, 145–146, 149, 150, 151, 170,
        176, 179, 180, 203, 205
languages, xix–xxi, 3, 4, 5, 24, 108, 138n, 144,
    148–150, 166, 173, 204, 234, 240, 241
    click, xix–xx, 5, 131, 142, 144
    Khoesan, xix–xx, 131, 144, 236
leaders, community, 36, 71, 196
leadership, 24, 25, 50, 51, 54, 61, 63–64, 72,
    109, 116, 121n, 122, 126, 137–138, 139,
    144, 146, 158, 161, 162, 164, 171, 177,
    180–181, 183, 184, 186, 187, 189, 190,
    191, 224, 234
    centralized, 62, 164, 188, 190
    formal, 72, 118, 181, 204
    informal, 63–64, 72, 116, 181, 204
    "leadership by committee," 138, 161
Lee, Richard B., 53, 58, 88, 181, 229

Legal Assistance Centre (LAC), 140, 199, 224
LIFE. *See* Living in a Finite Environment
    (LIFE) Project
life skills, 88, 100, 152, 157
lions, 10, 21, 47, 60, 67, 73, 74, 76, 83–84, 85,
    87, 94, 95, 96, 103, 105, 108, 115, 156,
    200, 204, 213
Living in a Finite Environment (LIFE)
    Project, 25, 26, 151, 187, 201–206,
    208–209, 212, 218, 220

mafisa (form of long-term loan), 46, 215
malaria, 228, 232
malnutrition, 65, 196, 222
Mangetti Dune, 11, 26, 36, *41*, 46, 147–148,
    149, 150, 189, 230–231
marriage, 9, 52, 53, 58, 93
Marshall, Elizabeth. *See* Thomas, Elizabeth
    Marshall
Marshall, John, 11, 12, 13, 17, 19, 20, 28, 44,
    51, 53, 56, 61, 66, 68, 69, 71, 76, 77,
    79, 80, 83, 84, 86, 87, 88, 89, 96, 97, 99,
    100, 116, 120, 121, 122, 132, 133, 134,
    136, 138, 140, 153, 154, 156n, 159, 160,
    161, 171, 175–176, 187, 193, 214, 216,
    218, 220
Marshall, Laurence, 7, 8, 68
Marshall, Lorna, 7–9, 40, 51, 76, 244
marula, 44
MAWF. *See* Ministry of Agriculture, Water,
    and Forestry
Mbanderu, 36
McIntyre, Claude, 10, 47, 116, 214
meat, 8, 47, 51–52, 83, 90, 95, 96, 102, 105,
    200, 208–209, 212, 214, 216, 221, 222
media, 46, 68, 96, 106, 132, 141, 157, 176, 224,
    234, 243
medicinal plants, 44, 228
melons, 42, 46, 48, 125, 217
MET. *See* Ministry of Environment and
    Tourism
MHSS. *See* Ministry of Health and Social
    Services
migration, 62, 83, 109, 128
militarization, 10, 11, 62, 114, 126
mining, 1, 3, 32, 39, 145, 218
Ministry of Agriculture, 109, 110
Ministry of Agriculture, Water, and Forestry
    (MAWF), 21, 43, 46, 212, 215, 216,
    222, 224n

Ministry of Environment and Tourism
(MET), 25, 47, 97, 201–202, 204–206,
208, 220, 222
Ministry of Health and Social Services
(MHSS), 178, 231, 232
Ministry of Lands, Resettlement, and Rehabilitation (MLRR), 46, 136, 138, 145,
147, 174, 203, 216
Ministry of Wildlife Conservation and Tourism (MWCT), 12, 13, 22, 104–109, 112
minorities, 1, 13, 74, 126, 141, 146, 148, 150,
234–235, 236, 239, 241
MLRR. *See* Ministry of Lands, Resettlement,
and Rehabilitation
mobility, 10, 54, 136, 150, 182, 196
mogau (poisonous plant), 40, 105, 213
mongongo (mangetti), 17, 44, *55*
morama beans, 39, 44, 47
mortality, 10, 13
Mount Burgess Mining company, 25, 199, 218
music, 244
MWCT. *See* Ministry of Wildlife Conservation and Tourism

N=a Jaqna Conservancy, 108, 223
NACSO. *See* Namibian Association of
CBNRM Support Organisations
N!ae, 243–244
Nama, xxi, 3, 75, 108, 150, 155
name relationship, 54, 58–59
Namibia, xx, 1–6, *7*, 8–9, 11, 14–17, 20–26,
28, 31–36, 37, *38*, 39–40, *41*, 42–43,
45–49, 50, *52*, *55*, 57–58, 60–63, 65,
67–68, 71, 73–75, 78–80, 82n, 86, 88,
90, 91, 97–98, 102, 107, 111, 113, 115,
118, 120–124, 126–127, 129, 131–132,
134–136, 138–139, 141–152, 153–157,
160, 166, 168, 170–176, 180, 194–195,
198–200, 201–202, 205, 206, *207*, 208,
225, 230, 232–243
government, 12–13, 23–24, 26, 29, 37, 46,
49, 63, 79, 97, 99, 111, 137, 139, 144,
146, 151, 154, 170, 188, 199, 201, 205,
209, 212, 217–218, 222, 224–225, 230,
237, 239. *See also* Government of the
Republic of Namibia
Namibia Country Lodges, 222
Namibian Association of CBNRM Support
Organisations (NACSO), *207*
Namibian Constitution, 32–33, 37, 188

Naro San, xxi, *6*, *52*, 53, 148, 150
National Development Plan (NDP) 1, 2, 3,
32–33
natural resource management, 12, 23, 24, 25,
27, 32, 38–39, 54, 64, 77, 82, 106, 109,
119, 148, 187, 198, 199, 200, 202, 203,
206, *219*
land, 12, 24, 32, 37, 106, 203, 205
wildlife, 24, 25, 90, 97, 106, 108, 151, 152,
157, 158, 179, 220
Nature Conservation Amendment Act, 25, 205
NGO. *See* non-governmental organization
NNC. *See* Nyae Nyae Conservancy
NNDFN. *See* Nyae Nyae Development Foundation of Namibia
NNFC. *See* Nyae Nyae Farmers Cooperative
N//oaq!'ae ("area of broken rocks"), 40
nomadism, 150, 228
non-formal education, 25, 151
non-governmental organization (NGO),
15–16, 21, 22, 26, 27, 29, 36, 43, 46,
48, 100, 104, 107, 114, 119, 121, 136,
150, 153, 155, 158, 167, 168, 199, 200,
202–206, 209, 213, 217, 223–225, 229,
230, 233, 236–237, 238, 239, 240
"Nordic initiative," 143, 147
n!ore (territory), 17, 18, 19, 21, 23, 29, 51,
54–57, 59, 61–62, 66, 69–70, 76, *81*,
82, 87, 89, 92–93, 98–102, 105, 107,
111, 115–119, 124–126, 129, 133–135,
139, 140, 143, 145n, 146, 150, 151,
159–165, 170–171, 175, 176, 177,
183–184, 188, 190–191, 199, 225, 235.
See also *n!oresi*
n!orekxaosi (owners), 160, 162, 205
n!oresi (plural form of *n!ore*), 17, 18, 20, 21,
26, 29, 36, 51, 54–58, 60, 61, 68, 69–70,
72–73, 76, 77, 78, 79, 80, 82, 93–95,
103–104, 107, 123–125, 128, 129n,
134, 136, 138, 140, 142, 149, 158–159,
161–164, 170, 173, 180, 181, 183–184,
186–187, 190–192, 214, 215, 225, 229,
235
North West District (Botswana), 198
North West District Council, 56
nutrition, 196, 222, 227–229, 232
Nyae Nyae, 1, *7*, 12–14, 16, 19–20, 22, 25–26,
28–30, 43, 48, 50, 54, *55*, 57, 59, 60–62,
64–66, 70–71, 76–80, 83–86, 89–91,
93, 96–98, 102, 106–109, 111,

Nyae Nyae (*cont.*)
    113–114, 117–121, 122–123, 125,
        127–129, 132–133, 135–143, 145n,
        146–147, 149–152, 154–160, 163,
        168–173, 175–176, 180, 183–196,
        198–214, 216–218, 220, 222–223, 227,
        229, 232–236, 238–239, 241, 243–244
    area, 1, 6, *7*, 8–9, 11–13, 15–17, 20, 23,
        28, 30–31, 35, 39–40, 42–43, 45, 47,
        48–49, 54–55, 57, 60–62, 66–67,
        70–71, 76–77, 79–80, 83, 85–86,
        91–93, 96–99, 102–103, 106–108,
        111, 115, 117–118, 124–125, 128, 138,
        140–141, 144, 145n, 146, 149, 154,
        156–157, 159–160, 169–172, 176–177,
        198, 199, 201, 203–206, *207*, 208–216,
        218, 220–223, 225, 227, 229, 230
    communities, 13, 15, 20, 26, 30, 47, 50,
        77–78, 80, 89, 96n, 99, 100, 103–104,
        114–115, 117–119, 121, 123, 127,
        133–134, 138, 150, 157, 159–160, 164,
        169, 180, 182–183, 185, 187–189, 191–
        192, 196, 198, 202–205, 218, 221–222,
        230–231, 233, 235–237, 239, 242–243
    pan, 55n, 208, 222
    people, 1, 6, 12, 15, 27–30, 43, 46, 48, 50,
        59–60, 65, 70–71, 77–79, 82, 84–85,
        87–89, 95–96, 99–100, 103, 105, 115,
        117–118, 126, 131, 135–136, 140,
        146, 150, 160–161, 163, 169, 176, 179,
        183–184, 189–190, 192, 196, 198–199,
        201–203, 205–206, 210–212, 217–218,
        222–223, 229–230, 232, 235, 243–244
    schools, 131, 190, 233, 234, 235, 238, 240,
        242. *See also* Village Schools Project
    traditional authority, 170, 174, 188, 224
Nyae Nyae Community Forest, 225
Nyae Nyae Conservancy (NNC), 26, 29, 61,
        64, 96, 101, 118, 120, 166, 172n2, 197,
        198, 206, 208–212, 216, 217, 218, *219*,
        220, 221–226, 227, 229, 231, 240
Nyae Nyae Development Foundation of
        Namibia (NNDFN), xix, 12, 16, 22, 25,
        44, 72, 103, 107, 140, 142–143, 146,
        147, 151–152, 153–158, 161–167, 168–
        171, 173, 176–187, 190–195, 198, 201,
        203–204, 206, 211, 214–216, 218, *219*,
        220–226, 230, 231, 233, 235–238, 240
Nyae Nyae Farmers Cooperative (NNFC), xx,
        22–25, 28–29, 57, 59, 61–62, 63–64,

78, 80, *81*, 82–83, 87–88, 90, 91–92, 96,
        101–112, 114, 115, 117–120, 122–124,
        127, 129, 130–143, 145, 146–149,
        151–152, 153–167, 168–193, 195, 196,
        197, 198, 201, 203–206, 208, 214–215,
        216, 220, 229, 230, 233, 235–237
Nyae Nyae Tape Archive, 79, 119, 171, 243

Odendaal Commission, 17, 35, 54, 82
Okavango, 6, 136
"Old Way," the, xix, 50, 51, 59, 60, 66, 95, 96
    =Oma Tsamkxao, 61, 93, 117, 159, 213
Omaheke region, 6, *38*, *41*
oral history, 51, 54, 93, 96, 237, 240
ostrich eggshells, 45, 54, 223
Otjozondjupa region, 6, 23, *38*, 39, 40, *41*, 49,
        144, 203, *207*
"outstation movement," 70
Ovambo, 3, 9, 35, 75, 144, 230

pan (stratum of soil), 8, 17, 42, 45, 51, 55n,
        62, 92, 98, 100–101, 160, 201, 206, 208,
        210, 212, 222
parks, 12, *34*, *35*, 39
    Boesmanland Nasionale Park, 104
    See also Etosha National Park; Kaudum
        National Park (Kaudum Game Reserve)
Parliament, 14, 119, 143, 174, 175, 205, 225
participation, 1, 12, 14, 15, 24, 25, 26, 27, 29,
        68, 72, 82, 88, 91, 94, 95, 97, 102, 103,
        104, 106, 109, 114, 122, 128, 129, 135,
        136, 139, 141, 145–146, 147, 150, 155,
        157, 161, 164, 177, 184, 186, 188, 192,
        194, 200, 203, 235, 237–239
pastoralism, 18, 62, 64, 88, 89, 90, 98, 141, 144
pastoralists, 15, 20, 23, 48, 62, 67, 88, 90, 117,
        138, 139, 141, 144, 170–172
peacekeeping, 29, 57, 110, 124, 166
pensions, 26, 151, 199, 211, 218, 222
photo-tourism, 27, 198, 208
poison, 40, 57, 83, 89, 105, 107, 212, 213
politics, 22, 63, 110, 114, 121, 122, 144–146,
        149, 165, 175, 189, 191
population, 3, 4, 5, 6, 7, 9, 10, 18, 26, 31–32,
        37, 39, 42, 45, 49, 51, 53, 62, 66, 67, 70,
        73, 83, 84, 85, 95, 96, 98, 102, 104, 115,
        129, 131, 132, 135, 139, 144, 145n, 146,
        148, 183, 186, 199, 200, 202, 206, 208,
        210, 211, 228, 229, 232, 233, 236
    density, 10, 39, 70, 144, 199

post-independence period, xx, 12, 14, 15, 16,
    22, 31, 36, 50, 61, 97, 99, 102, 104, 112,
    129, 135, 137, 139, 140, 141, 144, 152,
    154, 155, 156, 158, 165, 168, 169, 174,
    176, 201, 234, 236, 237
predators, 10, 20, 21, 45, 67, 83, 84, 88, 90,
    159, 212, 213, 214, 215
pre-independence period, 6, 10, 14, 15, 21,
    29, 62, 67, 78, 91, 95, 97, 103, 112, 113,
    114, 115, 116, 120n, 122, 129, 133n,
    135
prejudice, 66
public policy, 1, 14, 20
pumps, 13, 19, 44, 48, 60, 69, 71, *81*, 82,
    86–87, 125, 153, 155, 178
    hand, 69, 71, 82
    solar, 157
    water, 13, 19, 44, 48, 60, 69, 71, *81*, 178
    wind, 86–87, 125
punishment, 235

racism, 15
rada (council or council member), 10, *81*,
    182, 188, 189, 190, 225
radasi (plural form of *rada*), 10, *81*, 177, 189,
    190, 206
rain, 2, 17, 40, 42–43, 53, 57, 59, 90, 104, 133,
    144, 217, 221, 228
reciprocity, 10, 54, 59n
Red Line, 49, 67, 82n3, 90. *See also* veterinary
    cordon fence
Redbush Tea Company of London, 44
Regional Conference on Development Pro-
    grams for Africa's San Populations, 24,
    147–148, 151
Regional Councils Act, 37, 39
religion, 67–68, 142
relocation, 61, 74, 160, 220
Representative Council, 73, 80, *81*, 118, 119,
    177, 188, 203
resettlement, 6n, 9, 12, 15, 23, 36, 48, 61, 87,
    123, 142, 149, 215
resocialization, 185
risk reduction, 57, 59, 196
Ritchie, Claire, 12, 13, 17, 18, 19, 20, 28n, 53,
    56n, 61, 67, 68, 69, 72, 74, 75, 76, 86,
    87, 88, 89, 100, 133–134, 143, 153, 154,
    159, 160, 214, 215, 230, 231
road building, 11, 157, 178, 218
roots (tubers), 42, 44, 210

SADF. *See* South African Defence Force
San Development Program, 49
savanna, 42
Schoeman, P. J., 34
schools, xx, 24, 67, 131, 135, 151, 179, 190,
    223, 231, 233–236, 237–239, 242. *See
    also* Village Schools Project
sedentarization (sedentism), 9, 10, 54, 196,
    228, 232
self-determination, 99, 121n
settlement, 9, 11, 13, 18, 19, 21, 36, 40, *41*, 46,
    47, 59, 62, 69–71, 73, 74, 86, 99, 105,
    106, 119, 138, 140, 141, 147, 150, 179,
    180, 203, 214–216, 228, 229
sharing, 5, 10, 11, 18, 19, 23, 29, 30, 45, 47,
    51–52, 56–57, 59, 60, 63, 65, 66, 68,
    84, 90, 93, 98, 104, 106, 110, 115, 116,
    120n, 138, 161, 162, 163, 166, 185, 189,
    190, 192, 195, 196, 214, 224, 243
shebeens, 229
Shipanga, Andreas, 21, 67, 77–78, 84, 101
skins, 13, 47, 125, 172
social services, 77, *81*, 177, 178
social ties, 59n
society, 12, 28, 31, 50, 58, 62–63, 98, 113, 118,
    124, 134, 137, 138, 166, 168, 179, 181–
    182, 183, 185, 194, 196, 233, 237
socio-economic system, 9, 18, 26, 31, 58, 104,
    114, 228
South Africa, 1, *2*, 4, 6, 11, 14, 16, 24, 33–34,
    35, *38*, 67, 71, 74, 75, 78–79, 96, 113,
    120, 122–123, 124, 126, 141, 148, 150,
    154, 155–156, 234, 235, 236, 238, 239
South African Defence Force (SADF), 6,
    10–11, 14, 36, 62, 74, 78, 99, 101, 104,
    108, 114, 121–122, 125, 127–128, 130,
    134, 135–136, 149, 180, 189
South West Africa (SWA), *7*, 8–9, 13–15, 19,
    35–36, 47, 62, 65, 67, 71, 74–75, 76,
    78–79, 83, 88, 97–98, 100, 113–116,
    120, 121, 125, 130, 131, 135, 180, 234
South West Africa Administration (SWAA),
    8, 9, 10, 11, 18, 33–36, 40, 50, 54, 59,
    60, 66, 71, 73–74, 75, 77–78, 85, 89,
    92–93, 116, 129, 137, 214
South West Africa People's Organization
    (SWAPO), 12, 14–15, 21, 62, 74, 78,
    79–80, 109, 113–115, 120–123, 127–
    129, 130–132, 135, 136, 142–143, 149,
    175, 180, 234

South West Africa Territorial Force, 14
southern Africa, 1, 4–5, 8, 16n, 20, 24, 45, 51, *52*, 60–61, 64, 65, 87, 88, 115, 138, 148, 200–201, 205, 212, 229, 236, 239
squatters, 135, 147
Sub-Saharan Africa, 2. *See also* Angola; Botswana; Namibia; South Africa
SWAPO. *See* South West Africa People's Organization

TB. *See* tuberculosis
territory, 5, 6, 17, 18, 33, 40, 51, 53, 54, *56*, 57, 58, 65, 73, 126, 143, 171
Thoma, Axel, 138, 140, 143, 155, 165, 167, 173, 179, 193
Thomas, Elizabeth Marshall, xx, 8, 40, 47, 48, 50, 66, 83, 213, 214
tools, 14, 45, 49, 68, 69, 71, 82, 133, 172, 220, 221n
    tool-making, 85
tourism, 1, 23, 24, 25, 26, 27, 39, 83, 100, 105, 106, 108, 145, 151, 158, 178, 199, 201–202, 205–206, 208, 209–210, 216, 218, *219*, 220, 222, 223, 226
tourist lodge, 25, *41*, 223
tracking, 45, 94, 210
trade goods, 54
traditional authority/Traditional Authority, 23, 29, 170, 174, 206, 223, 224, 229
traditional healers (*n/omkxaosi*), 163, 228, 231
truffle, 44
Tsamkxao =Oma, 29, 39, 59, 71, 73, 77, 84, 87, 89, 92–94, 104, 109–110, 116, 117, 121, 124–125, 133, 137, 139, 148, 154, 159, 160, 163, 171, 173, 176, 224, 233, 235
Tsumkwe, 5–6, *7*, 9–11, 12–13, 17–19, 20, 21, 22, 25, 26, 36, 39, 40, *41*, 42–43, 46–48, *55*, 59–60, 61, 68–71, 73, 79–80, 84–85, 89, 101, 104–105, 109, 114, 115, 116, 118, 123, 130, 131–132, 134, 140n, 143, 144, 159, 162, 163, 170, 172, 173, 174, 178, 184, 188, 190, 198, 199, 201, 208, 213, 214, 215, 221, 222, 223–225, 228–231, 233, 235, 240, 241, 243
Tsumkwe District East (Tsumkwe East), 6, 39, 40, 43, 201
Tsumkwe District West, 5, 12, 26, 39, 40, 43, 48, 199, 213, 223
Tswana, *35*, 149, 170, 214

tuberculosis (TB), 165, 199, 224, 229, 230–232
TUCSIN (The University Centre for Studies in Namibia), 153

UN. *See* United Nations
undernutrition, 228
unemployment, 32, 82, 104, 183
United Nations (UN), 14, 33, 113, 123, 133, 156, 217
United Nations Declaration on the Rights of Indigenous Peoples, 33
United Nations Permanent Forum on Indigenous Issues, 25
United Nations Security Council (UN Security Council), 21, 78–79
United Nations Security Council Resolution 435 (UN Resolution 435), 21, 78, 113–116, 123, 125–126, 129n, 131, 180
United Nations Transition Assistance Group (UNTAG), 130–131, 133, 170
United States Agency for International Development (USAID), 25, 107, 151, 156, 187, 189, 201, 234, 235
University of Namibia, 216
UNTAG. *See* United Nations Transition Assistance Group
USAID. *See* United States Agency for International Development

veterinary cordon fence (Red Line), *41*, 49, 67, 82n3, 90, 223–224
village, 27, 56, *81*, 87, 92, 101, 115, 127, 131, 150, 160, 161, 163, 177, 178, 182, 188, 190, 191, 199, 208, 209–210, 212, 218, *219*, 220, 221–222, 225, 231, 235, 237, 238, 239, 242, 243, 244
Village Schools Project (VSP), xx, 100, 131, 137, 155–156, 180, 225, 234–241
violence, 10, 13, 190, 223, 229

war of independence, 10
water, xxi, 2–3, 9, 12, 13, 18, 19, 21, 23, 26, 40, 42–44, 48, 51, 57–59, 66, 69, 70, 71, 73, 76, 78, 82–83, 85–87, 90, 94, 101, 105, 115, 119, 132, 140, 150–151, 155, 159, 163, 173, 178, 199, 204, 206, 208, 212, 213, 214, *219*, 220–221, 222–223, 224, 225, 232, 234
    borehole, 10, 11, 13, 14, 16, 19, 21, 36, 40, 43, 47, 66, 69–70, 71, 82–83, 86, 90,

115, 119, 132, 141, 157, 159, 160, 169, 178, 206, 212–213, 225, 234
  for cattle, 18, 23, 49, 82, 164, 171, 173, 212, 213, 214
  for game, 13, 42, 82–83, 94, 96, 102, 160
  groundwater, 2, 40
  permanent, 17, 40, 43, 49, 55n, 66, 213
  power, 47
  rights, 19, 26, 57–58, 66, 70
  seasonal, 2, 40, 42
  sub-surface, 40
  surface, 2, 40, 42
  water point, 13, 18, 19, 27, 47, 66, 72, 88, 119, 141, 146, 200, 206, 208, 213, 216–217, 220, 221
  water pump, 13, 19, 44, 48, 60, 69, 71, *81*, 178
  water table, 2, 43
  waterhole, 40, 53, 62, 86, 92, 94, 159, 160, 176
  waterless, 36, 40, 66, 74
weapons, 107
welfare, 13, 151
well, 16, 40
  windpump, 86–87, 125
Western Bushmanland, 5, 10, 11, 18, 36, 39, 40, 66, 74, 87, 104, 108, 114, 135–136, 139, 142–144, 147, 149, 152, 179
Wiessner, Polly, 15, 44, 54, 185, 186, 210, 218, 221, 223, 229, 232

wildlife, 2, 12, 13, 24, 25, 26, 32, 39, 47, 48, 59, 62, 68, 77, 82, 83, 90, 91, 93, 97–98, 102, 106, 108, 109, 115, 151, 156, 157, 158, 175, 179, 199, 200, 202, 205, 206, 208, 216, 220, 224
wildlife translocation, 208, 220
WIMSA. *See* Working Group of Indigenous Minorities in Southern Africa
Working Group of Indigenous Minorities in Southern Africa (WIMSA), xxi, 5, 199, 224
Working Group on Indigenous Populations, 25
World Conservation Union, 26. *See also* International Union for the Conservation of Nature and Natural Resources
World War II, 35, 70
World Wildlife Fund (WWF) (US), 107, 187, 189, 202, 204, 222
worldview, 163

Xamsa, *41*, 69, 70, 86, 171–172, 176, 243
!Xun San, xxi, 4, 6, 10–11, 36, 39, 40, *52*

youth, 45, 58, 63, 65, 97, 107, 114, 117, 128, 130–131, 149, 159, 167, 172n2, 180–186, 188, 190–191, 193, 196, 228, 231, 235, 241–244